The Poet and the Gilded Age

The Poet and

Social Themes in Lat

he Gilded Age

9th Century American Verse

y Robert H. Walker

1969

OCTAGON BOOKS

New York

PS
310
.S7
W3
1969

Reprinted 1969
by special arrangement with the University of Pennsylvania Press

OCTAGON BOOKS
A DIVISION OF FARRAR, STRAUS & GIROUX, INC.
19 Union Square West
New York, N. Y. 10003

AM

62-11268

LIBRARY OF CONGRESS CATALOG CARD NUMBER: 77-96172

Printed in U.S.A. by
TAYLOR PUBLISHING COMPANY
DALLAS, TEXAS

For E.L.P.W. and G.V.B.W.

Preface

THE EXPLICIT PURPOSE OF THIS STUDY WILL BE
self-evident: to re-examine the Gilded Age in the light of the
verse produced by its citizens. This should tell us something
more about the age, and something more about the function of
poetry. There are also a number of implicit purposes to which
attention may be called. These tangential implications may be
located by considering this effort as a case study bearing on
three closely related problems.

Most obviously, this is a case study which bears on the
stature of the poet as a responsive citizen. It would be misleading to assert that the poet and his work had fallen into
neglect; rather, a great deal of critical attention has been
directed toward this literary form, dating at least from the
"poetry renaissance" of 1912. Much of this attention has taken
the form of detailed exegesis, exercises in etymology, or
hypotheses in applied psychology. The obscure, the personal,
the "private" aspects of verse have received preponderant
emphasis. This attention has been necessary, and its results
should be applauded; but the disproportionate stress applied to
these aspects of poetry has tended to remove it from its rightful
place as an important method of social communication. In too
many of our American newspapers poetry, as well as other
creative forms, is discussed—if at all—within the pages of the
woman's section. Robert Frost, during an interview at the
Library of Congress in the spring of 1961, complained that
whenever he discovered a man reading a volume of his verse,

the man would put down the book with shamefaced haste, covering his retreat with, "Ah, Mr. Frost . . . uh . . . my *wife* is a great fan of yours!" It may be that the kind of attention we have recently lavished on poetry has distracted us from some aspects of its historical importance.

Even in primitive cultures the poet was often set aside as an exceptional individual, exempted from the usual labors, and expected—in return—to respond to the needs of the group by explaining the meaning of human nature within its natural and social environment. The poet's audience prized him not merely as a musician of words, but as an interpreter of their past and an augur of their future. The mantle of prophet-priest has been the poet's special vestment throughout the ages. To recall this fact is to underline the public—rather than private—importance of poetry; to insist that verse ought to contribute to any broad understanding of a culture rather than solely to seminars in explication; and to remind us that poetry, although it may appear on the woman's page, does respond meaningfully to page one.

In setting up a case study of the poet's social role, it has been necessary to abandon many valuable approaches to the appreciation of verse. There will be no place here for biographical treatments, for explorations of poetic traditions and influences, for internal analysis, or for the application of regional criteria. To ignore the use of such methods represents a serious loss, but a loss for which other studies have abundantly compensated. To stress the poet's social value is to deprecate neither poetry's aesthetic qualities nor the traditional methods of analyzing them. By suspending some of our conventional preconceptions, however, we may discover important aspects of poetry which have received too little attention. At its best, poetry transcends the language of which it is composed; at his best, the poet is capable of expressing the preoccupations of his age more tellingly than the prosaic recorder. The poet who seriously accepts his special and historic role provides cultural insights of extraordinary value. To appreciate them entails some sacrifice, but the prize may justify the handicap.

A second aspect of this case study arises from the period to which it has been applied. The last quarter of the nineteenth century is in many ways crucial to the development of modern American civilization. One could, with some justice, complain that much of this crucial quality has been generally overlooked or misunderstood by historians. More to the immediate point, however, is the condescension and neglect with which the verse of this age has been treated. On purely aesthetic grounds this summary judgment may be largely deserved, but there remains the question as to whether the verse of this period warrants dismissal on the grounds of its supposed social irrelevance. While the prose writer was schooling himself in journalism and regionalism for the creation of a new and important strain of realism—so goes the accepted generalization—the poet was languishing in the afterglow of English romanticism, achieving at best but a derivitive excellence, and contenting himself with the polite parlor and the woman's journal for a resting place. If this poetry—supposedly so severely dislocated from the important concerns of the day—can produce any serious source of social understanding, what then could we expect from similar examinations applied to the verse of other, more promising eras? As a case study, this work assumes the task of unearthing social relevance from the poetic ground which has been advertised as least likely to produce that commodity. Under such conditions, even partial success might have some meaning.

The third aspect of this case study is the experiment in quantification described in the Appendix. This represents an attempt not only to control a large and unwieldy mass of material, but to describe it in a way which will be useful to anyone interested in these materials, regardless of his own training or purpose. Even in this age of communication only between like-minded specialists, the student of literature has been notorious for his inability to share the results of his studies with other students of the same society. Understandably hampered by subjective criteria, the historian of literature has not been helpful in producing the kind of generalizations and evidence which the social historian or sociologist could use. Somewhat by default, the "scientific" student of literature has attempted to solve this problem by employing such techniques as image-counting and content analysis, while the anthropologist has bypassed the problem by subjecting creative art to rigid and preconceived compartmental constructs. These efforts have answered some needs, but they have done so at the cost of fractionalizing these integral creative products and thereby robbing them of a great deal of their exceptional value. This study exposes itself to a similar pitfall, since very little of the verse has been quoted in entirety, and none of it has been treated with special respect for those qualities which make poetry unique in the creative sense. Yet it is the poetry itself which shapes and pervades this study. Its message reaches the reader not through a process of mechanical analysis, but through the filter of an individual mind, trained and especially interested in the medium of poetry in all its aspects. I have attempted to organize and quantify the verse; but I have also attempted to understand it as poetry, where possible, and to pass on this understanding through extensive and carefully selected quotations, paraphrases, and descriptive passages. Any case study aimed at increasing the possibility of communication between specialists is doomed to the failure of all compromise: it will please no one totally. Yet, if it opens new opportunities for using poetry, it may achieve its own sort of limited success.

The character of this study has dictated a few exceptions to conventional forms. The unusual number of citations has made advisable a footnote form which offers the most abbreviated yet unambiguous means of identifying the source. Volumes of poetry, for which full imprint data have been supplied in the Bibliography, have been referred to in a shortened footnote form. Other works not listed in the Bibliography have been identified fully in the footnotes. In view of the many and often deliberate exceptions to standard spelling and punctuation in the verse quotations, I have abandoned what would surely become a distracting use of the cautionary *"sic."* Apparent errors have been scrupulously preserved, however. Finally, for the sake of my own stylistic freedom and variety I have chosen to use synonymously and as collectives the terms "verse" and "poetry," "versifier" and "poet."

R.H.W.

Acknowledgments

It is a pleasure publicly to acknowledge some of the many important debts I have incurred in the course of this project. In earlier form it appeared as a doctoral dissertation at the University of Pennsylvania ("Social Themes in Late Nineteenth Century American Verse: A Quantitative Study," 1955), and therein I have gratefully described the helpfulness of several members of the Graduate Faculty at that University, and of David Jonah and his staff at the John Hay Library, where most of my reading was done. I owe a special and continuing debt to Robert E. Spiller, under whose specific direction the dissertation was completed.

In shaping the book to its present form I have had the help of three distinguished readers, Daniel Aaron, Anthony Garvan, and Henry Nash Smith, all of whom I thank most cordially. Ralph H. Gabriel, whose perceptive helpfulness is legendary, gave me the benefit of his reactions to one section of the manuscript, as well as to some of the larger ideas involved. The preparation of a manuscript was made financially possible through the generosity of Dean Robert H. Bruce and the Graduate Research Council of the University of Wyoming. The labor of typing was performed by two exceptionally competent and intelligent ladies, Mrs. Lydia Matthews and Mrs. Phyllis Stevie, who saved me from many errors. Mrs. Stevie carried the principal burden so skilfully and so encouragingly that I am at a loss for adequate thanks.

It was my privilege, during the final stages of my work, to

use the Library of Congress, where Harold W. Cumbo was especially helpful in making research facilities available. Morale and mind were both improved by the company of Roy P. Basler, the late Vincent L. Eaton, Robert H. Land, Donald H. Mugridge, and Edward N. Waters. Of the many helpful members of the Prints and Photographs Division, I would like particularly to thank Milton Kaplan for his imaginative advice in selecting the chapter headpieces.

It is natural that the staff of a good press should contribute to the quality of the books which they publish. I would like to acknowledge not only this expected help, but also the truly exceptional services of the copy editor assigned to my manuscript, Amy Clampitt. Both style and logic improved markedly under her direction; she deserves more credit than I can fairly record.

A few friends and colleagues have supplied, through their sympathetic presence and considerate acts, more help than they realize. They expect, I am sure, no formal recognition; but I would like to mention the names of at least a few of them: James H. Coberly, Charles W. Cole, Herbert R. Dieterich, Eugene N. Hardy, William R. Hutchison, Calvin D. Linton, John K. Mathison, and William R. Steckel.

For permission to reprint material which first appeared in article form, I would like to thank the editors of the *American Quarterly* and the *Mississippi Valley Historical Review*. Acknowledgment is also made of permission to quote short passages from the following works: Alfred Kazin, *On Native Grounds* (Harcourt, Brace, 1942); Arthur M. Schlesinger, *Rise of the City* (Macmillan, 1938); and Mark Sullivan, *Our Times*, vol. I (Scribner, 1926).

R.H.W.

Contents

Illustrations

All illustrations are from the Prints and Photographs Division, Library of Congress, Washington, D.C.

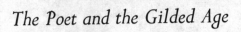

The Poet and the Gilded Age

I

The Poet and the Gilded Age

IN THE FOREGROUND OF THIS STUDY WILL BE THE question of what kind of America emerges from the pages of its poets at the end of the nineteenth century. In the background will be some equally interesting questions about the Gilded Age verse maker, his role as citizen and interpreter, his degree of similarity to that small number of better-known poets on the basis of whose output he is characteristically judged. In order to appraise the contribution of the poet, the specific character of the age must be recalled. What were the principal facts and conditions through which the poet, by noting and ignoring, by favoring and opposing, helped reveal the nature of this age and of his own relationship to it? What, first of all, do we mean when we talk about America's "Gilded Age"?

i

Even chronologically, this is a difficult question to answer. The term "Gilded Age" has been used with more than the historian's customary looseness—almost by default at times— to refer to a set of conditions which came into existence some time between the Civil War Reconstruction and the Edwardian or "Progressive" period which ushered in the new century. Although arbitrarily imposed, the scope of this study offers a reasonable opportunity for locating the Gilded Age with increased precision. Coverage begins with 1876, a year which witnessed the end of military and political Reconstruction, and which offered some notorious specimens of the political and economic problems which were to plague the coming generation. Coverage extends far enough beyond the turn of the century (1905) to make possible an appraisal of what brought about the change from a Gilded to a Progressive Age. Within this thirty-year range, the verse centers on twenty years (the eighteen-eighties and -nineties) which supposedly exhibited the characteristics representative of the Gilded Age. As a result of this chronological focus, we may be better equipped to locate the Gilded Age once we agree on its salient characteristics.

In this period of years, we find an era damned by those who have named it. "The Gilded Age," suggesting as it does a time when all was show and nothing substance, is only the most common designation for the years in question. With the possible exception of "The Tragic Era," or the "Age of Hate," which preceded and to a certain extent overlapped it, no era has received so unflattering a set of sobriquets. The general drift of such labels as "The Great Barbecue," "The Brown Decades," "The Mauve Decade," "The Chromo Civilization," as well as others less wholeheartedly damning—"The Buried Renaissance," "The Age of Innocence," and "The Gay Nineties"— is sufficient to suggest the kind of impression those years have made in retrospect: a tasteless time, surely; a time of pale and pretentious shades and shapes, false fronts and other artificialities. Beneath the surface? Corruption: a time when representatives of business and government joined hands to supervise the plunder of the public pocketbook, a time when public interest went unheeded in a market where the bids were high. And what was the public attitude toward all this misrepresentation and dishonesty supposed to have been? Uncritical, complacent, innocent acceptance. Yet to recall the existence of a Populist Party or a Pullman strike is to remind oneself that this period is not susceptible to so over-simple a characterization. What was it like, then? How can it be described?

The Gilded Age, as it reveals itself both in the manner in

which the poet recorded its principal conditions and in the nature of his reactions to these conditions, can best be understood as an era in which opposing forces and reactions were at work in almost every area of the culture. The events themselves reveal a series of countervailing tendencies; the public—to an extent which the verse may help us appreciate—was of two minds in its reaction to these events.

The divided nature of the Gilded Age reveals itself in so basic a factor as demography; for the two most important directions of population redistribution had quite different implications. The one, a movement toward the Western frontier, has suggested to most historians a continuing renewal of our basic national experience up to that time: a contact of democracy with the wilderness and an extension of the fundamentally agrarian nature of the republic. The contribution of this experience has been seen in the emphasis it placed on such traits of national character as individualism and self-reliance. The flux of American citizens toward the cities, on the other hand, suggests the emergence of an influence diametrically opposed to that of the frontier. The city denotes the coming of an industrial—rather than agrarian—condition and philosophy; in place of individualism and self-reliance the city demands a collective point of view and a state of mutual dependence. As the obvious line of frontier settlement became less clearly discernible, the opportunity arose for retrospective appraisal of this important element of national development. As the city's new prominence became impossible to ignore, there arose a parallel opportunity for assessing America's future.

Did the citizen of the Gilded Age take advantage of these opportunities? Did he record the latter days of the frontier as well as the rise of the city? How did he appraise the Western experience? Was the westward march for him an ennobling agrarian experience studded with episodes of embryo-democracy? Did he find the meaning of the West in political innovation, in applied materialism, in scenic geography, or in international implications? To what degree, on the other hand, did he find his age dominated by the mounting factor of urban culture? What sort of force was the newly dominant city thought to be? Which of its many features appeared most telling? Was the late-nineteenth-century citizen prepared to relinquish that historic portrait of America as the land of the independent, self-sufficient freeholder, blessed by nature and inculcated with all the virtues pertinent thereunto, for the sake of a new national environment of sidewalks and subways? Did he see that as America's past lay with the frontier, so her future lay with the city; and, if so, what sort of future did he imagine this to be?

Economically, even more than demographically, the Gilded Age was characterized by conflicting strains. Are we to understand this era primarily as one that had witnessed the triumph of American enterprise, that had lionized the entrepreneur and the engineer and elevated to the stature of unwritten law the Gospel of Wealth? Did the spectacular increase in goods and services justify to the consumer the system which produced them? Was poverty either taken as a consequence of natural law or remanded to the beneficence of a benign stewardship of wealth? Or are we to see as dominant economic traits those suggested by strikes and bombs, by marching armies of unemployed, and by increasing organization in the ranks of both industrial and agricultural workers? Did social Darwinism have a rival church in socialism?

In the closely related area of political activity the personality of the times was split in a similar manner. We may ask, on the one hand, whether the voter was successfully distracted from fundamental issues by the continued waving of the bloody-shirt Civil War issue or by the politically meaningless details of candidates' personal lives. Did the war-veteran-turned-professional-politician emerge an unscathed hero in the political arena? Were the major parties able, unnoticed or at least uncensored, to take turns at the till of public office, each conniving with business, each making its own mockery of civil service, and each determinedly avoiding commitment on the true and pressing issues? Or, on the other hand, how much of the true political picture of the period belongs in the album of such protesting splinter groups as the Liberal Republicans, Green-backers, Socialists, and Populists? To what extent can we understand the age in terms of sincere debates over taxes, tariffs, and currency policies? Was the political character of this period determined more by the corrupt and complacent spirit of the preceding decades or by the era of protest and reform which followed?

In the politico-economic nature of the times we see a carefully defined philosophy and technique—the Gospel of Wealth and the system of professional politics—designed to promote the continuing acceptance of unregulated laissez-faire and unchal-lenged two-party spoilsmanship. This fortress status quo was under siege by the often poorly organized forces of protest: Socialists, Populists, and other groups who shunned the two-party structure in order to oppose both political corruption and economic inequity. This warfare, which divided the Gilded Age into extremes as great as have ever existed side by side, had its prominent generals and chaplains. But where were the privates? Which side captured the support and sympathy of the public? What were the major battles? This crucial and divisive warfare still confronts us with its legacy.

A related skirmish in which the lines were far less clearly drawn involved the unceasing battle for a higher humanitarian level in the culture. From the welter of causes which might fall under such a heading—everything from beautifying the home to abolishing capital punishment—each age makes its own selections. One sees the character of the times not only in this selective process but also in the nature and extent of the argu-ments for and against such reform movements. Did the Gilded Age have its humanitarian side? What causes did it favor? What revealing assumptions were made by those who argued in these social debates?

The end of the nineteenth century we recall as a time of

shifting and broadening international horizons as viewed from American shores. Conditions changed, technologically and demographically; patterns varied, diplomatically and militarily; new ingredients appeared from all sources. These changes called forth new attitudes; problems arose whose resolutions were to form a bridge between the receding shores of the Enlightenment and the emerging coastline of the twentieth century.

America had long cherished her role as haven for the polyglot multitudes, although her experience with immigrant "hordes" had been largely confined to those from Northern and Western Europe. Now that immigration patterns had begun to change, what was to be her attitude? Would she court as eagerly the non-Protestant Southern European, the non-Christian Central European and Asiatic? Americans were forced to re-define themselves religiously and ethnically; some vitally important aspects of the nation's fundamental meaning were bound to emerge.

For the first time America became a major diplomatic and military force outside the immediate confines of her own continent. What kind of force was she to be? The spirit of the times was rife with ideas of national evolution, racism, imperialism; was America to accept the challenge of expansion, assume the onus of the white man's burden? Or was she to remember the days of 1776 and be true to the idea of the underdog as ruler in his own kennel? The facts of America's march into this new order of international affairs are well enough known, but we have less knowledge of the climate in which these decisions were reached, the nature and popularity of the various points of view, and the direction of the appeals put forth by those who argued for a specific commitment. The attitudes were various and the episodes were complex, both at home and abroad; but once again the memory of America's historic stand for independence and the right of self-determination was pitted against the fashionable expediencies of expansion and empire.

Since it is the poet of whom we shall be asking these questions
—the poet who sometimes plumbs, analyzes, parodies and
prophesies—we may venture beyond events and conditions.
We may not only question surface reactions, but we may also
discover preoccupations which help determine a mood, a temper
of the times. If the hallmark of the age was stamped by science,
if the proudest strides of progress were dictated by the applications of this branch of knowledge, then what were the consequences in terms of shaping the public mind? As carriages gave
way to steam-cars, were humanists to give way to scientists?
In welcoming the telephone, did the age also welcome a way of
thought which made its inroads on older habits and points of
view? Another characteristic of the age was its success in out-
doing former ages in things material and quantitative. Did this
condition open a new chapter in the history of American ideas?
If things were in the saddle, need materialists, in the narrow
sense, ride the national mind? Another dominant aspect of the
age was to be found in our international emergence. As the
doctrines of Roosevelt and Mahan replaced the doctrines of
Washington and Monroe, what happened to the idea of
American nationalism? As we stretched towards Cuba, Hawaii
and the Philippines, were we also reaching out for a new and
different definition of the nation? In raising such questions as
these one can come to terms with the meaning of the period in a
more basic and sweeping manner.

The immediate aftermath of the Civil War had ended; the
next twenty-five years were to be marked by the efforts of the
first generation of modern Americans to cope with such newly
dominant forces as large-scale manufacturing, commercial and
financial enterprise, and the mechanized super-city. Founded on
Enlightenment ideas, which were modified in turn by the
democratic waves of the 1830's, the United States had scarcely
found time for self-testing before the impact of disrupting
sectional strife shook its very foundations. With this matter at
least superficially resolved, the nation returned once more to

"Experiment America," only to find the laboratory unrecogniz-
ably re-equipped. The worlds of Washington, of Jefferson, even
of Jackson, gave way to a set of conditions which had hardly
been envisaged in earlier days. The post-Reconstruction generation had to face the question of whether a system conceived by
agrarians could work for industrialists; of whether blueprints
drawn in eighteenth-century, rural America could continue to
guide us in the urban world of the late nineteenth century; of
whether principles established in seclusion from international
pressures, with a wilderness at the back door, could be applied
in a time of disappearing frontiers and emerging international
involvements. Looking backward, this end-of-the-century
generation reveals an important tension between the facts of its
contemporary life and the institutions with which it was
expected to deal with them.

Looking forward from the Gilded Age toward our own, we
see another kind of significance. Any epoch casts its influences
unpredictably forward into time; one era, however, may
peculiarly influence a later one if it takes upon itself the resolution of civilization's recurrent problems in a context which
shapes them both. In twentieth-century America we are still
very much involved with the problems of adapting our individualistic democracy to the context of urban, industrial internationalism. May we not find, in fact, that the generation of
1880–1900 set us most firmly on our present course by taking
up *de novo* the very problems we now face and by reacting to
them in modern terms.

Our modern literature was rooted in those dark and still little-
understood years of the 1880's and 1890's when all America stood
suddenly, as it were, between one society and another, one moral order
and another, and the sense of impending change became almost
oppressive in its vividness. It was rooted in the drift to the new world
of factories and cities, with their dissolution of old standards and
faiths; in the emergence of the metropolitan culture that was to
dominate the literature of the new period; in the Populists who raised

their voices against the domineering new plutocracy in the East . . .
But above all was it rooted in the need to learn what the reality of life
was in the modern era.

In a word, our modern literature came out of those great critical
years of the late nineteenth century which saw the emergence of
modern America, and was molded in its struggles.[1]

ii

We have asked a great many questions about the essential
nature and significance of the Gilded Age; we have even
suggested, by quoting Alfred Kazin, that the writer was

seriously involved in determining and expressing the concerns of this day. But was the poet, as such, of any significance in this process? What sort of citizen was he? Did he notice those facets of his culture which either his contemporaries or his descendants might regard as important or revealing? How perceptive was his participation in those crucial years?

Were we to ask such questions of the historians who have told us most about the later decades of the century, we would probably receive responses unflattering to the reputation of the poet-as-citizen. Except for quoting a line here from "The Man with the Hoe" in illustration of agrarian discontents, or a line there from "Ode in Time of Hesitation," revealing America's reluctance to accept the imperial mantle, the historian seems unaware of any effective citizenship on the part of America's verse writers. Were we to ask such questions of the critics and chroniclers of America's letters, moreover, we would receive— if possible—an even less flattering testimonial to the poet's social perceptivity. If the historian had counted on the student of belles-lettres to show him evidences of social concern in our literature, surely he would have found none in literary histories of the Gilded Age.

A composite summary of the literary historian's view of late-nineteenth-century verse might include as many as three categories of verse writers, none of them calculated to arouse a more than belletristic interest if even that. First come the grand old men of ante-bellum reputation who continued to write poetry throughout much of the century: Holmes, Longfellow, Lowell, Whittier, and Whitman. These were, to be sure, major writers whose output is useful for many reasons; but, with the exception of Whitman, they made their important comments on the America of pre-Civil War days. For the student of the Gilded Age they have little relevance. A second group, achieving maturity around the outbreak of the Civil War, likewise represents a somewhat earlier generation, albeit one which continued productively till about 1900. Its leaders were Thomas

Bailey Aldrich, Edmund Clarence Stedman, Richard Henry Stoddard, and Bayard Taylor; and they gave us our closest approach to a true Victorian school of poets. But the literary character of each had been formed before the Gilded Age was ushered in, and the body of verse they left us can be understood more constructively as an extension of European literature than as a comment on late-century America. A third group is sometimes encountered: a seldom identified body of collegiate-bohemian poets who were united in their rebellion against Victorian verse conventions and in their admiration for Oscar Wilde. The pastel ephemera which fell from their pens demonstrated their delicacy with the triolet, their virtuosity with the villanelle. Dedicated to art for its own sake, they mirrored little of their social environment.

These three groups represent the extent of literary-historical interest in the late-nineteenth-century writer of verse. Whether or not, in terms of the limited materials on which it is based, such an appraisal is just, it offers little encouragement to one seeking further understanding of an age through its literary output. The literary historian, either by intention or by default, has consigned the verse of the Gilded Age to the limbo of social irrelevancy. How momentous a judgment this represents, even to the critic interested primarily in literary rather than social criteria, may be clearly seen through the eyes of Edmund Clarence Stedman, important to this age not only as a poet but also as an anthologist. In introducing his compendious collection of nineteenth-century American poetry he made the point that, next to its essential poetic quality, what marks a verse for distinction is "its quality as an expression and interpretation of the time itself." Further emphasizing what might fairly be called the social value of verse, he continued:

In many an era the second factor [social relevance] may afford a surer means of estimate than the first, inasmuch as the purely literary result may be nothing rarer than what the world already has possessed, nor greatly differing from it; nevertheless, it may be the voice of a time, of a generation, of a people,—all of extraordinary import to the world's future. . . . One who underrates the significance of our literature, prose or verse, as both the expression and the stimulant of national feeling, as of import in the past and to the future of America, and therefore of the world, is deficient in that critical insight which can judge even of its own day unwarped by personal taste or deference to public impression.[2]

Recognizing thus acutely the importance of literature as a voice of the times, Stedman then found fault with the post-bellum poets for being less demonstrably engaged with their social milieu than their predecessors had been.[3] Surely the many poems which he selected to represent the Gilded Age contribute little to an understanding of its conditions and concerns.

The relegation of the poet to this limbo of disaffiliation, then, is no small matter. While it is not the purpose of the present study to offer a head-on challenge to that verdict, some related and pertinent questions ought, surely, to be raised. Does the verse product of the age, considered as a whole, reveal the same characteristics as the quantitatively lesser sampling to which the critics have given their main attention? Is the poet of aesthetic distinction a different sort of citizen from his less successful literary contemporary? Or is it possible that what we need is not so much a new set of materials as a new point of view when approaching verse in search of its social meaning? We may perhaps be in a position to profit from further definition of our glib collective, "the poet," especially when speaking of his relation to the issues of his day.

NOTES

[1] Alfred Kazin, *On Native Grounds* (N.Y.: Harcourt, Brace, 1942), pp. viii–ix.
[2] Edmund C. Stedman, *An American Anthology* (Boston: Houghton, Mifflin, 1900), p. xxii.
[3] *Ibid.*, pp. xxiii, xxvi.

THE GREAT WEST

II

Westward to Destiny

THE CLOSING YEARS OF THE NINETEENTH CENTURY
represent an interesting and decisive era in the history of the
Western United States—an era replete with commemorative

occasions from whose vantage points diverse attempts were made to evaluate the distant and recent regional past. In the final eleven years of the century, seven new Western states were added to the Union. A series of pretentious expositions, beginning with the great "World's Columbian" at Chicago in 1893, called attention to cities which had been but frontier outposts not so long ago. San Francisco opened the first Pacific Coast international exposition in 1894; Omaha fêted the trans-Mississippi West in 1898; St. Louis adorned the largest acreage of all with its Louisiana Purchase Exposition of 1904; and in 1905 and 1909 Portland and Seattle once again drew attention to the Far West. If these celebrations needed a commemorative rationale, one could readily be found in the epochal report, drawn from the 1890 census, which seemed to herald the close of a frontier age.

Considering the attention which has been given to the influence of the Western frontier in American history—as fact, as myth, as thesis—the varied intellectual reactions to that region's passing are of particular importance. The poets who wrote at that time, although not necessarily exact reporters of events, were important among those who created abstract meanings out of the Western experience. They functioned as chroniclers, as intellectual historians, and as makers and destroyers of myths. What might one expect from the poet who sought to sum up the last decades of the nineteenth-century West? On the one hand lay a clear record of growth and progress. In spite of the lure of Eastern cities, the population west of the Mississippi had grown more than threefold from 1870 to 1900, while the other half of the nation had less than doubled. In the shifting demographic tides of those times, the West achieved a net gain of from two to four million people during each decade. The more spectacular of the mining "rushes" had either tapered off or ended entirely, leaving areas like Nevada with fewer people in 1900 than in 1870; but such losses were more than offset by a continuing regional growth in mineral productivity, by the settlement of such virgin areas as Oklahoma and the Dakotas, and by the fourfold growth in the population of such older states as Texas. In the last quarter of the century, perfected homestead entries totaled 77.6 million acres.

Statistics pointing to growth and achievement could be compounded endlessly, but they would not erase the other side of the Western picture, more vivid then than now. It was not only prospectors who often returned empty-handed; so did many plains farmers as well. For them, the West of the eighties and nineties meant drought, poverty, economic victimization, and political protest. Few cattle herders got rich on the back-breaking long drive; even mine owners and cattle barons fought nature and barbed wire with only intermittent success. These were the decades which, judging from experience, saw the often stern facts of the region replace the myth of the West as the world's equalitarian Eden, garden of plenty:

> Alas, in our Utopian West,
> Success, howe'er attained is best!
> An arrant knave may wear the ermine,
> And office honor is a jest!
>
> Behold the want, the greedy strife,
> The office-hungry harpies rife,
> The slaughters, lynchings, strikes and riots.
> The scorn of law and human life![1]

Yet the West as a source of positive inspiration was by no means neglected. The following, in its affirmative tone, is decidedly more representative than the disillusioned lines cited above:

> Turn Westward, and ye shall be (though weary ye were
>   and sad)
> Made one with the sea and sun, and the breezes that
>   woo the hills;
> And ye shall rejoice with men, who labor, yet who
>   are glad,
> Because they are free themselves . . .[2]

On these alternatives rested the poet's potential as chronicler and myth-maker. His choices were obviously conditioned by personal response to the realities of Western life; yet, when quantitatively assessed, his reactions reveal well-defined similarities of thought regarding the meaning and influence of the Western experience.

i

There were two clear sources of negative inspiration to the poet-observer of the frontier. One of these was the Indian, and the versifier reacted to this "noble savage" in a manner which firmly excluded him from a share in the magnificent Western legacy. Custer's Last Stand, that calendar-illustration event par excellence, allowed a score of poets the opportunity not only for obvious drama but also for appraisal of the contestants. Epithets applied to the Redmen, in this encounter, ranged from the relatively neutral "Fierce hordes of painted braves" to the damning "bloody Neroes."[3] Only two or three of these narrators in verse showed any sympathy for the Indian, and they cautioned that he was only, in the long pull, resisting the greater "destiny" of the new Americans.[4]

Following the lead of the dime and half-dime fiction, poets occasionally turned to narrations of that classic situation, the capture of the pioneer mother or daughter by the Indians.[5] These accounts, although not nearly so frequent in verse as in prose, contribute nothing at all toward the reader's esteem for the aborigines. But the extent to which the Indian was patronized can best be appreciated against the background of the Spanish-American War, that "splendid" occasion for celebrating the reunion of North and South and of black and white. Here the magically catalytic experience of military action under Old Glory was occasionally seen as strong enough even to "Americanize" the Indian! Thus "The Red Private" in Cuba was comforted, "Come home to your mother, the mighty West,/ Baptized a man and American."[6] The idea of the white American naturalizing the Indian, proposed with a perfectly straight face, demonstrated how small a part the Indian played in the poet's evaluation of the Western experience.

Another aspect of that experience which failed to provide affirmative inspiration to the poet was the plight of the farmer. This is not surprising when one considers the difficulties— drought, insect pests, dust storms—faced by the agricultural pioneer as he crossed the hundredth meridian into that treeless, subhumid area known as the High Plains. Even when crops prospered there were such factors as currency deflation,

European competition, the railroad, and the speculator to be
dealt with. But the poetic treatment of the farmer has unusual
interest in the light of the emphasis placed by Frederick Jackson
Turner and others on the agrarian element in the frontier
situation. Not only has the idea of free land to the west been
continually cited as an important safety valve for the oppressed
Eastern urban laborer, but the theory of the frontier as an
important formative element in the institutions and character of
the United States has always presupposed a strong connection
with the land and with farming. From Jefferson through Turner,
and even more recently, the importance of the frontier experience has called forth an image of the freeholding farmer,
economically self-sufficient, socially equalitarian, and politically
democratic.[7] That the poets, the myth-makers, were able to turn
this aspect of frontier life to no positive account is significant
indeed.

The rural verse of the eighties and nineties offers a mixed
bag. On the one hand the rustic bards upheld the farm against
the city with a vehemence sometimes born of desperation (see
Chapter III). On the other hand, an entire history of the agrarian
protest of this period could be reconstructed from the verse of
all regions of the country, featuring the Grange, the Wheel, the
Farmers' Alliance, and the Populist Party (see Chapters IV and
V). But the rural verse that was peculiarly Western struck
only one consistent note: failure.

Hopes were high as the agricultural pioneer wended his
westward way:

> A "PRAIRIE SCHOONER" creeping slow;
> A way-worn, jaded household band,
> In eager voices, speaking low—
> Thus we enter the "promised land."[8]

But hopes were not fulfilled. Only infrequently could one
discover a hymn to the satisfaction of toil amid nature's bounty
emanating from a Western setting. Where the prairie was made

to bloom, the event was regarded as the result "sorcery" rather
than a dependable annual recurrence. The enemies of man in this
setting included the dust storm, the blizzard, the tornado, the
grasshopper, the beetle, and the prairie fire; but by far the most
prevalent and devastating obstacle was the drought:

> Away to the east, brown ridges thin and bare
> Notch the blue burning sky;
> There is no motion in the quivering air,
> No wild bird hurries by.[9]

> . . . parched to death,
> And the shrivelled maize sobs dead,
> And the burnt wheat bows the head,
> And the gray dust stifles breath . . .[10]

These were more than the ordinary hazards of rural life. That
they meant not merely success or failure, but, in some cases,
literally life or death may be gathered from a poem titled "The
Grasshopper War," or from the truly epic terms in which a
seemingly ordinary prairie storm could be described when the
outcome might provide a life-giving rain.[11] Man was pitted here
against the elements, with no holds barred; the elements
enjoyed the position of odds-on favorite. Before the reader's
eyes, violently and dramatically, the myth of the Western
garden, gave place to the myth of the Western desert.[12]

Not only backs but spirits were being broken in the process.
In the unrelieved flatness of the prairie it was not difficult to
imagine oneself as "lonelier than God."[13] In the persistent heat
of a cloudless drought, one thought readily of "men/Whose
hearts and brains have been slowly seared"; and in the ever-
present wind one came to detect "a sneering sigh of ennui."[14]
Thus from the poetry emerged a saga of beleaguered humanity
struggling against the overwhelming forces of the plains frontier.
Until new tools and technology could be brought to bear on this
environment, the saga typically ended in failure or in that kind
of desperate stubbornness expressed by Hamlin Garland: " 'To

hell with your rain and your snow./ . . . despite of your anger
we go!' "[15] The testament is a shocking one. That it was
compiled by people who left the East full of confidence and
dreams of plenty, and whose plaints would only make them
appear misguided in the eyes of the stay-at-homes, or by people
from areas bent on proselytizing settlers, makes its negative
character even more remarkable.

ii

The manner in which the poetic recorders of the West
characterized their contemporaries constituted a middle ground

between the sources of negative and positive reaction; for the poet selectively depicted traits which were at the same time admirable and reprehensible, actions which were interpreted both constructively and destructively. The quality of fearlessness, an allegedly prime ingredient in the Western makeup, provides an excellent case in point. Credit was claimed by the West not only for feats of heroism on its own soil but even for those of Colonel Roosevelt and his Rough Riders in the Cuban campaign and of "The Montanas at Caloocan" in the Philippines.[16] A special case was made for the pioneer women, "Hardy of nerve and sinew," who were quick to adapt "to the rough, weird and new."[17] This case was occasionally developed to the discredit of the male (as in the ballad "Sweet Betsy from Pike") when the female fortitude proved itself over the obstacle of desertion by the male. The wife, having fed the young and fought off the Indians, might or might not receive back into the fold a returning, repentant spouse.[18]

The border line between courage and willful violence could be seen in a comic episode described by one poet. This narrative opened with the entry of a greenhorn into a mining camp where he received the gratuitous insults of harlots and gunmen alike. Presently the greenhorn revealed himself as a man of the cloth who had determined to make these untamed people repent of their sinful ways. He succeeded in gaining a hearing only when, after receiving further generous helpings of insult and ignominy, he mounted the bar of the saloon (the pulpit of the West, in this case) and threatened to dash to the floor a stick of dynamite clutched in his hand if he were not given a respectful audience. The choice between two approaches to the hereafter proved irresistible, and the preacher had his say.[19] Similarly, the morbid and sanguine side of Western fearlessness could be demonstrated by any number of colorful anecdotes, such as "How they Histed 'Chloride Joe' "—wherein "hist" is in fact a euphemism for "kill" since the cemeteries were on higher ground than the towns.[20] Fearlessness degenerating into lawlessness was depicted in the rough-and-tumble politics of the area where public welfare often went unheeded, and in the economic and social instability aggravated by clashing tempers.[21] Even cruelty was occasionally depicted as a Western trait, as in the account of a prairie farmer who turned away a shelter-seeking family to freeze in the gathering storm.[22]

Two other traits predominated in the poetic profile of the Westerner. One was greed, which the poet saw as tingeing the open-handed generosity for which the frontiersman was noted. The Klondike meant "Gold and greed"; from the mania for wealth, Cripple Creek became the "Curse of Colorado"; California was "Mammon's In Memorian."[23] The third Western characteristic, openness of nature, was also especially evident in the mining-camp environment. Here Uncle Sam's great melting pot could be seen to bubble contentedly over the evening fires as Irish, French, Negroes, and even Indians and Chinese—often received inhospitably in other Western settings —worked and lived together harmoniously over long periods of time in an atmosphere determined by the Westerner's easy inclination to take people as he found them. At the other end of the scale from nature's noble innocence was a foolish naïveté, fully and poignantly illustrated in the many tales of Westerners duped and fleeced by Eastern urbanites.

The contrast between East and West helped define the features of the Western portrait. In his reaction to the visit of Oscar Wilde, apotheosis of the effete East and Europe, that professional Westerner Bill Nye spoke for his own region:

> We yearn
> To put the bloom upon thy alabaster nose . . .
> With our free, untutored ways and wild . . .[24]

This composite portrait was drawn with a primitive, "free, untutored" hand. The virtues—fearlessness, innocence, and generosity—were primitive virtues; the vices—violence, cruelty, lawlessness, credulity, and greed—were primitive vices.

To arrive at the ideal American, the Westerner would have crossed John L. Sullivan with Buffalo Bill.[25]

Thus the poet found himself in approximate agreement with Professor Turner's idea that the frontier, through initiating a series of stages in society commencing with the primitive, would encourage the purification and improvement of American characteristics and institutions. With Turner's estimate of the eventual effect, as will be shown below, he was in total accord. But the poet saw, as far as Western character was concerned, no clearly ascending line of development. In fact, looking backward from this portrait of his contemporary Westerner, the poet recognized an earlier stage of the frontier experience as productive of a far more admirable type. In evincing more respect for his forebears than for his contemporaries, the poet interpreted the stages of character development wrought by the frontier as retrogressive in some respects.

iii

The character traits described thus far belonged to the Western farmer, rancher, miner, cowhand, businessman, and politician of the eighties and nineties. When the poet turned to the trail-blazers and settlers of earlier eras, he dropped his frank and colorful brush and palette and climbed a figurative Mt. Rushmore, mallet and chisel in hand. While less vividly perceptive than his contemporary portraits, his celebration of the pioneer furnished a voluminous source of positive inspiration for the poet of the West.

Although grandiloquent, these tributes have the ring of sincerity, often because the writer followed close enough in the wake of the revered pioneer to feel a literal indebtedness and to reap a tangible reward. "Theirs was the deed; the guerdon ours" ran the appreciative refrain:[26]

> O Pioneer, what task is set for thee!
> Not thine to taste the fruit, but plant the tree;
> The years of strife are thine . . .[27]

They rise to mastery of wind and snow;
They go like soldiers grimly into strife
To colonize the plain. They plow and sow,
And fertilize the sod with their own life,
As did the Indian and the buffalo.[28]

To celebrate this theme with proper scope and setting, the poet brought back to life and paraded before his reader a whole series of explorers and trail blazers: Coronado, a favorite among Spanish explorers; John Smith, Daniel Boone, John C. Frémont, and William F. Cody. Lewis and Clark were so highly regarded that the poet momentarily forgot his deep-seated prejudice against the Indian, and wrote appreciatively of their controversial guide, Sacajawea.[29] Groups, rather than individuals, were frequently chosen to personify the pioneer virtues. Those who sought to underline more blood-thirsty qualities most frequently chose the heroes of the Alamo as emblematic of hardiness, bravery, and martyrdom. Those who preferred exemplars of love and patience often chose the Franciscans of California. But with such a range of subjects, it is obvious that the poets were celebrating not so much specific heroes or events—whether remote or near at hand—as a quality that might be called the pioneer spirit, which itself was sometimes explicitly traced throughout the long history of man.[30]

Whatever the particular focus, the theme was constant: an appreciation for the "martyr lives" of those who were the "Vanguard of progress, heralds of time."[31] Often a comparison was made between the pioneer and his successor: "Bronzed, haggard men . . . with thirst a-moan . . . Rebuke the softness of modern man . . ."[32] This first wave of settlers conquered nature with persistence and courage; they worked hard; they lived austerely, with no use for fashion, leisure, or convenience. In contrast, the poet found a modern daughter spending as long at her coiffure as her mother did at baking the bread.[33] In the case of the mineral prospectors an interesting distinction was made: for, whereas the contemporary gold-seekers of the eighties and nineties were scorned as Mammon's greedy slaves, the early prospectors were classed as "argonauts" and given credit for trail-blazing and other pioneer virtues.[34] The contrasting artificialities of the Gilded Age were dealt with sternly, whether they manifested themselves in Eastern city or on Western farm. James Whitcomb Riley spoke with rude effectiveness for this point of view:

> I want plane facts, and I want plane words,
> Of the good old fashioned ways . . .
> Tell me a tale of the timber-lands—
> Of the old-time pioneers;
> Somepin' a pore man understands
> With his feelins's well as ears.[35]

An implied criticism of the ways of fashion and soft living could be read into many of these verses as the pioneer spirit was celebrated for itself, for its legacy, and for its contemporary relevance. Had their skill allowed it, these spokesmen would have gladly seconded the famous stanza of Katharine Lee Bates, doubtless italicizing the second word in the second line:

> O beautiful for pilgrim feet,
> Whose stern, impassioned stress
> A thoroughfare for freedom beat
> Across the wilderness.[36]

The second source of consistent pride in the West stemmed from the growth of cities and towns, commerce and industry; from the two samples which follow, the nature of this pride will be readily appreciated:

> O'er sunny Kansas
> Some commercial Cadmus,
> In days unknown,
> The teeth of golden dragons must have sown;
> For when the prairies
> Feel the breath of summer,
> The trowels ring,
> And from the soil the burnished cities spring.[37]

> Love to hear the hammers poundin'
> On the bitin' drills,
> Hear the dynamite a soundin'
> Through the 'tarnal hills. . . .
> Love to see the stir an' bustle
> In the busy town,
> Everybody on the hustle
> Saltin' profits down.
> Everybody got a wad a'
> Ready cash laid by;
> Ain't no flies on Colorado—
> Not a cussed fly.[38]

Most poems of this sort took the form of general tributes to civic and commercial aggressiveness in the best Babbitt-land style, but without many specific referents. The growth of commercial, and to some extent industrial, enterprise formed the specific subject matter; occasionally the prosperity of banks, real estate operations, mines, and railroads was catalogued. Indeed, some few of these verse pamphlets of Western booster-ism were directly sponsored by the railroads in order to point out both the scenic wonders and the commercial opportunities which lay along their right of way. Specific towns and cities, too, were sometimes eulogized in the manner of Kansas and Colorado in the lines above.

Obviously, the reportorial value of such testimony must be radically discounted since the object of so many of these verses was to encourage immigration, investment, or both. But it is interesting to note that when the poet set out to promote his Western home, whether he labored under subsidy or inspiration, he almost never boasted of agricultural prosperity or rural felicity. The rural scene in the eighties and nineties, as shown above, was a gloomy one; when the booster crowed he ignored this aspect of the Western appeal almost entirely, and concentrated on the urban, the industrial, and the commercial.[39] Without detailed local evidence one cannot leap to a cause-and-

effect conclusion; but the consistent focus of such verse does at
least suggest that if the West operated as an effective safety
valve for the Eastern laborer it probably did so by offering
opportunities not in the form of cheap land but in the realm of
trade and manufacturing. The pattern of migration from Europe
and the East suggested here becomes one of farm-to-town, or
town-to-town, rather than the customarily postulated town-to-
farm pattern. Here is a problem for the demographer rather than
the literary historian; but it is at least interesting that the
poetry consistently supported a pattern at variance with the
usual postulations as to the role of the West during these years.

Finally, and most importantly, the poets responded to the
natural aspects of the Western scene to produce a tremendous
corpus of inspirational verse which in quantity amounted to one-
third of all the poetry on the West, and which in tone was
affirmative in the highest degree. Its source lay in the scenic
geography of the West. One verse was reportedly chosen from
among four hundred submitted in a contest on the subject of
Pike's Peak.[40] At least thirty-two separate poems mentioned
some aspect of the Rocky Mountain chain, while thirty-nine
mentioned the Sierras. As a sort of inverted mountain, the Grand
Canyon produced its share of rhapsodies; and the giant sequoias
of California impressed the poet with their age and magnificence.
Even the level prairie became a "mystic, Western deep" for the
schooner to ply.[41]

As a mere picturesque travelogue such poems might have
little interest for the student of an era and a region, but the
poets only began with the scenery. From this awesome setting
they went on to enumerate what they felt to be the special
virtues of the region—everything from a salubrious climate
("Just give us one whack at your ailment,/And we'll knock it as
cold as can be."[42]) to the chance to live "Where Fortune's
favors wait upon the bold."[43] According to Hamlin Garland and
Eugene Field, two of the West's foremost bards, a prime
quality of the region was freedom and lack of restraint:

P.G.A.–D

I have no master but the wind,
My only liege the sun;
All bonds and ties I leave behind,
Free as the wolf I run.[44]

Give me no home 'neath the pale pink dome
    of European skies,
No cot for me by the salmon sea that far to
    the southward lies;
But away out West I would build my nest on
    top of a carmine hill,
Where I can paint, without restraint, creation
    redder still![45]

Many poets not only agreed with them but went on to cite
particular social and political benefits which this land of freedom,
populated with refugees from "Oppressions and plutocracy,"
would promote.[46] For one thing, it could become a melting pot
(as has already been pointed out with special reference to the
mining camp) for peoples of various nationalities and religions;
the admission of Mormon Utah to the Union was cited as a
case in point. Then, too, the admission of the "omnibus" and
other Western states with their advanced constitutions became
a token of the guarantees of popular sovereignty. In this same
vein, Texas, rightly or wrongly, was upheld as a guardian of
"equal rights . . ./Civil, and religious liberty"; Kansas was
applauded for its advances toward temperance (a doubtful ally
of freedom) and female suffrage.[47] Broadened opportunities
for women through a sophisticated acknowledgment of free
relationships between the sexes, unrestrained by the institution
of marriage, was demonstrated by the following parody titled
"Up to Date":

"Where are you going, my pretty maid?"
"I'm going to Dakota, sir," she said.

"May I go with you, my pretty maid?"
"Do you wish a divorce, too, sir?" she said.

"What is your fortune, my pretty maid?"
"My alimony, sir," she said.

"Then I can't marry you, my pretty maid."
"I'm already engaged, kind sir," she said.[48]

All of these rather miscellaneous attributes, some trivial, some important, were gathered up by the poets into a grand and fundamental assertion of America's mission in a Western setting. In these lines the West unhesitatingly took over the nation's role as open-armed receiver of the oppressed, polyglot multitudes, whatever their origin. There were many near parodies of the famous lines on the Statue of Liberty. Nor was the region encouraged merely to become a place of refuge; rather, Iowa was to develop a new Athens, California a new Italy. Rome, Greece, and the Holy Land were frequently alluded to as these verse-writers urged their contemporaries to aim for a civilization which would surpass the historic high points in our European and Hebraic heritage. Passion, enterprise, the sense of dedication were to supply the ingredients missing elsewhere as "This promised land beyond compare . . . shall the old world's youth renew."[49]

To believe in this magnificent eminence required no stretch of the poetic imagination; for the poets the place of the West was preordained by God and dictated by the splendor of the setting. Stimulated by the view from Pike's Peak, one poet imagined how the mountains had dwelt

> With their God, alone, in silence;
> How they, from their lofty station
> Looking downward, saw the progress
> Made by tribes and clans and nations,
> Watched the rise and fall of kingdoms,
> Till at length a fairer people
> Came to dwell beneath their shelter,
> And they too were lifted higher,
> Nearer to the great Creator.[50]

Sometimes this process of evolution was treated as a "natural" phenomenon in the Darwinian sense, as witness the attitude toward the Indians already alluded to; but more often it was ascribed to divine intent. The words "Eden" and "Paradise" occurred so frequently in this connection that there can be no doubt of this association; even such a title as " 'God's Country' —California" can be taken quite literally.[51] The idea of the promised land reached the comic level when a verse titled "California versus Heaven" compared these two to the advantage of the former and described the Californians as disinclined to make a trade.[52]

Thus the poets called attention to the idea of America as a promised land, to Americans as God's chosen people, and to the American experiment as the culmination of the long history of Western civilization. Thus did they reassert a belief in freedom and equality, a faith in progress and constructive evolution. But they did not stop here; to them the prairie schooner had been an "empire ship," leading the star of manifest destiny westward until, in California, the hammock swung symbolically from palm at one end and pine at the other.[53] A people so manifestly blessed as were the Americans of the West could hardly be expected to haul in their sails on reaching California, where

> The world shall press toward her. From the sea
> Awakened Asia shall demand her hand;
> While eager Europe, in the years to be,
> Shall seek alliance with this favored land.[54]

The sense of destiny, the mood of expansionism, the sentiment for empire was veiled ever so thinly, if at all. In such lines as these one can even see the idea of the "passage to India" restated in a new and richer sense. America now had become not merely a highway linking the rich continents of the Renaissance, but a civilization in its own right—one in which the best qualities of the Oriental and Occidental cultures could be united, recast, and given the vigorous stamp of the American West.

The poetic interpretation of the frontier placed such decided emphasis on certain aspects of the West that one may look with augmented understanding at the total picture as drawn from this as well as other appropriate sources. It is clear, for example, from the consistent despair in the poetic treatment of the agricultural aspects of the scene, that during these years the image of the "desert" had triumphed over that of the "garden," thus discounting, to some extent, the importance of the agrarian ingredient in our frontier experience. Although evidence in verse is admittedly less pertinent when one shifts from questions of myths and values to questions of social and economic development, it is nonetheless helpful in an interpretive sense to note how firmly there flourished in the poet's mind that optimistic picture of promise in town and city, in commerce and industry—as contrasted with the equally pervasive image of rural gloom.

But the most impressive pattern of reaction to the frontier relates not to contemporary facts and feelings but to the larger legacy of the Western experience in shaping American character and destiny. The poet, collectively, was not only willing but eager, during this period, to turn his back on the unpleasant facts of Western life: the agricultural depression, the unhealthy influence of speculations in land and commodities, the abuse of power in the hands of railroad tycoons and politicians. To such questions he preferred, as subject matter, the hardiness of the pioneers and the primitive character traits of later settlers—in both of which subjects he professed to see the hope of a re-vitalized culture. In great numbers and with sweeping en-thusiasm the poet turned to a dramatic restatement of the major articles of American faith as they appeared to him with renewed strength in this Western setting. In this light the frontier experience became positive and inspirational indeed. It not only demonstrated the mission of America and the process of constructive evolution, but breathed new life into an aged yet impressive heritage, pointing toward future triumphs of progress and manifest destiny wherein the passage to India was to be achieved in a vigorous and totally Western sense. To judge from the poetry, the prime impact of the Western experience lay not so much on internal questions as on the attitudes with which expanding America faced the world at the opening of the twentieth century.

NOTES

[1] I'Anson, *Vision of Misery Hill*, 105. The term "West" in these pages designates the trans-Mississippi West, although some few poets wrote retrospectively of earlier frontiers.

[2] Sutherland, *Songs of a City*, 88.

[3] Whitman, *Not a Man and Yet a Man*, 227; Ward, *All Sides of Life*, 112.

[4] Belrose, *Thorns and Flowers*, 121.

[5] See, for example, Williams, *'49 to '94*, 3–12; Taney, *Kentucky Pioneer Women*, 34–37.

[6] Cummings, *Flamborough Head*, 27.

[7] For the best recent interpretive summary of these ideas, see Henry N. Smith, *Virgin Land: The American West as Symbol and Myth* (Cambridge: Harvard University Press, 1950). My indebtedness to Professor Smith's interpretation will be seen throughout this analysis. For an account of the Turner Thesis and the ideas succeeding it, see Gene M. Gressley, "The Turner Thesis—a Problem in Historiography," *Agricultural History*, vol. xxxii, no. 4 (1958), pp. 227–249.

[8] Allerton, *Annabel*, 38.

[9] Smith, *Where the Sun Goes Down*, 26.

[10] Bates, *Songs of Exile*, 12–13.

[11] Brooks, *Poems, Ballads, and Songs*, 108–9; Fowler, *Poems*, 91–98.

[12] For the background and importance of these contradictory images see again Smith, *Virgin Land*, especially Chapter XVI. See also the title cited in the succeeding footnote for coincidental evidence.

[13] Huff, *Songs of the Desert*, 9.

[14] Fowler, *Poems*, 92, 94.

[15] Garland, *Trail of the Goldseekers*, 71, from a poem called "Relentless Nature."

[16] Coburn, *Rhymes from a Round-up Camp*, 127–30.

[17] Williams, *'49 to '94*, 3–12.

[18] Tripp, *Legends of Lemars*, 9–11.

[19] Griggs, *Hell's Canyon*.

[20] C. L. Miel, in *Celebration of the Thirty-Ninth Anniversary of the Admission of California into the Union*, 21–23.

[21] Dibble, *Prairie Poems*, 45–48, 49–54; Foss, *Back Country Poems*, 44–45.

[22] Allerton, *Walls of Corn*, 49–51.

[23] Folson, *Love Lyrics*, 25; Huff, *Songs of the Desert*, 56–57; Truesdell, *California's Hymn*, n. pag.; I'Anson, *Vision of Misery Hill*, 55.

[24] Nye, *Chestnuts Old and New*, 264.

[25] Osborne, *Quest of a Lost Type*.

[26] Waterhouse, *Some Homely Little Songs*, 97.

[27] Burgess, *Chant Royal of California*, n. pag.

[28] Garland, *Prairie Songs*, 29.

[29] Buchanan, *Indian Legends*, 9–10, 11–12.

[30] See Washington Ayer's two long verses in *Celebration of the Twenty-Third Anniversary of the Society of California Pioneers*, 17–23; and *Celebration of the Forty-Seventh Anniversary of the Admission of California into the Union by the Society of California Pioneers*, 24–30.

[31] Field, *Little Book of Tribune Verse*, 164; Gilman, *In This Our World*, 8.

[32] Burton, *Message and Melody*, 15–16.

[33] Ernest G. Fahnestock in *Prescott's Plain Dialogues*, 191–92.

[34] Hopkins, *Roses and Thistles*, 390–92.

[35] Riley, Ne[i]ghborly Poems, 53.

[36] This verse, from "America the Beautiful," by Katharine Lee Bates, first appeared in *Congregationalist*, July 4, 1895.

[37] Ware, *Rhymes of Ironquill*, 3.

[38] Adams, *Breezy Western Verse*, 88.

[39] Many poets, in describing Western cities, placed so much emphasis on parks, trees, and natural beauty in an urban setting that the city could be seen taking over the "garden" image which the farm had relinquished. For example: Berkeley was spoken of as a "bower" (Pinney, |*Within the Golden Gate*, n. pag.); Oakland as a "fair city of oaks" (Lambert, *Rhyming Oak Leaves*, 9); Los Angeles as a "garden paradise" (Mace, *Under Pine and Palm*, 131); while San Diego was actually called "Eden town" (Pelton, *Life's Subnbeams and Shadows*, 73).

In contrasting the poetry on rural and on urban subjects, a possible explanation of the poets' preference for the urban scene may rest with the rather surprising distribution of population in that region at that time. In 1890, for example, 44.8 per cent of the people in the Western United States lived in towns or cities; this percentage was higher than the national average and higher than that for any other region except the North Atlantic states. See Adna F. Weber, *Growth of Cities in the Nineteenth Century* (New York: Macmillan [for Columbia University], 1899), p. 30. Another useful clue in assimilating this rather surprising preference of the poet for town over country may be gleaned from David M. Potter's emphasis on abundance rather than free land as a more consistent determinant in the history of the United States, Western or otherwise. See his *People of Plenty* (Chicago: University of Chicago Press, 1954), pp. 158–60.

[40] Davis, *Davis's Poems*, 3–4.

[41] Mighels, *Out of a Silver Flute*, 9. On reading this paragraph, Professor Ralph H. Gabriel pointed out the apparent cultural immaturity of these poets who, obsessed by size, failed to make capital of the equally inspiring smaller details of Western flora and fauna. Not having been alert to this question as I examined the verse, I cannot document this interesting accusation; but it is true that these poets suffered from a "grandeur complex" whose principal effects I have tried to interpret.

[42] Mosher, "*The Stranded Bugle*," 45.

[43] Grant, *By Heath and Prairie*, 63.

[44] Garland, *Trail of the Goldseekers*, 229.

[45] Field, *Second Book of Verse*, 164.

[46] O'Brien, *Birth and Adoption*, 150.

[47] Terry, *Our Pumkin Vine*, 131; Campbell, *Land of Sun and Song*, 38–39.

[48] Burnett, *Love and Laughter*, 43.

[49] Burgess, *Chant Royal of California*, n. pag.

[50] Rice, *View from Pike's Peak*, 14–17.

[51] Kercheval, *Dolores*, 341.

[52] Nevill, *Some Little 'Rimes' Composed at Odd 'Thymes,'* 47.

[53] Waterman, *Book of Verses*, 42–43; Gunnison, *In Macao*, 6.

[54] Sutherland, *Songs of a City*, 81.

III

Gotham and Gomorrah

Two great movements of population charac-
terized the growth of the United States in the late nineteenth
century: one to the West, the other to the city. Captivated by
the idea of a truly continental nation, the poets of the day hailed
the filling in of America's political outline with messianic

enthusiasm. As poetic subject matter the city provided a
considerably more doubtful source of inspiration, albeit its
importance could hardly be denied. After a decade of minimal
increase from 1870-80, the city set out in earnest to dominate
the land.[1] At rates far exceeding the national norm, cities
increased both in population and in wealth; spurred on by im-
provements in transportation and manufacturing, abetted by
invention and technical advance, the city rose to mark the advent
of our new industrial age and to set the pattern for contemporary
America in ways too numerous and complex to analyze. By the
end of the century, as Professor Schlesinger stated at the close
of his social history,

The city had come and, it was clear to all, it had come to stay. Was
its mission to be that of a new Jerusalem or of ancient Babylon? The
answer to this question was the chief unfinished business of the
departing generation.[2]

This scholar's uncertainty notwithstanding, many of the departing generation had already made up their minds. If the West
was to be the new Jerusalem, as they had announced in terms of
undeniable affirmation, then the city was, no less clearly, to be
the new Babylon: "The City of Jerusalem is wrecked,/The City of
New York is built again," wrote one poet, while others spoke
of parallels with Babylon and Sodom.[3]

The era was important not only for its commemoration of
frontier landmarks, but also for its recognition of the new urban
hegemony. In reacting to the rise of the city, the poet expressed
a sentiment important not only for its vivid contrast with the
frontier myth, but also for its detailed and frequently prophetic
delineation of the city and its influence.

Before turning to the negative bill of particulars it must be
admitted that the verse picture was not wholly unfavorable;

nearly one in five poets who discussed the city had something
good to say about it, their comments ranging all the way from
the blindest boosterism to a determined devotion in spite of
fully recognized shortcomings. Many of these poets were struck

principally by the speed and magnitude of change (which they
classed as progress) involved in urban development:

> An alder swamp, in thirty days, would grow into a
>   public lawn . . .
> An' fox trails into public streets, an' cow paths
>   into boolevards!⁴

Fittingly, they paid tribute to the achievements of mechanics and engineering on which this growth depended. Large buildings, viaducts and bridges came in for prominent notice. But the poetic favorites were the new methods of transportation; and the poets were forever marveling at the subway, imitating the sounds of the "elevated," or joking about the trolley.[5]

Parts of the city set aside for nature and recreation were rarely omitted from the catalogues of city boosters, although the contrast between park and slum became a favorite device among the critics as well. When the city-advocate turned his attention to less forested parts of the city he found not squalor and overcrowding, but picturesqueness and local color. Verse in this genre, varying from imitations of the Bowery accent to fascinated descriptions of such areas as New Orleans' Vieux Carré, furnished a telling testimony to the heterogeneity of the city, a characteristic which sociologists also find important.[6]

Often the poetic partisans of the urban scene showed considerable ingenuity in turning to good account what was commonly recognized as evil: the smoke menace, for example. One poet, admitting that his city had always been smoky, held that this smoke had served as a beacon for the early pioneers and now rose as a signal to those who looked cityward for leadership.[7] For others, these rising wisps or clouds, especially when seen early in the morning, came to symbolize the aspiration of the community and its inhabitants.[8] In the hands of a skilled poet the tables could be completely turned and the smoke made into an aesthetic asset:

> The long rows of lights through the City
> In the twilight's deepening glow,
> Seem to tremble and wave through the shadows,
> As their rays gleam soft on the snow.
>
> And the smoke curling upward,
> Silent, soft and gray,
> Seems to carry its wreaths, with shadowy hands
> To crown the parting day.[9]

Most tributes were identified with particular cities, the larger and newer centers drawing the most comment. New York received the lion's share; but Chicago—with its fire, its prominence in labor disputes, and its World's Columbian Exposition—stood a close second. City expositions, counterparts to the rural-oriented county fairs, attracted attention to New Orleans, San Francisco, Omaha, Buffalo, St. Louis, and Portland as well. Philadelphia, its Centennial Exhibition past, practically disappeared from the poet's view; and the other leading Colonial city, Boston, received less attention than such recent arrivals as Cleveland, Cincinnati, and Detroit. The following excerpts, all pertaining to that supposedly archetypal American city, Chicago, illustrate the nature of these tributes:

> Erect, commanding, like a goddess born,
> With strength and beauty glowing in her face
> And all her stately form attired in grace,
> She stands beside her lake to greet the morn.[10]
>
> Suburban towns are thickly seen
> Like bees around their ruling queen . . .
> Self interest prompts to what is right,
> And weaker with the strong unite.
>
> Costly dwellings adorn the streets . . .
> Rich structure of ambitious man,
> Fit home for gods the heavens to scan . . .[11]

There was, then, some recognition of urban virtue in the historical sense, in the sense of the city as the cradle of civilizations from Memphis to Paris, as the center of wealth, learning, opportunity, and excitement. "Magnet of ardent souls," one poet called the city, "Focus of life concentric and of art!"[12] Thus was the lure of the city recognized, thus was its central place in the cultural life of the community at large established. The expanded horizons as well as the increased opportunities offered by urban life were dramatized in the following lines:

A busy town beside a rushing stream,
That stirred to briskness such slow-moving men
As late had left the plowshare for the din
Of countless shuttles in the new-made mills;
With local thrift and enterprise evolved
As in a night from village sluggishness;
With wants grown great with opportunity,
And sudden confidence that left small place
In all its scheme for failure.

    Here men rule
As rural nabobs, finding over-night
A new-fledged fortune in paternal fields;
Familiar pathways turned to streets, where broke
Strange sounds upon the ear, and hammers stirred
The ancient stillness with the din of work;
Till very rustling of the leaves rehearsed
The universal rise of property.
Young men from out-grown acres came, to pit
Their wind-blown vigors 'gainst the wealth of towns;
While old men, mourning losses, sought new homes
On peaceful outskirts of this clamorous life.[13]

The most effective partisans of the urban cause were those
who admitted its failings but who recognized values which
outweighed them. Professor Schlesinger, after a vivid catalogue
of evils, summarized the urban achievement of the late nineteenth century in terms not only of physical accomplishment
but also of "a spirit of impersonal social responsibility" directed
toward civic betterment.[14] This sense of good will was held
crucial by those poets who described the city as "swift to
grapple with giant wrong" or who ran off the trial balances
like this:

Though filled with the weak and the sinning,
Filled, too, with the good and the strong,
Each wail of thy misery winning
Its echo of strife against wrong.[15]

Thus the city received, if not its due, at least a modicum of
recognition for the dispatch and dynamism with which it pro-
gressed; for the marvels of engineering and transportation on
which it was based; for the beauty and picturesqueness of its
varied profile; for the role it enjoyed as cynosure of wealth,
learning, and opportunity; and for the sense of purpose with
which it attacked its problems.

ii

But "rural America, like a stag at bay," as Professor
Schlesinger wrote, "was making its last stand"; and in its

desperate answer to the lure of the city appeared much of the antagonism which was to cloud the urban image in the poet's mind.[16] The drama of the struggle between town and country revealed itself in three acts, the first of which stated the true source of this resentment:

> A sound is heard throughout the land
> Which causes vague alarms;
> You hear it oft, on every hand,
> "Vermont's deserted farms."
>
> Where once the strong Green Mountain boy
> Pursued his honest toil. . . .
> You now behold the shattered homes
> All crumbling to decay,
> Like long-neglected catacombs
> Of races passed away.[17]

Thanks to Madison Cawein, and to a lesser extent to Paul Dunbar, much of this verse pertained to the South, where images of "Decay and silence . . . rotting leaves" set the tone.[18] Whatever the region the titles remained the same ("The Deserted Farm," "The Desolated Homestead") as did the imagery of the rusted plow, the dulled scythe, the house taken over by wild creatures, and the slanted barn which once had strongly stabled the evidences of agricultural prosperity.[19]

Act two stated the argument, in the unsubtle language of propaganda, against further desertion of rural areas—"Don't Leave the Old Farm":

> The city has many attractions,
> But think of the vices and sins,
> When once in the vortex of fashion,
> How soon the course downward begins.[20]
>
> "To one having little or nothing to lose
> A city life might have a charm . . .
> BUT A FARMER SHOULD STICK TO HIS FARM."[21]

Over and again, the dreary round of pastoral chores was measured against the bright lights—and found superior. Not only were farmers themselves urged to stay behind the plow, but special pleas were frequently directed at their offspring to "Make the dear old folks happy by staying at home."[22] Yet a third act seemed typically necessary before a fitting denouement could be supplied. Here the country folk were observed transplanted into an urban setting, where they were plagued by strange noises and customs, and filled with nostalgia for the country food and air, the familiarity of chores and companions.[23] Occasionally a happy adjustment was achieved; but usually the outcome depended on the farmer's coming to his senses in time to escape the disappointment of menial work after high expectations, the imprisonment in "brick and granite," which epitomized the urban trap.[24] A truly happy ending could occur only when all the denizens of crowded alleys and filthy cellars traded their lot for the "thousands of life-giving acres untilled" which America still had to offer.[25]

Aside from the main drama, this conflict could also be seen in the accounts of mutual visiting between city and country dwellers. The story of the "rube" in the big city is an old one, and its retellings in the verse of the period added little to the genre except that by this time the bumpkin had not only speeding horses and falling refuse to contend with, but might even get picked up by a power shovel or frightfully ensnared in a piece of factory machinery.[26] Whatever the circumstances, he still returned home fleeced, flayed, and forlorn. The more frequent tale brought the "milk-white city clown" out to visit the farm.[27] Just as the farmer's openness, ignorance, and trusting nature had worked against him in the city, so did the city dweller's abstract learning, over-mannerliness, and fancy clothes invariably get him into rural scrapes. The slick drummer, the dude gambler, and the careless hunter were the stock villains of these pieces. When the urban and rural types were contrasted in a less malicious manner, it was to make the point that farm

life teaches the practical whereas city life teaches the superficial.[28]

More frequent than the tale with moral appendage was the
direct comparison between the two ways of life, a comparison
which consistently favored the rural. In such a context were
developed many of the complaints against the city which will be
treated under appropriate headings below. What should be
noted here is the intensity of these complaints lodged against a
myriad of urban shortcomings, real and imagined, and placed
against an idyllic counterfoil of rustic life—serene, secure,
ennobling, healthful, direct, and honest. Against one such back-
drop of bucolic virtue was presented the following urban
portrait:

> Contrast with this the city life
> With all its bustle and its roar;
> Its howling greed, its angry strife
> That tramples down each feeble life
> Which vainly struggles to the fore;
>
> Its brawling crime and snarling death;
> Its cries of want and wild despairs;
> Its dust and smoke which stifle breath;
> Its foul effluvia of death;
> Its catacombs of human lairs;
>
> Its seed of whirlwind, crops of tares;
> Its hells of woe, its devils' care;
> Its folly-shops of sham-faced wares;
> Its tolls, its panders and its snares . . .[29]

Personality types as well as physical and social caricatures
emerged from this verse of last-ditch rural defense as it added
severely and pointedly to the long list of urban evils.

Rural America, deviled by a host of problems, watched with
sick heart as, in many areas, the frontier experience reversed
itself, the wild returning to claim the cultivated and the civilized.

Not only was her land given back; often her best sons, discouraged by the unfavorable social and economic contrast between town and country, defected to the urban side. Those who remained found this a bitter pill indeed; and in their poetry could be seen a bewilderment that this should have happened in the America of Thomas Jefferson, that all the agrarian virtues should have been sold so readily for a mess of pavement. It was hardly surprising that the city, which seemed to gain from rural loss at every turn, should have felt the brunt of pastoral resentment.

iii

Yet it was not only the bitter farmer who reviled the town; poets in great number, of whatever origin and residence, joined forces to compile a complaint against the city as thorough as it was lengthy, and as shrewd in some cases as it was obvious in others. On the most obvious level the poets attacked the city for its unpleasant physical characteristics and for the evils which sprang directly from them. Hearing was the first of the senses to be assaulted, and the poet reacted strongly against the welter of noise which struck his ear: the "shrieking engines," the clatter of the "elevated," the "ribald song," which combined to compose a "vast unceasing din."[30] The effect of this cumulative complaint was to make "noisy" so common an epithet for "city" as practically to escape the attention.

Sight and sympathy were outraged by the prospect of "reeking slums" where "life grows fevered/With lack of air and sun."[31] Inseparable by-products of the overcrowded areas were disease, crime, want, and immorality. Most of the poets merely described these conditions, albeit in terms which clearly demonstrated the need for attention to such "festering" problems. Beyond description, the poet tended either to sentimentalize or to demand, rather mildly, some reform measures. Examples of both tendencies can be observed in these excerpts from a single volume:

In cities densely populated
The poor are apt to dwell,
And to describe their misery,
Is more than tongue can tell. . . .
We find no form of diction,
To adequately describe the poverty
Of a tenement-house eviction,

And thousands of such people,
In these rookeries die;
'Tis time we should pause,
And ask the reason why.
Why not condemn such places?
To exist they are a crime!
They make people old and delicate,
Who should be in their prime.[32]

To list the other poetic protests against the physical aspects of the city would be to catalogue all the unpleasant or unsanitary matter—solid, liquid, or gaseous—which may have covered the ground or polluted the water or tainted the air. One can be spared such a listing, but not without noting the intensity which characterized reactions to such conditions:

. . . the town
drench'd by a penetrant
wind-driven dust of rain,
fast-gluing to the walls soot-flakes
from grimy house-tops swept; . . .
a viscous mire; compacting
the smoke-roof, propped by the towers,
spires, factory-chimneys, that threaten
under the mass enormous
to topple, and smother all life
with gloom and stifling dismay; . . .
the dusk, wet, slime
of the hideous town . . .[33]

To the poet who wrote these lines, their impact was intended to stand for all that was repellent in our urban, industrial civilization; with less ambitious aims, other verse-writers seemed prone to revel in the ugliness which the urban scene presented to their sensitive view. The prevalence of this rather sordid school provoked one poet to chide his fellows for their addiction to this "curious cult of the Ugly" with its cheap effects produced by devotion to "Hovels where misery crouches in dull unmurmuring squalor," "black chimneyed factories," "Smut-faced factory girls . . . and the hot-lipp'd hiccoughing harlot."[34] Undoubtedly the temptation to produce an easy literary effect by playing up the unsavory glamour of the city was and is an appreciable one.

For the poet the city had a political and an economic identity as well as a physical one; and, although these aspects cannot be fully appreciated in this limited context (see Chapters IV and V), they should at least be acknowledged. Political reactions in the narrow sense—that is, comments on municipal government —were few, specific, and widely scattered both topically and geographically; although it is interesting to note that the one poet who applied himself to this subject in a general way concluded, in agreement with Lord Bryce, that "The science of government, as applied/To cities" was "a failure."[35] But in a broader sense, the basically economic reactions to the city contained powerful political ammunition.

Politico-economic protest at the end of the century resulted basically from the inequitable distribution of wealth. Where, more obviously and more dramatically, could one observe the meeting of financial extremes than in an urban setting?

> In a great, Christian city, died friendless, of
>   hunger!
> Starved to death, where there's many a bright
>   banquet hall!
> In a city of hospitals, died in a prison!
> Homeless died in a land that boasts free homes
>   for all!
> In a city of millionaires, died without money![36]

One reads so frequently of this "want and misery/Amid the wealth and splendor of the city" that, although this theme of protest spread far beyond the confines of the city, it is difficult not to suspect that the seeds of economic resentment had been sown in asphalt and cobblestone.[37] Poetic reactions to this inequity ranged from that classic melodrama of the ill-shod and hungry newsboy with drawn face pressed against the steamy window beyond which the wealthy sat warm and contented at the laden board, to outspoken tirades of hate addressed from poor to rich, and haunting nightmares of conscience which plagued the millionaire's slumber.[38] Thus the city, as the home of the hopelessly poor, the conspicuously rich, and the irritatingly foppish, served as a microcosm within which many a protest of larger significance was launched.

The meaning of the city to the American poet of this period cannot be fully appreciated without launching a full-scale discussion of contemporary political and economic issues, the temperance crusade, the status of women, the immigration question, and the theme of materialism. Yet the most remarkable aspect of the verse lay not in its contribution to subjects such as these, but in the extent to which it provided a full portrait, rich and shrewd, of the urban personality and its environment. It was a portrait for the rogues' gallery, only negative and questionable features having been recorded; but it was a portrait which anticipated by decades, in its completeness as well as its perceptivity, the profile drawn by the urban sociologist.[39] In the discussion thus far, certain obvious traits have already been noted: the city's heterogeneity and its "false-front," fashion-oriented, superficial character. Beside these, there can be developed at least a dozen recognizable urban characteristics, all acknowledged by modern students of the city and all fully documented by the poets.

Poetic responses are not, of course, the same as clinical reports; one cannot expect the same detail from the bard as from the interviewer or statistician. In some cases the poetic freedom provided insights valuable beyond the laboratory atmosphere, in other cases the lack of detail robbed the portrait of its convincingness. The latter was true when the poet took up his discussion of crime and delinquency, evils associated with the city for as long as it has existed. For, although the tendency to connect the words "crime" and "city" was as common among

late-nineteenth-century poets as it is among contemporary tele-
vision script-writers, the annals of this putative crime wave
were remarkably bare of detail. Except for a street fight or two
("De Dago cut me wid a knife") the poet kept his mysteries to
himself, writing of "Many a crime that is never told" or, even
more vaguely, describing the city as a blossom "Where Vice
and Crime conspire to fade the bloom."[40] Although the cry was
generalized, it was insistent. It included the delinquent
("Young savages in city cellars reared"), and it culminated in
a veritable "clamor of crime" at all levels.[41] The crime of
gambling was also noted, but this typically involved the pit and
the "big board," rather than the dice and the punch board.

As did the prohibition campaigner, the poet also associated
alcoholism with the city. One poem, entitled "A City Incident,"
featured the "maniac shout . . . 'Fill the bowl!' " and ended
with the child leading homeward the drunken father.[42] Another
enthroned King Temperance on a rural dais while describing
King Alcohol's city reign.[43] Whether or not the associations
with drink were pleasurable, and they usually were not, they
were consistently identified as urban in setting.

Some evidence points to the identification of sexual deviation
and promiscuity with the city, a connection the poet sought to
establish by depicting a "writhing city" fraught with "dark and
bestial sin."[44] Not only did the poet particularly abhor the "red
and beckoning light" of prostitution, but also the general
bawdiness of attitude as portrayed by this "Red-faced" slut,

> . . . her mouth all insult and all lies. . . .
> With ribald mirth and words too vile to name,
> A new Doll Tearsheet, glorying in her shame,
> Armed with her Falstaff now she takes the town.
> The flaring lights of alley-way saloons,
> The reek of hideous gutters and black oaths
> Of drunkenness from vice-infested dens,
> Are to her senses what the silvery moon's
> Chaste splendor is . . . to innocence.[45]

Secularism is another trait which sociologists ascribe to urbanites, and the poets seemed to agree here too. From the city they heard a welter of "sacrilegious babble" which showed this to be a place "where God is not."[46] True religion, as well as Christian ethics, had deserted the city, the poet found.[47] One spoke of a friend who had spent twenty years in the city: "We are pretty sure his soul, and we know his head, is grey.[48] Were Christ to descend upon an American city, be it Brooklyn or Chicago, the poet prophesied another crucifixion.[49]

The city was not only anti-religious, in the poets' view, but also "anti-natural," as Lewis Mumford would say. One or two of them felt that the city man's over-dependence on human control, his acceptance of artificiality, deserved drastic—if humorous— depiction. Complaining that the only sure sign of the arrival of spring in the city occurred when his fashionable neighbor ("Saphronia") left the house without her furs, one poet went on to assert that the flowers in the park were no longer to be trusted as seasonal reminders, since attendants made them bloom at the push of a button, turning them off at night.[50] Another maintained that the city-dweller needed specially developed varieties of trees and shrubs which would respond to life in small pots with wine instead of water for irrigation.[51] Natural beauty in the suburban and resort areas, many were quick to point out, had been blighted by urban commercial interests.[52] More serious, and more effective, were the poets who were made uneasy by the extent to which man-made mechanical devices had replaced natural ones. The complete dependence on such fallible media as the trolley and the "elevated" disturbed one poet; another condemned his own "Twentieth Century Home" because he had to reach it by trolley and elevator.[53] In such ways the poet made clear his accord with the sociologist who lists such urban characteristics as "artificiality" and "dependence on human control."

The idea of haste, or "time-consciousness," underlay a great deal of what was said about the city in meter. Most vividly it appeared in descriptions of living habits, such as this contemporary-seeming visit to "The Park Row Beanery":

> With crash and smash and splash and slash the
>   waiters sling the food
> And sing and yell like merry hell, so's to be
>   understood:
> "Ham and!" "Draw one!" "Brown wheats!"
> . . . "Pork n'Boston!"[54]

The degree to which the emphasis on speed had replaced the leisurely patterns admired by the poets was epitomized by the assertion that a modern, masculine deity, "hurry," had replaced the nine gentler female muses of old.[55] Riming "worry" with "hurry," the poets went on to agree with those who identify calculating and competitive characteristics with city life. Urbanites were depicted as "a curious canny folk" who "push and jostle and scheme and plot."[56] Their "artful wile" produced "snares" for a variety of unsuspecting victims.[57] More than by the canniness, the poets were oppressed by the "panting chase," the "mad conflict and unheeding crush" of the competitive strife which turned Broadway into a "mad river" where only the strong survived.[58]

> The City's roar is rising from the street;
> The old, bedraggled "types" are shuffling
>   through the strife;
> They plod and push, and elbow as they meet,
> And glare and grin, and sadly call it "life."[59]

The "worry" which rimed with "hurry" indicated more directly the accord of the verse-writer with social psychologists who define a city syndrome composed of insecurity, anxiety, and enervation. Even to be near the city's rushing torrent, to sense its impersonality, argued the poets, is to be robbed of peace and calm. The drain of this life made people old before their time; one described a city friend, looking worried, harassed, and weak, who was then quickly returned to stréngth, youth, and placidity by a removal to the country.[60] In the "tumult of the city," there was "neither rest nor peace," but a sort of mass anxiety which was summed up as the "agitations of innumerous souls."[61] With the hustle and bustle went a "shrug" of indifference; no one cared that his neighbor was racing nervously toward the end of his short, frantic life.[62]

It was this indifference, this threat to his own meaningful participation, which affected the poet most strongly; he responded subtly, elaborately, and in a manner which adumbrated most strikingly the observations of more scientific students of the city. These students tell us that urban life is characterized by social distance, by a preponderance of secondary relations, by a collectivistic rather than an individualistic frame of reference, and that these characteristics produce in the individual a sense of anonymity, often to a harmful extent. The poetry not only furnished evidence for such statements but also provided a reaction which is truly disturbing.

The idea of social distance, producing loneliness in crowded places, struck the poetic responsiveness to the paradoxical. Realizing that the city was not necessarily a warm and friendly place, for all its fire of activity, the poet pled for more satisfactory personal relationships:

> Alone I walk in the peopled city,
> Where each seems happy with his own;
> O friends, I ask not for your pity—
> I walk alone.[63]

He wrote of lonely bankers, lonely workers—all with plenty of people around them—and reminded his readers that it was the stranger "Alone in the City" with "no look of kind remembrance," and not the farmer, who was the isolated one.[64] The impact of this ironical solitude, of these secondary relationships, brought him to a reconsideration of values:

> One of the million, that am I;
> One of the million wondering why
> And what it is, and if it pays,
> This living in the city's ways.[65]

He pondered the impersonality of a New York hospital where people battled for life while external noises went on unheeding and uninterrupted; and sometimes he saw, in "the ceaseless lave/Of life and trade, the cities rave and'jostle," the death of his own identity: "egotism's own grave/Upon the pave."[66]

The city as a "labyrinth of human ways/Where footpaths meet and cross, and meet no more" preoccupied the poet as he faced the problems of collective life.[67] The coldness of a life where no one knew his neighbor, the irony of lovers passing within a few feet of each other and then missing connection because of the crowds—these were some of the manifestations of the city which impressed upon the poets the seemingly unpredictable impersonality with which the city treated its citizens.[68] Plagued by such impressions, the poet reverted to a strange language: a "City without a face," he called it.[69] And what could this mean—city without a face? No face where there were thousands? It meant, answered the verse, that the city was "jagged, formless"; it meant that the poet, his own sense of reality and identity threatened, was launching a counterattack, was attempting to take from the city those same qualities which he felt it had taken from him.

> I know my Boston is a counterfeit,—
> A frameless imitation, all bereft
> Of living nearness, noise, and common speech . . .[70]

A city without noise? Certainly this was unreal. In a more sinister frame of mind he went further, calling the rush hour movement a "river flowing evermore/Towards dim oblivion's ocean."[71]

The anonymity which the poet suffered at the hands of the city sometimes forced him into an eerie blending of the real and the unreal in framing his counterattack, plainly implying that the city itself did not exist. He coupled the "torrent of the living down Broadway" with the "myriad dead in unremembered graves" and pronounced, inscrutably, that "thousands tread/The City streets, who now are dead." [72] The occasion of hearing footsteps without seeing who made them, as one often does in the city, suggested further opportunities to blend the real and the unreal. One poet proclaimed that such sounds represented specters which raise themselves from the pavement at night to tell of foul deeds. [73] The decisive placing of the curse, the transfer of the individual's dilemma to the source, appeared as follows:

> But of the City: there alone exists
> True Beings and real Selves; Identities . . .
> That come and go, and are not and yet are.
> There also Powers . . . pass, abide, and brood,
> And bring forth awful births. [74]

Thus was the bill of particulars laid down. Against the small voice of those who found items to praise in the relentless rise of the city was raised the deafening plaint of its detractors. Incited in some cases by a rural partisanship, they scored the town for its unhealthy ugliness, for its example of economic inequities, for its affinities with crime, drunkenness, sexual excesses, immorality, and artificiality. Oppressed by its killing pace, they accused it of encouraging a craftiness and over-competitiveness which led in turn to insecurity, anxiety, and individual anonymity. With both aptitude and insistence, the poets constructed a myth of the city formidable in its detail and frightening in its intensity. Although not all of the city's critics intended to damn it, the preponderance of negative reaction was sufficiently decisive that one may fairly summarize the content of this urban myth with lines from verses which foresaw the modern metropolis inhabited by veritable satans, or turned to desert and peopled only with moths. [75] Pealing the great knell of doom, the

poets pointed out the city's materialistic greed and consigned it
to everlasting damnation:

> None shall put forth a hand and twist the brass
> That galls the neck of Liberty, none dare
> Avert the iron stigma of despair . . .
> The vengeance of the Lord has come to pass!
>
> They fester in the cities who have scarred
> The face of earth until her skeleton
> Is naked, and her breasts are dry and hard. . . .[76]
>
> Great is the City of a thousand streets,
> The greatest city in the modern land.
> Yet are the people blinded in their minds,
> By teachings false, the vainest ways of life.
> How many dream that money maketh rich.
> How many judge that learning maketh wise.
> How many cry: "Position giveth strength."
> Yet is it false, and all the world is fooled.[77]

Insomuch as America's future lay with the West, according
to the book of the poet, she faced a vista of sunny expansionism,
blessed by God's own hand; insomuch as the future lay with
urban leadership, this same hand of God seemed destined to
snuff out her brief, bright candle.

NOTES

[1] Adna F. Weber, *Growth of Cities in the Nineteenth Century* (New York: Macmillan [for Columbia University], 1899), 24–27.

[2] Arthur M. Schlesinger, *Rise of the City* (New York: Macmillan, 1938), vol. X in the History of American Life series, 436.

[3] Davenport, *Perpetual Fire*, 198; May, *Inside the Bar*, 17–20.

[4] Foss, *Back Country Poems*, 44.

[5] Bradford, *Around the Hub in Rhyme*, n. pag.; Kerr, *Cheery Book*, 64–65; Burdette, *Smiles Yoked with Sighs*, 73–74.

[6] McCardell, *Olde Love and Lavender*, 53–64; Lincoln, *Historical New Orleans*.

[7] Elmore, *Supplement*, 216–18.

[8] Emerson, *Love-bound*, 42–43.

[9] Carland, *King of the Land of Nod*, 25.

[10] Fiske, *Ballad of Manila Bay*, 71.

[11] Easton, *Chicago*, 4, 5.

[12] Thomas, *Cassia*, 77.

[13] Hayward, *Patrice*, 7.

[14] Schlesinger, *Rise of the City*, 120.

[15] Putnam, *Living in the World*, 55; A. C. J., *Heart Echoes*, 39–40.

[16] Schlesinger, *Rise of the City*, 53.

[17] Rogers, *Stray Leaves from a Larker's Log*, 27–28.

[18] Cawein, *Blooms of the Berry*, 49; see also Dunbar, *Lyrics of Lowly Life*, 158, as well as lyrics throughout Cawein's collections.

[19] Wheeler, *Home Poems*, 19–21; James H. Scott, *Poems*, 414–17.

[20] Alden, *Poems*, 34.

[21] Baker, *Marmondale*, 167.

[22] Woodruff, *Collection of Wild Flowers*, 17.

[23] See Currier, *Among the Granite Hills*, 82–83; Fairhurst, *My Good Poems*, 160–65; Tadlock, *Solomon Grinder's Christmas Eve*, 69–72, 106–9.

[24] Castelle, *Pedagogics Number One*, 52–53; Foss, *Back Country Poems*, 27.

[25] Davis, *Immortelles*, 113.

[26] Cox, *Hans Von Pelter's Trip to Gotham*.

[27] Morse, *Summer Haven Songs*, 66.

[28] Boynton, *Poetry and Song*, 34–48.

[29] Fleenor, *In Passing Through*, 61.

[30] Barrett, *Fugitives and Other Poems*, 93; Edmunds, *Songs of Asia Sung in America:*, 32; Darrow, *Iphigenia*, 59; Kenyon, *An Oaten Pipe*, 122–24.

[31] Malone, *Songs of North and South*, 40–43; Conant, *Field of Folk*, 48–51.

[32] McFarland, *Miscellaneous Poems*, 17, 22.

[33] Guthrie, *Songs of American Destiny*, 21.

[34] Peck, *Greystone and Porphyry*, 46–62.

[35] Schultz, *Course of Progress*, 72.

[36] Cake, *Devil's Tea Table*, 84.

[37] Donahoe, *In Sheltered Ways*, 55.

[38] Cook, *Fancy's Etchings*, 185; Lemon, *Ione*, 376–78.

[39] As a stranger in the world of urban sociology, I leaned on summaries presented in the following current textbooks: Noel P. Gist and L. A. Halbert,

Urban Society (New York: Crowell, 1956), Chapt. 14; Rose Hum Lee, *City* (Chicago, Phila., and New York: Lippincott, 1955), Chapt. 20; and James A. Quinn, *Urban Sociology* (New York: American Book Co., 1955), Chapt. 6. Readings collected by T. Lynn Smith and C. A. McMahan in *Sociology of Urban Life* (New York: Dryden, 1951), Chapt. 23, were especially helpful, as were earlier treatments such as Robert E. Park, Ernest W. Burgess, and Roderick D. McKenzie, *City* (Chicago: University of Chicago Press, 1925), Chapt. 1; Niles Carpenter, *Sociology of City Life* (New York: Longmans, Green, 1931), Chapt. 6. For my purposes, the single most useful summary proved to be an article by Louis Wirth, "Urbanism as a Way of Life," *American Journal of Sociology*, XLIV (July 1938), 1–24. Useful special approaches to the problem were found in E. S. Bogardus, "Social Distance in the City," *American Journal of Sociology*, XXXII (July 1926), 40–46; Lewis Mumford, *Culture of Cities* (New York: Harcourt, Brace, 1938); David Riesman, with Nathan Glazer and Reuel Denney, *Lonely Crowd* (New Haven: Yale University Press, 1950).

[40] Major, *Lays of Chinatown*, 23; Remick, *Miscellaneous Poems*, II, 141; Elshemus, *Songs of Spring*, 20.

[41] Malone, *Songs of North and South*, 40–43; Conant, *Field of Folk*, 48–51.

[42] Van Derveer, *Soul Waifs*, 94–96.

[43] Crosby, *Broad-cast*, 93.

[44] Griffith, *Trialogues*, 6; Huff, *Songs of the Desert*, 57.

[45] Remick, *Miscellaneous Poems*, II, 141; Cawein, *Weeds by the Wall*, 82.

[46] Le Gallienne, *English Poems*, 102; Waterhouse, *Some Homely Little Songs*, 90.

[47] Cole, *In Scipio's Gardens*, 99–100; Hills, *Echoes*, 74–79.

[48] McCann and Jarrold, *Odds and Ends*, 76.

[49] Davenport, *More Outcries from Brooklyn Hollow*, 9–11; Hirt, *Second Booklet of Social Poems*, 44–45.

[50] Martin, *Poems and Verses*, 41–43.

[51] Bangs, *Cobwebs from a Library Corner*, 61.

[52] *History of Coney Island in Rhyme*; Sweet, *Day on Coney Island*, 7–16.

[53] Elmore, *Lover in Cuba and Poems*, 132–34; Kenney, *Some More Thusettes* 115–16.

[54] Heaton, *Quilting Bee*, 137–38.

[55] Hayward, *Willoughby*, 3.

[56] Watres, *Cobwebs*, 11; Waterhouse, *Some Homely Little Songs*, 89.

[57] Nims, *Declining Village*:, 22.

[58] Walker, *Poems*, 16; Emswiler, *Poems and Sketches*, 42; Kerr, *Jests, Jingles and Jottings*, 22.

[59] Bridges, *Bramble Brae*, 84.

[60] Collins, *Poems, Sketches*, 37.

[61] McCarthy, *Round of Rimes*, 34; Nesmith, *Monadnoc*, 52.

[62] Gaylord, *Heart Echoes*, 170.

[63] Conover, *Via Solitaria*, 5.

[64] Minkler, *Songs in the Night*, 22.

[65] Hall, *When Love Laughs*, 12.

[66] Blount, *Poems*, 28; Brooks, *Poems*, 221.

[67] Fearing, *In the City by the Lake*, 15.

[68] Grant, *Little Gods-on-wheels*:, 28; Loomis, *Sunset Idyl*, 92–93; More, *Great Refusal*, 19–36.

[69] Crosby, *Swords and Plowshares*, 60.

[70] Robinson, *Torrent and the Night Before*, 33–34.

[71] Chittenden, *Ranch Verses*, 172.

[72] Richard Hovey in Carman and Hovey, *Last Songs from Vagabondia*, 52; Davenport, *Visions of the City*, 4.

[73] De Kay, *Hesperus*, 78–80.

[74] Davenport, *Visions of the City*, 9.

[75] *Tour of Prince Eblis*, 11; Le Gallienne, *Robert Louis Stevenson*, 9–10.

[76] Lodge, *Song of the Wave*, 114.

[77] Davenport, *Perpetual Fire*, 55.

IV

Progress and Protest

THE POETS OF THE LATE NINETEENTH CENTURY HAD
more to say about economic conditions than they did about the
city and the West combined; in fact, they reacted to events and
ideas in this area more fully than to any other specific subject.
Just as the verse reaction to the two major movements of
population during these years split itself into an inspired
approval of the American West and a violent disapproval of the
city, so the picture of our economic well-being was split into
two distinct profiles. Nor was this dichotomous response
surprising, in view of contemporary conditions and events. The
years in question saw, for example, not only the introduction of
the telephone, but also the outbreak of the Great Strike of 1877;
not only the laying of nearly 200,000 miles of railway track, but
also the conduct of the Granger cases enforcing regulation of

railway practices; not only the formation of Standard Oil, Inc., but also the recruiting of Coxey's army. Industry, abetted by invention, government subsidy, and virtual freedom from restraint, unified the nation and changed its way of life to an impressive extent. It was apparent that the best minds and imaginations of the day were attacking problems of engineering and industry, rather than of government or scholarship. Furthermore, it was observed in 1890 that one-eighth of the population had come to own seven-eighths of the nation's wealth. If industry had brought tinned foods to the pantry shelf and fast trains to the station, it had also wrought changes of deeper significance. During these years Americans began to notice, to describe, and to protest against the stamp which uninhibited free enterprise was placing upon our society.

These years witnessed, then, some of the greatest achievements and some of the greatest abuses on the part of American enterprise. Attendant upon these achievements there appeared the Gospel of Wealth with its overtones of social Darwinism, the triumph of the fittest, and the stewardship of the elect. The abuses produced the revolt of the farmer and laborer which led, in turn, to the reform activities of the Progressives during the early years of the twentieth century. In handing down sanctions and censures, the poets participated abundantly in summing up America's economic character at the turn of the century. From their writings one can personify and particularize both the Gospel of Wealth and the literature of protest; and from their work as a whole can be read a judgment, an answer to the question of whether this economic and material progress had been worth what it had cost.

i

Satisfaction with the status quo, and thus at least tacit approval of American progress under the guiding hand of free enterprise, was expressed most voluminously in those lines which enumerated the vast material achievements of the day. Looking backward from the apogee of our first great age of invention and applied science, the poets' catalogue of progress included everything from the friction match to a motor for towing canal boats. For all the heterogeneity of the lists, the subjects of poetic praise can be arranged in three general categories. One of these included such feats of architecture and engineering as bridges (especially those of Brooklyn and St. Louis), viaducts, tunnels, and asphalt roads. An ode "To a Modern Office Building" demonstrated how the "poetry of height" had replaced the skylark and west wind with such subjects as

> Labor's cathedral, castle of finance!
> No medieval masterpiece of stone
> Lifted a grander pile to face God's glance
> Than thou upholdst to the heavens alone.[1]

Improved means of communication received even more praise; included in a lengthy list were the typewriter, the new typesetters, the phonograph, the steam press, and the fast mail. At the top of the list, consistently, was the telegraph with its rhythmic message so suitable for poetic reproduction:

> And so I hate thee, telegraph!
> Of madness being on the border.
> Thy *click, click, click,* when working well;
> Thy *clank, clank, clank,* when out of order![2]

But it was the telephone and the Atlantic cable which most thoroughly captured the poetic imagination. All kinds of powers, including mutilinguicity and the possession of a soul, were ascribed to the former; whereas Cyrus Field's achievement in perfecting the cable was likened to that of Columbus:

> And o'er this turnpike Morse's steeds shall leap;
> Mermaids shall hear the lightening stage-whip crack—
> Ho, Neptune! make your loafers clear the track![3]

This new link between the continents, it was prophesied, would "fire with hope the struggling millions to be free."[4]

In the third and most prominent category of poetic favor were advances in transportation: steamships, steam-cars, elevated railways, cable and electric cars, interurban railways, subways, bicycles, and even a triumphant railway—never executed, of course—designed to lift ocean-going ships over the Central American isthmus. The poetry of movement was exemplified by a prophetic selection titled "The Automobile"

> I am the movement
> Of the time to come;
> And in me motion finds
> Its rhythm and its poesy . . .
> I am The Thing.[5]

But throughout the world of industrial and engineering accomplishments the poet seemed to have been saving a special place in his heart and in his verse for one phenomenon, the railroad. The number and variety of ways in which he celebrated it indicated not only his admiration for this achievement but also the impressive extent to which he had adopted the railroad as the dominant symbol of his age.

Marking the path of civilization, the railroad thundered across the plains until the buffalo "hold up their heads in wonder."[6] Its "Generals of Progress," Huntington, Hopkins, Crocker, Gould, and Vanderbilt, were among the most consistently praised of the leaders of American industry. On the other hand, these roads were railed against for destroying natural beauty, for discriminating in rates and routes, and for offering poor service; the palace car and the railroad pass soon came to stand as symbols of luxury and special privilege. The smoking car became a target for those who preached tobacco-temperance; and by 1890 technical railway language had even, in Palmer Cox's widely read "Brownie Books," penetrated to the level of children's verse. A title such as "English Bonds and Grade Crossing Murders" showed that the railroad was used not only to air economic grievances but also to provide the ever-sought note of melodrama. The train wreck, a favorite subject in its own right, revealed a distinctly maudlin taste for gory descriptive passages, featuring the plummeting of the iron horse and its carriages from bridge or trestle, whereupon

> The river seems a stream of blood and flame . . .
> A few are saved; but oh! what horrid cries
> Come from the wreck, and terrify the heart![7]

Often these disasters were used to score the railroad for its lack of safety precautions or for its low pay scale; but at times the aftermath of a wreck could even illustrate the road's efficiency; and usually the incident merely underscored the heroism of the locomotive engineer, that faithful pilot "With an arm that's strong and steady,/And a heart that knows no fear" who guided his precious cargo through the long and lonely night, risking, when necessary, his own life for the safety of his passengers.[8] He was, attested the poet, "a nobler knight in his toil-stained blue/Than th' Cavalier in gold."[9]

Metaphorically, the railway represented everything from parts of the human body to spiritual values. There was "The Gospel Railway" whose track was laid on rock, as opposed to "Satan's Railway" with its "Drinking Car," "Smoking Car," and "Murder Car"; there was the "Train of Life" which led either to greed or to eternity; there were railways built by Jesus and railways leading to other heavens (' "Next stop, Parnassus.' 'Ding-ading!' ").[10] The locomotive and its train became "God's own trusty savior,/Helping to redeem mankind" and even threatened to replace the "old/Bewailed divinity."[11] Thus the railroad, as did to a lesser extent the other achievements of industry and invention, peopled both the heaven and earth of the poets. As a mark of progress, as material for melodrama, as a soapbox for political and economic oratory, this favorite of the versifiers summed up the era:

> O brazen monster bellowing by
> Art thou indeed our century?[12]

The poets had their brush with the rise of American commerce as well as of industry, although this was a minor skirmish by comparison. Aided by dependable means of transportation and communication, the local peddler of former days emerged into the more widely traveled "drummer" whose way of life provoked some not-always-respectful comment:

> Oh Posen, fair Posen,
> Your Sammy has "rosen,"
> The ladder I've climbed mit a dash,
> I vonse was a "drummer,"
> But now I'm a "hummer,"
> Und piziness is strictly "Spot Cash."[13]

But the salesman was not always the object of deprecating humor. Just as frequently his "commercial smile" was called "distinguished," and he was lauded for his "good, warm heart" or for his Yankee shrewdness.[14] The rising world of advertising brought out criticism for the ugliness of its photographs and for its abuse of the language. Shakespeare, on behalf of the poets, was made to query,

> Why shouldn't I praise the bilious pill . . .
> And make the popular heartstrings thrill
> With a poem on soothing syrup?
> . . . the soap muse brings me shekels.[15]

But the poet also offered parables proving the value of advertising; and if one counted up the number of poets who sold their dubious talents for the promotion of railroads, malt beverages, and other products and services, it would be readily discernible that the versifier had made a profitable peace with the Billboard Goddess.

As has already been intimated, industrial progress and advancing commercialism was not, to the poets, an unmixed blessing. Specific complaints were filed against the sewing machine as a dubious labor-saver, against the electric light for

its lack of dependability, against the automobile for leaving
"Suicides, murder trials, hell in its wake."[16] The cumulative
confusion attendant on the mechanization of life had left "the
earth no happier/Than in the silent days."[17] Thoreau-like,
another complained, "The world is drunk with rapid transit.
. . ./Everybody wants to be somewhere else."[18] The great
majority of those who described the contributions of science and
industry did so, however, in the spirit of sincere tribute. These
contributions were given a central place in centennial recollections and chauvinistic boastings; poetic dreams of the future
emphasized the mechanical super-convenience to come; verse
histories leapt from one invention or engineering achievement
to another; industrial progress was treated as synonymous with
prosperity. Machine power was a noble innovation, come as a
David to rule mankind:

> Quick he stills the mocking rabble,
> Yields his might for nobler causes,
> Speaks to man from purer motives.[19]

For such a summit of achievement, the poet was bound to
give due credit. Sometimes the triumph of the machine was
broadly attributed to "the mind of man" or to "science" or
"inventiveness."[20] In the same vein, praise was given to
particular inventors—Edison, Morse, Fulton, Brosius, Volta,
Henry, and Franklin, to list the most popular. When the poet
spoke of the achievements of industry, however, he frequently
made it clear that he referred neither to inventiveness nor to
business enterprise, but rather to the collective strength of the
laboring man:

> O we are knights of an iron crown;
> No golden sword we wield!
> We stand on earth, the free man's throne,
> With labor, skilled, our shield! . . .
> And where the engine whistles scream,
> Our labor, there, is seen!

> We've caught the light'nings from the sky,
> And bound them to the earth . . .
> The cities of all nations stand
> A glory to our name . . .[21]

Even though these poets chose to honor the laboring man rather than his employer, they did so without any sense of class struggle and without any intention of dwelling on abuses suffered by the wage-earner. Such verse in praise of labor in the abstract readily turned to sentiments like the following:

> Contented be with toiler's humble lot,
> Free from pomp and ostentatious life,
> Let thy home be the workman's tidy cot,
> Thy best friends thy children and thy wife.[22]

Such lines as these serve to introduce the existence of a recognizable body of verse which filled out, as it were, the oft-neglected lower region of the portrait of the Gospel of Wealth. If the leaders of commerce and industry furnished the opportunity, then labor stood to profit by it. "Labor is but capital unhatched," wrote poets who thought in this vein; and they warned the "extremists" who pilloried capital that they were wringing "the neck of the goose/That lays every day a bright golden egg."[23] If labor hoped to improve its lot, the remedy lay not in agitation but in looking to one's own house first:

> If the laboring man would be
> Independent, strong, and free,
> First, with all the foes within,
> He the warfare must begin,
> With envious low desires,
> And with passion's baleful fires . . .[24]

The opposite of labor, for this group of versifiers, was not capital but idleness; their lines hardly furnished ammunition for those who proposed more militant methods of raising the workers' standards. The extent to which some poets, many of them doubtless laborers themselves, resisted efforts to dramatize their need can be seen most strikingly in the rural setting.

Edwin Markham's "The Man with the Hoe" was surely the most celebrated item in the literature of protest on behalf of the agricultural laborer. If not a truly great poem, at least it is powerful in its impact, and its sympathies are hard to mistake:

> Bowed by the weight of centuries he leans
> Upon his hoe and gazes on the ground,
> The emptiness of ages in his face,
> And on his back the burden of the world.
> Who made him dead to rapture and despair,
> A thing that grieves not and that never hopes,
> Stolid and stunned, a brother to the ox?
> Who loosened and let down this brutal jaw?
> Whose was the hand that slanted back this brow?
> Whose breath blew out the light within this brain? . . .
>
> O masters, lords and rulers in all lands . . .
> How will you ever straighten up this shape. . . .
> Make right the immemorial infamies,
> Perfidious wrongs, immedicable woes? . . .
> How will the Future reckon with this Man?
> How answer his brute questions in that hour
> When whirlwinds of rebellion shake the world?[25]

Although he dealt with the farmer in stark and unflattering terms, Markham furnished in labor's cause a document of unmatched potency. But the farmer-poet, his sense of inferiority aroused by rural hardships and by the losing battle between farm and city, reacted not to Markham's espousal of the agrarian cause but to what he read as an insult:

> How false the note of him who sings
> That toiling hand lends sloping brow,
> But brutal minds behind the plow;
> His soul may soar, but not on wings.[26]

" 'The man with the hoe,' but not 'a clod,' " one poet reprimanded him, while still another corrected, "Kin to the eagle,

not brother to the ox."[27] Thus, in ways both trivial and touch-
ing, did the intended recipients of Markham's sympathies shrug
them off with petulant objections. Evidently conscious that his
intentions had been misapprehended, Markham sought to
clarify his message by offering in his next volume an obvious
sequel to "The Man with the Hoe," called "The Sower" and
based, like its predecessor, on a painting by Millet. Here he
spoke of the farmer returning in the twilight "with hero step"
and called him

> . . . the stone rejected, yet the stone
> Whereon is built metropolis and throne.
> Out of his toil come all their pompous shows,
> Their purple luxury and plush repose![28]

Yet by 1901 it was apparently too late; there were no retractions
in the verse of those who had taken Markham to task. Even by
pointing the finger at the farmer-hero, by taking his side against
the city and the idle rich, he was unable to retrieve or mollify
his intended audience.

The moral of the Markham episode is not that there was a
lack of agrarian protest literature during this period, but rather
that there was a sizable group of versifiers who were totally
unwilling to deal with the workingman's plight in any but the
most pallid and sentimental terms. In contrast to the complaints
against the hardships of farm life which will be discussed below,
the group which reacted to Markham's violent images refused
to abandon the stereotype of "The Happy Ploughman."[29]
Instead of owning up to the presence of rustic pitfalls, these
poets sung on with an imperturbable bucolic serenity:

> How sweet to lean on Nature's arm,
> And jog through life upon the farm!
> Merchants and brokers spread and dash
> A little while, then go to smash;
> But we can keep from day to day,
> The even tenor of our way.[30]

Even that most depressed of all farm laborers, the Southern
Negro, did not escape the blandly sentimental pen: "Nigger
mighty happy w'en he layin' by co'n . . ."[31]

Whether their setting was agricultural or industrial, these
poets preached the dignity rather than the degradation of labor.
In their texts they provided the high priests of the Gospel of
Wealth with a willing and cooperative congregation:

> Wealth is the power,
> Poor men the machinery;
> While all work together
> The world moves harmoniously . . .[32]

There was also, as these lines suggested, a related and partially
overlapping subject to be found in the condition of poverty. If
the laborer complemented the entrepreneur, the poor man
complemented the man of wealth. (If there existed a Gospel of
Wealth, there was also a "gospel of poverty.") Most poets who
wrote about the poor were concerned with the sorry side of
society's lower levels; but a few not only proclaimed the dignity
of labor but also the dignity of poverty, thus vitiating to some
extent the impact of protest poetry.

Poverty, it was maintained, promoted beauty in women and
fostered "Truth, Honesty, Sincerity" and greatness in men.[33]
The lot of the poor worker, far from being hopeless,

> Is freer from that constant strain
> That comes from greed and love of gain;
> And 'tis a question all in all
> On which the richest blessings fall.[34]

In contrast to this "virtue of poverty" school of thought there
was also the "sin of poverty" persuasion which paralleled the
writings of those poets who urged labor to look to its own
improvement. Not many poets were disposed to blame the poor
for their own condition; but a few did, citing over-large families,
drinking, laziness, and lack of religion among the causes.[35] Just

as there were "deserving rich" there were also "deserving poor," each group bearing the responsibility for its own fate. Obviously, the verse which sprung from such sentiments as this, acknowledging as it did the attitudes of social Darwinism and accepting the status quo, went a long way toward accounting for conditions which the Gospel of Wealth produced at the bottom of the economic scale. Although not abundant, relatively speaking, there was perhaps a surprisingly persistent verse sentiment which tended to withdraw from the impoverished laborer any grounds for complaint or militant action.

The disposition of the poet to provide constructive sympathy for the oppressed worker was bounded on one side by the temptation to sentimentalize the ennobling effects of poverty and labor and on the other by a horror of militant radicalism and the possible consequences thereof:

> But when I [labor] rule,
> I am a master and a tyrant then
> That overthrows all order,
> Crushes men,
> Starves helpless little ones,
> Wrecks homes,
> And ruthlessly tears down
> All I have builded up.
> Unreasoning
> I run my course . . .[36]

The stimulus which might incite the American worker to such an attitude was typically attributed to "Europe's nihilistic bands," who were particularized as "social cranks . . . Russian Nihilists . . . Irish Patriots . . . French Communists . . . Italian Carbonari . . . who all the time/Proclaimed free labor a capital crime."[37] The foreign connection was not always expressed, but was usually implied. The poet's favorite villain was that "anarchistic spoiler,/Cursing the hand that feeds"; but he readily extended his blame to the nihilist with "Pistol, bomb, and dirk," to the Godless Socialist, and to the Communist who exploited the poor and wished only "to live without work at our ease!"[38] Although exaggerated, some of the poetic horror may well have stemmed from just cause; but what seems unfortunate in retrospect is the way in which this suspicion spread to include a prejudice against the organization of labor for whatever purpose.[39] Pathetically indicative of a fear of guilt by association were those partisans of labor who prefaced their remarks, however mild, with such phrases as, "Now I'm no Debs or Coxeyite; But . . ."[40] A self-styled "honest Socialist" complained of being called "crank, and idiot, a fool,/A communist, an anarchist . . ."[41] The lines below, in rejecting the hated labels one by one, illustrate the nature of the particular cross borne by spokesmen for the workingman:

> We be workingmen, we! . . .
> Still, though toil be paid with scorn,—
> Independent we!

> Not of the commune, we! . . .
> Heaven helps them that help themselves. . . .
> Not of the anarchists, we! . . .
> Not of agrarians, we!
> Labor is not all a curse!
> Toil is hard, but crime is worse![42]

That even identification with the "agrarians" should be feared! Not many poets concerned themselves explicitly with the question of radicalism, but with the foregoing as background one can better understand the caution which so many poets saw fit to employ even when speaking on the side of organized labor:

> Pluck down the monarchs from their seats—set sons of
>   freedom in their stead! . . .
> Equal born with equal ballot . . .
> But with dynamite and pistol do not try to force your way;
> Wrong with wrong you cannot conquer . . .[43]

With the laboring poor placated and cautioned, the poets of the Gospel of Wealth turned to even more appealing subject matter: wealth, that "gigantic arm/That wields the National sword."[44] We must attempt to understand the rich as we do the poor, they said:

> Rich men we have among us,
> Have to toil as others do,
> If they reap the world's approval,
> And be counted good and true.
> Many eyes on them are watching,
> For some favor or some trade,
> And too much is oft expected,
> Things the weak and poor evade.[45]

For these were the men who, through their "schemes that bring about/Great booms of enterprise," provided the music for the "grand hymn of Industry" and thus brought prosperity to all.[46] When it came to appraising the contributions of individuals, the poets drew a clearly visible line between the industrialist and the financier, centering much of their praise on the railroad builders mentioned above. Even a figure of such mixed repute as Jay Gould received praise for developing the Missouri Pacific Railroad ("We'll ever remember our friend J. Gould") and was rated as a "spirit born to lead and master men . . . a true aristocrat of intellect," though he was scored on other counts for his financial practices.[47]

As will be shown below, the poets as a group took unkindly to the idea of great wealth and to the idea of tainted-money charities perpetuated with reputation-saving motives. There were at least a few, however, who were prepared to judge the rich with favor not only for the way they made their fortunes, but for the way they spent them. As an answer to economic disorder one poet saw simply the need for more multi-million-aires, each "Eager to share/The bounty which he holds in sacred trust . . ."[48] The doctrine of stewardship, thus stated, was applied most fully and specifically in these lines in praise of one of its most insistent spokesmen, Andrew Carnegie:

Lord Rector of Saint Andrews University
Giver of Organs and Libraries
Promoter of Peace among Nations
The American People having, of their Generosity,
Granted to you a magnificent Share in the Natural
Monopolies of the great Country, you have accumulated
   a colossal Fortune which you have splendidly
   recognized as a sacred Trust to be administered
   for the
Benefit of your Fellow Men . . .[49]

More generally, the principle of charity was sometimes cited as the natural way to "heal the ghastliest wound" in our economic corpus:

Young men and women leaving ease and comfort and
   idleness to live in the slums of our great cities;
Sacrificing self, because they cannot do otherwise;
Yet living gladly, finding new, undreamt-of joys in life.[50]

In this manner were great remedies offered without hint of altering nature of the system.

The poetic case for the Gospel of Wealth, while less powerful than its counterpart of protest against economic wrongs, was still impressive in its own right. Calling on the widespread American respect for applied science and material advance, the poets in this camp praised the considerable achievements of industry during the last decades of the nineteenth century. With the railroad providing the major drama and the telephone offering new puns to play with, the poet readily absorbed the achievements of the new age into his vocabulary and meter. As a defender of the status quo, he was quick to sentimentalize the poor and to blame the worker for his own plight; as a defender of the dignity of poverty and of labor, he was hypersensitive to complaints of economic injustice; as a defender of the American Way, he was avid in his censure of foreign ideologies which he feared might breed discontent and violence; as a philosopher of capitalism, he urged more industry, more millionaires, and more enlightened stewardship of wealth. America, in his grateful judgment, rested safely in the hands of the inventor, the entrepreneur, and the public-spirited man of wealth.

ii

If this was a period of awesome achievement, it was also a time when suspicions arose to the effect that the fruits of that achievement were not being properly shared. These protests far outweighed the literature urging acceptance of the status quo or attacking the attackers thereof. While at its most effective the poetry of protest was specific and constructive, much of it did little more than establish a mood of discontent; but if the poets were often vague in the particulars of their criticism, they were not always mild in their language:

> Labor . . . is simply going to swarm on its own roads,
>   occupy its own homesteads, enjoy its own pleasure,
>   work out the measure and shape of its own will,
>   and leave you to fall in line in the one way that
>   will assure you against annihilation.[51]

P.G.A.–G

Ultimatums were delivered in sinister contexts ("Upharsin is
writ on the Wall!") and refrains succeeded one another with
ominous emphasis (*"The laborer is worthy of his hire"*).[52] But as
the object of these portentous protests, the reader was frequently
given only a seldom-specified "Company of Oppressors," a
villainous but anonymous roost of capitalist buzzards, or a
stereotyped assemblage of soulless businessmen.[53]

Among the purveyors of this vague unrest were numbered
many followers of socialism and of the Single Tax who, although
they adopted the watchwords of these schools of thought,
nowhere took the trouble to endorse the specific policies
associated with them.[54] Whatever their point of departure,
however, these men left no doubt as to the center of their
sympathy. Their methods were sometimes ironic:

> But down with the doubt! Why it's atheistic
> To hint that the system which men adore
> Needs a turn from the cranks that are socialistic:
> It's perfect now, and it can't be more.[55]

sometimes religious in their reference:

> . . . ye that have heired the purple! . . .
> Though you laugh in your pride exulting . . .
> The God who numbers the sparrows,
> Has counted the common herd![56]

but most often simply militant:

> Ye sons of toil, awake!
> Your bondage break,
> Your children free;
> Created by your hands
> Your tyrant stands,
> Plutocracy . . .[57]

As did the exponents of the Gospel of Wealth, these poets saw
a "new day coming"; but, in contrast, this was not to be a new
day of sunny skies and smiling workmen. Rather, it was to be a

day of retribution for the wrongs which labor had suffered throughout the long years.

This retribution and these wrongs were particularized in a number of ways. Those who spoke for the farmer were involved in several questions, some of them primarily regional (see Chapter II), some of them demographic (see Chapter III), and some more political than economic (see Chapter V). But the determining elements in the rural scene were chiefly economic, and the verse to be discussed here concerns this aspect of the agricultural frame of mind. The poetry also gives insight into the kind of economic figure the farmer-poet thought himself to be. It may be logical, for example, to think of the farmer as having more in common with the small businessman than with the laborer, as sharing the concerns of the creditor and employer, as well of the debtor and the employee. Following this line of thought, historians have attempted to account for the failure of rural and urban labor interests to unite for their common benefit. But those who spoke for the farm interest in verse expressed no such confusion as to status or identification. The farmer, as he appeared in these lines, was a son of toil, not a master of means; he shared with the urban laborer not only long hours of work with little remuneration, but also the curse of common enemies: the Eastern financier, the speculator, and the politician who represented them. The literature of agrarian protest not only added another dimension to the economic picture, but did so in the spirit of dissatisfaction with the status quo and of sympathy with the "have not" side of the economic debate.

The rural disposition toward protest was somewhat vitiated by that hypersensitivity to criticism which has already been mentioned in connection with Edwin Markham. As social protest it was also vitiated by the fact that a good many of the hardships encountered by the farmer were natural rather than man-made: heat, cold, dust, wind, gophers, insects and fire. Yet, when such discouragement as the following resulted, it made little difference, in one sense, where the villainy lay:

> The farmer scanned his fields so bare,
> And sighed that mercy was no more;
> While Famine whined, he thought, in air,
> And crouched around the opened door.[58]

> "Our fields lie waste, no toiler's hand has reaped
> Aught for his labor, empty are our barns,
> Our stock unfed. God give us strength to bear
> Not want alone . . . but . . . to sustain our shrinking
>   souls . . .[59]

> A life-long labor spent upon the sod
> That yields him scarcely half enough to eat . . .
> There *must* be justice in the halls of God![60]

This appalling discontent with things as they were often led to despair of finding earthly remedies; and, as the last line quoted above suggests, the "The Sod-House in the Sky" became an oft-promised haven of final rest and retribution.[61] Hamlin Garland's powerful lines served not only as further illustration of this tendency, but also as a reminder of the monotonous drudgery and the peculiar hardships of women which were depicted in rural plaints from all sections of the country:

> It ain't been nothin' else but scrub
> An' rub and bake and stew
> The hull time, over stove or tub—
> No time to rest as men folks do.—
> I tell yeh, sometimes I sit and think
> *How nice the grave'll be, jest
> One nice, sweet, everlastin' rest!*[62]

Although many of these verses were not directly focused on economic causes or effects, they did constitute a shattering attack on the status quo, and they did provide a fertile field of unrest in which the seeds of more specific protest could be sown.

Nor were particular targets lacking, as witness this complaint against two rural villains of long standing, the tax agent and the moneylender:

An' there ain't very many farmers but what feel the lash
Of poverty—'bout Tax Time . . .
The mortga*gees* hide their money bags so's not to
    pay no tax,
While the mortga*gors* most haf' to sell the coats from
    off their backs
To raise the wind—'bout Tax Time.[63]

Speculators in farm commodities were a special target of the rural spokesmen; in "Smith's Corner in Hay," Mr. Smith was outfitted in the well-worn whiskers of Simon Legree.[64] The railroads, whose routes and rates spelled the difference between success and failure, were viewed with awe and antipathy, often through the symbol of the grain elevators, "Castles . . . that . . . compel men's fear."[65] The farmer had some special enemies and some special problems (over-expansion, the decline in land values, and the decline in the purchasing power of the farm dollar) to which he gave particular attention in his verse; but his major protest, against the background of discontent indicated above, will be considered below as a part of the general reaction to economic conditions.

As might be inferred from the preceding chapter, the outcry against poverty, against poor living and working conditions was louder and more detailed in the urban-industrial context than in the rural setting. Here one finds that large but uninspiring group of melodramatic narratives suggested by such titles as "Newsboy's Christmas," or "Match Girl's Thanksgiving." Although they called attention to the contrasts between wealth and poverty, they stood on the border line between the poetry of sentiment and the poetry of protest. The transition from the story of the sentimentalized waif, laboring ill-clad through snow and ice on a mission in support of a crippled and chair-bound mother, to the literature of more outspoken protest could be seen in the lines of a verse entitled "The Flower Girl." Beginning like any other melodrama, toward its finale it rose to a complaint of "want and misery Amid the wealth and splendor

of the city," and concluded with the plea: "How long, O Lord,
will evil rule the earth?"[66] The phrase, "How, long O Lord
. . ." was virtually thematic with these versifiers who stood in
awe of the misery borne by the poor and the patience required
by this burden. Some went so far as to remind the rich that if
the poor were not noble and Christian neither they nor their
wives would be safe.[67] Reacting against the apologists for
poverty, they reviled rich and church alike for attempting to
cover an ugly situation with quotations from the Bible. "God's
poor," a phrase popular with poets who defended the status quo,
was called blasphemous by another who argued that it was not
God but society who made them poor.[68] Also attacked were
those who hid behind Malthusian theories in their justification
of the condition of poverty.[69] Most of the versifiers who called
attention to the outrages of poverty did so through vivid
portrayals of the "children of hunger" in their "stifling dens"
and "quarters of want."[70] Whatever the technique, or the
specific approach, the theme of social responsibility received
constant emphasis:

> O'er our beautiful earth hangs the shadow of death,
> And the air hath a taint of the pestilent breath
> Of dense-peopled cities; where want and oppression
> Are a withering blight on the face of creation.[71]

Although this period included two severe depressions, there
was no general tendency to connect poverty with unemployment; nor was there, in the lines of those who did make this
connection, any concrete suggestion as to how unemployment
could best be overcome. The workingman, out of a job, was
passively depicted "with his idle arms crossed/By the want-
stricken hearth, with a sigh in his breast." Such catch-all terms
as "prosperity" and "brotherhood" measured the extent of the
remedies proposed.[72] Perhaps it was significant that even one
poet, in the years following the panic of 1873, placed the
responsibility on "Uncle Sam" to "Contrive some plan to help

us through.''[73] More poets associated poverty with charity and
looked for "relief" as a supplement to prayer.[74] Although there
was some cynicism directed at organized charities (" 'Popular
Aid Societies care not for the human cause,/But work for self
. . . vain applause . . . pelf.' ''[75]), dire consequences were
nonetheless predicted for those who did not go out to help the
poor:

> I tell you the rage of the ages waits
> And crouches low at your mansion gates;
> God's brotherhood only its thirst abates,—
> Go forth in the name of Him![76]

In discussing poverty, unemployment, and charity, the spokesmen for the urban poor cultivated, alongside that of his rural
neighbor's, a field of economic discontent which was to bear its
own crop of more particularized protest.

The protest against poor living conditions has been sampled
in connection with the poet's profile of the city (see Chapter
III), but this subject took on a special pertinence when the poet
surveyed the scene from the point of view of the "working
class." Here the most persistent complaint was against inadequate housing and unhealthful environment: the "hovels, dens,
and ditches" in which the workers were forced to live, and the
tenements in which they were forced to sleep often "Three or
four in a single bed."[77] Diet, perhaps oddly, received little
attention unless it reached the starvation level; but other aspects
of public health were criticized in some detail. The most often
repeated grievance was against the pollution of air and water by
the factories—air and water which the factory workers, if no one
else, were forced to breathe and drink:

> A thousand factories poured a noisome flood
> Of foul off-scorings and of poisoned waste
> . . . Till the clear stream grew turbid, rank, and foul . . .[78]

The smoke which grimed the workers' faces and shut off the
"pleasant glow of sunny skies" was railed against so often that

the ugly black smokestack atop the factory became directly associated with "dank disease for the toilers."[79] Seldom specific, the outcry against conditions leading to poor health among the workers was shot with such phrases as "unnamed stenches," "Dark pollution," and "tasteless, shoddy, adulterated products."[80] But the language of sickness and disease was sufficiently present to be used in even larger discussions, as illustrated by these lines from a verse called "The Mill on the Damn-Side":

> A corporation skirts the town,
> Polluting every germ of health
> By hiring children scarcely grown
> While they [the owners] speed on toward wealth.[81]

Questions of housing and health led easily into questions of morality:

> The foulest home and brutalizing lives,
> Which bring forth brutal lives to fill the street,
> Growing in moral filth, amid the cursed
> Environment of shame and hate and sin.[82]

Reacting to a moral problem attributable to economic causes, the poet was strongly drawn to the defense of the fallen women who married for money, let themselves be kept, or entered houses of prostitution because *"they had no choice."*[83] The economic orientation of this problem was brought out most emphatically by a poet who based his comments on a newspaper article which he quoted as follows: ". . . shop girls are often insulted on the streets by men who assume that they are immoral because they are poor."[84] Honesty, as well as virtue, was felt to be inhibited by the worker's environment:

> Right in the heart of sin and poverty,
> Where Vice, unblushing and unvisored, walks
> With his dark consort, ignorance, up and down,
> Quickly devouring up each little grain
> Of virtue that dares sprout amid the filth,

Leering at laws and laughing down reforms;
Here where serfs of labor sometimes dream
Of being men and women some bright day
When they less hardly feel the cursed grind
Of getting honest bread. . . .[85]

In the battle for existence necessitated by such an environment,
a general atmosphere of violence and lust prevailed. The young
tough was pictured, cigar in mouth, lying and stealing as if by
nature.[86] The prevalence of broken homes and the need that
compelled mothers to go to work, thus denying normal family
affections, led some poets to condemn parents for begetting
children under slum conditions. Beauty was kept out of the
workers' lives by the "windowed ugliness . . . appalling
blackness" of both factories and dwellings.[87] Even religion, that
final consolation of the oppressed, was feared lost in the extreme
poverty that could not afford to buy pews or make offerings, and
would therefore feel unwanted in the house of God.[88]

The poets sympathized not only with the social consequences
of female and child labor, but also with the hardships which these
workers endured. "The Wheel of Child Labor" became a cruel
"wheel of fire and it burns to the very brain."[89] Also appealing
were the images of children shut off from nature, God, and
family behind the prison door of the factory or the adit of the
mine. Verses on this subject, as might be expected, verged on
the maudlin and the melodramatic; but their sincere sympathy
is hard to question.[90] Lines concerning the exploitation of
women could be equally moving:

. . . women working where a man would fall—
Flat-breasted miracles of cheerfulness
Made neuter by the work that no man counts
Until it waits undone . . .[91]

As had the question of living conditions, the working conditions
also led the poets to consider the problem of female morality.
One verse sympathized with the girl employee in a candy store

who was compelled to endure the playful advances of her wealthy customers:

> These she must suffer, and things more cruel
> From the hand of commerce-hardened man,
> And still remain an unsullied jewel
> 'Mid the world's garbage—if she can.[92]

"No wonder," speculated the poet, "they turn to the lurings of shame."[93]

The 1880's and 1890's did not signal the entry of women into mills and factories, although the number of female industrial laborers continued to increase; but these years did witness the arrival of a new field for female endeavor. The telephone and the typewriter had begun to furnish opportunity for labor where physical endurance under industrial conditions was not required. But the advent of the switchboard girl and the female stenographer raised further questions in the Victorian mind concerning the propriety of placing isolated women in the predominantly male surroundings of the office. The switchboard operator, for example, received sympathy for having to cope all day long with male rudeness, if only over the wires.[94] There was also some recognition of the monotony of this occupation, although complaints about the hardships of office work were less likely, with the possibility of comparison with the lot of the seamstress and factory worker forever at hand.[95] For this reason the general comment on this new branch of female labor was relatively mild. The woman in the office was assumed to have honest motives and was appreciated as a cheerful influence in an otherwise drab setting.[96]

Protests against long hours and low wages, as might be expected, occupied the bulk of the verse comment on conditions of labor. Complaints against hours of labor were most spectacular, whether they pertained to home labor—

> My eyes are aching, my brow's on fire,
> I work through the night till my thin hands tire;

> I lie down to sleep on the wooden floor,
> Where my lamp burns low by the cellar door.[97]

—or to the factory girls who stitched from dawn till dusk.[98] The figure of labor in chains, a common one, arose from the idea that long hours on the factory treadmill completely dominated the worker's life and left room for nothing else, not even thought or prayer.[99] The language used in protests against low wages tended to be relatively undramatic, doubtless because the figures cited were considered striking enough:

> Fourteen cents are all the wages
> One can earn in the longest day.[100]

The underpayment of labor figured importantly in the more detailed reactions to economic and political conditions which will be treated below; but it should already be clear that the poet did heartily condemn the state of the world which called for long exposure to fatigue, poor health, and demoralizing conditions for so small a compensation.

This body of verse also reflected a strong indignation at the unsafe and unsanitary conditions under which labor was typically forced to work at this time. On both these counts the miners, trapped "like moles" in "dull and damp" air, received special attention.[101] For the miner, "grim death is near,/Unseen and terrible, alert to smite," and the occasions when death did smite were important ones for the poets.[102] Mass deaths due to explosions or cave-ins testified to the small regard in which the operator held the lives of his employees. The "death in the mine" school of verse, like the "death on the trestle" school, valued melodrama, individual heroism, and wholesale gore above the idea of social protest. All of these elements were developed—to take one instance—in the story of "Miner Jim," who saved the lives of an elevator load of his fellow workers by shoving his arms into a defective winch to serve as a brake.[103] Another common object of the poet's pity was the child worker, as seen in this lament for Charlie the slate-picker:

> He watched the cogs at their iron dance;
> 'Twas such fun to see them whirl and spin;
> He touched them, and, quick as a reptile's glance,
> The treacherous things snapped Charlie in.
>
> They caught the child in their deadly grip,
> They crushed his bones in their wild embrace.
> The great wheels halt; they delay the trip.
> There's one more slate picker's vacant place.[104]

Outside the mine, the place singled out for its unsanitary conditions was the "reeking basement," with its poor light and "poisoned vapors," in which the tobacco-stemmer worked; although tirades against the pervasive gloom and filth of factories of whatever sort were abundant.[105] The cotton mill and the railroad bore special opprobrium for the maiming accidents they caused.[106] The railroad, as was shown above, served as jumping-off place for greatly varied comments; under this heading it should be noted that some poets specifically indicted the railway for such willful negligence as poorly set rails, soft embankments, inadequate safety precautions, and the general exploitation of life for profit:

> Only a company getting rich!
> In an undertaker's style,
> With a life for every switch
> And a funeral for every mile![107]

As was evidenced by the stanzas cited in connection with the mining tragedies, the poets exhibited an increasing awareness of the unequal battle between man and machine. Shaking their heads over the insistent machine-made racket, the poets complained of the "anvils' ceaseless ringing," the mechanical needles that "buzz in monotonous hum," and the constant clack of the telegraph, "Of madness being on the border."[108] Among the poets, Ernest Crosby recognized most vividly and accurately the effects, both physical and psychological, of machine on man. Long hours of monotonous application produce "high tension," he wrote; and he capped his analysis with the statement—intended to be taken literally—that machines "have eaten up the men and women."[109] Many of the poets realized that men of flesh and blood were being asked to keep pace with the tireless machines, and that the result, over long hours, could only prove disastrous for the human mind and body. The opposition of the mechanical to the human could be dramatically set forth in such verses as the one which described a factory boy who was able only through death to trade the harsh and angular shapes of the machines in the dark shadows of the shop for the splendors of natural beauty among which he was buried. As the lad found final rest from his harassed and artificial life, the poet wrote as epitaph, "And the great wheels are still!"[110]

The interest of the poet in the "other half" was voluminous. Whether his subject was rural or urban, he reacted with a sense of unrest based on the prevalence of poverty and of bad living and working conditions. His individual attitudes ranged from a stereotyped sentimentalization of poverty to an acute examination of the complicated effects of machines upon men. The tone pervading these verse discussions was sometimes strongly moral, sometimes predominantly sociological. A distinct body of protest verse dealt harshly and specifically with such matters as long hours, low wages, and unsafe or unsanitary working conditions. The poet was manifestly disturbed by what he saw in the lower economic strata; his appraisal of this situation, in composite terms, showed a readiness to reconsider some of the basic facts of economic America.

For some poets the "other half" meant the top fraction of the economic stratum; and they were as disturbed by their examination of the behavior and environment of the rich as others had been by the behavior and environment of the poor. These protests became most vivid and varied when they dealt with the extremely rich. Jay Gould, Andrew Carnegie, William H. Vanderbilt, the Rothschilds, and John D. Rockefeller, in that order, were the favorite subjects for verse comments; and the poet's evaluation of these men epitomized his attitude toward the economically triumphant.

The names which sprang into verse most readily as suggestive of over-opulence or of questionable financial practice were those of Gould and Vanderbilt. The couplet, "The vampires Gould and Vanderbilt,/Have all the people's life-blood spilt!" typified the use of these names, as did a remark in a verse dialogue addressed to a glib and hypocritical character named "Mammon": "You could give lessons to Jay Gould."[111] When the plot of a narrative verse, "The Lambs," called for an innocent to be shorn, he was led to his financial slaughter by reports of investments by Gould, Vanderbilt, and "the Dutch."[112] As for over-opulence,

> In New York City, people say,
> That Mr. Vanderbilt does pay
> Eight thousand dollars every year,
> And doesn't seem to think it dear,
> To get a certain person to
> Cook . . .[113]

The Rothschilds belonged in the same general class with Gould and Vanderbilt, according to the poets, but they bore the added stigma of being foreign and of meddling in political affairs. The following words were made to emerge from the mouths of President Grant's backers:

> Don't forget to remember that our foreign friends,
> Are the six Baron Rothchilds [*sic*] whose money we use,
> To push on our scheme. They are ready to lend
> All the money we want—and they are all Jews . . .[114]

It depended strictly on the poet whether the Rothschilds were to be exceptionally abhorred because they were Jews or because they were English.[115]

The treatment of Rockefeller brought into focus the question of how individual riches had been accumulated. One particularly vengeful versifier traced a never-named Rockefeller from his industrial beginnings in Bradford, Titusville, and Oil City, through his achievements in horizontal and vertical monopoly, to a final judgment of his business practices which sentenced him to boil eternally in his own oil.[116] Here Rockefeller was condemned for his ruthless monopolism rather than for his mere accumulation of wealth. The poets drew a clear line, as has already been noted, in appraising these economic successes. Men who were self-made (such as Carnegie), or who had done something physically constructive and beneficial to the community (such as Gould and Stanford with their railroads), were criticized less severely than the men who were thought of primarily as financiers and speculators, such as William Vanderbilt and the Rothschilds. In the case of Gould, where both aspects were prominent, the poets praised his industrial achievements and condemned his financial practices.

A citation in defense of Gould will serve to bring up the question of the charities of these men of means:

> He surely did not rob the proletaire,
> But sharply sapped his brother millionaire!
> And, unlike them, he built no library,
> College or cathedral as a bribery
>
> To buy the "good will" of the middle class . . .[117]

The question of the stewardship of wealth arose most often in connection with the charities of Carnegie and Rockefeller; and, although some poets saw fit to praise these activities, as noted above, most commentators on the subject were uncharitable to the idea of "tainted money" gifts. The following comment, more detailed than most, may be taken as typical of the attitudes expressed:

> The speculator, pious and knowing,
> Will give to his scheme so good a showing
> That people get mad as crazy March hares,
> And all rush in to suscribe for the shares.

But when they are sold he pockets the cash,
And the great speculation goes to smash.
He then builds, by way of apology,
An institute to teach theology;
Or, as a kind of restitution,
Founds a Young Men's Christian Institution.
Sometimes after wrecking two or three banks,
He will, on his knees, give Providence thanks;
And to show he is not mean nor greedy,
Will freely give to the poor and needy,
Or found a mission with half what he took
To send the heathen the Holy Book . . .[118]

Libraries, educational and philanthropic institutions, as well as other charities effected by this group, were consistently judged as apologies designed to atone for the financial abuse of widows and orphans. In tune with Finley Peter Dunne, the poets looked these gift horses searchingly and embarrassingly in the mouth.

From the examination of the wealthy, both specifically and in general, there arose two prevailing themes, both best identified in Veblenian terms. The first was what Veblen labeled "conspicuous consumption"—castigated by the poets in such phrases as "ostentation of dress," "sordid vanity and show," "lavish luxury and taste . . . extravagance and waste," "vulgar millions," or "gold, pomp, and glitter."[119] Sometimes specific luxuries were itemized—Newport mansions, "steam-yachts and auto-cars," or excursions to Europe.[120] The railway's palace car, as mentioned above, frequently symbolized ostentatious luxury; and the over-lavish houses of the rich were classed as "mansions reared to dull self-adulation . . . [which] only tell of fortunes misexpended."[121] Also of interest was the manner in which some poets attacked the "gilded churches" for deserting the poor in order to capitalize on their lucrative friendship with the rich.[122]

Not only the consumption itself but also the conspicuousness thereof sometimes attracted the attention of the poet, as in the case of one "John Moneybags." Here was portrayed not only a city villain (from New York), and a gesturing villain (he "rubbed his fat hands"), but also a man bent on being a public villain. His curtains were fashioned so that "folks in the street,/ Might see the room's toilet, clear down to its feet." When he opened his blinds, it was made clear that he did so not so much to observe as to be observed.[123]

The second prevailing theme is not necessarily to be traced to the writings of Veblen, but it did correspond quite exactly with his emphasis on a leisure *class*, a group which had come into being during more crudely atavistic times and whose continuing existence had become inimical to society. Evidence for the poet's consciousness of a separate class made up of the wealthy stems from works which scored the rich for their mimicry of the upper classes in more formally stratified societies. The recurrence of such phrases as "brutes in princely garb," "Lord and Peasant; Social Contrasts," and "Fawning courtiers" made the intended accusation clear.[124] Living "like a king" took on an almost literal meaning, as did the branding of rich homes as "palaces."[125] Not so royal in their reference, but equally connotative of rigid class structure were such frequently used labels as "autocrat" and "Swell-Plutocracy."[126]

What, besides wealth, brought about this acute sense of class on the part of the poet? First of all the idea, so repugnant to busy Americans, that the rich were living as idle parasites— "human rats," "robber drones," in the words of the poets themselves.[127] But it was especially the adornment of that idleness—the fashionable, foppish frills—which aroused the critics. They abhorred the "youthful swell with rattan cane in hand" who might change his clothes "at least three times a day" and who represented a class with "pipe stem" muscles, who took for a model the effete of the English upper class.[128] This set of habits formed a distinctly unfavorable contrast with those of the honest workingman who "hasn't time to swing a fan or downward pull a vest."[129] Again in a setting built on economic contrasts, a snobbish slimming party was described as "Wasp-waisted, spindle-shanked, and baby-faced"; and these repre-sentatives of the upper crust were roundly condemned by the slum denizens as "but tailor's dummies widout brains."[130] Thus not only were idleness and effeminacy stressed, but also the uselessness of what little activity was indulged in by this class. The money spent on the clubs of the rich, it was pointed out,

> Could be better spent by far,
> In getting up communion
> With the furtherest fixed star.[131]

The poet could dislike, yet tolerate, a class which built its life around "clubs . . . cognac . . . cards" only so long as he was convinced that such activity did not come under the heading of "wanton cruel pleasures" which created "all poverty and crime as well."[132] Many poets took the latter point of view, fearing that the rich man's air of nonchalance and philosophy of *sauve qui peut* showed that he not only lived off the workers but also was inclined to "hate all those greasy mechanics" and to exert the pressure of his wealth to keep them "in their place."[133] Into the mouth of "The Modern Pharisee" the poet placed his estimate of this class-oriented point of view:

> I soar above the mass,
> Look down upon the poor;
> I try to keep them where they are,
> In poverty secure.[134]

The poet's outrage at this attitude was exhibited in stinging lines which pitted the "aristocrat" against the "howling mob," or bemoaned the existence of a "fawning lapdog race" literally enslaved to the rich.[135] As vivid as any, and more eloquent than most, was Stephen Crane on this subject:

> The successful man has thrust himself
> Through the water of the years,
> Reeking wet with mistakes,—

Bloody mistakes;
Slimed with victories over the lesser,
A figure thankful on the shore of money.
Then, with the bones of fools
He buys silken banners . . .
With the skins of wise men
He buys the trivial bows of all
. . . and makes . . .
A coverlet for his contented slumber.[136]

Out of this background of complaint against conditions at both extremes of the economic scale, many poets developed what might be very broadly termed economic philosophies. As might be expected, relatively few of the versifiers offered constructive critiques of the system, but great numbers came forth to locate the source of the inequities they found around them. Among specific targets, the large-scale business unit drew most of their fire. Although the term "monopoly" was hit most frequently, the poet also aimed at trusts, corporations, combines, pools, and syndicates, apparently distinguishing not at all among these various types of business combinations. Any group or single organization which had grown sufficiently large to dominate its field was considered fair game. The Standard Oil Company, the Sugar Trust, the "Coal Barons," and the "railroad monopolies" were sighted by poetic snipers, but as a group the poets preferred to fire random salvos at all over-large comers.[137] Epithets such as "monster Corporation," "the Octopus," "hydra-headed monopoly," and "monopoly's shark" indicated the tenor of their sentiments.[138] Added to these grisly associations was the connection of the trusts with the pirates of old and with greed and misused wealth in general:

Would you build up great trusts and throttle the law,
And sacrifice nature's good instincts to greed . . . ?
Would you have all the wealth possessed by the few,
Treat merit and honor with neglect and scorn . . . ?[139]

Monopoly was regarded as anti-democratic, and the fear of its power was graphically depicted:[140]

> Onward unceasingly moves a huge cylinder,
> Grinding, levelling city and field. . . .
> Falling beneath it, merchants, workmen,
> Helplessly struggle,
> Quickly to yield. . . .
>
> Wrecks of the workshops, factories smokeless;
> Crumble before it, waiting decay;
> Factories greater, rising behind it
> Glow with the furnaces,
> Capital centered, massing, in union,
> Handle the levers,
>
> Quickly to sway nations and laws in their way.
> Ruthless Monopoly, thou art the cylinder,
> Moving, grinding, levelling all. . . .
> Either the people, through ballot or battle
> Handle the levers,
> Or in the fall—slaves they are all.[141]

As this selection so well illustrates, the large business unit was pictured not only as synonymous with power and greed, but also as literally destructive to the competitive system; many of the complaints against it centered on this aspect. The tentacled prehensile beast became a cylinder, as above, or a great wheel, grinding the small businessman into extinction.[142] The "heartless Trusts/That kill all competition" limited production for their own advantage, engaged in shoddy practices unknown in times of free competition, and used their unfair size to upset the natural economic balance.[143] There were those who upheld the economic status quo, or who showed an implicit acceptance of the role of big business; but very few actually rose to the defense of large-scale enterprise. If the reaction of the poets is to be regarded as significant, it would appear that the proponents of social Darwinism had failed to make a case for their philosophy. One poet debated that very rationale:

> Brothers, shall we place reliance
> On the men of modern science,
> Who commend the great corporations
> To subserve the public good?
> Or bewail their power controlling,
> As the knell of freedom tolling . . . ?

From the loading of the question, the answer supplied is not surprising:

> Ne'er before has time recorded
> Such increase of millions hoarded,
> Such a fierce and bitter struggle
> Of the weak against the strong;
> Men with itching palms unheeding
> Freedom's right or poor man's pleading
> As their stocks and shares they juggle,
> In a carnival of wrong.[144]

The phrase "as their stocks and shares they juggle" calls attention to another example of economic turpitude already suggested in several of the previous quotations. As American enterprise moved from the industrial to the financial stage, an impressively large group of poets stood ready to denounce the symptoms of that change. Overlapping slightly with the anti-monopolists and representing rural as well as urban points of view, this group underlined the responsibility of those who sought to control the economy by purely financial, rather than industrial, means. Their villains were the "money kings," the "usurers of banks," and the "Corporation lords who . . . water stock/With sweat of others' brows."[145] The figure of Shylock, "tightening his screws" to the discomfort of everyone, was recalled; and such contemporary counterparts as Hanna and Morgan were shown playing similarly reprehensible roles.[146] The banker became a "vulture" perched amidst "Envy and Pride and Lust and Greed."[147] The bondholder was accused not only of "grade crossing murders" but also of keeping the

farmer a slave to debt.[148] Illustrating the special antipathy of the
rural citizen to the financial class came the following lines:

> He [the farmer]'s opposed by a class with a stealthy-like
>   tread,
> And cruelly swindled by base financiers—
> That great moneyed power which companies wield
> For their profit, alone, and the husbandman's harm,
> Possesses itself of the fruits of his field,
> And afterwards pockets the whole of his farm.[149]

These men who controlled the money were accused of
conspiring to limit its circulation (as were the political "gold-
bugs") in order to hoard it in their "marble grotto."[150] Nearly
all of these condemnations centered on the deification of money
to the detriment of public welfare:

> Money is our dream ideal; money is our highest goal;
> Money—money—and for money we crowd out the human
>   soul. . . .
> Stocks and bonds are more than honor. If our brother's
>   blood is shed,
> We will overlook the murder, if they pay us for our dead . . .
> . . . If workmen ask for higher pay
> We will shoot them down like cattle on the open, broad
>   highway.[151]

Grouped with the banker, the bondholder, and the moneylender was the speculator. Sometimes he was pilloried in a
deceptively friendly manner as in this spelling-book catechism:

> Is it a-live?
> Oh yes, it is a-live: it is a stock-bro-ker.
> What can he do?
> He can knock off hats.
> Why is he so proud?
> He is not proud, he is on-ly calm.
> Will he take an or-der?
> Oh yes, you bet he will take an or-der!

Oh fie! See the fight!
No, it is no fight; the men are on-ly bus-y.
Does it hurt to be there?
No, it does not hurt; it is nice to be there.
The stock is up an eighth.
Are they go-ing for the stock?
Oh no, they are go-ing for the eighth.[152]

More often the attack was overtly malicious, as when the "stock wizards" were cast as the witches of *Macbeth*, in which roles they brewed "Workman's savings, workman's bread," "a miner's sweat and blood" in a broth of gain and fraud.[153] In better days, according to one poet, "Stock gambling and Futures, and Corners in Food" would have been punished; several of his colleagues joined him in specially deploring any gambling affecting the national food supply and the precarious well-being of the marginal farmer.[154] Sympathy was accorded both to the poor, who would have to pay a penny a loaf more for their bread on account of "A Corner in Wheat," and to the farmers who were often victimized by speculation in grains.[155] Although speculation in agricultural commodities captured the most attention, manipulated booms in land and natural gas were also condemned.

Wall Street, as the home of the financiers, came to have a pejorative connotation all its-own. At his mildest, the poet spoke of it as a place where education was dearly bought; as his temper rose, he linked its "Great mausoleums" with that calamitous Black Friday of 1869.[156] Morbid as are the following lines from a verse called "The Genius Loci of Wall Street," they are by no means unrepresentative of the collective poetic reaction to the coming of the great age of finance capitalism in America:

Down in a wonderful city, near to the foulest slums,
Where squalor and crime are rife, and the tide flows
  turgid with greed,

> Where all are greedy and blatant, where peacefulness
>   never comes,
> There squats a ravening reptile, Arachne, the Spider
>   Queen. . . .
> Her prey is human muscle, with the products of honest
>   toil . . .[157]

This "Spider Queen," the poets feared, was about to devour the
land of the free.

iii

Some poets, although they were relatively few, sought to do
more than place the blame for economic inequities. As they
developed what often amounted to social philosophies some of
them stressed political aspects (and will therefore be discussed
in the next chapter), while some stressed the economic. Several
among them indicated their beliefs and recommendations simply
by endorsing one of two spokesmen for the "have nots": Henry
George and Edward Bellamy. These two were rivaled only by

Peter Cooper—who was given credit for the "altars to Labor he reared"—as constructive thinkers whose ideas, if pursued, were to have rescued the dispossessed.[158] Henry George received the greater poetic acclaim; one entire volume of verse was devoted to celebrating both major and minor events of his life.[159] Unfortunately the acolytic zeal of his explicators tended to render his ideas less meaningful than they originally were. One poet, on the other hand, had the temerity to accuse "Mr. Buncombe George" of talking cant, and even he diluted his criticism through the device of an imaginary dialogue between George and the Pope.[160] Henry George's death, although it did not lead to any clearer understanding of his ideas on the part of the poet, did lead to his virtual canonization in the halls of verse. Richard Hovey called him the "Bayard of the poor," and other poets underlined his role as prophet and martyr:

> We had a prophet and we knew him not.
> Another age will rate thee at thy worth,
> . . . And, O the poor,
> How true a friend they've lost in thee!
> Who ever plead their cause with tongue and pen,
> And gave a plan to help them and the race. . . .
> He was a martyr to a holy cause. . . .[161]

References to Edward Bellamy were neither so numerous nor so enthusiastic, though the cry of "make haste, deliver us, O Bellamy," did sound in the work of one poet.[162] The interest here was in a work rather than a man, and that work—*Looking Backward*, published in 1888—had attracted an impressive amount of attention by the end of the next decade. There were enough verses and volumes which borrowed Bellamy's title, even, to make *Looking Backward* second only to "The Man with the Hoe" as a popular catch-phrase among poets interested in the economic scene. Since the followers of Bellamy did not personalize their loyalties, and thus avoided the messianic intensity of the Georgeites, their contributions mirrored their model more faithfully and contributed more rationally to the discussion of economic issues.[163]

In order to appreciate the poet's basic economic position, we need not go deeply into the details of the Single Tax movement or the non-competitive utopia described by Bellamy. In essence the poet had but two constructive plans: one called for increased participation by the government in the economic arena, and the other for the organization of the workingman. The first of these proposals—often couched in terms more political than economic—was stressed by many of the followers of George and Bellamy, as well as some factions of the Socialist persuasion.[164] The specific demands made by this group centered on state control of railroads and mines or government intervention on behalf of labor.[165] The role of the government in national finance was also thrown open for prolonged discussion; suggested revisions ranged from the plea that the state take currency control out of the hands of the private banks, to a panacea based on a drastic corporation tax which was to have provided the government its entire revenue.[166] One of the more interesting verses in this category pointed out that the proper political leadership for the country should involve not only skilled statecraft but also a sound grasp of the techniques and problems of science and industry.[167] Too often, however, the comments in this category were frustratingly vague, as witness one verse which merely queried "Is it not time to think of those who labor?" or another which contented itself with calling on Uncle Sam to "Contrive some plan to help us through."[168] Frequently fuzzy and widely varied in detail, this comment had in common a conviction that increased governmental control over economic measures was necessary in order to lessen the differentiation between the extremes of wealth and poverty, and to moderate between the camps of capital and labor.

The most positive and aggressive answer to the economic questions of the day emerged from those, once again relatively few in number, who advocated the organization of the laboring force. The urge to organize was expressed in agriculture as well as industry, albeit the rural movement, diluted as it was by educational and social emphases, took on a considerably milder tone. The Farmers' Institute, beginning in the 1880's, stressed the economic betterment of the rural citizen through education; the poets participated by urging attendance and by describing the proceedings. The semi-social occasion of the Institute's meetings brought forth some light joshing, under which lay a profound respect and appreciation for its basic function:

> But science came, a shining light,
> And stayed our hands from toil,
> And taught us how to do things right
> And till the virgin soil . . .[169]

From the comments of the versifiers it would appear that the Patrons of Husbandry, or Grange, founded in 1867, in many neighborhoods remained predominantly a social institution, frankly stressing "social mirth and friendly glee" while featuring marvelously complicated secret initiations.[170] It also fostered the interchange of serious ideas, prayer, and oratory. This last, judging from the verse, must have served mightily in shoring up the sagging rural ego:

> Time was when rich men and esquires
> Were held in great renown;
> Today, before the farming world,
> The greatest men bow down.[171]

In most localities, however, verses read at Grange functions or signed by Grangers reflected a much greater social consciousness. "The Ploughholders Ride in the Bondholder's Wake" was the title of a poem read at a Grange picnic in 1877, and other verses associated with Grange occasions complained of speculation or agitated for higher prices for farm commodities.[172] The membership was sometimes exhorted on the advantages of a united front in a manner more often associated with pleas to the industrial worker:

> Farmers often work eighteen hours a day . . .
> Farmers, 'rouse to your noble stand,
> Others have rights which they demand,
> Why not you have a rightful share,
> When it is honest, just, and fair ?[173]

Others, alerting the Grangers, dwelt on the advantages of rural cooperatives or fomented group resentment against such miscellaneous "serpents" in the farmer's Eden as trusts, monopolies, boards of trade, stockyards, railroads, capital, whiskey, fashion, and pride.[174] Verse pertaining to the Agricultural Wheel, the Farmers' Alliance, and other rural organizations also appeared, but was predominantly political rather than economic in its appeal. The shift in such organizations from an economic emphasis to one that was primarily political was evident in lines such as these:

> The Lights are out in Grangers' Hall;
> But in the campaign next fall
> They'll come again, for be it known
> Young blood will henceforth rule the town.[175]

Some of the verse pertaining to the organization of industrial labor paralleled its rural counterpart in stressing social rather than economic activities. One poet advocated the establishment of a "People's Institute," analogous to the Farmers' Institute, aimed at the betterment of the worker primarily through education.[176] Where specific unions were concerned, as for example the Ancient Order of United Workmen or the Brotherhood of Locomotive Engineers, the poetry typically commemorated the social rather than the aggressive aspects of unionization. The Knights of Labor, who boasted 700,000 members by 1885, were apt to be the subject of kindly comparison with knights of more chivalric days. The American Federation of Labor, founded in the mid-eighties and claimant of one million members by 1902, was virtually ignored.

Although the poet failed to identify himself with the cause of particular unions in any way that would have pleased a labor organizer, he did sound a clear, if generalized rallying call to the cause of union:

> Let workers unite!
> The brain and the hand
> Be nerved for the fight
> Now shaped in this land.[177]

Sometimes he made his point for organization simply by addressing workingmen as "brothers" or "comrades," or by prophesying the coming of a "Lincoln of Labor" to free the wage-slave.[178] The attitude of those who dealt with organized labor tended to be one of encouragement capped with caution. The workers, to quote a representative verse, had the right "To band together in their own defense,/Or with the money magnates unite" to end "industrial civil wars"; but they must never "scorn the public" in a selfish battle for wages alone.[179] Labor's association with "radical" ideologies, as was shown above, automatically invoked the disapproval of most poets, however sympathetic they might else have been to the general cause of the worker.

It was in his successive reactions to the three major events on the labor front that the poet demonstrated his increasing sympathy for the laborer. The Great Strike of 1877 provoked very few comments, and these few centered on the "waste of so much precious wealth" and the lawless commotion which "chills the circling life of enterprise."[180] Although no poet rose to defend the victims of the Haymarket Affair in 1886, at least one poet tried sympathetically to understand the anarchic impulse which was reputedly involved.[181] A more pointed defense of labor's side of the case was exhibited in a verse titled "Dynamite" and dated 1886. Here the explosive was termed the friend of hunger and poverty, and the verse concluded:

> Your gold can bribe me not, I [dynamite] fling your
>   chains away to rust;

I sweep the earth with giant gales—remember ye are
    dust![182]

And, at a greater chronological distance, another poet robed
Governor Altgeld in lavish praise for his pardon in 1892 of the
anarchists who still remained in jail.[183] By the time of the
Pullman strike the poets were alerted in greater numbers, and
most of them stood ready to extend some measure of encouragement to the strikers. At one extreme protests were penned
against the "spirit of evil" shown by the strikers "Who vent
their spleen with torch and force"; while at the other extreme
the strikers were completely vindicated.[184] A middle position
between these two extremes reveals a notably increased willingness to uphold the cause of organized labor as compared with the
days of 1877:

> "The Pullman strike, the sympathy attests,
> By carping Lords aroused, in workmen's breasts;
> Through injudicious, as most men concede;
> Yet its inauguration proved the need
> Of broader avenues to life's supplies."[185]

These sentiments in behalf of organized labor combined with
those in favor of governmental participation on behalf of the
dispossessed to express the poet's program for righting the
economic imbalance of his times.

In the poetry which addressed itself to the economic conditions of the late nineteenth century there existed a reasonably
complete record of the major events, personalities, and movements. More important, the poet, collectively speaking,
developed a well-elaborated bill of particulars in support of the
Gospel of Wealth, on the one hand, and in support of the
sentiment of protest on the other. These two general reactions
to America's economic system and status, however, were by no
means evenly balanced; both in the consistency of his approach
and eloquence and in the sheer quantity of his dedication, the

poet expressed a decided preference, amounting to a judgment on the relative values in our economic life. His satisfaction with the status quo was outweighed by his sometimes unfocused but clearly discernible sense of unrest; his defense of the dignity of poverty and labor gave way before his attack on the degradations inseparable from poverty; his paeans in praise of the achievements of industry were grossly tainted by his protests against poor living and working conditions. While with one hand he upheld the captains of industry and their benign stewardship of accumulated wealth, with the other, more potent hand he smote the leisure class for its conspicuous consumption and its hypocritical charities. Any overt defense of inequality which sought authority in the writings of Malthus or Darwin he quickly discarded. Against those who argued that prosperity should be equated with strong industrial leadership, he countered that the monopolist and the financier were about to crush the competitive system forever; and he consequently urged the government to take a more active role in guaranteeing economic equity. Although he feared the influence of foreign radical thought on the American system, he nevertheless offered increasing support for the agressive organization of labor.

Thus the poetic judgment weighed heavily against those who would let free enterprise run its course unfettered, and heavily in favor of those who objected to the inequities which this permissiveness apparently entailed. This sentiment strongly supported the growing Progressive program in its insistence on a closer regulation of business and a more active protection of the citizen's stake in the economy. The rising stature of organized labor, also characteristic of the period, may be more readily explained in the light of this poetic mandate. The idea of America as the land of the almighty mogul and as the source of economic opportunity for all gave way, in the verse of this period, to an impression dominated by the sense of struggle wherein antagonisms were recognized and inequities freely admitted.

Notes

[1] Knowles, *Love Triumphant*, 120–21.

[2] Mackintosh, *Memorial*, 75.

[3] Aiken, *Collection of the Poetical Writings*, 146.

[4] Davis, *Among the Muses*, 69.

[5] Lampton, *Yawps*, 103.

[6] Winslow, *Poems*, 165.

[7] Goss, *Vision of Tasseo*, 215.

[8] Cavaness, *Poems by Two Brothers*, 47.

[9] Cake, *Devil's Tea Table*, 91.

[10] Eisenbeis, *Amen Corner*, 188–92; Franklin, *Mid-Day Gleanings*, 11; Gailey, *Wreaths and Gems*, 97–103; Miller, *Parnassus by Rail*, v.

[11] Fairhurst, *My Good Poems*, 238; Furman, *In Vales of Helikon*, 57.

[12] Farquhar, *Libyssa*, 131.

[13] Curtis, *Legend of Sam'l of Posen*, 36.

[14] Wharf, *Promiscuous Poems*, 3–5; Emerson, *Patriotic Songs and Poems*, 36; Kaplan, *Jonathan's Dream*, n. page.

[15] Munkittrick, *Acrobatic Muse*, 114–15.

[16] Kenney, *Some More Thusettes*, 31.

[17] Dorr, *Babylon*, 120–21.

[18] Crosby, *Swords and Plowshares*, 59.

[19] Montgomery, *Lilies from the Vale of Thought*, 28.

[20] Adams, *Songs and Sonnets*, 97; Holden, *Many Moods*, 32, 33.

[21] Adams, *Siouska*, 315.

[22] McCabe, *Poems of Home and Fireside*, 11.

[23] Schultz, *Course of Progress*, 50; Smith, *Libertas*, 60.

[24] Armstrong, *La Porte in June*, 39.

[25] Markham, *Man with the Hoe*, 15, 17.

[26] Leary, *Toil*, 7.

[27] Davenport, "A Sweet and Hallowed Time," in *Norwalk after Two Hundred and Fifty Years*, 161; Granniss, *Boy with the Hoe*, n. pag.

[28] Markham, *Lincoln*, 5.

[29] Gould, *Autumn Singer*, 56.

[30] Allerton, *Annabel*, 101.

[31] Harris, *Tar-Baby*, 151.

[32] Davis, *Kingdom Gained*, 106.

[33] Cross, *Pygmalion*, 167–69; Mattocks, *Songs of Help and Inspiration*, 86–87.

[34] Dean, *Poems*, II, 46.

[35] Hoffman, *Poems*, 30–31; Kiser, *Ballads of the Busy Days*, 118–19; Fletcher, *Thousand Songs*, 298.

[36] Lampton, *Yawps*, 153.

[37] Welburn, *American Epic*, 260; *Devil's Visit*, 77.

[38] Skidmore, *Roadside Flowers*, 9; Gregory, *Beauty of Thebes*, 37; Huckel, *Larger Life*, 127; Price, *Poetical Works of Peter Peppercorn*, 105.

[39] See Haywood, *Peter Duikel Spiel*, n. pag.; Lawrence, *Day Dreams*, 66–67.

[40] Lozier, *Your Mother's Apron Strings*, 23.

[41] Watson, *To-Day and Yesterday*, 94.

[42] Martling, *London Bridge*, 11–12.

[43] Shaw, *Forward Forever!*, 12–13.

[44] Davis, *Kingdom Gained*, 106.

[45] Doeman, *Poems*, 353.

[46] Doeman, *Poems*, 313; Armstrong, *La Porte in June*, 20.

[47] Cole, *Colonel*, 135–37; McCann, *Songs from an Attic*, 121.

[48] Holden, *Ode*, 5.

[49] Dole, *Peace and Progress*, 5.

[50] Crosby, *Plain Talk in Psalm and Parable*, 39.

[51] Traubel, *Chants Communal*, 67.

[52] Voldo, *Poems from the Pacific*, 152; Cheyney, *Poems*, 72.

[53] Stevens, *Song of Companies*, 32–39; Mak, *Ekkoes from the Hart*, 54; Smiley, *Meditations of Samwell Wilkens*, 90.

[54] See, for example, Johnston, *Pagan's Poems*, and Sosso, *In the Realms of Gold*.

[55] Austin, *In the People's Name*, 31.

[56] Goodenough, "*Blossoms of Yesterday*," 21.

[57] Brooks, *Margins*, 27.

[58] Hartzell, *Wanderings on Parnassus*, 28.

[59] Miller, *Gallery of Farmer Girls*, 29.

[60] Mifflin, *Slopes of Helicon*, 35.

[61] Mills, *Sod House in Heaven*, 11–17.

[62] Garland, *Prairie Songs*, 143.

[63] Templer, *Some Rustic Rhymes*, 46–47.

[64] Spalding, *My Vagabonds*, 38–40.

[65] Upson, *Westwind Songs*, 21.

[66] Donahoe, *In Sheltered Ways*, 55–56.

[67] Dawson, *Poems of the New Time*, 77–78; Hewetson, *Strike*, 19.

[68] Clark, *Poems*, 42.

[69] Higgins, *Looking Backward in Rhyme*, 9.

[70] Claflin, *Thoughts in Verse*, 88.

[71] Davis, *Immortelles*, 111.

[72] Armstrong, *La Porte in June*, 19.

[73] Fry, *Poems*, 168.

[74] Bridges, *Lights and Shadows of Life*, 262.

[75] Gorton, *Drama of the Cycle*, 95.

[76] Putnam, *Memories and Impressions*, 38.

[77] McGaffey, *Poems*, 32; Crosby, *Broad-cast*, 29.

[78] Perry, *By Man Came Death*, 15.

[79] Plimpton, *Poems*, 40; Peck, *Greystone and Porphyry*, 48.

[80] Crosby, *Swords and Plowshares*, 90.

[81] Kirschbaum, *Prose and Poetry*, 54.

[82] Perry, *By Man Came Death*, 22.

[83] Sloan, *Telephone of Labor*, 223.

[84] McElroy, *Poems*, 52.

[85] Fearing, *In the City by the Lake*, 167.

[86] Fairhurst, *My Good Poems*, 145–48.

[87] Watson, *Songs of Flying Hours*, 91.

[88] Roberts, *Short Poems*, 37–39.

[89] Lemon, *Ione*, 235.

[90] See Milne, *For To-Day*, 67–68, 69–72.
[91] Robinson, *Captain Craig*, 21.
[92] Austin, *In the People's Name*, 30.
[93] Hemstead, *Musings of Morn*, 151.
[94] Friselle, *Kismet Poems*, 252–53.
[95] Barrows, *Friendship and Wayside Gleanings*, 54.
[96] Dorr, *Babylon*, 215–16.
[97] From "A Sewing Girl's Temptation," in Dodge, *Poems and Letters*, 32.
[98] Hinckle, *Life's Blue and Gray*, 45–46.
[99] Emswiler, *Poems and Sketches*, 57.
[100] Marshall, *Launching and Landing*, 169.
[101] Dole, *Peace and Progress*, 15; Mackley, *Idle Rhymings*, 79.
[102] Barrett, *Fugitives*, 42.
[103] O'Byrne, *Song of the Ages*, 106–9.
[104] Barrett, *Fugitives*, 78–79.
[105] Ware, *Some of the Rhymes of Ironquill*, 53.
[106] Crosby, *Broad-cast*, 32.
[107] Kirschbaum, *Prose and Poetry*; from "Only a Brakeman," 32–33.
[108] Cook, *Fancy's Etchings*, 216; Granniss, *Skipped Stitches*, 18; Mackintosh, *Memorial*, 75.
[109] Crosby, *Swords and Plowshares*, 79–82.
[110] Gustafson, *Meg*, 236.
[111] Savage, *Poems*, 166 (although typical of many poetic attitudes, these lines do not reflect the opinion of the author cited); Welburn, *Amercian Epic*, 236.
[112] Grant, *Lambs*.
[113] Archibald, *Some Scribbles*, 68.
[114] Nickelplate, *Story of a Broken Ring*, 16.
[115] See Gregory, *Beauty of Thebes*, 35–36.
[116] Robinson, *Dream*.
[117] B. F. Clark, *Poems*, 43.
[118] *Devil's Visit*, 58–59.
[119] Hewetson, *Strike*, 18; Trueman, *Philo-Sophia*, 71; Colby, *Rhymes of the Local Philosopher*, 198; Greene, *Cloudrifts at Twilight*, 54; Coughlin, *Songs of an Idle Hour*, 156.
[120] Crosby, *Swords and Plowshares*, 91; Gorham, *Bosky Dells and Sylvan Roads*, n. pag.
[121] Sloan, *Telephone of Labor*, 117; Davenport, *More Outcries from Brooklyn Hollow*, 16.
[122] Fetterman, *Street Musings*, 7.
[123] Drew, *Spiced Thought-food*, 97–100.
[124] Holbrook, *Ruth Haight*, 71–72; Kelso, *Poems*, 87; Swartz, *Poems*, 43; Kenney, *Some More Thusettes*, 18.
[125] Carter, *Log Cabin Poems*, 40; Horton, *Songs of the Lowly*, 44.
[126] Coyle, *Promise of Morning*, 25; Treuthart, *Milliad*, 296.
[127] Stout, *Poetic Works*, 229; Nevill, *Some Little 'Rimes,'* 46.
[128] Evans, *Fashion*, 24, 21; Hill, *History and Origin of the "Dude,"* n. pag.
[129] *Holiday Souvenir*, n. pag.
[130] Major, *Lays of Chinatown*, 41.
[131] Hillhouse, *White Rose Knight*, 75.
[132] Grissom, *Beaux and Belles*, 16; Cloyd, *Voice*, 33.

133 Carter, *Duck Creek Ballads*, 25–27; Price, *Poetical Works of Peter Peppercorn*, 107.

134 Wright, *Grandpa's Rhymes*, 7.

135 Currie, *Sonnets and Love Songs*, 7.

136 Crane, *War Is Kind*, 45.

137 E. A., *Yale Jingle Book*, n. pag.; Helmer, *Child's Thoughts in Rhyme*, 36; Hylton, *Knights of the Plow*, 23.

138 Hanna, *My Early Random Hits*, 23; Johnson, *Songs of the G. O. P.*, 71; Major, *Peril of the Republic*, 3; Kenney, *Some More Thusettes*, 24.

139 Freeman, *Reminiscences of Farm Life*, 36.

140 Donaldson, *Poems*, 142–43.

141 Valentine Brown, *Poems*, 66–67.

142 Norwood, *Political Poems*, 13.

143 Bullard, *Cupid's Chalice*, 64; Hirt, *Social Poems*, 66; Cruff, *Poems and Squibs*, 10–11, 37–39; Kirschbaum, *Times*, 9–11.

144 Grant, *By Heath and Prairie*, 89.

145 Crosby, *Plain Talk in Psalm and Parable*, 25.

146 Rubottom, *When I Was Living at the Grange*, 12; Kelley, *Age of Goid*, 12.

147 Viett, "*Thou Beside Me Singing*," 132–33.

148 Hubbell, *Various Verses*, 89–90; O'Connor, *Works*, 259–60.

149 Rice, *Rural Rhymes*, 186.

150 Terry, *Our Pumpkin Vine*, 49. See also Chapter V.

151 Edgerton, *Songs of the People*, 57–58.

152 *Stock Exchange Primer*, 1, 11.

153 Kercheval, *Dolores*, 431–33.

154 *Proceedings at the Semi-centennial Anniversary of the connection of Caleb Arnold Wall* . . ., 27.

155 Horton, *Songs of the Lowly*, 36; Spalding, *My Vagabonds*, 38–40.

156 Doyle, *Haunted Temple*, 70; *Centennial of the Providence National Bank*, 37.

157 Sears, *Forest Runes*, 67.

158 Rich, *Dream of the Adirondacks*, 138.

159 Milne, *For To-day*.

160 Flattery, *Pope and the New Crusade*.

161 Hovey, *Along the Trail*, 104; Edgerton, *Voices of the Morning*, 97.

162 Holden, *Many Moods*, 102.

163 For the best example, see Higgins, *Looking Backward in Rhyme*.

164 Versifiers who called themselves Socialists made up a variegated group. Some were primarily labor organizers, some wrote in terms of political movements, while others assembled under the Socialist flag a miscellany of personal protest impossible to categorize.

165 Sloan, *Telephone of Labor*, 108; Crosby, *Broad-cast*, 31.

166 Marshall, *Launching and Landing*, 173–77; Welburn, *American Epic*, 270.

167 McElroy, *Poems*, 82–83.

168 Schafer, *Thoughts on Social Problems*, 9; Fry, *Poems*, 168.

169 From "The Farmer's Institute," in Elmore, *Lover in Cuba*, 131.

170 Lambie, *Life on the Farm*, 72; Sprague, *Billy Dash Poems*, 107–10.

171 From "Rumford Grange Field Day," in Howe, *Home Songs*, 145.

172 O'Connor, *Works*, 259–66; Rubottom, *When I Was Living at the Grange*, 12; Thorndyke, *Simply Stuff*, 87.

173 Case, *Grange Poems*, 45.

[174] Wharf, *Promiscuous Poems*, 23–24; Temple, *Sheaf of Grain*, 249–50.
[175] Parmelee, *Then and Now*, 93.
[176] Fearing, *In the City by the Lake*, 167.
[177] Creamer, *Adirondack Readings*, 60.
[178] Van Derveer, *Soul Waifs*, 73; Lloyd, *Red Heart in a White World*, 3; Rule *When John Bull Comes A-Courtin'*, 25.
[179] Whitaker, *My Country*, 131–32.
[180] Welburn, *American Epic*, 233; Whitman, *Not a Man and Yet a Man*, 252–53.
[181] Higgins, *Looking Backward in Rhyme*, 27–29.
[182] Malone, *Songs of Dusk and Dawn*, 144–46.
[183] McIntyre, *Sun-Sealed*, 68.
[184] Emswiler, *Poems and Sketches*, 4–7; Dawson, *Poems of the New Time*, 69–70.
[185] Treuthart, *Milliad*, 367.

V

Statesmen and Spoilsmen

THE POLITICAL CONNOTATIONS OF THE PERIOD BETWEEN
the administrations of Ulysses Grant and Theodore Roosevelt
are various and often conflicting. Mention of the Gilded Age is
most likely to recall the cynicism and corruption of the "spoilsmen" who ran the political show for victory rather than for
principle, for the advantages of patronage and subsidy rather
than for the application of statecraft to the pressing problems of
the age. From Grant's deference to Conkling the political boss
and Fisk the millionaire down to McKinley's subservience to
Hanna—who was both millionaire and boss—the White House

rarely failed to recognize the influence of the machine politician
or the industrial and financial leader. The scandals of the Grant
administration, whose exposure marked the opening of the
period, had their later—if less spectacular—counterparts. Such
damning phrases as "De Golyer contract," "Gold-bugs," and
"embalmed beef" echoed throughout the remainder of the
century as an indication of business influence in the halls of
government, while the party. leaders, distracting the public
with the "bloody shirt" of Civil War memories, continued to
roll the pork barrel and carve up the plunder.

On the other hand, the same period saw the passage of
several notable landmarks on the road to political and economic
reform. The Pendleton Act formed the basis for a federal civil
service; the Sherman Anti-Trust Act and the newly established
Interstate Commerce Commission represented efforts in the
direction of governmental control over large-scale enterprise;
and the Wilson-Gorman Tariff, before it was modified, attacked
vested economic interests by reducing protection and providing
an income tax. More realistically indicative of the rising
progressive temper of the times was the activity of the many
minor parties and factions in rough-hewing many of the important political planks which were to compose the platforms of the
major parties after the turn of the century. This activity moved
toward a "purification" of the democratic process by placing
political power directly in the hands of a broadened electorate,
with the intention of undermining the power of the professional
politician and the industrial and financial elite.

The poets of this period illuminated both sides of this portrait
by commenting on political personalities, on the state of
politics, on the efforts of minor parties, and on the primary
issues of the day.

i

One widely accepted generalization concerning political life
in the late nineteenth century holds that the voter was con-

sistently separated from the true issues of the day by two
overlapping devices: a rehearsal of Civil War records and
allegiances, and the exploration of the candidates' personalities.
It is true that nearly all the major aspirants for office ran on
Civil War records and often precious little else, and that their

private lives often seemed to overshadow more relevant political
issues. Since more than half the political verse of this period
focused on specifically named or unmistakably identified figures,
it would seem at first glance that the poet-as-voter had been
captivated by the question of personality and had—to that
extent—escaped involvement in the more pressing problems.
Before such an estimate can be supported, however, the nature
of this verse comment on the political figures of the era must
be examined.

Two political figures had what amounted to a monopoly on the attention of writers of verse: Ulysses S. Grant and James A. Garfield. The latter, the more popular of the two, achieved his eminence in verse neither by acts of monumental statehood nor by artifice at election time; his appeal as lyric subject matter arose from a single event: his assassination. Writing on such an occasion the poets were, predictably, attracted less by the possibilities for political comment than by the elements of drama and pathos implicit in the event and its aftermath. The suspenseful waiting, while doctors wore down the President's naturally strong constitution by persistent probings after the spent ball, drew particular attention, as the following sequence of titles indicate: "The Nation's Prayer," "The Morn of Hope," "The Angel Escort," "Dead," "Burial."[1] Adding to the poignancy was the suffering and bereavement of the two Mrs. Garfields, one the "lone watcher" who was his wife, and the other, his beloved mother.[2] This was the President, be it remembered, who at his inauguration "Kissing the Holy Book . . ./ Then turned aside . . ./To kiss his mother's brow."[3] Sentimental Americans who had been thrilled by this act of filial homage did not forget the woman's side of the picture, and whole volumes retelling Garfield's life were dedicated to this famous mother.

In spite of the temptations of the melodramatic and the sentimental, the occasion of Garfield's death furnished, theoretically at least, an opportunity for politically relevant remarks—of which, however, the poets took little advantage. The chance to re-assess Garfield's career and his political environment was bypassed in a wave of mourning. The consistency of over-laudatory estimations of the man's political role could best be observed in the reaction of one poet who found himself unwilling to go along with the tide:

> Yet though a little power was thine,
> Garfield, I will not worship thee. . . .
> Thy worth I gladly, freely, own,

And mourn a nation's loss in thee;
But cannot say with thee has flown
All that was and shall noble be.[4]

If it was in fact Garfield's death at the hands of a "disappointed office seeker" which furnished the final impetus toward a workable civil service program, there is absolutely no evidence to that effect in the verse of the time. The only generalized theme connected with the occasion grew out of the hope for restored unity. The poets suggested not only that the tragedy might lead to a reunion of the factions within the Republican Party and a healing of the old wounds remaining from the Civil War, but even that it might bring harmony within the "ocean-sundered Saxon race," with the ultimate result that all nations might be prevailed upon to "bury all their spite."[5] Obviously, the grief did not prove sufficiently universal.

Unfortunately for his posthumous reputation, the man second only to Lincoln as a Civil War hero died a natural death. But the end of Grant's life, however unspectacular, signalled the beginning of a poetic re-appraisal of this General-hero, strong in war and firm but merciful in peace. The praise accorded him was often extravagant, linking his name with that of Washington, of Lincoln, or of his Homeric namesake. What startles the reader of this mass panegyric is not the magniloquence of encomium for the General, but the absence of any reference whatsoever, in nearly half these verses, to the subject's political career, even though all were published after he had served his eight years as the nation's President. In seeking to praise, the poets sought their subject's strength; but in avoiding something as obvious as the presidency, they only called attention to Grant's weakness.

While a numerical majority of the assessments of Grant's political career—whether written before or after his death—were more or less favorable, individual criticisms were often bitter and detailed. One volume, eighty-eight pages long, was devoted entirely to exposing the "ring" of financiers and party bosses who planned Grant's tour of the world as a prelude to foisting him on America for a third term—a term these backers intended to utilize for unprecedented accumulation of spoils. Their choice of Grant as a front was explained by their ability to keep him controlled with "a padlock of gold."[6] Exposures of other "rings," rampant during Grant's Presidency, were brought to light in verse along with the names of those involved: "Orville, Belknap, Babcock, McDonald and McKey."[7] Some mocked his ambition:

> At Washington they offered this same Grant
> Some bull pups. He took them just took quick!
> Was this ambition? Correct![8]

Southerners spoke of "that hated Grant" and his "shot-gun rule," while temperance advocates, of whatever section, found fault with that "expensive old codger [who] . . ./Smokes his chops that are well soaked in whiskey."[9] Many poets were particularly disturbed by the General's inelegance and lack of presidential stature:

> Fit but for camps, he adds disgrace
> To glory, in the statesman's place.
> What gentleman is not ashamed,
> When his administration's named?[10]

The critics of Grant stressed his stubborn tolerance of corruption in his own political family, his intolerance of Southern political rights, his lack of dignity and judgment.

One poet called the General a man "By statesmen admired" and referred to his administration as "eight blissful years"; but he was practically alone in offering a positive defense of Grant as a political figure.[11] In sum, the praise of Grant as President was so faint, the whitewash so transparent, that it told against him almost as heavily as the criticism. Both typical and revealing were the following lines:

> Let mankind, then, deal justly with the dead.
> Not all are faultless in this day.

> For errors that unthinking clay has made
> Blame not the spirit, but the clay.[12]

Anxious to speak no ill of the dead, the poets tended to forgive Grant his political sins of omission and commission, and to commemorate his role as the military savior of the Union. Finding difficult the task of praising his political career, half the poets who wrote on Grant simply ignored this aspect; while the other half damned him either with faint praise or with calculated abuse.

After Garfield and Grant, in the order of their popularity as subjects for poetry, came McKinley (another martyr), Cleveland, Blaine, Bryan, Harrison, Hayes, Arthur, and Hanna. In appraising these men the poets showed more inclination to write politically rather than personally, although the tendency did not show itself with any real prominence until the elections of 1896 and 1900. The administrations of Hayes, Garfield, and Arthur were regarded with mild but by no means unanimous approval. There was sympathy for Hayes because of the awkward circumstances surrounding his election (see below) and because of his reconciliatory attitude toward the South. The short tenure of Garfield was lent a generally roseate hue by the drama of his assassination, and Arthur received the benediction due a little man trying his best to handle a big job. In reacting to Benjamin Harrison the poets were unusually vague, preferring to write of his wife or his grandfather; whereas Cleveland became the subject of widely varied comments. He attracted slightly more censure than praise, and with the poets was likely to stand or fall on the basis of his tariff policy or his conduct toward the opposite sex.

The end-of-the-century elections, involving as they did three personalities attractive to the verse writers, produced more elaborate comment. Those who wrote about McKinley before his death tended to picture him as a "shrinking spaniel" on the leash of the self-interested Hanna, given to vacillation on important issues, from monetary policy at home to the Cuban

and Philippine questions abroad.[13] A duplicitous record in both
Congress and the White House revealed, his critics maintained,
consistent sacrifice of public interest for the benefit of his
moneyed backers.[14] The praise McKinley received on domestic
politics seemed to stem either from party loyalty or from
disgust with the trouble-fraught administration of Cleveland
which preceded his election:

> I pray the Lord to give me strength to live
>   again and vote
> And cram the Free Trade falsehood down the
>   Democratic throat. . . .
> Protection fills the dinner pail, Democracy
>   the graves.[15]

In such a tone did many poet-citizens align themselves on the
side of the Ohio Major, without contributing any very positive
evaluation. But war and the assassin's hand served to trans-
figure the McKinley reputation; what before had been weak and
undecisive behavior became, in the afterglow of martyrdom, an
example of calm and judicious restraint.[16] The retrospective
evaluation came thus to resemble that of Garfield.

Even without the advantages of martyrdom or Civil War
service, the figure of William Jennings Bryan appealed to the
verse-voter more vividly, albeit to a lesser extent, quantitatively
speaking, than did his rival's. "When other leaders fail,"
averred one poet, "Loved truth brings forth a BRYAN to
prevail"; and another thanked God for Bryan, "Standing firmly
erect, untrammelled and free."[17] Warnings against this man
were equally striking in their abhorrence of the "trackless ways"
and "chaos" which marked the path "Where Bryan leads."[18]
Where issues were concerned he was more frequently associated
with silver and the Philippines—subjects which will be treated
in their full context below.

When the poets dealt with political figures by name, they
were apt to treat them kindly if unrealistically. Exceptions to

this rule, such as John Sherman, Matthew Quay, Thomas Reed, and Richard Bland, arose to serve as passing targets for the expression of particular grievances. Marcus Hanna, the closest thing to an antitype for the hero Garfield, received almost nothing but abuse from the poets; this universal attack, however, was symptomatic more of poetic disgust with a condition (which will be discussed in the next section) than with an individual.

The poet, to judge by the national voting record, went along with his fellow citizens in his reaction to the succession of presidents. Except for Cleveland's second term, all administrations were accepted with at least tacit approval. The only vigorous debate occurred when Bryan and McKinley were opposing each other.

But was the poet distracted from the political issues by the personality of the candidates? An examination of his comment on the leading figures indicates that such a generalization is probably unwarranted. Had it not been for the assassination of two presidents and the death of a military hero, the proportion of his political comment would have favored the conditions and issues rather than the figures per se. As does the entertainer, the elected official depends for his livelihood on public attention; that personality should constitute a relatively prominent ingredient in the political situation is inevitable. But the poet was not distracted to any great extent at election time; it took the occasion of a notable or dramatic death to plunge him into personal considerations. Although his comments on these individuals as such were not always discriminating, they do show that he was relatively unmoved by the superficial distractions of election years, and they do not lessen the importance of his contribution to the discussion of conditions and issues of the day.

ii

When the poet treated the statesman as an individual personality, he was apt to ignore the seamier side of the political environment; but when he approached the individual via the political context, his attitude underwent a marked change:

> See the first official record
> Of the President [Grant] gold elected,
> See the bill which demonitized silver,
> See the fraud in the West Indies
> Floated thither on wings of Ulysses,
> See the Whiskey Ring and stealing,
> See De Golyer capture Garfield,
> See the gold on that Black Friday . . .[19]

As this sample suggests, the poet never really got beyond the Grant administration in his specific considerations of scandal and fraud. A few scattered Democrats used more recent materials in an attempt to establish a formula of fraud-by-association for the entire G.O.P.; but most poets contented themselves with reviewing such items as the Credit Mobilier, the salary grab, the treasury scandals, and the various rings—especially the Whiskey Ring—which operated in the early 1870's.

One particular scandal, perhaps because it arose from the Centennial Year presidential election, shocked the poet with special force:

> Oh, Jubilee Year! the first notes of thy song
> Are minor keyed melodies, sad to the soul,
> For the strong men have given their strength
>   to the wrong. . . .[20]

What was this wrong?

> The people voted Tilden into place;—
> But, now an act of national disgrace
> Proves, cumulatively, virtue's decay . . .
> Electoral returns, forged past cognition,
> Force three raped states to vote adverse
>   to their volition.[21]

The disputed election of 1876–77, capping as it did a series of unsavory exposures, struck the poet as an appalling miscarriage of the democratic process. Even verse-annalists, who sought merely to recount our history in as detached a manner as possible, referred to this election in terms of "Conflicting questions" or a "disputed seat."[22] Judging from the verse, no one was completely satisfied with the way in which the problem was solved; whenever blame was placed, it was assigned to Justice Bradley or to his fellow Supreme Court committeemen whose votes were crucial in validating the conflicting electoral returns.[23]

But the poet was far more impressed by the general unsavoriness of the political diet than by the Hayes-Tilden stew or by any other entree on the carte du jour. Usually without naming names, dates, or places, he brewed his own seething caldron of outrage at the politician, the party system, the process of legislation, and even the sanctity of the bench. His outrage savored of disgust at the materialism, hypocrisy, and self-interest which the poet felt pervaded the atmosphere where political cooking was done.

Addressing an individual known variously as "the politician," "the candidate," or "the officer-seeker," the poet chided him for his dual personality. Before an election, the candidate was described as beaming ubiquitously, proffering drinks and cigars along with flattery and promises. Once the votes had been counted, the poet seldom saw him. "The workingman's friend" cannot be found just now, but "he'll be 'round next election."[24] With "greed of office" as his sole motivation, and victory as his single aim, the office-seeker's stated principles were secondary and readily changeable:

> The Politicians in our day
> Oft seek office for the pay,
> And if emergencies require,
> Will pull or push at either wire!
> And if they think 'twill break or bend,
> They're apt to take the strongest end.[25]

Impressed with political insincerity, one poet composed an "Adjustable Campaign Song," in the meter of a popular air, accompanied by a variable vocabulary of "nonsense" words which could be substituted to make the song answer all foreseeable campaign contingencies.[26]

The campaign, in its failure to offer opportunities for the serious discussion of major issues, had sunk to the level of a cruel, dishonest farce. The cruelty took the form of a continuing mortification of "old wounds . . ./Lest haply they might heal as time went by."[27] Reaction to the campaign emphasis on the "bloody shirt" of Civil War memories, as well as to the blatant dishonesty of electioneering methods, was typified in the following lines:

> If you want an office talk loudly of gore,
> And swear by the God of the cannon's loud roar,
> That over your boots in blood you will wade,
> The foe will resign ere you start on your raid.
>
> Don't wait the slow process of counting the vote,
> Just grab the incumbent thief by the throat;
> Jerk him out, and teach him the jim-jam waltz,
> Then scoop out the coin in the treasury vaults.[28]

Yet, so expensive was the cost of campaigning that even with the spoils of office at his disposal, the successful candidate might still wind up a *"badly busted man."*[29] A further campaign hazard was illustrated by the failure of a candidate, perfectly suited for politics in his ability to "calculate/A living at the crib of state" and "Of different minds [to] agree with each," who lost out because "The whiskey made him sick."[30]

Of notable concern to the poet was the manner in which politically irrelevant aspects of the candidates' lives were substituted for more important criteria:

> No candidate is safe from fierce attack,
> His private life is probed from birth to date,
> Repressing truth, with lies he's stabbed in back.[31]

"The Puzzled Voter," complained one poet-citizen, must choose between such statements as "A. has been caught stealing chickens" and "B. is just no man at all."[32] Scandal attached to the personal lives of the entrants into the political arena had become such an effective offensive weapon that the "whitewash-brush" was recommended as a constant necessity in self-defense.[33] The true shame of this degradation of politics to the petty and the personal arose not only from the unnecessary strain it placed on men in office, but also from the manner in which it discouraged well-qualified citizens from entering politics:

> "Mr. Chairman, I deem it more honor to till
> My farm here, if I shall till it well, than to fill
> The position of Congressman, even." . . .
> "When a man can take office for good of the state,
> And not pledged to sink honor and soul in the dust,
> I should proud be to hold a position of trust . . ."[34]

The ardors and pitfalls of the campaign, however shameful and fraudulent, only reflected the conditions of officeholding. Neither the knack for evasiveness nor the penchant for dishonesty was apt to desert the candidate once elected, according to the poet. One pictured a successful officeholder, once a "corner loafer," who had risen by stuffing ballot boxes and falsifying returns; the key to his eminence lay in his ability to

> Shun work, and honesty likewise . . .
> Cheat, steal, and lie, and bum around;
> Drink whiskey in addition:
> Because the bigger fraud you are,
> The better politician![35]

Such diatribes were most frequently directed at minor or local officials, but the reader was often reminded that the objects of general censure included the high as well as the low. An unnamed governor, for example, was depicted proclaiming that "right an' wrong are nothin' but/Inventions o' the Sophists" and that by catering to the prejudices of the electorate he could "fatten on their folly."[36] The poet's prayerful entreaties for divine help in guiding the trembling arm which ruled the state make the reader suspect that even our most exalted leaders had not been received with any notable confidence or respect; here this feeling was made most explicit:

> Behold the statesmen who strut forth to-day,
> So finely moulded, yet how base the clay!

Compare McKinley with our statesmen past,
Can he with Jackson or Monroe be classed?
As well call eagles from their lofty flight,
To mate with owls and hoot the livelong night. . . .
True, statesmen of to-day require no skill,
Nor wit nor wisdom, fortitude or will;
Just sense enough a minor part to play,
Look wise or solemn, sorrowful or gay,
Just as required, as farce can sometimes be
Played to the limits of a wide degree. . . .[37]

In addition to attacking individuals, named or unnamed, candidates or officeholders, the poet singled out for abuse three institutions: the political party, the state and federal legislatures, and the judiciary. The party, complained the poet, made a mockery of the franchise by offering the voting public but a choice between knaves, by fixing the results and distributing the fruits of victory in violation of public interest.

Constitution ne'er was so betrayed:
Officials high and petty, daily break
Their oaths to honor and support it, swayed
By greed or by the party spirit of the times . . .[38]

Thus the party and its bosses created a "vitriol sea" of chaos out of the corrupt machinations of spoils politics.[39]

The legislative process, both in state and national capitals, evoked a reaction like this one:

Corruption and bribery have entered the hall
Where state legislators and Congressmen meet,
And sad is the sight, when our law-makers fall
And worship the gold that us laid at their feet;
Their trust is betrayed, and our interests are sold . . .[40]

Describing the legislator as a man with a "mind far-reaching in its plans for gain" and a "conscience feeling money-loss alone," the poet urged him to turn to "Deep-lurking dangers, social ills" instead of determining to become a millionaire on "five thousand salary."[41] In an atmosphere of sycophancy and sybarit-ism, the legislatures—the poet feared—had committed them-selves to the preservation of privilege instead of the popular will. The mysterious ways of the bribe, the lobby, and the cloakroom, though often poorly understood, were clearly identified as the tool by which the people's representatives were brought into the service of the moneyed interests. As a fair sample of the poet's picture of the legislative process, witness the chronicle of Judge Boodle, a "cunning chief in caucus," whose fiancée would marry him only if he could recover her claim against the government (for a horse her grandfather had allegedly loaned to George Washington).

> So Boodle every wire did pull,
> Rolled logs with all creation,
> And piped our glorious Capitol
> To push his legislation.
> Another tax! another loan!
> The syndicates made honey;
> The people drained out, groan by groan,
> John Boodle's darling's money.[42]

Boodle's victory, happily for the right, became a hollow one when his bride climaxed the wedding feast by turning into a witch and disappearing forever.

As the choice of Judge Boodle's title indicates, the judicial stood alongside the legislative in the poet's target range. Judges were labeled "corrupt, malignant and vile"; juries were blamed because they "do not dare condemn/When by the rich men they are paid."[43] It is gold that buys justice, complained the poet, pointing to the Supreme Court where Jay Gould was able to purchase a seat for his ex-attorney.[44] Justice had become an outworn concept, and force and fortune ruled the land:

> The meanest man I ever saw
> Allus kep' inside the law;
> And ten-times better fellers I've knowed
> The blame gran'-jury's sent over the road.[45]

It is clear from the foregoing examples that everything connected with politics, and not merely a few specific abuses, had come to be regarded as deserving of the poet's contumely. The degree of his horror is to be seen in the use of such metaphors as "a sewer wide and deep" where "microbes, revelling, are feeding cheek by jowl" "as they stench for stench oppose."[46] If not a disease, politics was a senseless and destructive conflict:

> I hear the sound of guns afar
> Like pulses on the trembling air,
> Dread messengers of civil war,
> Convulsive throbs of freedom's death,
> Throes of a nation's dying breath.
> Though feeble now and far away
> May nearer come as goes the day . . .
> The foremost nation of the world
> By faction, to destruction hurled,
> Hissed on by those who knew no right,
> But for the spoils of office fight.[47]

That through connivance and corruption the politician was seen as having shattered the American dream, is made painfully vivid by the intensity of these Centennial lines:

> *Oh! what does this mean?* Oh! beautiful years!
> Where did ye gather such terrible pain?
> . . . such sorrowful tears,
> The days are foul with such horrible stain!
> Blood, blood,—all your garments are reeking and red,
> . . . where are the flowers that blossomed . . . ?[48]

Throughout the poet's nightmare visions ran the persistent image of the elected officeholder selling the interest of the many into the moneyed hands of the few:

> Shall we talk of choice and suffrage, and of
>   freedom loudly brag,
> While the demagogue wears velvet and the working
>   man a rag?

> Shall we talk of right and justice, while our
>   sovereigns steal men's votes?
> By the aid of gold and station forging fetters
>   round their throats?
> Shall we dream of ballot's power, while our votes
>   sell for a song?
> And, when cast with truest motive, venal vikings
>   count them wrong?[49]

Thus the most intense and consistent comment on the politics of the Gilded Age was wholly negative. Politicians, parties, lawmakers, judges—the tactics, principles, policies, and general behavior—all were assessed, and all were found wanting.

iii

In approaching the poet's constructive comments on the political scene, one meets the question of "third" or minor parties. Although many saw in adherence to one of these parties a remedy for the widespread ills described above, the poets as a group, by a ratio of about three to two, disapproved of such aberrations from Democracy or Republicanism. The reaction to minor parties, while significant on the one hand as constructive political protest, would thus appear to be chiefly indicative of our deep fundamental commitment to the two-party system. To at least some degree the explanation for the poet's rejection of these movements could be found in the plethora of such groups, in their shifting and often illogical alignments and alliances, and in the inconsistency of their behavior when seen from a national point of view:

> Mebbie I *am* a sort of
> A Farmers'-Alliance-Citizens'-
> Alliance-Knights-of-Labor-
> National-Industrial-Anti-
> Monopoly-Single-Tax-

Prohibition-Woman-Suffrage-
Greenback-Free-Silver-
Potato-Currency-Socialistic-
Grand-Old-People's party . . .[50]

Out of this welter of possibilities, the poets selected three
groups for extensive comment: Populists, Socialists, and
"liberal" Republicans, in order of frequency of mention.

Of these three groups, only the Socialists received predominantly favorable comment, and even here the verdict was
close. This subject, disappointingly, brought forth little in the
way of specific political debate. Although the Socialist Party

was sufficiently well organized to offer a presidential candidate as early as 1892, one finds no verse urging Socialist votes in this or subsequent elections. As was suggested in Chapter IV, criticism of this movement was apt to center on its reputation as a radical, foreign philosophy antipathetic to the "American way"; whereas the defense of Socialism occupied itself with denying this stigma. One complained that he was "an honest Socialist" who wanted only to help the "trodden down, the overworked," but that he found himself labeled "crank and idiot, a fool,/A communist, an anarchist . . ."[51] Socialism, another pointed out, is not "Un-American," but "A champion of all men's liberty."[52] Nevertheless, detractors persisted in thinking of a "Socialist class" (responsible for Garfield's assassination) committed to an immoral attempt to reform man in non-Christian as well as non-American ways.[53]

For the persistence of this reaction, the poetic proponents of Socialism were at least partly to blame. Their continued vagueness, their characteristic tone of idealistic religiosity did little to show their countrymen concretely where they stood:

> "I am a Socialist;
> Seeing that men are neither more nor less
> Because of riches, office, birth or name. . . .
> I am a Radical,
> Because I know that all beliefs are dead . . .
> I am a Liberal;
> Because I'm Christian . . ."[54]

Such grand but misty paradoxes could hardly have been expected to convert hard-thinking Americans, much less to produce party platforms or get out the vote. The Socialist-poet consistently failed to attach to his watchwords any concrete program of political action; he was typically content to leave his philosophy as a promising but unformed dream in the mind of the working-man.

In contrast the Populist program was presented with utmost plainness:

> If the People's Party was in power, 'twould
>   be an easy trick
> To turn our projuce into cash most everlastin'
>   quick . . .[55]

> "We'll go and vote with the Populists,
> We'll then monopoly fight."[56]

> The most important planks of all
> Is money, transportation and land . . .[57]

The spokesmen for the Populists represented a clear voice on behalf of the "have nots," especially the rural depressed, proposing easier credit, cheaper land, and opposition to the Eastern moneyed interests. They drew only scant support from their fellow versifiers, however, and toward the end of the period laments could be heard for the times "when we Pops were young and gay" and the fight against the "Octopus" was "part of our religion."[58] As the nineteenth century waned, the detractors of the Populists waxed. There had always been some suspicion of the "crazed populist/Who stored his grain lest millionaires would grow,"[59] and of his political and economic acumen:

> I love to see a granger
> Who doesn't know a pine refrigerator from
>   a legal
> Maxim, discourse on finance, whittling on
>   a store box.[60]

Even those who had agrarian interests at heart often wondered whether the party was representing or merely exploiting the farmer.[61] The disaster of the Populist merger with the Democrats in 1896, and the adoption of the cause of free silver, cost the Populists the respect of many poets. Derision toward "Demulist" and "Popocrat" swelled into an anthem of ridicule as the party was warned that its attempts to force a "silver wedding" would come to naught.[62]

The Liberal Republican movement of 1872 left its record in one of the more impressive pieces of political poetry of the Gilded Age. Titled "The Cincinnati Convention," it began:

> In from the farm and cattle-range—
> Something in politics new and strange—
> Men with their faces bronzed and set,
> Common men . . .
> Angry men with sense of wrong . . .
> Yet, in spite of their schemes of folly,
> Something of deepest melancholy . . .
> For his hopeless life and his mortgaged farm,
> Stirs within us to know
> The party has left him so . . .[63]

Aside from this single specimen, attention to Republican splinter-group activity was focused on the "Mugwump doings" of the 1880's. Sympathizers urged their readers not to fear the Mugwump label and concentrated on placing honesty above the spoils of party politics:[64]

> Let's strike for better government by having
>   better men.
> We will have to be all mugwumps, it can't be
>   done till then.[65]

Censure of defection from party discipline keynoted the verse which attacked this "rash and stumbling" chameleon party.[66] The anti-Mugwump camp was swelled by a one-man army in the person of Eugene Field, who volubly expressed his disapproval of "All Mugwump sycophants," and who took particular pleasure in pointing out that their maneuvers had thwarted Democrats as well as Republicans.[67]

Reaction to these minor political movements helped to pinpoint poetic attitudes. In supporting the Socialists the poet attacked special privilege and the failure of economic democracy; in advocating Populism he listed specific planks on behalf of the depressed farmer; in adhering to liberal Republicanism he voiced a protest against the dishonesty of party politics. In attacking these minor parties, as he did more often than not, the poet rejected what he considered radical ideology, political disorganization and temporizing alliances, and—most strongly —any departure from the two-party system.

iv

In coming to grips with the real issues of the day, rather than with individuals or labels, the verse-commentator demonstrated more clearly than anywhere else his concern with economic aspects of American political problems. In a period when the single most important government activity revolved around the struggle to establish—one way or another—a working relation with the economy, it is not surprising that the major issues were all financial in nature: the money question, import tariff, and domestic taxation.

Within the broad confines of the currency question the poet expressed himself most volubly on the proposition of free and unlimited coinage of silver at a ratio of sixteen to one. The inclusiveness of the claims put forth by the supporters of this proposal may be judged from these lines:

> Silver's day is bound to come,
> And cause all idle mills to hum . . . [and it]
> Will help the farmer pay his debt. . . .
> Will lift the mortgage off the farm . . .
> Will give employment to the masses;
> Restrict the greed of money classes;
> A bloodless revolution cause,
> Restore to Code once-honored laws. . . .
> Bryan and Free Silver shall succeed![68]

On neither side of these financial questions—but least of all among the supporters of free silver—did the poets employ economic logic to any great extent; rather, as the lines quoted above indicate, they relied on flat assertions or frankly hortatory language. Advocacy of free silver was urged for one of the following reasons: that Bryan was a good man; that McKinley was a weak man; that control of finance should be taken from the hands of Eastern bankers; that the miner and farmer needed help; or that more money meant prosperity for all.[69] These arguments were refuted by asserting that Bryan was a fool or

McKinley a man of wisdom, or that the "poor" silver baron
needed no more help than the Eastern banker.[70] In defense of
the Eastern banker the anti-silverites cited Morgan's redemp-
tion of the nation's honor by sh ing up the gold reserves in
1893–94.[71] The silverities, accused of attributing to the "Crime
of '73" all evils from Noah's flood to "the London plague and
fire," were reminded that this "crime" had not driven silver
from the market but had merely "recognized the fact of its
disappearance."[72] Seemingly more sure of their economic
ground, the poet-critics of free silver warned against dangerous
devaluation of the dollar and predicted that any attempt to
establish artificially fixed relationships between the value of
gold and silver would lead to dire consequences.[73]

For better or for worse, the silver question pervaded the
poetry in many and various ways, among them a series of un-
rewarding allegories identifying gold and silver with the sun
and moon. By the end of the century, however, the versifier
indicated that enough had been said on this subject. There
appeared a description of a pointless barroom brawl occasioned
by "Everybody, but Casey" having been for silver; and a
farmer's family complained that the head of the house spent all
his time talking "16 to 1" instead of attending to the chores.[74]
A public speaker ended his occasional verse by demanding thanks
for "omitting all reference . . ./To the great silver question,"[75]
and a voice in dialect pronounced the final obituary:

> An' hit ain't de so't o' money dat is
>   pesterin' my min',
> But de question I want answehed's how to
>   get at any kin'![76]

Those who addressed themselves to the greenback question
occupied less space than the silver-debaters, and tended to argue
questions which had already been settled for the nineteenth
century by the resumption of specie payment in 1875. Attackers
of the greenback wrote deprecatingly of "ragged scrip" and

"A pocket full of trash," or referred sinisterly to the "Green-back-Grayback [Confederate] alliance."[77] Since the real crisis in the greenback debate had passed with the dangers of post-Civil War inflation and with the 1875 solution, it is not surprising that this issue was increasingly ignored as the period advanced. Although the Greenback Party ran presidential candidates up through 1884, the versifiers paid little attention to either campaigns or nominees.[78]

While the special debate over the greenback question was disappearing, the general arguments in favor of fiat currency evolved into a financial philosophy of much broader implications, an attitude which led directly to our present institution of Federal Reserve banks and notes. The body of verse which dealt with this evolution reflected a common resentment of the control exercised over the nation's economy, under a strict gold standard, by private financial magnates. Antipathy toward gold, which "has always robbed the poor," was emotionally expressed and was extended to include those who wielded the power of gold: Wall Street speculators and their cohorts in the Senate.[79] History, maintained these poets, had proved the value of a currency based not on any one or two metals but on a national credit that could expand or contract in relation to the fiscal needs of the moment.[80] The particular need for an expanding system of currency in a growing nation was stressed, and the mysterious advantages of the "power of circulation" were celebrated by this cult.[81] A dislike for gold, and the system which its exclusive usage was thought to have fostered, formed a more consistent common denominator than did the promotion of the greenback or any other specific plan for increasing the amount and flexibility of the currency. Many of these arguments will appear specious to latter-day economists, but in urging more active governmental participation in the economy, and in emphasizing the advantages of a flexible currency controlled by public authority, these poets embodied one of the more progressive politico-economic attitudes.

As did the silver question, the tariff debate pervaded the poetry to the extent that American visitors to Europe were spoken of as free trade items, and the title *A Poet's Appeal for Protection of Home Industry* covered a discussion of the importation of British verse.[82] Also parallel was the versifier's eventual satiety with this subject, evidenced by his complaints against "The Tariff Fiend" whose arguments were apparently as interminable as those of the silver advocate.[83] On the side of protection the arguments tended to be calm and minimal, suggesting that these partisans would have preferred to keep the discussion from becoming a major issue. Advocates of high tariff warned that the free list on the "Democratic Tariff" would give British manufacturers a dangerous edge over home industry; they reminded the still undeveloped nation that protection remained a necessity; or they attempted intellectual coercion, assuring their readers that the college professors were teaching the protectionist point of view.[84] Eugene Field, again adding the weight of his pen to the orthodox Republican stand, typified in some respects the half-hearted approach of the apologists for protection, secure in their confidence that the Congress would uphold their interests. "An Ohio Ditty" sympathized with a Mary who was forced to eat her lamb when a protective tariff on wool was repealed, while an otherwise purely sentimental verse about "The Tin Bank" revealed a preference for "McKinley tin" over "British steel."[85]

In contrast, those who argued for low tariff (for revenue purposes only) or for free trade did so in significantly larger numbers and with markedly greater intensity. Under the "watchword of 'Reform' " reduction in tariff was sought as the nation's due, while a spokesman for the Grangers scored all tariff and called "reciprocity" a dodge.[86] The dominant argument of the free trader, whether rural or urban, centered on an unhealthy link between protection and misused power in the hands of the moneyed interests. "There's no Union if 'Protection' be right," because it makes everyone a slave to "a fell

money-curst Oligarchy," was the assertion of one poet, who
pursued his argument in Civil War terminology.[87] Another
identified the tariff, foisted on the nation (he said) by Webster
in league with the South, as the original sin which led to the
many economic ills of the century, including the dominance of
monopoly through the influence of "corrupted public men."[88]
His views were not unshared:

> The big schemer the nation robs;
> . . . by tariff swindles . . .
> He pockets millions at public expense—
> All, of course, it is understood,
> Expressly for the people's good.[89]

Joining the advocates of fiat currency in their defense of the
economic dispossessed, the attackers of protective tariff associated their target with the creation of millionaires and monopolies. Befriended by corruption in high places—both economic
and political—this tariff was condemned as a major obstacle
preventing an equitable distribution of wealth.

The attack on excessive and inequitable domestic taxation
was led, as might have been expected, by the rural versifiers
who sought to warn the government against taxing wheat and
raising paupers.[90] "Those men who are making the laws," one
verse opened, "might give the poor farmer a chance" by not
"taxing property twice."[91] Blame for this condition was laid at
the feet of either the "infernal" political machine or the government itself, which had lured agricultural settlers onto the new
lands and then taxed them off again.[92] Through this cloth of
complaint ran a thread of strangely colored individualism which
rebelled against taxes and government aid alike, suggesting
that taxes on land or home were contrary to the American way.[93]

Those who treated taxation as a constructive issue did so
with the consistent objective of providing for a broader sharing
of the national wealth. In order to "take th' burden off th'
people's backs" it was recommended that assessment be

increased on railroads, "moneyed corporations," and "Bond-holders, usurers, and gold rings."[94] The income tax, shown in one place as preferable to a whiskey tax, protective tariff, or national indebtedness,[95] was a favorite recommendation with these poets, as was the corporation tax:

> To[o] long have riches dodged taxation,
> Your railroad, trust, and combination,
> And dogged the poor to prone vexation
> To pay it all . . .[96]

Traveling, perhaps consciously, in the company of Henry George, many of these versifiers left the impression that their pronouncements on taxation were intended to form the basis of a total political philosophy. Loaded with unpoetic detail and exact formulae, verses of this type left little to the imagination:

> From ev'ry dollar of the capital
> Of money making trusts and syndicates,
> And other corporations that get gain,
> Collect three mills in each and ev'ry year.
> If more is needed for the public use,
> Collect it from existing capital.
> Less than a thousand dollars should not pay
> A cent into the public treasury.
> A hundred should pay double tax;
> One million should pay double that again,
> Over ten millions double that high rate.
> Except tobacco and intoxicants,
> Let nothing pay tariff or excise tax.[97]

As this passage shows, the prevailing tone of the taxation issue too was one of protest, and its central emphasis rested on the redistribution of wealth, lest "the people tax themselves un-awares,/To create a class of millionaires."[98]

The political age in question might be said to have centered around two major issues: the establishment of a workable system of government in an era of public apathy and professional politics; and the achievement of a functional balance between business and government in an age of extraordinary economic opportunity, and of increasing concentration in large-scale industrial and financial units. The poet made a significant comment on both these problems. Finding his political environment both brutal and sickening, the poet characterized the practicing politician as a dishonest, opportunistic materialist, whose institutions—the party and the legislature—reflected the individual officeholder's willingness to sell the interest of his constituents to the highest bidder. Although the poet himself went in heavily for discussion of the personalities in the political arena, he did so largely to honor the martyred dead or the military heroes of the Civil War; at campaign time he lamented the distraction of the voter through the extension of the Civil War as a political issue and the injection into election debates of petty and personal matters in place of more vital issues. In everyone from the humblest ward worker to the most exalted Supreme Court Justice, the poet found nothing but scandal and unworthy behavior. Although he did not campaign explicitly for civil service reform or for a "Progressive" movement which would bring better men and better laws, his testimony revealed a background of intense discontent on which such measures were subsequently built.

As for the second major issue, the poet agreed that the principal questions of the day, outside the generally sorry state of politics, were all economic in their nature. Even though, collectively, he denied that a third party offered the solution of the American dilemma, he espoused both specific proposals and general ideologies which had their basis in the conviction that our wealth was not being properly shared. As the partisan of corporation and income taxes, of free trade, and of fiat currency, and as a receptive listener to socialistic platforms, he urged the government to enter the economy in order to wrest financial control from the private sources which had abused it, and to guarantee the underprivileged citizen a fair share of the national abundance.

As was suggested at the beginning of this chapter, the Gilded Age in the history of American politics has a double character; and at this point there should be little doubt as to which side the poet emphasized. Except for the occasional verses written in commemoration of deaths and assassinations, and except for the stubborn rejection of third parties as effective political forces, the verse literature here represented was one of consistent and violent protest. It carried a sincere concern for the economic dispossessed beyond the confines of the more purely economic issues discussed in Chapter IV. Along with the preceding chapter it explains the emergence of that great period of politico-economic reform which was to follow.

Notes

[1] Smith, *Day Lilies*, 265–73.
[2] Barton, *For Friendship's Sake*, 117–18.
[3] Lozier, *Your Mother's Apron Strings*, 77.
[4] Taylor, *Original Poems*, 120.
[5] Engle, *Poems*, 265–70; Parrish, *Echoes from the Valley*, 40; Holford, *Cofachiqui*, 142; Toms, *Sacred Gems*, 17.
[6] Nickelplate, *Story of a Broken Ring*, 32.
[7] Cudmore, *Poems and Songs*, 3–11.
[8] Johnston, *Pagan's Poems*, 171.
[9] Temple, *Sheaf of Grain*, 138; O'Connor, *Works*, 239.
[10] Sloan, *Telephone of Labor*, 176.
[11] Brown, *Ernest and Madeline*, 121–26.
[12] Lee, *Dreamy Hours*, 14.
[13] Van Slingerland, *Love and Politics*, 283ff.
[14] Johnson, *Songs of the G.O.P.*, 31–38; Wiley, *Song Book*, 16.
[15] Hubbell, *Various Verses*, 47.
[16] Fitzpatrick, *Passing of William McKinley*, 17ff.
[17] Currie, *Sonnets and Love Songs*, 22; Hunt, "*The Writing on the Wall*," 7.
[18] Wright, *Under the Red Cross*, 14.
[19] Brown, *Bullion in the Campaign of 1880*, 22.
[20] Armstrong, *La Porte in June*, 19.
[21] Treuthart, *Milliad*, 288.
[22] Adams, *History of the United States in Rhyme*, 68.
[23] Treuthart, *Milliad*, 289; Cudmore, *Poems and Songs*, 43.
[24] Scully, *Songs of the People*, 70.
[25] Kirschbaum, *Prose and Poetry*, 85; Boyd, *Poetical Works*, 248.
[26] Nye, *Chestnuts Old and New*, 265–66.
[27] Gosse, *Royal Pastoral*, 180.
[28] Dickson, *Farmer's Thoughts*, 28.
[29] Crewson, *Old Times*, 121.
[30] Smith, *Wayside Poems*, 108.
[31] Maline, *Nineteenth Century*, 26.
[32] Sprague, *Billy Dash Poems*, 94–95.
[33] Bien, *Oriental Legends*, 122.
[34] Waite, *Helen*, 261.
[35] Price, *Poetical Works of Peter Peppercorn*, 101–3.
[36] Grant, *Yankee Doodle*, 22, 25.
[37] Kelley, *Age of Gold*, 17–18.
[38] Bowen, *Losing Ground*, 3.
[39] Ware, *Rhymes of Ironquill*, 19.
[40] Rice, *Rural Rhymes*, 186.
[41] Campbell, *Civitas*, 101; Austin, *Devil's Football*, 13; Donaldson, *Poems*, 120.
[42] DeForest, *Poems*, 91–97.
[43] Cornaby, *Autobiography and Poems*, 95; Dennehy, *Convict's Story*, 24.
[44] Kelley, *Age of Gold*, 40–42.

[45] Riley, *Home-Folks*, 119.

[46] Dorr, *Babylon*, 96.

[47] Rorer, *Pastime Poems*, 53.

[48] Dennis, *Asphodels and Pansies*, 62.

[49] Martin, *Vistae Vitae*, 13.

[50] Lampton, *Yawps*, 149–50.

[51] Watson, *To-day and Yesterday*, 94.

[52] Dawson, *Poems of the New Time*, 65.

[53] Suttill, *Works of the Poet Coachman*, 119–20; Huckel, *Larger Life*, 127–33; l'Anson, *Vision of Misery Hill*.

[54] Davenport, *Perpetual Fire*, 20.

[55] Hussey, *River Bend*, 134.

[56] Henderson, *Thoughts at Random*, 60.

[57] Johnson, *Poems of Idaho*, 126.

[58] Wilson, *Troubles of a Worried Man*, 144–45.

[59] Conway, *Thrice Words*, 142.

[60] Moulton, *Kansas Bandit*, 5.

[61] *Ibid.*, 4ff.

[62] Buck, *Silas Balsam's Letters*, 6–9; Kenney, *Thusettes*, 60.

[63] Miller, *Verses from a Vagrant Muse*, 75–76.

[64] Osborne, *Quest of a Lost Type*, n. pag; Jackson, *Poems*, 152–55.

[65] Dean, *Poems*, II, 125.

[66] Wolcott, *Song-Blossoms*, 161–62.

[67] Field, *Sharps and Flats*, II, 174, 37–38; *Culture's Garland*, 285; *Hoosier Lyrics*, 109.

[68] Jepson, *Pot-pourri*, 45–46.

[69] Cole, *Colonel*, 15ff., 120ff.; Henderson, *Thoughts at Random*, 53–56; Seymour, *Pen Pictures*, 100–103; Warman, *Mountain Melodies*, 60.

[70] Bixby, *Driftwood*, 4–5.

[71] Kenney, *Thusettes*, 87.

[72] Burgoyne, *Songs of Every Day*, 62–63; Franklin, *Free Silver*, 10–11.

[73] Dresser, *Captured and Bound*, 20; Cleveland, *Scarlet-veined*, 87; Elmore, *Love among the Mistletoe*, 52–53.

[74] Carey, *Barnstormer's Companion*, 43–45; Moore, *Collection of Jewels*, 84–89.

[75] *Centennial of the Providence National Bank*, 38.

[76] Dunbar, *Lyrics of the Hearthside*, 144.

[77] Alden, *Poems*, 3; Price, *Poetical Works of Peter Peppercorn*, 219; Coan, *Better in the Mornin'*, 64.

[78] Peter Cooper, the 1876 nominee, was a prominent figure in verse, but not in this connection (see Chapter IV). Weaver and Butler, the nominees in 1880 and 1884 respectively, were mentioned only five times in all.

[79] Brown, *Bullion in the Campaign of 1880*, 5; Norwood, *Political Poems*, 3ff.; Chase, *Rough Notes in Rhyme*, 14–15; 16–19.

[80] Marshall, *Launching and Landing*, 132–84.

[81] Brown, *Bullion in the Campaign of 1880*, 26.

[82] Osborne, *Quest of a Lost Type*, n. pag.; Belrose.

[83] Foss, *Back Country Poems*, 108–9.

[84] Mosher, *"The Stranded Bugle,"* 63–65; Fitzpatrick, *Passing of William McKinley*, 13ff.; Seymour, *Harrison and Reid Campaign Song Book*, 30–31.

[85] Field, *Sharps and Flats*, I, 184–85; II, 240–43.

[86] Mattie N. Brown, *Poems*, 135; Hylton, *Knights of the Plow*, iii.

[87] McIntyre, *Sun-sealed*, 75–76.

[88] Treuthart, *Milliad*, 197ff., 293.

[89] *Devil's Visit*, 314–15.

[90] James, *Poems*, 48–49.

[91] Schafer, *Thoughts on Social Problems*, 4–5.

[92] Heylmun, *Musings on a Locomotive*, 125–26; Elmore, *Love Among the Mistletoe*, 91.

[93] Davenport, *Perpetual Fire*, 45–47; Bowen, *Losing Ground*, 41.

[94] Cudmore, *Poems and Songs*, 30–32.

[95] Currie, *Sonnets and Love Songs*, 21.

[96] Musser, *Poems*, 213.

[97] Welburn, *American Epic*, 270.

[98] *Devil's Visit*, 367.

VI

Wine and Women, a Song of Reform

THE QUESTION OF REFORM AND THE REFORMER MAY be related in its large sense to a state of mind or a broad social attitude. Some socially conscious poets of the Gilded Age selected this generalized approach, hailing a "sun of reform for freemen now rising"[1] or characterizing the reformer as a

> Grand man, who, standing forth to view,
> A full head higher than his peers,
> Whose eye, undimmed by veils of gold,
> Looks through the future like a seer's . . .[2]

The reformer was, for these poets, an oft-martyred foe of tyranny, an enemy of "Oppression, Injustice and Fraud . . . Greed" and "Cant."[3] With Jesus Himself as prototype, and with the "Mammonite" as antitype, the reformer was an inspired individual bringing "God-like Love" and progress to the "Devil's stronghold."[4] Although most spokesmen for the principle of reform stressed divine and inspirational sanctions for the social crusader, some preferred the weapon of irony as a counterattack against those who characterized reformers as

> . . . busy-bodies here below
> Who prate of change and progress, thus and so;
> Who loud proclaim that, as the planets bear
> Their torches up the age's pathway, there
> Will be new realms of truth discovered, and
> The vision of a more contented land.
> They dare to think the sons may wiser be
> Than were the fathers . . .

WOMANS HOLY WAR.

Grand Charge on the Enemy's Works.

They are disturbers in these latter days,
And turn the earth from out "the good old ways." . . .
And with an egotism most intense
They talk of science—call it common sense. . . .
They doubt if our commercial ways are just
And would upset the basis of our trust.
The state they shock with their *reform* assaults,
And dare assert a politician false.[5]

As these defensive lines suggest, there were an equal number of poets who considered the "magic watch-word" of reform as something less than spellbinding. To some the reformer was well-intentioned but hopelessly frustrated by the realities of his environment; to minds more Thoreau-like the reformer was a rude, unattractive, over-serious busybody who made otherwise innocent people conscious of sin. Reform was to them a misdirected waste:

Mankind could save one-half its wasted labor
Would each but heal himself and spare his neighbor.[6]

Even more serious attacks were leveled at hypocritical advocates of political reform who, once in power, readily sold out to opulence and corruption; who planned orgies of "Occasional Reform" simply to make vice more attractive and lucrative by clothing it with the glamour of the forbidden; or who backed reform on principle but shied away when interests close to home were threatened.[7] The reformers' self-righteousness was castigated—

The ground is firm beneath their feet,
No stain can come their garments nigh,
What may it matter then to them
That some poor sinful ones should die?[8]

—and the total effect of reform was sometimes estimated as decisively negative:

But you have really got an awful squad
Of villains who richly deserve the rod.

And among the worst, in every case,
Are the "special friends of the toiling race"—
Self-dubbed reformers, selfish and lazy,
With morals loose, and intellects hazy—
Who, by stimulating discontent,
Make impossible good government.[9]

General attitudes toward reform, however, were far less important—at least numerically—than were specific issues. Applications of the reform temper to urban, economic, and political problems have been dealt with in the foregoing chapters; subsequent chapters will include consideration of peace movements and moral reform. Verse to be considered in the present chapter belongs in the tradition of humanitarian reform which had its first full flowering in the decades immediately preceding the Civil War, and which embraced such areas as education; treatment of the handicapped, the insane, and the criminal; temperance; woman's rights; and antimilitarism. Several leaders in this first widespread expression of the reform impulse, among them Wendell Phillips, Elizabeth Cady Stanton, and Susan B. Anthony, were still alive and active. But for most reformers—and for the public as well—the impulse which had lavished its energy on so many diverse causes in the general campaign for human betterment seemed to have spent itself in one supreme crusade, that of freeing the slaves and saving the Union. As the twentieth century approached, the public disposition toward reform gathered renewed strength, and the Progressive Era—that landmark of wholesale reform in many directions—arrived as proof that crusades for mankind could yet prosper. But for most poet-citizens, at least, the last quarter of the nineteenth century was a time of fence-mending and the re-grouping of forces. In the area of humanitarian reform the signal fires were kept alive with fuel from two causes: woman's rights and temperance.

Before dealing with these twin aspects of the movement, it should be noted that a multitude of causes—from pleas for sanitation and better medicines to lessons on home beautification —caught the attention of isolated versifiers. Aside from the two major subjects of temperance and woman's rights, however, only one area attracted sufficient comment to require mention— namely, that concerning the treatment of the criminal. It was approached in a variety of ways. Some poets promoted prison reform and encouraged rehabilitation of offenders so as to prevent the perpetuation of a class of social outcasts.[10] "Judge Lynch" was excoriated in Western as well as Southern settings; capital punishment was called "legal revenge" or termed a "throwback" to less civilized times; and specific methods of inflicting legal death—including as "advanced" a device as electrocution—were rejected as horribly cruel.[11] One versifier even sought to persuade his readers that crime should be treated as a disease rather than a willful act.[12] Salted in among such enlightened comment inevitably appeared the reactionary who favored a return to the "ancient whipping post" and the well-applied lash in order to make "hoodlums grow rare."[13] The pervasive tone, however, was one of outrage at a society which refused to entertain a constructive attitude toward the criminal and his problems; as for the taking of human life, that was for God, not man.[14]

i

Throughout the later years of the nineteenth century the American woman steadily broadened her fields of activity and improved her status. The growth of the city, the development of the department store, and the increasing use of the typewriter and telephone gave her the opportunity for economic self-sufficiency without the hopeless drudgery of farm or factory labor. These circumstances had provided an unarguable basis for female emancipation; it remained for social and political attitudes and institutions to recognize these economic facts. In many areas, signs of recognition could be noted: in education (by 1894 there were 84,000 women in normal schools and colleges); in labor (the National Woman's Trade Union League was founded in 1903); in journalism (enlightened periodicals such as *Woman's Home Companion* and *Ladies' Home Journal*, founded in 1873 and 1883 respectively, were replacing the sentimental magazines of mid-century); in organized social activity (the period saw the founding of a myriad of women's clubs, including the Eastern Star in 1876, the Daughters of the American Revolution in 1890, and both the Colonial Dames of America and the United Daughters of the Confederacy in1891); and in political rights (by 1900 five states had allowed woman the ballot).

The leading feminists, anxious to accelerate the recognition of woman on all fronts, had waited impatiently till the Civil War should end, anxious lest some hard-won gains of the forties and fifties should be lost in the welter of post war questions. Abundant evidence attests to the efficacy of their reorganization. The scope of this post-bellum movement is suggested by the statement of purpose carried on the masthead of *The Woman's Journal*, founded in 1870 under the editorship of Mary A. Livermore, Julia Ward Howe, Lucy Stone, William Lloyd Garrison, and Thomas Wentworth Higginson. This periodical announced itself

devoted to the interests of Woman, to her educational, industrial, legal and political Equality, and especially her right of Suffrage.

Although woman's rights was a prime question in the socially-oriented poetry of the late nineteenth century, it was not treated with anything like the zeal which led to the organization of elaborate annual conventions or which produced the weighty, multi-volume *History of Woman Suffrage*. Nor did the scope of the verse mirror the concerns enumerated on the masthead of *The Woman's Journal*. The poets did, however, agree with the *Journal* editors, and with most feminists of the period, that the important item on the woman's agenda was the suffrage question.

Very few verses on the franchise question were as militant as one titled "Victory Shall Be Our Watchword" composed for the Nantucket Woman's Suffrage Convention;[15] most were contentious. Some of the arguments were well taken, pointing out the

THE AGE OF BRASS.
or the triumphs of Woman's rights

increase in female education as a preparation for active citizenship; but most of them foundered on extremely petty points. Justifiably piqued by the assertion that women should not be allowed the vote since they did not bear arms in war, suffragists retorted with equally puerile logic, proposing to deny male franchise since men did not bear children![16] Such phrases as "less brains than breeches" indicated the infantile name-calling to which these supposedly serious political discussions frequently descended.[17] Victorian prejudice further distracted some proponents of the woman's suffrage by leading them into attempts to prove that the purity of womanhood would not be violated through accepting the vote.[18] Thus, although a respectable number of poets jumped on the suffragette bandwagon in the hope that the addition of the female to the electorate might bring an end to the long reign of male corruption and introduce an era of sweetness, purity, and enlightened prosperity, much of the constructive reasoning behind such a proposal was vitiated by small-minded simpering and schoolyard logic.

One particular aspect of the woman's rights question on which the poet expressed a proportionally greater interest than did the orators and essayists had to do with the relation between the sexes. Attracted by the sentimental and dramatic possibilities of the subject, the poet undertook a re-appraisal of American heterosexual behavior. In emphasizing the need for a new freedom only one poet went so far as to sing the joys of free love—"Divine Promiscuity," he called it—but many others showed a clear resentment at the constraints of Victorianism superimposed on Puritanism.[19] In his rebellion the poet accorded sympathy to the unwed mother and even to the wife who accepts a lover.[20] These unfortunates were by no means forgiven their transgressions, but their dilemmas were regarded with an understanding which would have been unlikely in earlier decades. The poet was not entirely consistent in his efforts to encourage an increased latitude of accepted behavior; he was consistent, however, in his demand for a more reasonable understanding of the situation involved, regardless of blame. He distinguished, for example, between the woman seduced out of innocence, and the mature woman fully responsible for her actions.[21]

The problem of prostitution received especial emphasis. Taking Christ's pardoning of Mary Magdalene as an example of the triumph of mercy over self-righteousness, the poet scorned the "Sham-Virtue" of those who flatly condemned the "fallen woman."[22] These daughters of Eve were excused on account of economic necessity (*"for they had no choice"*), and the argument of social responsibility was strongly presented: "Together we rise, or together we fall."[23] The defense of the prostitute led readily to a general attack on the whole concept of the "double standard" of sexual behavior. "Fallen man/No better is than fallen woman," proclaimed one verse, while another particularly dramatic episode pictured a young woman receiving a new tar-and-feather coat as a reward for her loose behavior, while her male partners "silently . . . slink away."[24] If the women were condemned, why not the men, they reasoned; if "shameless" were so glibly applied to "courtesan," why not then to her partners in misbehavior? Through episode and analogy, an argument was made for understanding over taboo, for a sense of social responsibility instead of self-righteousness, and for a willingness to end arbitrary distinctions between male and female in judging patterns of sexual conduct.

Aside from these two strong emphases on matters political and sexual, the poet was inclined to participate in the woman's rights crusade on a general level, rather than as an advocate of any particular measure. Specific causes such as divorce, birth control, and professional and educational status, were mentioned occasionally but received no concerted support and were no more than incidental to the general expression of sympathy for the lot of unemancipated woman. Although generalized, this sort of comment often contained very positive assertions, linking national advancement with feminine status, or labeling as backward any conception of "Woman's Sphere" as delimited by the kitchen walls.[25] Woman was urged to claim what was rightfully hers:

> Woman, didst thou but know thy power
> To claim thy birthright and thy dower,
> Thou would'st o'erleap the gulf that lies
> Twixt thee and thine own paradise . . .
> Instead of cowering 'neath the rod.[26]

Deeds of physical valor performed by heroines of the past served as exemplars for exhortation: Kentucky pioneer women such as Elizabeth and Frances Callaway and Jemima Boone, who had been captured by the Indians; California heroines such as Mary Pollack; "The Cuban Amazon," Inez Cari, who led five hundred black women against the "cruel Weyler" in a martyred cause.[27] As less spectacular but more pertinent examples of female fortitude, the grand old ladies of American reform were apotheosized: Elizabeth Cady Stanton, Lucy Stone, Margaret Fuller, Susan B. Anthony, and Harriet Beecher Stowe.[28] Attacking the idea that woman must forever remain inferior to man on account of Eve's sin, her partisans pronounced that she had now served her penance and overcome the handicap with which she had started the human race.[29]

As the century neared its close, the arrival of the "new woman" was hailed:

> She studies all the questions of the day,
> And gives these problems of her earnest thought;
> Wise plans for woman unto her are brought,
> Which shed new light on her advancing way.[30]

> She looks straight at the deeds of men,
> And judges them by what they do
> In council strife, with tongue or pen . . .[31]

"Emancipated . . ./Erect, self-poised," she "stands beside her mate, companionwise."[32] The future will reveal her man's equal, versed in science and the arts, and fit to occupy with credit "Pulpit, platform . . . Presidential chair."[33]

But there were those who said, "To the Coming Woman," "*Don't you come!*"[34] To nearly 40 per cent of those who wrote on this subject, visions of the "new woman" were frightening indeed:

> Then shout hurrah for the woman new,
> With her rights and her votes and her bloomers, too!
> Evolved through bikes and chewing-gum,
> She's come! . . .

And shout hurrah for the woman new!
Who wants a new Bible to suit her new view,
And writes for the papers and eats at the club
Her grub.[35]

This reference to "a new Bible" indicated that the foes of feminism believed the Bible—through God's judgment on Eve and through the words of St. Paul—had spoken once and for all on the subject of female status.[36] If the American woman thinks she is without rights, she should look to the Orient and be thankful for her relatively high place.[37] If, instead of accepting her place, woman insists on entering new and unsuitable areas, she will only lose the virtues for which she is needed and cherished:

But much I fear this business life,
In which they're striving to outdo man,
Will soil the charms of maid and wife,
And dwarf what we admire in woman.[38]

"Shall Women Vote?" asks one verse, and answers yes; women should vote affirmatively to accept marriage proposals and forever hold their peace.[39] For as a wife and mother, ran this argument, woman has all the place and power one could wish. In guiding and counseling her husband, in teaching "mercy, purity, and love" to her children, woman assures us of a new generation which "will not fail."[40] "Think you the forum, or the badge of state,/Or steel would bring you increment of power," queried one poet, when woman already controlled the "law of love."[41]

Humor was one of the most powerful and popular weapons in the hands of the anti-feminist. "The New Woman's Mistake," for example, described in ludicrous detail the duel between a fire-armed feminist on one side, and on the other side—a mouse![42] The title "Emancipated Woman," in some instances, led only to the discussion of woman's emancipation from her household duties which made her husband, unfed and uncared for, the true "Suffragist Sufferer."[43] Following this direction of humorous attack, the poet unhesitatingly brought to bear that classic comic cliché involving the reversal of male and female roles; thus the Supreme Court appeared in delicate finery, exchanging gossip; women made small talk over stocks and bonds; and men were left to worry at the household chores.[44]

But the sense of annoyance often overcame the sense of humor. One poet finally threw up his hands and decided that life was too short to include worry over "What old maids in bloomers proclaim";[45] while another shouted a testy "hands off!" to the interfering females:

> Do not demand, ye women, then,
> To add to complications,
> Forego your sentimental talk
> Of legal "Prohibitions."
> Just leave the ship of state alone,
> Rest easy on your oars—
> While Uncle Sam with practiced hand
> Shall steer for calmer shores.[46]

The most intense protests were penned by men and women who saw the new woman as a crass product, forced on an unwilling market, who might drive from circulation the tender sweetheart, the precious wife, and the loving mother of pre-emancipation days. Women who cherished the traditional female virtues became the most effective opponents of the more militant of their sex. An example of protest from within the ranks appeared in a long verse called "Woman" and written as an answer, according to the poetess, to Pope's "Essay on Man." After flailing the male for his encouragement of woman's weakness and frivolity, she then took on her contemporary feminists in this surprising vein:

> With "*Woman's Rights*,"—in modern parlance stated,—
> I have no sympathy; but deem them mated
> With arrogance and folly;—none more blinded

Than those denominated "the strong minded;"
And "Woman's Rights," so called, were they secured,
Must be considered *ills* to be endured.[47]

The "woman movement" had some effective opposition, especially from the sex it sought to liberate, but both sides helped keep alive this commanding nineteenth-century debate. The contribution of the poets was limited and selective; but it was, in spite of the criticism, a positive part. Much was said—although too often with dubious effect—on the side of woman suffrage; with greater effect, the poet contributed to an impressive analysis of woman's social and sexual role.

ii

The related causes of temperance and prohibition, overlapping somewhat with the woman's movement, provided the staple crop in the harvest of humanitarian reform, albeit these causes were in a somewhat depressed state compared to their high yield both before and after the Gilded Age. Ante-bellum temperance activity, its evangelical flavor salted with the mass conversions of Father Theobold Mathew and peppered with the lurid confessions of the reformed drunkards of the Washington Temperance Society, provided some of the more highly seasoned dishes in our social history, and led, by 1855, to temperance legislation in every Northern state but New Jersey. Public enthusiasm proved short-lived, however, and by 1868 all states but Maine had repealed their temperance measures. Moreover, the twenty years prior to 1880 saw a sevenfold increase in the amount of money invested in the liquor business.

The peace and prosperity of the rum-seller was not undisturbed, to say the least. The "Woman's War" of 1874 led to the closing of over three thousand saloons, and heralded the militant awakening of the dormant enemies of the bottle. The founding of the Woman's Christian Temperance Union, in that same year, augured both for careful organization of temperance forces and for an enlightened approach centered on the social causes and effects of addiction to alcohol. That religious and moral appeals for temperance would still be prominent was assured by the continuing activity of Protestant church groups,

especially the Methodists. The important shift in the character of the crusade against alcohol revealed itself behind the superficially similar stereotypes of Frances Willard, marching on a Pittsburgh saloon in the late 1870's, and Carry Nation, swinging her hatchet in Medicine Lodge in the late 1890's. But Miss Willard and her W.C.T.U. educated toward temperance, while Carry Nation and her Anti-Saloon League, founded in 1893, made the uncompromising demand for total prohibition and promoted it with a determined use of pressure-politics.

Two things are of primary interest in the verse pertaining to temperance and prohibition: first, that it made up two-thirds of all humanitarian reform sentiment and thus served a major function in providing a continuing focus for the reform-minded in an era when humanitarian causes in general were not notably prosperous; second, that it exhibited a wide variety of interesting approaches which help reveal the fundamental identity of the reform spirit in these shifting times. Here, then, is an important key to a major puzzle. By examining this verse from the standpoint of its basic appeal one can learn not only what motivated the reformer, but also how he hoped to move his fellow citizens.

Perhaps surprisingly, in the light of the well-publicized activities of the W.C.T.U. and the Anti-Saloon League, temperance verse was dominated not by a social or political approach but by a moral and religious emphasis supposedly more characteristic of the ante-bellum crusades. Dogmatic pronouncements on the evil of drink, enlivened by the singing spirit of a religious army, characterized this extensive collection of arguments in verse which could be epitomized in a phrase from one of them: alcohol "Hates Christian men—despises God!"[48] Biblical strictures against drinking were frequently cited, even to the extent of advocating the unfermented wine allowed in Isaiah, or arguing that the flushed faces of the wedding guests at Cana resulted from inspiration rather than alcohol.[49] That liquor is in league with the Underworld was also made laboriously clear. Alcohol was called the "child of Satan's breath" and its birth was depicted against the background of yawning hell, where Satan planned the ruination of mankind.[50] Busily tempting susceptible victims, the archfiend and his lieutenants worked with the confidence that the drunkard's "one sin" would consign him to eternal perdition.[51] More Christian in spirit were the gentler poets who sought converts through "Faith, Hope, and Charity" in service of a cause which "soars beyond this mortal scope."[52] Resorting to prayer in behalf of John Barleycorn's victims, poets in this camp made explicit their interpretation of applied religion: that the *"only sure basis of Moral Reform"* is temperance.[53]

The revival spirit of those who approached the temperance question as a religious crusade was most manifest in hymns and parodies clearly intended for group singing, preferably on the march. Thus "Rally 'Round the Flag" became the "Temperance Flag"; "Yield Not to Temptation" lent itself readily to a temperance version; and another favorite hymn became "Stand up, stand up,/For temperance true . . ."[54] Popular tunes as well as hymns gave way to parody: "Coming through the Rye" became "Drinking on the Sly"; "The Battle Hymn of the Republic" was made to open "Mine eyes have seen the coming of a hideous dragon form"; and the familiar "cup o' kindness" was deleted from "Auld Lang Syne," which was then made to conclude, "We'll reach the han' to brother man,/That's in the power of wine."[55] As some of these verses suggest, this temperance spirit was not only vocal but militant as well. The same inspiration which labeled the "Woman's War" produced such titles as: "Glorious Temperance Army," "Temperance Armor," "The Temperance Fight," "A Temperance Battle Hymn," and "The Temperance Soldier."[56] In a poem entitled "To Arms!" one poet referred to the temperance cause as a "holy war."[57]

Two categories of temperance argument which suggest, logically, emphases other than religious, turned out in verse to rest on moral suasion. The "water versus wine" school, although it utilized arguments from nature and although it stressed the factor of health to some degree, took its fundamental strength from the assertion that water was the beverage "distilled by God" and should therefore be preferred to less pure, man-made liquids.[58] Water was, put simply, holy; alcohol was immoral. The many poets who approached temperance through attacks on the rum-sellers and their allies did include arguments which could best be described as economic, political, or social. The manufacturers and dispensers of alcoholic beverages were condemned for profiteering from a trade which brought poverty, disease, and death; and those who protected their interests in political circles were roundly reviled. But here too the basic and consistent approach was dependent on the identification of the rum-seller and his wares with moral wrong. With the poets the rum-seller was the man "who, from thirst of gold, to all doth sell/*Distilled damnation filled with fires of Hell.*"[59] In a number of ways, some of them unexpected, the poets of temperance stressed moral and religious arguments.

The second major temperance argument placed the use of alcohol in a social rather than a religious context. Clearly in the van of this phase of the movement was Frances Willard, whose "Christ-like life, and deeds of love" aimed at "elevating manhood" were duly and conspicuously praised.[60] As an obvious landmark of the progress of the W.C.T.U. there appeared verses recommending education as the prime method of reform; others were directed specifically at the nation's youth and composed for classroom use.[61] Another indication of socially oriented temperance thinking appeared in those verses identifying the evils of drink with a particular group, most often the city dwellers. This urban-focused verse makes clear one important distinction between the two most pervasive temperance arguments. Those who considered drinking a crime against God were relatively unconcerned about where and by whom the drinking was done; those who considered drinking a crime against society were greatly concerned. Thus one can recognize verses associating "The Accursed Cities" with the blight of alcohol, "the drunken dancer's breath," and the "reek of hideous gutters and black oaths/Of drunkenness from vice-infested dens" as indicative of the social approach.[62] One version of the tale of the child come to the saloon to lead home a drunken father was titled "A City Incident."[63]

Melodramatic narratives, such as the one just alluded to, were to the socially oriented temperance poet what hymns and marches were to the evangelistic school. "The Drunkard's Lament, or the Bottle" featured the latter as the cause of murder.[64] A messenger took "The Fatal Drink" and failed to prevent a train wreck.[65] "The Drinker's Child" made her father kneel beside her and take the "solemn pledge"—just after he had killed her mother while inebriated.[66] With plots that improved not at all on "The Face on the Bar Room Floor," and with no greater aesthetic distinction than the hymn-parodies of the marching crusaders, these narratives succeeded one another with predictable monotony, alike in their maudlin demonstration that the person who drinks to excess is bound to bring harm to those around him.

But if their verses were no more distinguished, at least the reform poets who thought in social terms showed a great deal more understanding for the drunkard's plight than did the proponents of the "devil-in-the-bottle" approach. "The Drunkard's Club," for example, showed how polite tippling among the educated could lead to social damage no less great than in more humble strata.[67] The melodramas typically stressed the drunkard's role as social menace; other verses, however, examined the other side of the coin, placing responsibility for alcoholic excesses on the society rather than the individual. Furthermore, argued these poets, social causes indicate social remedies. Not only must we encourage a set of living patterns at all levels which will combat the bottle's lure, but we must realize that the addict will be cured not through legislation nor through a conversion experience, but only through the sympathetic understanding of those around him.[68]

In an age which took its patriotic anniversaries seriously, many poetic pleas for temperance reflected a nationalistic tinge:

> If e'er our land had need of honest men . . .
> 'Tis now, to-day, this year of glory when
> We boast ourselves the sons of patriot sires.

> And yet we mourn a nation steeped in sin;
> Soaked half in fraud, the other half in gin.[69]

Representative of this point of view were verses which pointed to America's achievement in overthrowing monarchy and slavery; how depressingly ironic, the argument continued, that we should bow before King Alcohol's throne and tolerate slavery to rum.[70] In one sense these patriotic persuaders formed a group unto themselves, wherein the use of liquor was tantamount to treason; but in another sense they were only arguing from the point of view of an enlarged social group—the nation as a whole. Their goal was a nationwide—or even worldwide—social evolution leading to a "Temperance Millennium" when man would at last fulfill his promise.[71] In this sense they made up a rather grandiose adjunct to those who based their appeals on education, environmental rehabilitation, and specific exhortations of the social conscience.

When political rather than social boundaries were mentioned, however, it was usually a sign that the versifier had grown impatient with the limited objectives of the temperance movement and had enlisted his pen in the cause of the prohibitionists:

> Talk for Temperance seems but folly,
> When a license can be bought;
> Hence, to kill the License System,
> Hardest battles must be fought. . . .[72]

This third, and last, of the major arguments against alcohol occupied itself with political action; readers were urged to *"vote* for *men* and *measures* that will keep this curse away."[73] As for measures, the Maine Law represented the chief triumph and served as a rallying cry throughout the era, albeit local victories from Kansas to Massachusetts were likewise celebrated in rime. Detailed reasoning, such as the attack on the license system cited above, was infrequent, the poets usually contenting themselves with getting out the vote for whatever temperance or prohibition measure was on the ballot. When it came to men,

the poets plugged hard for Prohibition candidates. That un-
successful presidential candidate on the 1904 Prohibition ticket
with the unfortunate name of Silas C. Swallow had caught the
attention of at least one versifier by 1897.[74]

Toward the end of this period the good will of these poets,
who had been indefatigably rallying at election time and loyally
consoling in defeat a party which never received more than 2.2
per cent of the national vote, began to wear a bit thin. Some
began to revile the major parties ("Honest Republican party,/
Your talk is very cheap") for their failure to adopt a prohibition
plank, and for their use of liquor to influence elections.[75] The
party which had freed the nation from slavery was asked to free
it from drink as well, and that "glorious day" was hailed when
Republicans, Democrats, and Prohibitionists would "All stand
on one platform."[76] But until that day, the Prohibitionists
complained with some bitterness, the token vote hardly paid:

> When Democrats vote for the cause so true,
> And Republicans vote as the Democrats do,
> Why then I'll vote Prohibition, too.[77]

The sweet smell of victory was at times only faintly perceived
by the poets of prohibition.

In addition to the three major approaches to temperance and
prohibition—religious, social, and political—two minor arguments appeared with sufficient frequency to command interest.
One of them, based on the harmful physical effects of drink, was
surprisingly small in this nation of hypochondriacs and in an era
when applied science held immense prestige. Within this
category occurred some facetious fun-making, as when a Devil,
downing a slug of bar whiskey, found that it had "burnt his
tail off close to the chair."[78] This nursery-rime parody, too,
seems hardly calculated to terrify:

> Little Jack Horner
> Ran round the corner,
> And bought him a bottle of rye;

>   But when he had some
>   He was sullen and dumb,
>   And then he began to cry.[79]

But for most of these versifiers alcohol was more than a temporary depressant or the subject for a joke. The list of maladies seriously—even morbidly—attributed to alcohol included hobnailed liver, heart failure, delirium tremens, blindness, softening of the brain, and insanity. "Hand not the Cup to Me," for it is "full of death within" might have been a motto in this camp, and one not to be taken lightly.[80] Though these verses realistically warned that alcoholic excesses might lead to the dilution of talent and premature death, they did so in a melodramatically exaggerated manner which was seldom physiologically accurate. As a group they saw alcoholism as a crime—not against God, nor society, nor the body politic, but against the body physical.

The other numerically minor approach to the problem of drink provided an interesting link between the ante-bellum activities of the Washington and Father Mathew temperance societies and the present-day activities of Alcoholics Anonymous. Emphasizing the glorious state of the individual saved from the bonds of Barleycorn, poets who chose this approach also favored melodramatic verse with such self-explanatory titles as "The Drunkard Redeemed," "The Drunkard's Reform," or "Father's Home and Sober."[81] Reminiscent of former days were tributes to John B. Gough, the star speaker of the Washingtonians;[82] whereas lines like the following foreshadowed more modern methods of dealing with the reformed addict:

>   To tell a rummy he *cannot* drink when he feels
>   a strong desire,
>   Is like telling a hero he cannot fight when
>   you call him a sneaking liar![83]

In addition to these three major and two minor temperance schools there existed a variety of individual points of view too numerous to catalogue. Before leaving this subject, however, it would be unfair not to mention a composition on behalf of temperance which has a certain claim to uniqueness. It was the work of a convict who boasted at some length on his record of unfailing abstinence; that he compiled this record in surroundings where the only bars were iron, and where his weakest moment could have brought him no temptation, entered the picture not at all.[84]

For the relief of the thirsty reader it should also be noted that one in ten of the verses on temperance took an unsympathetic stand on the curtailment of drink. Taking their precedent from odes to Bacchus and the spirit of Omar Khayyam, many poets found in the consumption of alcohol a positive good—although only Eugene Field went so far as to insist that he found enjoyment in hangovers and hallucinations as well.[85] More commonly the idea of reasonable indulgence was advanced: money, women, and whiskey are all "beneficial when properly used," "Should *all* be prohibited because they're abused?"[86] One poet who was also a physician praised the delights of drink and fellowship at his favorite tavern; a statistics-minded bard used death-rate data to quiet alarmists.[87]

Twitting the reformers provided an outlet for those who could not become aroused over the temperance crusade. One told of a saloon-keeper who routed an army of female prohibitionists by loosing some mice from under a box, where he had presumably kept them in anticipation of just such an emergency.[88] Others, more seriously irritated, took a firmer view:

> Smash, Smash, Smash!
> List to the war cry in Kansas!
> Amazonian bands
> With hatchets in hands . . .
> Though evil exist,
> You girls must desist
> From joining the list
> Of disturbers.[89]

More fun was had by turning the watchwords and precedents of the crusaders to opposite ends:

> Have You Heard that Saloons are a Hell?
> That's what All Prohibitionists Tell.
> Now We've cried, "Down with Rum"
> And We've Downed it, by Gum!
> Hell is Not half as Bad as they Tell[90]

> "Did God set grapes a-growing, do you think,
> And at the same time make it a sin to drink?"[91]

> "Look not on de wine cup," is what de Word tells me,
> Well, don't dat mean to drink it? 'Tis plain ez plain ken be.[92]

Many were the arguments turned, either seriously or in jest, against the enemies of drink; but the most impressive of all was that which sought to put the problem of temperance in a large perspective. Thus, as one poet wrote, it is not wine this nation is drunk with, but

> Cursed inebriate nation,
> Lo! where she wallows in gold;
> Drunk with the dollar's damnation,
> Withered and sottishly old.

> Crazed by the absinthe of riches,
> Bleared and bewildered she goes;
> Shrieks, as she staggers and pitches,—
> Money will solace my woes.[93]

Anti-temperance versifiers are not easy to catalogue; usually they responded directly to attacks on what they regarded as an important freedom; seldom did they originate constructive arguments of their own.

A noticeable segment of temperance verse was directed not at the abuse of alcohol but at the abuse of tobacco. Foreshadowing modern concern over the physical damage attributable to smoking, some poets listed disorders in an inclusive manner reminiscent of the anti-alcohol writers.[94] Others reacted against the foppishness and effeminacy of the cigarette or protested against the filth of the tobacco-chewing habit.[95] The defense of the "kind narcotic," however, amounted to nearly as many lines as did its condemnation.[96]

As with other humanitarian causes, that of temperance operated at a low ebb compared with the pre-Civil War crusades and the political triumphs of the twentieth century. Perhaps one clue to this failure could be found in the dominance of religious and moral arguments employed in these verses. Here was an attitude closely related to Protestant fundamentalism and to the revivalist spirit. In an America where the urban was rapidly replacing the rural, where the new immigration patterns heavily favored cultures and religious groups antipathetic to the fundamentalist Protestant ethic, and where the social climate was increasingly characterized by a confused struggle with a new "sophistication," this strictly moral approach—better suited to older and simpler times—faced diminishing prospects for success. The persistence of this old-time-religious line of reasoning throughout the era not only helps explain the lack of temperance success but also points, perhaps, to a continuing strain of puritanism in the American character, which makes itself felt beyond the mid-twentieth century when the climate would seem to have become even more unsympathetic.

The basically social orientation of the next largest category of temperance verse presents one of the frequent puzzles in the history of humanitarian reform. Framing their arguments in terms of group responsibility, with stress upon education, the versifiers in this liberal camp appear in many ways more enlightened and more modern than their contemporaries. Helpfully calling attention to areas where the work or reform was in general demand, as in the urban slums for example, they went beyond their fellow writers on temperance in promoting a spirit of altruistic interest rather than an obsessive devotion to an often narrow cause. Perhaps it was this very breadth and reasonableness which vitiated the practical effectiveness of this movement; for, as the nineteenth century waned, so did the power and prevalence of the more temperate advocates of temperance. Their function, apparently, was to prepare the way for the more politically knowledgeable and single-minded crusaders who rose in their wake.

The emergence of such a group within the camp of humanitarian reform was apparent before the end of the Gilded Age. Such were the prohibitionists who, at their height, had mastered a lobbying technique which became the envy of many less nobly motivated groups. More than the socially oriented temperance versifiers, these poets of prohibition represented a blend of idealism and practical action which we like to consider a peculiarly American mixture, and which manifested itself so positively in the decade before the first World War. Representing a less-than-dominant force in the Gilded Age, the prohibitionists had at least laid a firm foundation for the intense campaign which was to follow.

The end of the century saw the temperance crusader looking in two directions. Looking backward he clung to his old rugged cross of fundamentalist Protestantism, drawing converts from the audiences which responded so readily to such evangelists as Moody and Sankey. Looking forward, he rode the brief swell of social emphasis and swung alertly to the possibilities of political realization.

One finds in the woman's rights movement many of the tendencies evident in the temperance verse. The predominance of the suffrage question showed the feminists proportionately more politically advanced than the temperance advocates, although this is hardly surprising considering the basic importance of the vote. The extent to which those who discussed the woman's movement alluded to religious arguments and Biblical precedents furnished additional evidence for the dominance of the moral element in American reform: not because these instances were so numerous but because they intruded in such unlikely and illogical ways. That such arguments appeared at all suggests the strength of such an orientation. If moral and religious elements dominated the humanitarian reform crusades of the Gilded Age, then socially oriented arguments furnished the most enlightened comments, not only on alcoholism and the double standard, but also on the treatment of the criminal and on other topics mentioned only infrequently.

From a modern point of view one might be tempted to place more value on a handful of these enlightened treatments of woman's social role, of the problem of alcoholic addiction, or of the need for prison reform, than on all the welter of moral pronouncements, the plethora of gauche melodramas, or the superabundance of coarse parodies and feeble puns. But it was, after all, the temperance songster and the suffrage campaigner who provided the continuity for the drama of American reform; and it was in the strength of moral conviction and in the awakening of the public mind to political possibilities that the verse contributed to the character and understanding, as well as the persistence, of our tradition of humanitarian reform.

Notes

[1] Donaldson, *Poems*, 182.

[2] Crozier, *Songs in Earnest*, 5.

[3] Mattie N. Brown, *Poems*, 133–35; Price, *Poetical Works of Peter Peppercorn*, 144–48.

[4] Koopman, *At the Gates of the Century*, 45; Davenport, *Poetical Sermons*, 84–85.

[5] Savage, *At the Back of the Moon*, 16–17.

[6] Putnam, *Memories and Impressions*, 29.

[7] Carter, *Log Cabin Poems*, 37–41; Smith, *Some Simple Rhymes of Leisure Times*, 78–79; Davies, *Success*, 34–35.

[8] Beattie, *Poems*, 50.

[9] *Devil's Visit*, 37.

[10] Smith, *Jets of Truth*, 84–88; Norwood, *Political Poems*, 65; Riley, *Afterwhiles*, 89–90.

[11] Price, *Poems*, 18–21; Darling, *Messages from the Watch Tower*, 13–15; Hirt, *Social Poems*, 61–64; Hubbell, *Midnight Madness*, 89–90.

[12] Croffut, *Prophecy*, 114.

[13] Devens, *Selections of Prose and Verse*, 20.

[14] Campbell, *Queen Sylvia*, 305–6.

[15] Gardner, *Golden Rod*, 12.

[16] Croffut, *Prophecy*, 60.

[17] Allis, *Uncle Alvin at Home and Abroad*, 231–33.

[18] Scholes, *Thoughts in Verse*, 87–89.

[19] Lloyd, *Psalms of the Race Roots*, 40.

[20] Cawein, *Garden of Dreams*, 95–97; Allerton, *Annabel*, 9–32.

[21] Praigg, *Almetta*, 154–55.

[22] Elshemus, *Moods of a Soul*, 82; Dozier, *Galaxy of Southern Heroes*, 195–96; Spollon, *Mary Ann*, 27.

[23] Sloan, *Telephone of Labor*, 233; Darling, *Messages from the Watch Tower*, 17.

[24] Dearing, *Lost Chords*, 105; Allerton, *Walls of Corn*, 84–85.

[25] Bowen, *Losing Ground*, 45; Campbell, *Queen Sylvia*, 220–21; Savage, *At the Back of the Moon*, 24–25; Scarff, *Grinding of the Mills*, n. pag.

[26] Sisco, *Gems of Inspiration*, 155.

[27] Taney, *Kentucky Pioneer Women*, 34–37; Williams, *'49 to '94*, 3–12; Boylan, *If Tam O'Shanter'd Had a Wheel*, 14–18.

[28] Rich, *Murillo's Slave*, 27–31, 38–40; Taylor, *Captive Conceits*, 98–105.

[29] Collier, *Lilith*; Nicholson, *Whispers of the Pines*, 40–42.

[30] Commelin, *Of Such Is the Kingdom*, 84.

[31] Siegvolk, *Few Verses*, 55.

[32] Dawson, *Poems of the New Time*, 80.

[33] Painter, *Lyrical Vignettes*, 26; Shirley, *Everyday Rhymes*, 74; Van Nostrand, *Poems*, 26–27.

[34] Wise, *Optimist*, n. pag.

[35] Baum, *By the Candelabra's Glare*, 39.

[36] Alden, *Poems*, 14–17; Gregg, *Poems in Three Departments*, 134–35.

[37] Leonard, *My Lady of the Search-light*.

[38] McCourt, *Treasures of Weinsberg*, 141.

[39] Evans, *Sir Francis Drake*, 51.

[40] Fuller, *Venture*, 179–81; Bonney, *Meditations*, 19.

[41] Crowninshield, *Pictoris Carmina*, 63; Cornaby, *Autobiography and Poems*, 94–95.

[42] Helmer, *Child's Thoughts in Rhyme*, 50–51.

[43] Bixby, *Driftwood*, 21–23; Griggs, *Lyrics of the Lariat*, 114.

[44] Brown, *Chieftain*, 115–34; Fordham, *Magnolia Leaves*, 74–75; Heaton, *Quilting Bee*, 133.

[45] Conners, *Wreath of Maple Leaves*, 88.

[46] Teetzel, *Vagrant Fancies*, 33.

[47] Baldwin, *Flora*, 59.

[48] Ward, *All Sides of Life*, 173.

[49] Woodward, *Miscellaneous Poems*, 8–11; Swartz, *Poems*, 175–79.

[50] Eisenbeis, *Amen Corner*, 148; Carter, *Poems and Aphorisms*, 60–61; Ludlow, *Original Rum Convention*.

[51] *Rather Restful Rhymes*, 38–40; Craig, *Rough Diamond*, 208.

[52] Baldy, *California Pioneer*, 33–37; Bielby, *Poems*, 10.

[53] Barton, *For Friendship's Sake*, 30.

[54] Butters, *Harp of Hesper*, 123; Brown, *Golden Rod*, 64; Nichols, *Iron Door*, 12–13.

[55] Nichols, *Iron Door*, 5; Radford, *Court of Destiny*, 153; Campbell, *Blue Ribbon Lays*, 23.

[56] Gates, *Musings*, 112; Dodge, *Echoes from Cape Ann*, 128, 137; Beebe, *Prairie Flowers*, 155; Beard, *Choice Poems*, 27.

[57] Hobbs, *Poems*, 128–31.

[58] Adams, *Siouska*, 321.

[59] Wing, "*Pluck*," 133.

[60] Gorham, *Bosky Dells and Sylvan Roads*, 103; Lippincott, *Visions of Life*, 317.

[61] Tripp, *Around the Fireside*, 133–34; Griffin, *Our Treasure Chest for Girls*, 163; Ruddock, *Temperance Poems*, n. pag.

[62] Huff, *Songs of the Desert*, 57; Rule, *When John Bull Comes A-Courtin'*, 28; Cawein, *Weeds by the Wall*, 82.

[63] Van Derveer, *Soul Waifs*, 94.

[64] Holden, *Original Poems*, 87.

[65] McCoy, *Buds and Blossoms*, 207–12.

[66] Conway, *Complete Poems*, 158–60.

[67] Houghton, *Poems*, 73–75.

[68] Tillotson, *Poems*, 104–5.

[69] Rude, *Magnolia Leaves*, 98.

[70] Peckham, *Welded Links*, 177–79; Thompson, *Simplicity Unveiled*, 100–2.

[71] McKinnie, *From Tide to Timber-line*, 64–65.

[72] Spencer, *Opening for a Candidate*, 56–58.

[73] Allis, *Uncle Alvin at Home and Abroad*, 142–48.

[74] Sours, *Tax-Payer's Songster*, 9, 14–15.

[75] Norwood, *Political Poems*, 20; Kelso, *Poems*, 122–28.

[76] Hager, *Forty Years with the Muse*, 20–22; Richmond, *Free America*, 10.

[77] Abbott, *Wild Roses*, 52.

[78] *Tour of Prince Eblis*, 20.

[79] Wright, *Mother Goose for Temperance Nurseries*, 5.

[80] Vinton, *Vinton's Poems*, 75.

[81] Stout, *Poetical Works*, 169–71; Sprague, *Billy Dash Poems*, 96–97; French, *Stray Leaves and Fragments*, n. pag.

[82] Fennall, *Lyrics and Poems*, 149–53; Scribner, *Ode on Temperance*, 17.

[83] Woorster, *Random Rhymes*, 95.

[84] Dennehy, *Convict's Story*, 51–53.

[85] Field, *Second Book of Verse*, 35–38; *Songs and Other Verses*, 44–45; *Clink of the Ice*, 59–62.

[86] Donaldson, *Poems*, 217.

[87] Major, *Lays of Chinatown*, 11–13; Bixby, *Memories*, 73–75.

[88] Sears, *Forest Runes*, 205.

[89] Kenney, *Some More Thusettes*, 12.

[90] Donaldson, *Apropos Alphabet*, n. pag.

[91] Bundschu, *Happy New Year to All!*, n. pag.

[92] Davis, *'Weh Down Souf*, 121.

[93] Brooks, *Margins*, 78.

[94] Waugh, *Autobiography*, 282.

[95] Kerr, *Cheery Book*, 98–99; Hollister, *Sunflower*, 63–64.

[96] Doggett, *Hugh Allone*, 73.

VII

Immigration and Internationalism

No ASPECT OF THE POET'S COMMENT ON AMERICA'S
Gilded Age offers such striking immediacy to the mid-twentieth-
century reader as that dealing with foreign countries, citizens,
and causes. Here America, firm in her expansionistic sentiments,
exuberant with her new industrial power, confident from her
conquering of a continent, faced the world in a mood to dismiss
old allegiances and to test her new-found strength. How was she
to react as individual crises appeared? Was she, who had freed
herself from empire and her slaves from bondage, to be the
friend of refugees and revolution still? Or would she begin to

build a bastion of conservatism, limiting immigration and using her international influence to preserve the status quo of national sovereignty?

The events and circumstances of the years between 1876 and 1905 offered abundant opportunity for comment and interpretation; the poet responded with principle and with prescience. Both in dealing with foreign minorities within the United States and in developing a general attitude toward the continuing reception of such groups, he expressed an elaborate view of America's place in the international scheme of things. Further, in response to the pleas of those who struggled for self-determination and freedom from foreign domination during this period—the Cubans, the Irish, the Boers, the Boxers, and the Filipinos—he developed his own interpretation of America and the continuing world revolution for national independence. The American government showed a fair degree of consistency in dealing with these questions; the poet—representing a selective and relatively enlightened public view—showed an even more consistent attitude which diverged from the official acts and policies at almost every turn.

i

Throughout the period under consideration, overwhelming waves of immigrants inundated increasingly widespread areas of the United States; meanwhile, participants in earlier migrations either accepted or resisted the process of acculturation. The poet of the Gilded Age, writing both as immigrant and as resident, reacted to the abundant stimulation of this subject. As America held wide her gates, the poet-citizen could be seen discussing—often in connection with particular national groups—special problems resulting from this virtually indiscriminate acceptance of Europe's multitudes. Surveying the scene as a whole, he expressed a clear general philosophy.

National groups which had been prominent, proportionally, in the days of early America and which had ceased to number significantly in nineteenth-century patterns of migration—such as the Scottish and the French—were mentioned favorably and infrequently. The two groups from Northwest Europe who

UNRESTRICTED IMMIGRATION AND ITS RESULTS—A POSSIBLE CURIOSITY OF THE TWENTIETH CENTURY.
THE LAST YANKEE.

dominated migration statistics to the United States throughout the nineteenth century—the Irish and the Germans—occupied the major attention of the poet when he wrote on national groups from this general area. Both of these groups—according to the poet—raised special problems in acculturation: the Germans a religious and the Irish a political one.

With the German, the problem centered on the clash between the free and easy "Continental Sabbath" and the strict, restrained observance of Sunday laws in many parts of America. Germans were warned to "leave Teutonic heresies at home," to learn to appreciate the freedom America did offer.¹ Apart from this major issue, the stolid "Dutchman" was occasionally pictured as too impossibly slow-witted for survival amid America's urban bustle; but seldom were "Yockop's Troubles in America" sufficiently serious to send him packing for the homeland.² More typically, the German was praised for his thrift, honesty, and industry, and welcomed as a useful infusion into America's lifeblood.

If the resident American poet had entertained any serious Papist fears he might have considered the Irish potentially more dangerous than the Germans; if he had read the superpatriotic outpourings of the Irish poets in America or thought back to the Fenian raids on Canada in the 1860's, he might have considered the Irish a dangerously incendiary minority. Apparently he did neither, for the only reservation expressed toward the Irish immigrant applied to the apparent ease with which he had been organized into a political bloc, and to the disproportionate power represented by "filthy Cork,/With tripled vote."³ In the repeated depiction of the nostalgic son of Erin who preferred his beautiful green isle even to California, one might detect some reservations concerning Irish adaptability; but, as with the German, the typical reaction was one of acceptance. The Irishman was credited with being a hard worker who usually succeeded, sometimes becoming "as rich as a Jew."⁴

The Jew, seldom identified by national origin, became for the poet a prototype, second only to the Chinaman, of the true alien whose culture clashed strongly with his own. Those who disliked the Jew depicted him as a cunning, covetous usurer and dispenser of shoddy merchandise who, when selling a suit of clothes, might grasp "a handful in the back" to prove " 'It's shust a fit for you!' " or who, when lending money, might unashamedly charge 9 percent interest, confident that God, looking down from above, would mistake the 9 for a 6.[5] The symbolic Shylock, already mentioned in Chapter IV, condemned —for the poet—not so much the Jew as the banker and speculator; but there is no denying the persistence of this appellation nor the anti-Semitic effect of its usage:

> The Jew at his best and worst, Jesus and Shylock
>   stand;—
> Galilee bred the one, the other a Christian land.[6]

As these lines show, the Jew was likely not only to be rejected as a type but also to be accepted as a type. Although the poet's response to the Jew shows a dismaying lack of experience with or knowledge of Jewish people, it is comforting to note that—even on this distant basis—the poet was generally disposed to accept rather than to reject. The preponderance of pro-Semitic poetry seemed to spring from three circumstances. First, the trial of Alfred Dreyfus, a Jewish French Army officer accused of treason, dragged itself out during these years and created a pro-Semitic cause among the many literary defenders of this unjustly accused man. Second, the persecution of Jews in Russia at this time added to the fires of indignation on behalf of that beleaguered people. Third, the first large-scale Jewish migration to the United States turned the poet's attention to the history of this interesting minority. Whether he decided, viewing the mass migration, that the Jew was cursed to wander the earth forever as a penalty for Jesus' death, or whether he decided that the Jew should be welcomed as Christ's fellow Hebrew, the poet typically concluded by offering the Jew his sincere if distant sympathy.

The most significant trend in the history of immigration during this period was furnished by the shift from the older sources of immigration in Northwest Europe to the "new immigration" from Southeast Europe. This latter group, which had comprised but 18.3 percent of our total immigration in the 1880's, rose to 51.9 percent in the 1890's and continued its dominance in the new century. Although some of his verse—particularly on the labor question—showed an awareness of this shift, the poet reacted to the national groups in this new immigration principally by ignoring them. The Jew, who figured heavily in the new immigration, attracted considerable attention, but was either identified as ·German or—more usually—mentioned without any national affiliation. Russians, Poles, Austrians, and other nationalities prominent in the new migration were barely noticed. Italians were the only group treated more than once or twice, and they attracted predominantly unfavorable attention. Italy was labeled proud, ignorant, and politically corrupt.[7] The undemocratic heritage of the Italian Carbonari was taken exception to, as were the tactics of Italian labor leaders.[8] "The Dying Gladiator" of a slum area moaned, "De Dago cut me wid a knife."[9] In fact only one poet, the settlement worker William E. Davenport, wrote of immigrant Italians with anything warmer than neutrality. In this unsympathetic reception of the newer immigrants may be seen the incipient attitudes which led to the quota system favoring the citizens of Northwest Europe.

Since the only important immigration law passed during this period was the Chinese Exclusion Act of 1882, it is not surprising that the poet recognized the issue by discussing the Chinese more extensively than any other national group. Even more than the Jew, the Asiatic was treated as a prototype of an alien culture; furthermore, the Chinese question was complicated by both economic issues and regionally differentiated attitudes within the United States. Poets in the far West were apt to insist that the "inferior blood, yellow, brown and tan" of the Chinese would taint our racial purity and that our only hope lay in stopping "Mongolian immigration."[10] Opening all the stops in the organ of xenophobia, the poet hid his fear of competition from Oriental labor behind accusations of opium addiction and barbaric eating habits ("grilled rats and mice"), or exploitations of cultural differences such as religious faith and female status.[11] "Bully for Blaine," cried the Californians, when that noted Republican spoke out against treaties with the Chinese which by allowing immigration would confront the American workingman with the prospect of "dire starvation."[12]

As one moves eastward in surveying this verse, a marked change can be noted. Writing from Chicago, a pro-labor poet was capable of distinguishing between racist and economic arguments:

> Here Labor stands, with back to wall.
> Behind her Asia's hopeless thrall,
> Whose limbs grow fitted to his chain,
> Whose dead nerves have lost sense of pain . . .
> Whose food is vermin, love is lust . . .
>
> Welcome, O! Brothers, free Chinese . . .
> He too, "pursues his happiness."
> But stem with all your force the waves
> Of immigrating Mongol Slaves . . .[13]

Reaching the Eastern United States, one is met by a wave of self-righteous disgust at the racism of the West Coast, a sentiment which barely exceeded that against the Asiatic. Eastern poets praised the Chinaman for his thrift, his industry, his lack of guile, and his acceptance of Christianity.[14] The West was condemned for using the Chinese worker to build railroads and then casting him aside like an "orange you have sucked," and for that mock justice which prescribed six months in jail for stealing a horse, "For killing a Chinaman—three!"[15] Underlining their arguments with references to America's traditional role, these poets told their contemporaries that Asiatics were no less acceptable than Europeans, and that the land of plenty and freedom had no right to hoard her treasures or deny them to any particular group.[16]

From this analysis of the poet's attitude toward particular groups of foreign origin, one may fairly judge the tenor of his general statements on tolerance and immigration policy. Toward those who had already arrived on American shores, the poet offered a sweeping benediction:

> I love you all, Mohammedan or Jew . . .
> For we are way-worn comrades and I go
> To share a splendid destiny with you.[17]

Uncle Sam was said to abhor "The Color Line" ("The sun shines on all, yellow, black, red, and white . . ."), to welcome "clans of every race, creed and color,"[18] and to treat them fairly:

> All nations gather on his lawn . . .
> And Irish, Dutch, or Chinaman,—
> He gives them all a chance, sir.[19]

Inspired by the exhibits from varied nations represented at the many fairs held during these years, the poet pointed with pride to the muti-national beginnings and continuings of his own country. As remarked in Chapter II, the American West was upheld—in spite of its attitude toward the Chinese laborer—as an unusually happy example of the melting pot at work. Kansas boasted that "Russian, Norwegian, German—all bloods under the sun/Here meet and mingle kindly."[20] Eugene Field, although outspoken against the Oriental, composed a series of lusty mining-camp ballads and a series of tender lullabies inscribed to various races and nations, both of which movingly exhibited an acceptance of Americans of whatever origin.[21] San Francisco's "International Settlement" furnished a continuing source of pride; endless lists of its component nationalities were triumphantly tabulated as California pictured herself a piebald mother to all.[22]

Some protests were heard from the "hyphenated bubbles" in Uncle Sam's melting pot who felt threatened by "Each jealous breeze" of dissension:

Must we always be aliens?
We men of foreign birth
Who have foresworn allegiance
To potentates of earth . . .
Must we be Scotch or Irish
When strife is at its worst?
Be Germans, French, or English,
When war-clouds o'er us burst? . . .
To love the songs of country,
The memory of hills
Whereon our feet have trodden,
No thought of wrong instills . . .[23]

The problem of whether the foreign-born citizen would, or even
could, adapt himself satisfactorily to the ways of his new land
was held a serious one by some poets; but even the author of
the lines quoted above placed much of the blame for hesitant
assimilation on the immigrant himself, and the poets who raised
this problem cast little doubt on America's tolerant acceptance
of her newest arrivals.

Almost inseparably related to this attitude toward foreign
minorities on American shores was the poet's appraisal of
continuing immigration. Within this latter framework more
varied and more serious reservations were expressed. Some
objected to unrestricted immigration as a continuing policy on
religious grounds, fearing the "heathen hordes" who were
thought to oppose our "Sabbath, Church, and school."[24] Some
objected on political grounds to "Europe's nihilistic bands,"
going so far as to blame Garfield's assassination on the whole
"foreign brood" who came here their "hellish plans to nurse."[25]
Some opposed on sociological grounds the foreign masses who
overcrowded our coastal cities and supported a breed of
"drunkards, thieves and harlots."[26] But the only sustained
reasoning against immigration came from those who opposed it
on economic grounds:

Europe's cheap labor market has supplied
Huns, Slavs, Poles, and Italians, untried,
On freer citizenship's higher plane.
Our native laborers cannot sustain
Their comfort-loving families on the wage
As left by blighting foreign competition;
Hence strikes, fights, violence, mark their debased
    condition.[27]

While Europe pours her scum upon our shore,
Mere vassals to some foreign prince our power,
To drive hard laborers' wages lower and lower,
And help retard Hope's great triumphal hour,

The people calmly sit and wait, for what?
Simply to see our country overflow
With men who seek to set our laws at naught.[28]

Aside from those who saw the continuation of unlimited immigration as a threat to American labor, no major objection was raised. Even those who seethed with indignation over the spectacle of "debased, illiterate" hordes succumbing to political exploitation still clenched their teeth and determinedly pointed out our duty to "keep ope the friendly door" so as to "purify the Earth."[29] Easily outnumbering the critics of immigration were those who felt that to keep "eager, thronging pauper feet" from our shores was tantamount to refusing a drink to the thirsty Jesus.[30] People of all lands were urged to consider America as a special place of refuge where they need fear "No despot's power."[31] Nor were the advantages of immigration confined to the newcomer. The United States would continue to benefit, the poet held, from infusions of "Alien blood" which would keep her "from content's anaemic sleep"; and tributes were penned in the Whitman manner to the "strong and beautiful" youths of other lands who would continually re-generate the native race.[32] One interesting point of view pre-ferred the "varied loveliness' resulting from immigration as opposed to the standardized crudity of paring "All shapes to market-needs" which would take place were new blood excluded.[33]

Thus the few sour notes of xenophobia were drowned out by a harmonious choir of mixed voices in praise of the value of foreign groups as American citizens, and the splendor of America's role as the unquestioning asylum for the oppressed, the land of unparalleled opportunity for the ambitious. While Congress was turning its back on the Chinese, the poet continued to open his heart—and to advocate the opening of his land—to immigrants of all races and colors, to future citizens from virtually all nations and climes. Trumpets sounding the call to America's international mission were never clearer or better tuned.

ii

The poet took note of five separate occasions when various groups raised the issue of national self-determination and freedom from what they considered to be foreign domination. Each of these occasions offered its own complexities; it is as impossible now as it was then to determine the "right" or the "wrong" of the insurgent or imperial side. What can be determined is an attitude. In all but one of these instances the government of the United States either turned its back on the nationalist group or else actively sought to subdue it; whereas the poet, in all but one of these instances, lent his voice to the support of the nationalist cause in question. If the American government was turning toward a defense of the international status quo, at least the American poet was consistent in upholding our revolutionary role as the friend of the oppressed, the foe of empire.

Two of these instances, involving Cuba and the Philippine Islands, will be treated in the succeeding section along with the other manifestations in verse of our war with Spain. Two of the others—the movement for Irish independence and the Boer

War—involved strong anti-English sentiment. Although many of these verses were written by recently removed sons of Erin; although many a Gilded Age politician made election-time capital by twisting the tail of the British lion; although the

From Erin's soil the Saxon foe
In shame shall be forever driven;
From Erin's sons who bear the woe,
The tyrants chain shall soon be riven,
And Erin's emerald isle shall be,
The Grand Freedom in the sea.

FREEDOM TO IRELAND.

Then up and arm at Erin's call
Ye FENIAN sons of Irish sires,
On every hill and mountain tall,
Arise and light your signal fires.
And swear to win with heart and hand,
The Freedom of your Native land.

Alabama claims and the Venezuela boundary dispute contributed notably to unfriendly feelings toward the English, it is still something of a shock to encounter strong Anglophobia in American verse. In this English-speaking land the poet learned his craft at the feet of Shakespeare, Milton and Wordsworth.

This indebtedness, made clear in numerous odes and sonnets of principally aesthetic significance, obviously did not prevent the poet-citizen from turning to fresh criteria as he judged the political behavior of nations.

Practically all the abundant collection of verse on the Irish question took the side of the oppressed Emerald Islanders. The protest ranged from humble pleas for food to militant demands for independence. Eulogies to Emmet, Parnell, O'Connell, and Tom Moore were joined with lists of Irish contributions to independence, both here and there. Appealing to common elements in the past of both countries, the Irish-American poet attacked without restraint an England

> So cankered with Commerce, so corrupted with gold,
> So hungry for Empire, so thirsty for blood,
> So cruel to man and so false to God![34]

With varying degrees of subtlety and from differing points of view, the poets expressed their grief for an unfortunate land:

> Oh, when shall be surcease of thy bitter wrong? . . .
> Of Famine, of Slaughter, and sore feudal blows;
> And misrule and greed are joined hand in hand . . .[35]

Some called "upon her children,/Exiled" to keep alive the cause of the homeland.[36] Others coyly raised the possibility of American aid, publishing poems to Emmet and to Erin alongside such statements as: "Uncle Sam needs more expansion/For a giant of his size."[37] As the prospects for American intervention in Cuba increased, a parallel with the plight of Ireland was developed. The following lines could easily have been applied to either cause:

> While o'er our land the stars and stripes
> Float freely far and wide,
> Oppression holds an iron sway
> Upon the other side. . . .

> Let justice crush beneath her heel
> Bold tyranny and pain . . .[38]

As some poets saw Cuba, so others saw "The Emerald Isle" as an Ariadne, enslaved and awaiting a "true Prince in armor,/ From out of the west."[39] Direct demands for action ("America . . ./Reach out your hands with help to us")[40] became more outspoken after the outbreak of hostilities with Spain:

> Erin . . .
> Has been troubled by tyranny;
> I wish that Erin was in Cuba,
> And then Erin would be free . . .
>
> O Ireland is weeping
> Looking for her freedom . . .
> But let Dewey cross the Irish channel,
> England then is bound to go.[41]

By thoroughly squelching the Fenian attacks on Canada in the late 1860's, the United States government showed what it thought of militant action on behalf of Irish nationalism. By putting the Irish in the same category as the American revolutionaries of 1776 or the oppressed Cubans of 1898, the American poet took a vigorous stand on the side of free and independent Eire.

For many poets interested in promoting Ireland's cause, the Boer War simply furnished a new vantage point from which to continue the attack on England and empire. Discussing "Kruger's Enemy," one poem moved readily from cursing the English in Africa to complaining of "murdered Irish mothers— murdered with their babes unborn."[42] England was chided for her land policies in Africa and Ireland, and verses supporting the Boers appeared side by side with such titles as "The Spirit of Erin."[43]

But whether or not the poet favored the wearing of the Green, the English actions in Africa sat ill with him. Only one poet defended the English course of action, as against the many who blushed "for the shame of Saxon sin" as they pictured the Boers standing firm for freedom against British "bullies maddened with thirst for gold!"[44] Placing the Dutch in South Africa in the same category with Negroes under slavery or Cubans under General Weyler, the American poet implored,

> Shall hatred, greed, and wrong,
> And cruel ignorance bear rule?
> How long, O Lord, how long![45]

The prevalent poetic attitude toward this issue, as well as the extent of interest aroused, may be judged from the career of one John F. Sleeper, who must merit the title of American poet laureate of the Boer War. In several closely printed pamphlets (two of which, according to the publisher, sold over nine thousand copies) he kept the American public informed of the march of events, consistently interpreting them as a dishonor to Victoria's reign, and attributing them to that "evil Arch Plotter," Joseph Chamberlain.[46] The Afrikander, on the other hand, evoked a sympathetic chord which, the poet felt, would echo long "in every Freeman's heart."[47] The resentment at British imperialism lay so deep in another poet's consciousness that he predicted as its consequence a major war which would change the face of civilization.[48] As an issue the Boer War was peculiarly complicated, for the Dutch in South Africa were also empire-builders of a sort, who practiced a policy of enslaving the natives. To the poet, however, the debate simplified itself into terms of empire (British) versus national self-determination (Boer); and he beat the drum loudly and steadily on behalf of the latter cause.

The third episode was one which provoked the only use of American arms during this period other than in Cuba and the Philippines; and while brief, it was complex, involving as it did not only the Chinese government but most of the major European powers. Here the issue of empire versus national interests was clouded by the sporadic and seemingly senseless activities of the Boxers, who, to Western eyes, offered no discernibly constructive program; besides, America herself was involved. Nevertheless the Society of the Harmonious Fists, as they were sometimes called, did represent an open resentment of foreign encroachments; and had the poet extended his arguments on behalf of the Irish and the Boers, he might logically have sympathized with the Boxers. One poet did so, asking "Are Our Motives Pure?" and questioning whether it was "sheer virtue with no hope of gain" which prompted our intervention in Peking.[49] Among a mere half-dozen voices raised on this issue it is doubtless significant that even one questioned intervention at a time when American lives had been lost and American honor was presumably at stake. The others sided with the government in censuring the Boxers and praised McKinley for his attitude toward this uprising. Only in his reaction to the Boxer Rebellion did the poet agree with official policy in encouraging the suppression of a group which fought against the inroads of foreign imperialism; and here the evidence was quantitatively meager and not unanimous.

Other episodes on the international scene elicited scattered response and further developed the consistency of the poet-commentator's attitude. His reactions to the Venezuelan boundary dispute underlined his antipathy to England and to empire.[50] Even though he strongly favored the idea of an Isthmian canal, his respect for the national rights of Nicaragua and Panama was sufficiently sincere to provoke criticism of high-handed American measures aimed at obtaining canal rights from the countries in question.[51] Respecting the Monroe Doctrine as an anti-imperial measure, the poet was quick to condemn his own nation when he thought she might be taking undue advantage of her relations within the hemisphere. Thus, the poet-statesman wrote with remarkable consistency on the side of local freedom and independence and against foreign domination, whether diplomatic or economic, whether British or American, and whether within or without the hemisphere.

iii

To the poet the cause of the oppressed Cubans appeared at least as attractive as that of the Irish or Boers—and so much more convenient! Happily in accord, for once, with both popular sentiment and government policy, he joined with vigor the ranks of the Hearsts and Pulitzers in pointing out to Americans their duty in the Caribbean, in sharing their horror over the *Maine* disaster, and in enjoying the splendid spring skirmish which ensued—and waxed as confused as the politicians over the Philippine dilemma. His comment on this entire chain of events —from the earlier Cuban insurrections to the subjection of Aguinaldo and his men—accounted for nearly half the verse dedicated to foreign questions.

Ill feeling between Cuban patriots and their Spanish rulers had been evident at least since 1825, and even in the verse published after 1876 expressions of sympathy for the Cubans appeared long before the revolt of 1895 which led to the Spanish-American War. A volume published in 1896, for example, praised a General Lopez who transported troops from New Orleans to aid the beleaguered Cuban patriots in 1851, and who was executed for his pains.[52] The revolt which lasted from 1868 to 1878 came closer to involving the United States than any previous outbreak, the House of Representatives going so far in 1869 as to pass a resolution expressing sympathy for the Cuban insurrectionists. The outbreak of this revolt was recorded in one volume,[53] while another contained the following lines dated 1873 (the year of the *Virginius* episode):

> Lift up a wailing voice, ye waters,
> And cry aloud, O, earth! to God;
> Nor cease till are avenged His children,
> Whose life blood freshly stains the sod.[54]

In a verse dated 1875 a poet offered abuse to Spanish tyranny and praise for the patriot leader Alaro;[55] in 1878 another poet chided the United States about her "younger sister," Cuba, who lay "gashed and bleeding" and "implored thy aid":

> Where now, Columbia, is thy prideful boast,
> Late voiced to all the winds . . . that nevermore
> Beneath the flame from Freedom's banner tost,
> The slave should crouch, nor proud oppression's host
> Beat down the helpless?[56]

The next year Columbia was again implored to reach out her "powerful hand" to aid that "Poor, bleeding Isle," and murmurings against Spanish tyranny were heard again in 1880 and 1883.[57] Between the mid-eighties and 1895 the published verse was free from references to Caribbean troubles, but a considerable backlog of partisan protest had already been accumulated before the outbreak of the crucial revolt of 1895.

Although it is difficult to pin poems to the calendar with any precision, it is plain that a great many verses were either written or published between 1895 and the entry of America into armed conflict, and that the poet therefore played a role in encouraging his country to come to the aid of the beleaguered Isle. The usual content of such verses may be gauged from the extracts cited in connection with earlier Cuban revolts, pointing as they did to a land "dissevered by crimes mountain high" committed by that "brigantine Spaniard."[58] The particular villainy of "Butcher" Weyler was frequently specified in connection with the *"reconcentrados,"* while Weyler's counterpart, the Cuban leader Maceo, was attracted considerable praise and encouragement even after his death.[59] The Cuban cause, ran the reasoning of the poets, shared much with that of the patriots of 1776 and the defenders of the Negro; it represented "The spirit of Freedom [which] rests couchant—unawed, unfrightened, serene" and which would never be defeated.[60]

But did we declare war on Spain to bring freedom to Cuba or simply because we were provoked? There is, of course, no final answer to such a question; but it may be worth our while to determine which motivation dominated the poetic mind; for, after all, an idealistic aim such as succoring the oppressed differs greatly from automatic vengeance. One or two poets were provoked by imputed Spanish slights on American valor and responded with taut-lipped threats:

> We are not a warlike nation;
> We love living more than dying;
> We have little time for swagger,
> And the military strut. . . .
> But . . .[61]

The loudest cries for retribution, however, arose after the sinking of the *Maine.* Most poets bent on either urging or justifying our entry into war mentioned both the cause of Cuban freedom and vengeance for the *Maine,* but the relation between these two appeals was a varied one. For some,

"Remember the *Maine!*" was simply a rallying cry, marshalling us toward our important objective:

> Ye who remembered the Alamo,
> Remember the Maine!
> Ye who unfettered the slave,
> Break a free people's chain![62]

Or, similarly, the sinking of the *Maine* could serve as an excuse for following the dictates of a deeper conscience:

> Shud Uncle Sam find out
> Dem Spanyerds sunk de Maine,
> An' blew dem sailors in de sea,
> A great big wah wud kum 'bout—
> Like cullud men in Linkum's reign,
> Dem Cubans wud be free.[63]

On the other hand, a mother might tell her children that daddy had gone to "avenge the *Maine's* murdered dead," while seeming almost incidentally to add, "Down-trodden Cuba we must set free."[64] Even a causal connection was suggested: "Freedom for Cuba, the price of the Maine."[65] The extreme was represented by those who ignored the Cuban natives entirely, calling the sinking of the *Maine* a "Colossal crime! blackest in history!" and accusing Spain of deliberate intent.[66] Poets in this camp set up a bloodthirsty howl for retribution and were only satisfied when they could label Dewey the "avenger of the *Maine*" or credit the ghost of this sunk ship with the victory at Manila.[67] Numerically, however, (at a ratio of about three to one) the profounder motive of concern for Cuba outweighed the arguments of those who demanded an eye for an eye.

For whatever reason they urged our entry, most poets were impatient for the shooting to start; and they criticized both Cleveland and McKinley for delaying the cause of justice. Cleveland was rebuked for the "rust" on his executive pen;[68] McKinley was urged to get together with Hanna and resolve on action:

> Poor spent Cuba, starved Cuba, is bleeding
> And for our intervention is pleading
> And why mock we her grievous suspense?
> Why McKinley sits on the fence
> Awaiting events![69]

More than by political inaction, the poet was infuriated by the suspicion that America was being kept out of the war for economic reasons:

> Shall half a gross of merchants—
> The Shylocks of the trade—
> Barter your heart, and conscience, too,
> While Freedom is betrayed?[70]

Conversely, the suspicion of economic interest provided an even stronger argument for those few cool heads who opposed the declaration of war. The "Wall Street clan" was suspected of wishing to humble Spain in order to preside at the division of spoils; arguments in favor of war were said to include pork profits, wheat corners, and "fortunes . . . in lard."[71] "I want fair Cuba for my trade, that's all," "Imperial Sam" was made to boast as the poet expressed his dread of both economic and political aggression:[72]

> Cuba, contiguous to a great grasping nation!
> Thou fair, fertile island, we must thee obtain!
> 'Twill cover with glory the administration,
> To extort thee from old, emasculate Spain. . . .
> A whole party's hounds bay for thee in chorus;
> The party is dominant, efficient, and brave . . .[73]

Although this fear that America might be turning into a greedy, grasping nation appeared with much greater insistence in connection with our resolution of the Philippine dilemma, one poet—as early as 1896—was ready to apply the curse of jingoism to our attitude toward Cuba:

> A jingo, in his fighting gear,
> Swept with his eye the earthly sphere. . . .

He saw the sword and burning brand
Turned loose on many a helpless land,
And, fired with zeal, he cried, "What bliss!
Our country must get in on this."[74]

America was once the enemy of "wars/For greed of gold or land," but now

She is become an armed, imperial power,
Crushing a weaker people to her will.
Let freedom's banner then to earth be hurled!
And raise the despot's flag of the grim old world.[75]

Those who sought to place a cool hand on America's fevered brow, anxious for the war bonnet, did not deprecate the plight of the Cuban patriots. They did argue, however, that Spain should be given a chance to settle her own difficulties and that Americans should be persuaded to take a more reasonable attitude toward the *Maine* disaster. The following lines, dated Good Friday, 1898, spoke for the minority who opposed the war:

Subdue Thy people's fiery will,
And quell the passions in their breast!
Before we bathe our hands in blood. . . .
Speak from Thy throne a warning word
Above the factions' din.[76]

Once the bugles had sounded, however, the poet bent himself to the task of providing words for our marching songs:

Behold! we have gathered together our battleships
   near and afar;
Their decks they are cleared for action, their guns
   they are shotted for war:
From the East to the West there is hurry . . .
Of hammers in port and shipyard . . .
Thou are weighed in the Scales and found wanting, the
   balance of God, O Spain![77]

Most of the lines devoted to the war, both during and immediately following it, addressed themselves to apotheosizing America's newest rank of heroes, among whom Admiral Dewey was proclaimed the grandest by far. Hailed as victor and agent of the Gods, welcomed home with lavish encomiums, encouraged to political aspirations, Dewey was subjected—after this first wave of sincere admiration—to perhaps the most outrageous series of puns, distortions, and other light-hearted indignities in the history of American verse. The possibilities latent in his name proved irresistible; the poet succumbed to temptation with such phrases as "Yankee Dewey Dandy," "Dew-way with the Spaniard," and "The doughty deed that Dewey did."[78] Obviously carried away, the poet even made light of his before-breakfast victory at Manila: " '*Damn the fishballs! Go ahead!*' "[79] Fortunately, the inevitable reaction soon set in, as one sated bard claimed superiority over his colleagues for not celebrating Dewey "in a lot of limpy verse."[80]

After the Admiral, other heroes paled by comparison; but it might be worth noting that the poet's second favorite was Lieutenant Hobson of the *Merrimac*; that McKinley—third in popularity—was the only war figure to receive any adverse comment; and that this uncritical attitude extended even to Sampson and Schley, who doubtless deserved less than total praise but who were next in favor with the versifier. Colonel Roosevelt, who received more attention than any of the regular army officers, was here described "As his men see him":

> Open's the field for the future fight,
> Teddy's the lad we're after!
> Level his head; he'll uphold the right—
> Teddy who fought with Shafter.[81]

Mentioned as often as Teddy himself, and with fewer political overtones, were the Rough Riders, those brawny "Centaurs of the West" who rode "reckless of the rein" to victory.[82] Clara Barton and her Red Cross workers completed the ranks of those singled out by the poet-historian of the war for special honor.

Besides canonizing America's heroes, the poet summed up the war in a number of ways. The principal effects, he noted, were the realization of a "Cuba Libre" ("freedom has come to the slave") and "The Passing of Spain from the Western Hemisphere" as a consequence of God's righteous judgment.[83] To those who took note of internal affairs there was heartening evidence of reunion between North and South, as the Negro soldier proved his loyalty and courage, and as "Fighting Joe" Wheeler assumed a command alongside his erstwhile Northern foes.[84] To those who looked toward international affairs there was a whetting of appetites for further extension of American power and influence. Here a poet explained to Russia, Germany, France, England, as well as Spain, that the world had better make room for America:

> E'en as men grow, so do nations; all expansion
>   leaves behind
> Narrow mind and narrow limits for the wider lands
>   and seas . . .[85]

For some our motives had been justified:

> For plunder Caesar's countless legions died,
> Napoleon made war to feed his pride;
> But thou, Columbia, girdest on thy sword
> In freedom's cause, to battle for the Lord.[86]

Others took a soberer and more negative view, calling victory "A lying, leering, loathsome mockery"[87] and mourning the dead of both sides:

> Tho' we boast of Manila—
> And remember the Maine—
> There is mourning at home,
> There is mourning in Spain![88]

> There is "great rejoicing at the nation's capital,"
>   so says the morning's paper.
> The enemy's fleet has been annihilated.
> Mothers are delighted because other mothers have
>   lost sons just like their own.
> Wives and daughters smile at the thought of
>   new-made widows and orphans . . .
> This is life—this is patriotism—this is rapture![89]

The more humane of the war-inspired quotations, "Don't Cheer, the Poor Devils are Dying," rose to precedence over more savage battle cries,[90] as prominent poets, including Stephen Crane, gave voice to the inevitable disillusion with violence:

> Do not weep, maiden, for war is kind.
> Because your lover threw wild hands toward the sky
> And the affrighted steed ran on alone,
> Do not weep.
> War is kind.[91]

In this mood of disenchantment the poet re-appraised the causes and conduct of the war, ascribing to necessity what he had formerly held as heroic, honoring the gallant of Spain—especially Admiral Cervera—alongside the brave of America. Instead of valor in battle he was apt to focus on examples of mismanagement—such as the "embalmed beef" scandal—or to insist that the steady competence of the regular soldier was worth more than the flashy heroism of the volunteer.[92] As a final sign that the war had settled into perspective, the poet returned once more to the problems of domestic economy and a struggle which captured his more abiding interest:

> Remember the Maine, but do not forget
> The miners shot down in the street;
> Remember the starving Cubans—yes!
> And the battle for bread and meat.[93]

The war with Spain had come and gone. In spite of a few sober and dissenting notes it had found the poet ready to interpret America's mission as an active one in behalf of nationalists struggling for independence; and for once the government agreed. Although the poems which expressed a resistance to the dominant mood may be more impressive at a later date, it is true that the poet urged us to war with enthusiasm and impressive unanimity, that he encouraged us in battle and enjoyed the victory to the fullest, and that the outcome left him in a mood for the further extension of American influence. This mood must be fully appreciated before the significance of his reaction to the next problem on the international scene can be understood.

This next problem—what to do with the Philippines—came into view almost before the wreckage of the Spanish fleet ceased smoking in Manila Bay. As the poet saw it, this situation differed from the Cuban question in two important ways. In the first place these islands lay well beyond the jurisdiction of the Monroe Doctrine, and their acquisition was impossible to justify, at that time, in terms of national defense. In the second place the Philippine natives, unlike the Cuban patriots, had never sought our intervention, and considered American rule just as antipathetic to local interests as the dominion of Spain had been. These two differences made the Philippines a new kind of problem, albeit one we have faced repeatedly since, one with striking mid-century parallels in Japan, Korea, and Southeast Asia. The debate in which the poet engaged over this crucial problem remains both moving and timely; the steps our government took commit us still.

In spite of the full head of expansionistic steam with which the poet cruised the waters of his day, less than half the verses written on the Philippine question indicated a willingness to steer the course prescribed by the government in its determination to quell the resistant natives. Support for the official position would have been decidedly meager had not a good many poets felt sympathy for the forgotten man of that hour—the

American soldier engaged in this unpopular war. In seeking to credit the efforts of those who fought against the Tagals, some poets felt called upon to defend the cause itself as worthy.[94] Seemingly hard pressed to discover advantages in American possession of these islands, the poets mentioned their beauty, their advantages for Oriental trade and their attractiveness to European empire-builders. The principal arguments in support of American action, however, developed in three directions. The first, and the most crudely provincial, worked up a magnificent resentment against the aborigines for their failure to appreciate the advantages of what we were offering them:

> Say, Aguinaldo,
> You little measly
> Malay moke,
> What's the matter with you?
> Don't you know enough
> To know
> That when you don't see
> Freedom,
> Inalienable rights,
> The American Eagle,
> The Fourth of July,
> The Star-Spangled Banner . . .
> All you've got to do is ask for them?
> Are you a natural born chump
> Or did you catch it from the Spaniards?

"We'll civilize you Dead or alive," concluded this verse, as Aguinaldo was threatened with extinction unless he awoke to his "golden glorious opportunities."[95] As much as these lines may read like satire, they do represent the strong conviction of one group of poets that anyone who resisted American culture— even though it had been delivered without request—should be ranked as an utter ingrate.

A closely related argument was expressed by the "little brown brother" point of view:

> Talk of government by consent of the governed?
>   that is well,
> You who take the Declaration for the sole true
>   guiding star;
> Do you govern so your children till they learn
>   to read and spell?
> Filipinos are but children and half-savage—
>   there you are.[96]

Poets who argued in this manner also resented, of course, the failure of the Filipinos to welcome us with open arms. Rather than argue with them as equals, they preferred to think of disciplining them as one would one's children. This attitude was, to be sure, hardly less provincial or condescending than the one expressed above, albeit less violent. The third argument in support of quelling the Philippine insurrection was the simplest and perhaps the weakest of all: something started must be finished. "Y've got tu lick 'em now," ran this line of thought; and the job had best be done quickly and forcefully.[97]

In contrast, the majority point of view in opposition to American policy in the Philippines followed but one main argument: a protest that we had sold our most cherished principles for the benefit of special interests.

> To hell with "national honor" that needs
> A triumph over a stripling nation!
> For "national honor" say "syndicate greeds,"
> And you've hit the nail on the right location.[98]

There was outrage at pumping "the beggars full of slugs" for the benefit of "impatient" missionaries and eager salesmen, and there were accusations that the "money-changers" had lured us onto "imperialist shoals" by hypnotizing us with "the luring voice of avarice."[99] But the central complaint was not directed merely at our apparent commitment to economic imperialism; rather, it was the reversal of our traditional international role which most upset these poets:

> Lies! Lies! It cannot be! The wars we wage
> Are noble, and our battles still are won
> By justice for us, ere we lift the gage.
> We have not sold our loftiest heritage.
> The proud republic hath not stooped to cheat
> And scramble in the market-place of war;
> Her forehead weareth yet its solemn star.[100]

Expressing his shocked disbelief at our refusal to defend the oppressed against more powerful forces, as he recalled our doing in our own Revolution, the poet flatly stated that the "blue-coats of Manila are the red-coats of King George."[101] As the foe of liberty we would become, he feared, an empire replete with "barbarous wars," a "President King" to die for in an ungrateful cause, wicked wealth, deceitful pomp, and "An Ireland of our Own" in the shape of the Philippines.[102] We had betrayed not only our political but also our religious heritage in our unchristian behavior toward the Tagals, thus meriting "The brand of Judas and of Cain, my country and my shame!"[103] In discarding both our Christian and libertarian heritage we were doing in the Philippines exactly what we had gone to war to stop Spain from doing in Cuba.[104]

Once dedicated to a policy of might over right and of greed over benevolence, America could not be trusted either at home or abroad. Armies could be turned on American citizens with as much justification as they had been turned on the Tagals, the poet feared; and, looking into our international future, he prophesied that

> We will give the Declaration,
> And the Constitution, too,
> To possess Zamboangan,
> And the Island of Sulu.[105]

One of the most interesting comments on this whole sequence of events in the Caribbean and the Pacific was contributed by that eminent Spanish-American, George Santayana. Under the title

"Young Sammy's First Wild Oats" he pictured an adolescent America consorting with three mulattoes: Cuba, Porto Rico, and "Filipina." Playful in its mood, this poem regarded American behavior with a surprising indulgence when one considers the likely sympathies of the author. But when the subject turned to "Young Sammy's" treatment of Filipina, the mild and indulgent tone completely disappeared; for, when Filipina shrank from Sam's caress,

> His contemptible demeanor
> Isn't easy to express,
> First he bought her, then he kicked her;
> But the truth is, he was drunk,
> For that day had crowned him victor,
> And a Spanish fleet was sunk.[106]

The poet, reversing his stand in support of American intervention in Cuba, found himself once again at odds with his government, albeit consistent with his own interpretation of America as the friend of those who struggled against foreign domination. That a majority of the poets could overcome the rising tide of expansionistic sentiment—even within their own ranks—and express themselves critically of America's precedent-setting commitment in the Philippines, showed a strong devotion to a certain concept of America's revolutionary tradition and a powerful sense of the ultimate consequences of our actions in the Pacific.

In passing favorable judgment on most of his foreign-born neighbors, and in expressing a strong belief in toleration and unrestricted immigration, the poet showed his dedication to the idea of America as the welcome haven for the world's oppressed. While his government felt the need to protect the country from the peaceful invasion of Oriental labor, the poet felt that America need strengthen herself only by continuing to admit and to absorb the varied races of the globe. Whereas the advent

of support for the restriction of immigration might have been
detected in the poet's hesitant reception of the advance guard of
the "new" immigration, still as a group he would overwhelmingly have seconded Emma Lazarus in her famous greeting:

> . . . Give me your tired, your poor,
> Your huddled masses yearning to breathe free,
> The wretched refuse of your teeming shore.
> Send these, the homeless, tempest-tost to me,
> I lift my lamp beside the golden door!

The poet urged the expansion of his country not only through
absorbing emigrants from whatever land, but also through the
extension of American influence to such places as Cuba, Ireland,
and even South Africa. While the official American attitude
toward such groups as the Irish and the Boers was not favorable,
the poet maintained that these people were engaged in a fight for
freedom against empire, as we had been engaged in 1776, and
that it was an American duty to abet all such causes. If the
beginnings of America's conservative international role could be
seen in governmental policy at the turn of the century, at least
the poet held high the torch of idealism, reminding his fellow
citizens of their commitment to those who struggled against
foreign domination toward national freedom. In such a mood
the poet readily distinguished between imperialism and his own
brand of expansionism. He did so by taking England roundly to
task for her attitude toward the Irish and the Boers, and in the
Venezuelan boundary dispute; nor did he hesitate to condemn
his own country for what he considered the imperialistic aspects
of her behavior, principally in the case of the Philippine insurrection, but also in Cuba, Central America, and even China.
Tempering his mood of expansionism with his fear of materialistic and militaristic behavior, the poet contributed an eloquent
statement in behalf of the spirit which had fought against
empire and freed the slaves.

NOTES

[1] *Last Strike for Liberty*, 44–45.
[2] Cox, *Hans Von Pelter's Trip to Gotham*; Butterfield, *Poems* (1887 edition), 107–8.
[3] *Mugwumpiad*, 3ff.; Sloan, *Telephone of Labor*, 167.
[4] Fuller, *From the Cradle to the Grave*, 51.
[5] Elmore, *Love among the Mistletoe*, 103–5; Wolcott, *Song-Blossoms*, 173–74.
[6] Koopman, *Morrow Songs*, 51.
[7] Butterfield, *Poems* (1880 edition), 6–7; *Burlingtoniad*, 5.
[8] *Devil's Visit*, 77; Haywood, *Peter Duikel Spiel*, n. pag.
[9] Major, *Lays of Chinatown*, 23.
[10] Cudmore, *Poems and Songs*, 71, 53.
[11] *Gynberg Ballads*, 5–8; Sutherland, *Songs of a City*, 89–90; Buell, *Kodaks*, 83; Field, *Little Book of Tribune Verse*, 176–77.
[12] Kercheval, *Dolores*, 378; Cudmore, *Prophecy of the Twentieth Century*, 21.
[13] Sloan, *Telephone of Labor*, 70–71.
[14] Sproull, *Hours at Home*, 22–25; McCardell, *Olde Love and Lavender*, 86; Meeser, *Sweet Memories*, 52–53, 89–91; Tarbox, *Songs and Hymns of Common Life*, 252–53.
[15] Howell, *Next door*, 80–83; Howard, *Later Poems*, 95.
[16] Ball, *Merrimack River*, 5–6; Davenport, *Perpetual Fire*, 48–50.
[17] Putnam, *Banquet*, 37.
[18] Hildreth, *Echoes from My Song Realm*, 167; Blagden, *Some Sweet Poems*, 75.
[19] *Yankee Doodle*, n. pag.
[20] Allerton, *Walls of Corn*, 46.
[21] Field, *Little Book of Western Verse*, 1–17; *Second Book of Verse*, 124–25, 151–52.
[22] Williams, *'49 to '94*, 2–12.
[23] Bryce, *Random Rhymes*, 53–54.
[24] Richards, *Shifting Scenes*, 120; Lozier, *Your Mother's Apron Strings*, 70–73.
[25] Welburn, *American Epic*, 260; Suttill, *Works of the Poet Coachman*, 119.
[26] Carter, *Duck Creek Ballads*, 114; Lampton, *Yawps*, 36.
[27] Treuthart, *Milliad*, 295.
[28] Allsworth, *Tales and Legends of Two Republics*, 44.
[29] Crowninshield, *Tales in Metre*, 115.
[30] Wise, *Optimist*, n. pag.
[31] Smith, *Libertas*, 46–47; Scholes, *Thoughts in Verse for Kind Hearts*, 187.
[32] Crowninshield, *Pictoris Carmina*, 11; Davenport, *Beggar-man of Brooklyn Heights*, 6.
[33] Crowninshield, *Painter's Moods*, 88.
[34] Realf, *Poems*, 95.
[35] McKinnie, *From Tide to Timber-line*, 34.
[36] Ryder, *Verses and Prose Selections*, 43–44.
[37] Joyce, *Complete Poems*, 83–84, 86–87.
[38] Ford, *Garlands of Thought*, 45.

[39] Collins, *New Year Comes*, 63.

[40] Magee, *In the Fields*, 142.

[41] Herrald,*Herrald's Book of War Songs*, 46, 47.

[42] O'Brien, *Birth and Adoption*, 181.

[43] McIntosh, *Songs of Liberty*, 34; Golden, *Criticism of Things in General*, 21, 22, 23. For similar associations, see Coates, *Mine and Thine*, 114–16; Dozier, *Galaxy of Southern Heroes*, 17–24; McCarthy, *Round of Rimes*, 26ff., 86ff.

[44] Harman, *Freedom's Footprints*, n. pag.; Crosby, *Swords and Plowshares*, 45.

[45] Henderson, *Bit Bookie of Verse*, 61.

[46] Sleeper, *Freedom's Triumph*, 7; *March of Oliver*, 7.

[47] Sleeper, *Tocsin*, 19.

[48] Thorwis, *Cumaean Sibyl's Prophecy*.

[49] Currie, *Sonnets and Love Songs*, 17, 18.

[50] Kenney, *Some More Thusettes*, 10; Major, *Lays of Chinatown*, 76.

[51] Terry, *Our Pumpkin Vine*, 55; LaMarsh, *Lux Christi*, n. pag.

[52] Pelton, *Greenwood*, I, 213–14.

[53] Ewing, *Poems on United States History*, 196.

[54] From a verse titled "Cuba's Victims," Hoffman, *Memorial Songs*, 17.

[55] Conway, *Complete Poems*, 67–101.

[56] Johnston, *Galileo*, 65.

[57] Menard, *Lays in Summer Lands*, 22; Donahoe, *Pedro and Miguel*; Day, *Lyrics and Satires*, 22.

[58] Robinson, *New Woman*, 284.

[59] Foss, *Dreams in Homespun*, 213–14.

[60] Hale, *Autumn Lane*, 136.

[61] Rogers, *For the King*, 57.

[62] Hovey, *Along the Trail*, 4–5.

[63] Beard, *Life Lines*, 121.

[64] Woodward, *Darkness and Dawn*, 27.

[65] Wingard, *Echoes*, 34.

[66] Leighton, *Prairie Songs*, 115.

[67] Marine, *Battle of North Point*, 93–95.

[68] Cleveland, *Scarlet-veined*, 90.

[69] Van Slingerland, *Love and Politics*, 283.

[70] Major, *Lays of Chinatown*, 78.

[71] Kelley, *Age of Gold*, 20–21; Shadwell, *America*, 1.

[72] Swift, *Advent of Empire*, 10.

[73] Gill, *Musings by Pequit Brookside*, 119.

[74] Burgoyne, *Songs of Every Day*, 125. By the time America declared war, however, this poet had swung to an attitude in support of our policy.

[75] Shadwell, *America*, i.

[76] Dandridge, *Joy*, 195–96.

[77] Cawein, *Idyllic Monologues*, 99.

[78] Harris, *Uncle Sam's Latest Yankee Doodle*, n. pag.; Cake, *Devil's Tea Table*, 144; Bangs, *Cobwebs from a Library Corner*, 90.

[79] Bangs, *Cobwebs from a Library Corner*, 61.

[80] Bixby, *Memories,* 117–18.

[81] Norys, *Flag That Won*, 40–41.

[82] Van Slingerland, *Love and Politics*, 311, 212.

[83] Atwood, *Kansas Rhymes*, 55; Cole, *In Scipio's Gardens*, 89–92.

[84] Bush, *Original Poems*, 8–10; Reidelbach, *Bubbles from Tippecanoe*, 123–25.

[85] Savary, *Poems of Expansion*, 5–9, 10.

[86] Hawkes, *Songs for Columbia's Heroes*, 44.

[87] Butler, *Isle of Content*, 91.

[88] Eldred, *Poems without a Muse*, 41.

[89] Crosby, *War Echoes*, 3.

[90] Johnson, *Now-a-Day Poems*, 15; Buchanan, *Indian Legends*, 87–88.

[91] Crane, *War is Kind*, 9.

[92] Brooks, *Pickett's Charge*, 52; Belknap, *Canalero*, 89–90.

[93] Claflin, *Variety from a Canvasser's Note Book*, 14.

[94] Elmore, *Twenty-five Years in Jackville*, 191–92; Gorham, *Bosky Dells and Sylvan Roads*, n. pag.

[95] Lampton, *Yawps*, 120–21.

[96] Savary, *Poems of Expansion*, 23.

[97] McGlumphy, *Village Verse*, 45.

[98] Putnam, *Lafayette Ode*, 30.

[99] Terry, *Our Pumpkin Vine*, 117; Thaw, *Poems*, 89; Dibble, *Prairie Poems*, 33.

[100] Moody, *Poems*, 15.

[101] Hunt, "*The Writing on the Wall*," 21.

[102] Morgan, *Morning Echoes*, 11; Swift, *Advent of Empire*, 12, 26; Dooling, *Rhymes without Treason*, 6.

[103] *Indictment*, 3.

[104] Milne, *For To-day*, 119; Crosby, *Swords and Plowshares*, 24.

[105] Dooling, *Rhymes Without Treason*, 3.

[106] Santayana, *Hermit of Carmel*, 212. ·

VIII

For Darwin, for Mammon, and for Country

IN ORDER TO ACHIEVE A TRULY REVEALING PORTRAIT, it is necessary to probe beneath surface features. Thus the poet contented himself not merely with strikes and elections, growing cities and flying temperance banners, but also labored toward a more fundamental representation of his age. In so doing he revealed a preoccupation with the impact of science, the inroads of materialism, and the interpretation of the national mission. Each of these subjects relates closely to specific conditions; each arose quite naturally out of the poetic response to the contemporary scene. On the other hand, the mood determined by these preoccupations had its indubitable effect upon the events themselves and upon particular reactions to them, so much so that these more abstract attitudes deserve their own important biographies and histories within the poetic consciousness. In coming to understand them, one comes also to appreciate most directly the character of the age.

i

In a span of years which saw the staging of the Agassiz-Gray debates, the coming, by way of German scholarship, of a "scientific" school of history, the founding of the magazine *Science*, the chartering of the "Church of Christ, Scientist," and the advent of the new sciences of human behavior, psychology and sociology, there can be no disputing the impact of the scientific habit of thought. The verse of the Gilded Age reflected this impact in a number of ways. In paying tribute to the achievements of industry (Chapter IV), in chronicling the rise of the city (Chapter III), and in recording reactions to the numerous international fairs, the poet dwelt at some length on the triumphs of applied science—the railroad, the telephone, the telegraph, the tall buildings and bridges, the rapid transit, the dynamos and steam engines. In discussing America's destined triumph over Indian and Spaniard (Chapters II and VII), in justifying or attacking her financial and industrial system, he showed his awareness of social arguments based upon evolutionary theory. But his susceptibility to the same influence was revealed in ways even more direct: not alone in the use of scientific words and phrases, but in his conscious determination to enter the debate concerning the ultimate effect of the new theories on man's picture of himself and his universe.

The invasion of the realm of poetry by the world of science manifested itself in some strange ways. A verse titled "Reflection," for example, opened with a testimony to the importance of "scientific questions," skipped glibly through a discussion of atoms and molecules, and then burst into a narrative concerning two clandestine lovers, caught in the act through their reflection in a mirror. It was ignorance of science which brought their downfall, moralized the bard, for they did not know that "the angle of incidence was equal to that of reflection.''[1] This verse illustrates two general ways in which the poets showed their awareness of science. One involved the deliberate concoction of usually humorous *jeux d'esprit*, often composed in the spirit of parody. "Darwinism in the Kitchen," for example, told the story of a servant girl who innocently picked a flea from her bonnet only to see it change before her eyes into a cricket, a frog, a monkey, and a man—whose presence she tried vainly to explain to her mistress.[2]

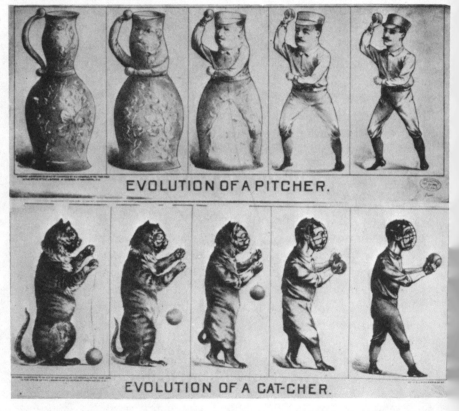

EVOLUTION OF A PITCHER.

EVOLUTION OF A CAT-CHER.

The second and more common device simply involved the intrusion of technical vocabulary into meter: "Paleontology

. . . Ozone . . . Neoplastic . . . Electrology.' "[3] Sometimes this new vocabulary added accuracy and vividness to the métier, as when the poet wrote of "Horrible disease, where microbes swarm."[4] Often the vocabulary of science only offered new ways of saying old things: "A laboratory is the universe . . ./Directed by the Master Chemist—God."[5] Humor was more typically the intended beneficiary of the verse-science merger: the class-reunion laureate could quip about the "Survival of the Fattest"; the upperclassman could identify the freshman as "a green, unknown,/Inorganic (?) moving substance"; and anyone bent on light-hearted vilification could label his target a "missing link."[6] Occasionally a superficial awareness of some scientific process could provide the poet with a serious and effective theme, as witness a verse springing from "A Lump of Carbon" burning in a grate to a description of "two Ichthyc beasts" who might have struggled under the ancient tree out of which was formed the poet's lump of coal.[7] As with the poet's adoption into his medium of new mechanical devices such as the railroad and the telephone, his blending of science and poetry was notable not for any spectacular enrichment of the verse but for evidence of the poet's growing consciousness of these new approaches to depicting the world in which he lived.

Of some interest in determining the nature of the attraction felt by poet is the manner in which he distributed his attention among the various branches of science. Chemistry and physics were ignored, relatively speaking, as was that new "science," psychology, about which a 1900 college yearbook had this to say:

> There once was a psychological lad,
> To whom "Movements of Mind" was a fad.
> On "The Theory of Dreams"
> He wrote wonderful themes.
> Why, they taught this same stuff to your dad.[8]

The occult sciences came in for their share of attention, as phrenology, astrology, and spiritualism were defended and attacked in roughly equal proportions. The major attractions, however, were astronomy, geology, and medicine—in order of ascending popularity. When the poet looked heavenward he did so either to inform his readers of celestial events—the approach of planets and comets, the occurrence of eclipses—or to draw comforting evidence of universal grandeur and divine glory in relation to man's tiny but unique role. Combining these two impulses, one poet held that "The Comet of 1882" demonstrated God's presence, while another praised the installation of a more powerful telescopic lens as a step toward His world.[9] When the poet looked earthward, he concentrated on explaining to his readers some phase in the development of the planet and the life it contained. Sometimes tempted by the urge to be facetious, he more frequently evinced a serious attitude toward his geologic materials, usually bringing into focus their significance in relation to the role of man. In tracing the geologic development of types, for example, a poet might pause to express the hope that man's usefulness would surpass that of the wingless bird.[10] Verse devoted to matters medical often offered nothing more than mnemonic devices for mastering elements of biology or anatomy, although pleas for better sanitary measures and more careful regulation of food and drugs were also voiced. Riming "morbific," "vivific," "splenic," "septicaemic," the poet of Hippocrates peppered his verse with more scientific terminology than any of his colleagues.[11] Comparable with today's "virus," the microbe of the Gilded Age enjoyed a celebrated ubiquity all its own, dominating verse-diagnoses while it worried the layman with its ability to inflate the doctor's bill.[12] Whether playful or purposeful, the verse relating to medical science was painfully specific, whereas the poetic excursions into astronomy and geology tended to bear on general problems related to man's place in time and the macrocosm.

The poet's interest was centered not upon any particular branch of science but upon a theory based principally on evidence from biology, though also relevant to findings in geology and astronomy. This was the theory of evolution—usually called Darwinism regardless of the relation of the particular item under discussion to the writings of the famous biologist. Nearly one-third of the poetry of science bore on this question, and roughly two-thirds of the writers who commented on evolution did so with an attitude of acceptance or approval. Specific tenets of the theory of evolution received verse support, and their principal propagator, Charles Darwin, was hailed as a man of great wisdom. On the other hand, this theory was labeled "Vain in each wild speculation" and flatly denied as a failure in attempting to explain the earth's origin and history.[13] "Evolution; by an Evolutionist" concluded that all is still "Unknown and all unknowable"; and the idea of natural selection was rejected as "Reversing facts in nature."[14] But the central objection to Darwinism arose from a misleading oversimplification of Darwin's ideas:

> We *never will* believe
> That man—was once a *monkey !*[15]
>
> . . . man did not spring from monkey,
> But *monkey descended from man !*[16]

To these poets the idea of kinship with the ape, however remote, proved too much to accept, and they exercised their ingenuity to the utmost in casting hypothetical dramas in the animal kingdom with the purpose of embarrassing the disciples of Darwin. "An Evolutionary Tradition," for example, pictured a convention of monkeys whose leader advised the assembled multitude to cut off their tails so that their brains would grow![17]

Much of the battle over evolution was fought not on scientific grounds but with regard for its social applications. In Chapter IV, it was noted how the poet introduced, then rapidly dismissed, the idea of social Darwinism as an explanation for economic inequities. Under the title "The Survival of the

Fittest," for example, a poet compared the millionaire's wealth to the bear's protective coat of fur, and then concluded that money alone would not insure survival.[18] In general, the poet refused to apply these impersonal theories as a social explanations because he felt them to be inhumane as well as inaccurate:

> Malthusian are the laws of life,
> And want doth ever check increase;
> A Darwin sees within such strife
> Conditions so selecting life
> The ill-adapted gasp and cease![19]

The most favorable adaptation of social Darwinism was made by the poets who urged America's destiny at the price of suppression of Indian or islander. The following lines expressed this point of view most fully:

> . . . peoples in process of selection,
> By virtue of "survival of the fittest,"
> On islands developed by accretion
> Still live, notwithstanding their condition,
> And that evolution by its latest
> Consigns them to certain extinction.[20]

The most extensive, and also the most violent, debate over the efficacy of Darwinism took place in the religious context. One extreme was exemplified by those poets who considered Darwinism as an outright competitor with religion. Writing of "Evolving worlds to perfect man," they gave to the "Light of Evolution" the credit for teaching man to play the "god-like part."[21] Claiming evolution as man's greatest heritage, they interpreted it as a force leading from materialism to wisdom and culminating in

> the last act
> of hell,—heaven's first:
> the deification of Man![22]

Not only was evolution adorned with attributes usually reserved for more spiritual ideas, but religious beliefs were also directly attacked. A faith in the Biblical version of the creation was accounted a hindrance to knowledge; and even improvement in the church itself was taken as an effect of evolution rather than a cause for religious belief.[23]

In numbers almost as great, however, poets declared their refusal to compromise religious and moral preconceptions for the sake of a lot of monkey business:

> I hold my grip on Genesis,
> And own it makes me spunky
> When these Darwinians try to trace
> Our species to a monkey.[24]

Now rationally attacking evolutionary hypotheses, now defiantly filling their pages with insults to Darwin, the poets who defended religious dogma based their rebuttals on their disappointment in the barren, amoral world they beheld through the eyes of the evolutionist:

> Such is the Evolutionist's theory!
> If such be true life indeed is dreary.
> Good and evil become the same,
> Oblivion o'er past and future will reign.[25]

> Thenceforth to evolution's
> Geology we say,—
> Nothing have we gained therefrom,
> And nothing have to pray. . . .[26]

If evolution brought knowledge—which to these poets was doubtful—it did so at the cost of faith, hope, and morality.

For every four poets who wished to reject evolution for religion's sake there appeared five who were ready to stand behind these new theories even at the cost of invading holy ground. Both camps were concerned with human progress and with the sources of knowledge; their debate concerned, essentially, the relative worth of evidence compiled by man as against

the revealed word of God. Between these two camps stood a
group of referees who proposed that one could profit from both.
Accepting the geologic concept of time, they made it a tribute
to the Bible's grandeur; accepting evolutionary theories of
creation, they moralized on both the insignificance and the
dignity of man; accepting natural selection, they pointed to
Christian progress from the cannibal to civilized man.[27] In
general, these reconcilers of evolution and religion endorsed
scientific postulates, with the reservation that the idea of
ultimate control and motivation be left to faith. The first "little
wave of motion/In a protoplasmic speck" was not impersonally
ordained, they argued, but was "Born of a divine impulsation."[28]
All evolution, this argument continued, had been carried out
"beneath God's thumb"; and the entire process may have been
nothing more nor less than a manifestation of the mind of God.[29]

Whether the poet argued in defense of evolution or of
religion, or whether he sought to reconcile the two, he showed
a great respect for—or a great fear of—these theories fostered
by science. This attitude was also reflected in the even greater
number of verses wherein the debate was transferred to a more
general level. Here the whole idea of science—rather than
simply the theories of evolution—was weighed and measured.
Typically it was either crowned with lavish praise—

> Only through Science can mankind
> Towards knowledge of the God advance;
> And not by theoretic chance
> The esoteric mystery find.[30]

—or flattered but warned to stay within its own realm:

> Teachers of science, minds profound,
> You chase the heavenly bodies 'round,
> Scan earth, rock, sea, heat, air and light,
> To prove your novel theories right.
> Test by God's word ere you can know
> That Science may not further go.[31]

Both approaches illustrated the profound respect in which science was held. Among the many ways in which the poets exhibited this respect—plainly apparent in both the acceptance and the rejection of science's ever-widening domain—two are of particular interest in exposing the underlying currents of the Gilded Age.

Most of the verses which placed a restraining hand on the proponents of the scientific approach did so in the fear that its increasing impersonality would abandon man to a dreary and hopeless materialism. The "dusty heap of facts" admired by science may keep us from the deeper thoughts of a Dante, complained one, in tones reminiscent of reactions to evolutionary theory.[32] Two others struck almost the same note of outrage at the theft of imagination's treasures by the cold hand of reason:

> You glibly settle things and say:
> From atoms grew,
> The great round world . . .
>
> The bed that science makes is short,
> It cramps me so . . .[33]
>
> Arcturus is his other name,—
> I'd rather call him star!
> It's so unkind of science
> To go and interfere![34]

Whether he pursued his plaint in a jocular vein—hoping the scientist would not proscribe kissing in sanitation's unsentimental behalf—or soberly regretted science's gift of iron where gold was sought,[35] the poet clearly disdained the material prizes with which science sought to distract him from race-old dreams of greater things:

> Man listens—ear to earth, and laboring buys
> Success with Science; yet how distant lies
> The glorious height to which his steps aspire![36]

To these poets, science, though feared and respected, told only the material half of the story, dividing the world into knowledge and myth, removing "hope, faith, patience . . . love."[37] The things that made life worth while for the poet—the mystery of creation, the meaning of the infinite, the fire of youth and love— would lie forever beyond the ken of the scientist, whether he admitted it or not. From ever-varying points of view these poets—even in the acceptance of some of science's accomplishments—warned their readers of the materialistic trap which lay ready for those who sought in science their ultimate sanctions and solutions.

The second point of interest in the poet's approach to science lay in his tendency to accept it—when he did so—in terms of thinly disguised nationalism and expansionism. In making this application he utilized a fallible logic, but he showed a spirit which stood ready to absorb questions however universal into the terms of American destiny. His reasoning ran as follows. In the first place, science was taken as an agent of man's regeneration:

> The outcast from the gutter, washed and trained,
> Infused with science, to his mind explained,
> Enthusiastic for the common weal,
> No longer left to starve, or beg, or steal,
> Shall show what man regenerate can do . . .[38]

In reclaiming society's outcasts, educating them to work for the common welfare, science especially benefited a nation which rested on a broad citizenry and which absorbed the world's refugees. And in elevating the depressed, science further served America by promoting equality and brotherhood:

> Our scientific progress
> Makes every man a man.

> We equalize resources
> By our scientific gain,
> Uniting men as brothers . . .[39]

Finally, science—as the enemy of oppression and the friend of truth—would best serve the land where oppression had been routed and truth enthroned; thus America, reasoned the poet, would be uniquely benefited.[40]

The verse of the Gilded Age exhibited a broad commitment to the ideas and vocabulary of science—theoretical and applied. The poet admired the convenience and prosperity which such developments had brought him, and he used scientific arguments to justify and to promote American expansionism. His majority report accepted the measures and meanings bequeathed him by the medical scientist, the astronomer, and the geologist as well as by the evolutionary theorists. But—even though he almost universally respected the authority of science within its own realm—he refused to apply social Darwinism to his domestic environment, and he voiced a vigorous minority protest against the limitations of a world defined solely in material terms. It is important to note that even his reactions to the general worth of science were often formed in a context of expansionism and materialism.

ii

Overlapping somewhat with the poet's interest in science was his concern with materialism. This theme—plainly visible in the reaction to every major movement and condition of the Gilded Age—was at least twice as important, numerically, as the reaction to science. It is impossible to characterize the poet's position without reviewing a great deal of what has gone before; but there is also much new testimony to be heard on this most important negative comment, a comment which in one sense supports the naming of this period, as we have, the Gilded Age.

Not all of the verse reaction to the materialism of the day was negative, however. To a noticeable extent certain poets accepted the material criteria which the greater number of their col-

ECKER, BOTH & KATZER's beautiful "STAR LAMP" is sent to any address, the world over, by THE SUPPLY AGENCY, 317 Lexington Avenue, New York.

THE GREAT BARTHOLDI STATUE,
LIBERTY ENLIGHTENING THE WORLD;
WITH THE WORLD RENOWNED AND BEAUTIFUL
STAR LAMP.

Showing, also, the Russian Corvette "STRELOK" (1); the British War Ships "GANNET" (2) and "CANADA" (3); also the U. S. Frigates "MINNESOTA" (4) and "OMAHA" (5), which saluted the "Liberty" bearing French Frigate "ISERE" (6); with New York City and Brooklyn Bridge—the largest in the world—in the distance.

The Statue of Bartholdi, 151 feet in height, is erected on Bedlow's Island, New York Harbor, and is mounted on a Stone Pedestal, 155 feet above mean low water, making the extreme length 305 feet. The "STAR LAMP," seen in the hand of "Liberty," DISPLAYS THE MOST POWERFUL LAMP LIGHT IN THE WORLD, AND THE Statue presents by night, as by day, an exceedingly grand and imposing appearance.

leagues so blatantly abhorred. In boosting the new West and the burgeoning cities some poets have already been revealed as devoted to that "wad a'/Ready cash laid by" or to those "Costly dwellings" by which achievement might, in their view, be justly measured.[41] Their acceptance of the politico-economic status quo often took the form of an endorsement of the materialist's emphasis on ruthless competition ("Root, Hog, or Die"), upon the necessity for narrow specialization ("The reason he makes money so,/He knows just what he needs to know"), and the willingness to applaud "an age of iron and steel" as superior to "an age of gold."[42] In recommending foreign expansion or in urging the exclusion of foreign labor, some poets were more than ready to couch their arguments in frankly materialistic terms. And when the occasion presented itself—frequently in the guise of a patriotic anniversary—for appraising the nation's achievements, it was not impossible to find America's virtue summarized in terms as crass as these:

> *Uncle Sam* is by option a son of high heaven,
> Inherits he all things by Deity given;
> Since firstly the kingdom of heaven he sought,
> All these things were added, joint-heirship he got;
> Some eighty-four billions of dollars to hold,
> With billions increasing to riches untold.[43]

Few tributes were so outspoken in their obsession with the measure of money as this one, but there were at least a few poets who saw the glory of their nation in terms of gold and gadgets.

This obsession with the material and the monetary became more blatant as the poet turned toward the discussion of abstract values. One may read, for example, that civilization needs to be defined in terms of *"comfort,"* or that gold provides the "measure of the most holy Toil."[44] One poet retold the story of Adam's fall in terms of debts and mortgages, while another saw the dollar bill as symbolic of independence, courage, and strength.[45] Devotion to the dollar may best be exemplified by a volume entitled *One Dollar's Worth*, whose title page took the form of a check for $1.00 made out to the reader, signed by the author, and explained in the preface as follows:

Without apology we rise to remark that experience is valuable, as it costs men much money and time to attain it. The author's experiences have been various, varied, and variegated. A large block of it, as chronicled herein, is offered to you, dear reader, at the ground floor price of one dollar. You pay your money and get the experience; we take your dollar. A fair exchange is no robbery.[46]

There are, clearly, many ways of doing business with the muse!

In spite of the impressive extent to which the poet's adoption of material standards may be documented, this testimony made up only the most minute fraction of his total reaction. The poet's protest against materialism became, on the other hand, the subject of an outpouring which was both elaborate and voluminous. In interpreting our Western experience, for example, he condemned the gold-seekers for their mercenary motives and upheld the pioneer frontier virtues against the materialistic ways of the Easterner, the urbanite, and the late comer. In reacting to the rise of the city, furthermore, he bemoaned the conflict, haste, greed, and artificiality which accompanied the chase after cash. Among the actors on the economic scene he hissed the rich man, the miser, the financier, and the fop for their devotion to Mammon, while in the political drama he cast as principal villain the representative of the people who betrayed his responsibility for financial gain. Even when discussing humanitarian reform he extended his disapproval to the mercenary ways of the prostitute and the rum-seller, as well as to the reformer who sold out to vested interests. Condemning international greed, the poet upheld Ireland and the Boers against England and warned the United States to leave Cuba, the Philippines, China, and Central America alone. On patriotic anniversaries he mourned a nation where "The dollar's almighty monopoly/The people's blood is distilling."[47] Finally, he protested against an applied science which had defaced his beloved nature, and against a set of scientific theories which had dehumanized the role and destiny of man.

A summary of the entire poetic reaction necessarily touches upon aspects of the Gilded Age which have already been discussed. But it is impossible to overemphasize the poet's vast sense of outrage. Much of his comment was centered not so much upon particular issues as upon a general diagnosis of the ills of his age and his country. The following citations may indicate the reiterative force of this message:

> Money is, I ween, the center
> Of the nineteenth century,
> 'Tis the nucleus that's forming
> Caste and aristocracy.[48]

> The age is sordid: gain and greed replace
> The virtue of the people . . .[49]

> The greatest curse of man to-day
> Is love of gold and its pursuit;
> The littleness that holds the sway
> Of wills . . .[50]

> Merciless, soulless, sordid, the science of
>   selfish greed
> . . . deaf to the voice of need.
> And you prate of the wealth of nations, as if
>   it were bought and sold!
> The wealth of nations is men, not silk and
>   cotton and gold.[51]

> The greediness of gain that here prevails
> Will undermine the virtue of these States.[52]

> The flattering nations look from afar,
> Freemen we seem, yet slaves we are,
> Ironed with hateful gyves of greed . . .[53]

> Cursed inebriate nation,
> Lo! where she wallows in gold;
> Drunk with the dollar's damnation,
> Withered and sottishly old.
>
> Crazed by the absinthe of riches,
> Bleared and bewildered she goes;
> Shrieks, as she staggers and pitches,—
> Money will solace my woes.[54]

Again and again the poet cursed an environment which had substituted the quest after material advantages for the higher ideals of former days and nobler climes. Instead of honor and altruism, he moaned, we have cultivated insatiate greed, patrician scorn, plebeian hate, and have encouraged vice and crime.[55] Typical of warnings against the vanity of riches was E. A. Robinson's famous portrait of the charming Richard Cory, "richer than a king" and endowed with all the material graces, who nonetheless "Went home and put a bullet through his head."[56] And an equally famous figure, writing in 1900, penned this poetic prophecy of the inroads of American material advance upon her distinctive heritage:

> Mid Uncle Sam's expanded acres
> There's an old secluded glade
> Where grey Puritans and Quakers
> Still grow fervid in the shade . . .
> Yet the smoke of trade and battle
> Cannot quite be banished hence,
> And the air-line to Seattle
> Whizzes just behind the fence.[57]

Seconding this sweeping damnation of the age, many poets went into some detail concerning the manner in which material values seemed to be undermining our institutions and our way of life. As suggested in Chapter V, the poet presented a strong case for the disruption of political democracy through the agency of Mammon. Praying "God Purge Our Politics!" he underlined the "avaricious greed" which had led our political leaders astray:[58]

> Constitution ne'er was so betrayed:
> Officials, high and petty, daily break
> Their oaths to honor and support it, swayed
> By greed . . .[59]

> . . . scoundrels hold our politics in sway,
> And ruin morals for their base desire
> Of lucre . . .[60]

Everywhere he looked, from courtroom to legislature, the poet observed material considerations overriding both principle and the popular mandate. Instead of government by representation, discussion, and legislation, he saw only a series of transactions wherein the popular will was sacrificed to the interests of highest bidder:

> Go view the scenes along Atlantic's shore;
> Where cities flourish and where men decline.
> Where wealth accumulates and hearts repine;
> Where trade's proud monarchs hold majestic sway,
> And servile statesmen tremblingly obey;
> Where plaint knaves proclaim in tones of awe
> The sacred purpose of each bribe-passed law . . .[61]

This type of protest vilified not only the "pliant knaves" in office, but also those who used "unscrupulous gold" to purchase favor.[62] Both our political and our economic institutions, complained the poet, had become subservient to that "fell money-curst Oligarchy" with its materialistic obsessions.[63] In order to combat this seeming defeat of the ideal by the dollar, the poet was willing to consider revising our whole economic system and —if necessary—our political system as well.

Mammon's curse on American economic life, in the poet's mind, extended well beyond the corruption of our democratic institutions. Many felt, for example, that materialistic standards were being employed to justify inequitable distribution of wealth:

> 'Tis the curse of the day, I sing in my lay
> This great disregard for the poor of our clan—
> Where gold in our sight, makes greater our right
> And the owner by far a much better man. [64]

In the pursuit of wealth the businessman made for himself a world which was "hard, inhuman steel . . . soulless in its search for gold," inconsiderate of right and wrong. [65] Within this world there was no room for sentiment, for humanitarianism, for charity—no room for anything, indeed, beyond blind worship of the material:

> Money is our dream ideal; money is our highest goal;
> Money—money—and for money we crowd out the human
>   soul. . . .
> Stocks and bonds are more than honor. If our brother's
>   blood is shed,
> We will overlook the murder, if they pay us for our
>   dead . . . [66]

The widespread addiction to this single-minded idolatry was producing, the poet feared, a new and unbecoming pattern of behavior in many areas. The characteristics of this way of life, some of which were suggested in particular connections above (see especially Chapter III), were treated here in a larger framework. When he told the "Nineteenth Century," "Thou hast transformed this drowsy, languid world," his imagery was that of the city; but often he placed less blame on the environment than on the general subservience to greed and gain. [67] The ubiquitous obsession with speed, the destructive clamor of "these modern onrushing machinery times" and "the brutal rush and hullabaloo/Of this practical world" applied not just to city life but—for many poets—to a truly national condition. [68] Of even more concern to the poet than the resulting hurry, noise, and physical ugliness, were the inroads of materialism upon American beliefs, values, and behavior. In the increasing bustle and brouhaha he saw symptoms of a ruthless competitiveness which threatened not only the leisurely life of his remembered childhood, but also the important public virtues which he associated with the national tradition. Instead of showing consideration for the rights of the individual, "Each must grab the mighty dollar, though his brother-man be crushed."[69] Instead of standing for peace and altruism, wrote another poet, we have become like a species of goose which, instead of eating the food nature provided it, "Deemed each other's life blood much more sweet."[70] In a similar vein, Stephen Crane drew his parable by contrasting a man who "toiled on a burning road,/ Never resting" with an ass which rested, eating grass and herbs. Said the man, " 'It will not suffice you.'/But the ass only grinned at him from the green place."[71]

Materialistic standards were found to contribute not only to an atmosphere of haste and turmoil among those seeking Mammon's rewards, but also to a useless condition of idleness and foppery among those who enjoyed the blessings of material abundance. As symbols of conspicuous waste and consumption, everything from "Pepsin Gum" to the "best brand of Champagne" drew the wrath of poetic pens.[72] As described in Chapter IV, this attitude was represented fully by those bards who condemned the behavior of our upper classes in expressing disapproval of our economic system. The three lines which follow show how this point of view, centrally important in the class-oriented economic protest, involved also a protest against the Gilded Age itself:

> Is it wise to make a sphinx of gold,
> To be adored by those, who, lacking grace,
> Flaunt satins in the pauper's care-worn face![73]

Many poets condemned our economy for specific abuses. Many more went beyond particularized protest, and leveled their criticism against the unquestioning adoption of materialistic standards which promoted an inhumane competitive condition at the bottom of the ladder and a wasteful idleness at the top. Mammon's power, they wrote, was absolute; yet nowhere did it bring the sort of life which the poet found admirable.

More subtle were those verses which linked materialistic criteria with certain other basic changes in our way of life:

> The same monotonous routine
> Of business, grinding like a mill,
> The noblest natures down to mean.[74]

> Not mere commodities,
> Stupid and salable,
> Wholly available,
> Ranged upon shelves;
> Each with his puny form
> In the same uniform,
> Cramped and disabled;
> We are not labelled,
> We are ourselves.[75]

Monotony and standardization one could find at any economic level; to the poet these by-products of materialism were also affecting our way of life, seriously and adversely. Under the title, "Specialists," for example, the poet described a process of grinding which left nothing but the "rind" of man.[76] The more severe resentment arose from those who felt that modern life threatened to rob man of everything that distinguished him from the machines which worked for him:

> I am living in the end of the nineteenth century,
> I've been trained and educated like the rest
> To perform my simple art in a way that's masterly—
> And expected too, to do my very best.
> Working in the system,
> Working in the system—
> An automaton in all the term may mean,
> And doing what I'm told
> I ask no questions bold,
> For I'm only just a wheel in the machine.

> I'm one among the millions of no personality,
> And my spirits have been crushed too as well,
> I've been subject to the square and the plane,
>   as you may see,
> 'Till I fit the little niche in which I dwell,
> Working in the system,
> Working in the system—
> 'Till a part of which at last I've come to be—
> Just toiling to exist,
> I never shall be missed,
> So I guess I'll make a break for liberty.[77]

With graceless effectiveness these lines bring forth the poet's horror at materialism and industrialism compounded; quite literally they catalogue the symptoms of the "automaton" within whom there yet stir more exalted instincts, but for whom there may be no true escape from monotonous uniformity and over-specialization.

But perhaps the most basic questions concerning the "system" were raised by those who balked at accepting contemporary definitions of success:

> How often the poor are despised and neglected,
> For no other reason except they are poor;
> How often the rich are beloved and respected,
> Because they have uncounted wealth at their door.[78]

In banner-headline style ("Success not the Test of Merit!"[79]), they exposed the false god who demanded lies, artifice, and brute force. Stephen Crane, once again, wrote eloquently in a direction taken by many of his colleagues:

> The successful man has thrust himself
> Through the water of the years,
> Reeking wet with mistakes,—
> Bloody mistakes;
> Slimed with victories over the lesser,
> A figure thankful on the shore of money.[80]

Turning his back on opulence and power, the poet sought rather the contentment symbolized by the forty-acre farm—the idea of having just enough to provide a living. He pointed to the wealth which is in nature and which all may share, and to the rewards of the life concerned with beauty rather than bank balances. In the last analysis, he wrote,

> Failure, success are terms but relative;
> They are not measured in the Mind Divine
> By such poor standards as our earthly are.[81]

Those who considered themselves successful by worldly standards would find that immortality was not for their kind but for the Homers; while in "The Great Procession" Croesus and the beggar would march side by side.[82] Materialism, in short, had warped our ideas of successful living until we no longer directed our lives toward appropriate goals.

Poets would not be poets if they did not delight in contrasts between the material world on the one hand and the world of God, love, and nature on the other. Verses of this sort often reveal only doubtful social relevance; no attempt was made, for this reason, to catalogue all imitations of Wordsworth's "The world is too much with us . . ." Less patently derivative, and thus of more interest to the student of the Gilded Age, is the poetic testimony to the corruption of religion and human affection as exemplified in the institutions of the church and marriage. "Spirituality," wrote one poet, is "pure externality."[83] The demands of competitive capitalism have driven religion from our lives, wrote another:

> Six days they worship the great god "Biz,"
> And notes and gold are their offering;
> To the early riser his favor is,
> And groans of toil the hymns they sing;
> But on Yadnus' day [Sunday] they lie abed . . .[84]

According to the poet, however, the church had not unerringly lived up to its mission as a bulwark against gold and godless-

ness. "Money is king!" began one verse; the "parson vows to
it" and the "Pope bows to it."[85] Instead of battling the inroads
of materialism, greedy parsons haggled publicly over salary
matters. Instead of exemplifying an unpretentious simplicity,
the great churches have come to rely upon stained glass, giant
organs, and elaborate architecture which, the poet felt, only
distracted worshippers from truly religious feelings. Finally, in
catering to the rich not only in social "tone" but even in
interpreting the gospel, the church had turned its back not only
on the poor but—in so doing—on all humanity.

That love between the sexes, not less than the love of God,
had suffered the effects of materialism, is suggested by such
titles as "Gold vs. Love," "All for Gold; or Clara's Unhappy
Marriage," or, more didactically, "Don't Marry for Money,
Girls; Marry for Love!"[86] Marriage for money meant unrelieved years of bondage:

> I'm linked to a loathsome, human brute,
> By strong, gilded, jeweled chains
> Which leave on my body, my heart and life,
> Their hateful, sensual strains.[87]

The poet saw the world swarming with the corrupters and the
corrupted: women who sold themselves in marriage; prosti-
tutes, panders, and their customers, whom the poet condemned
for bringing into the market place a commodity which did not
belong there. But almost beneath contempt, in poetic eyes, was
the preoccupied businessman who cared more for the price of
stocks than for a "lover's fond caresses"—the man to whom
love was merely an "unsound investment."[88]

Most dismaying of all to the poet was the impact of this
sweeping materialism upon the arts, especially his own:

> I hate the vast array of "modern" things,
> Gilt and pale purple, yellow, pink, and white;
> Dull imitations . . .
> . . . the years of good Queen Bess

Are made the dull philistine's property;
And Burns is "popularly" sent to press.[89]

"Art in a Sordid Age" is reduced to "Vending some trifle that none keeps nor seeks" while the grand march proceeds along the gilded road.[90] The poet who responds to the inspiration of the age uncovers a "jangling nerve," while the poet who honors his great tradition is "drowned in Mammon's roar."[91]

A poem dipt in flame sublime,
Its heights in scaling—call a senseless rhyme;
Would do for women or a few,
But they—they want but journalistic brue.
Their skies are dark o'er streaked with red,—
The breasts they suck protrude, by vitriol fed
Which burns away or sears their soul.[92]

Thus, according to the poet, if one wrote verse of excellence he would only be ignored by his contemporaries; on the other hand, to respond to popular taste was to degrade the art. Only one verse of any interest seems to call for a poetry of the age:

This is a practical age and it longs for a
practical poet,
One who will sing of the themes that are hot
in the hearts of the toilers,
Sing for the Utilitarians, sing for the makers of Money. . . .

But even this sentiment soon turns into sneers at the "curious cult of the Ugly"; the poet who revels in the filth of slums or in the "muck that reeks in the redolent barnyard" will succeed, we are told, not in mastering his art, but only in pleasing "the greatest numbers." He, and his readers, will be no better than a warpt Caesar, mad with lust for the material, who wallows unclothed in his hoard of gold.[93] The true call was for a poetic savior who could understand the age in a grander sense:

What does it mean, this barren age of ours?
Here are the men, the women, and the flowers,—

The seasons, and the sunset, as before.
What does it mean?—Shall not one bard arise
To wrench one banner from the western skies,
And mark it with his name forevermore?[94]

Both directly and in connection with many other subjects of social import the poet developed a detailed comment on that way of life which emphasized the material. Some of the verse-writing brotherhood accepted what they found around them, and couched their own sentiments in terms which offered a frank recognition of gold's domain. This fraction of the fraternity, however, was minute indeed. In reacting to the advent of industrialism and urbanism, especially, as well as in chronicling many other late-century developments, the poets wrote with nearly unanimous antagonism against the changes in American values and behavior which they saw resulting from public commitment to materialistic criteria. As a result, they withheld nothing of the pen's might as they scored the nation, the age, and the institutions through which these expressed themselves. From the brutal strife and squalor of the urban industrial worker to the heedless idle waste of the wealthy scion; from the corrupt public servant to the power-mad commercial titan; from the prostitute who sold love for gold to the clergyman who sold grace for favors—across the breadth of his society the poet saw an ubiquitous subservience to Mammon which he did not hesitate to upbraid in the strongest of terms. No other reaction by the poets was so widespread or so vehement; no other protest shows so clearly why this age was labeled "gilded."

iii

Quantitatively the most important theme to appear in the poetry of the Gilded Age pertained to the identification of America's mission. As prelude to this theme, there recurred the vision of a nation emerging triumphantly, after years of preparation under the guiding hand of destiny, into a position unique in the history of the world. As shown in Chapters II and VII, this vision revealed itself in connection with particular events, both domestic and foreign. The spirit of expansionism, firmly rooted in the experience of populating a continent, further nourished itself on such aggressive attitudes as Seward's

toward Mexico, Santo Domingo, and Alaska; brooked no discouragement from the failure of purchase treaties for Santo Domingo and the Danish West Indies; and attached itself to the cause of the Cuban insurgents, the Boers, the Irish nationalists, and oppressed peoples everywhere.

At home the atmosphere was more than congenial to the expression of patriotic sentiment, expansionistic or no. With

President Cleveland showing the way, Americans renewed the patriotic emphasis on such holidays as the Fourth of July and Thanksgiving, formed societies for honoring the nation's flag and history, and pulled vigorously at the bellropes of filiopietism on the many centennial anniversaries of landmarks in our nation's founding. Nor was the satisfaction of reunion after the bloody years of civil strife absent from these testimonies to a united faith in the federal government. Yet no commemorative occasion or acquisition of territory seemed necessary to the poet-prophet of America's mission; in fact, this love of nation with its inseparable sense of a special destiny enjoyed an independent vitality all its own, springing not so much from particular events as from a continuing state of mind.

Its least controversial expression took the form of tributes to that "blessed Utopian dream," that "land of milk and honey, rich and fair," "pride of the world," and "Wonder of the glorious West."[95] In laying this foundation of patriotic sentiment on which the structure of expansionism was inevitably to be raised, the poet emphasized varying aspects of American excellence:

> Columbia, gem of the West,
> A Continent, whose vast domain
> Is studded o'er with pleasant homes,
> Most fair to see; The happy land . . .[96]

> Time moves apace! . . .
> A highway built across a frozen land,
> And links of steel the distant ends command . . .
> And tillage spreads abroad o'er hill and glen,
> And harvests gather to industrious men . . .
> And enterprise transforms to bustling marts.[97]

> Supreme greatness of our independent country,
> Most unsurpassing seaport harbors to our clime,
> Most extensive breadth of land to our boundary,
> Pre-eminence of Americans for all time.[98]

P.G.A.–R

Such was the poet's assessment of his country—her size, her natural advantages and mineral resources, her material and mechanical progress, and the blessings of her institutions: "Free schools—free thought—and free people."[99] Extending the catalogue, he found many sources for national pride beyond the material: wise men and universities, an enlightened concept of justice, a devotion to truth and science, and—above all—a matchless "heritage of promise" which "Yet augments the nation's grandeur, growing still to more and more!"[100] But whether the poet found his inspiration in the Pilgrim fathers or in the steam engine, his conclusion was pretty much the same:

> Blest country of the West,
> Of all the lands the best
> Under the sun.[101]

Most poets were not content merely to praise their country, no matter how extravagant the terms. Rather, they built upon this foundation of virtue and achievement a monument to the special mission of their land:

> Americans, on you devolves a trust
> The grandest, noblest, and best
> That ever a people possess![102]

Led by "god-like destiny" with "the court of nations at thy feet" the America of these poets was singled out for leadership:[103]

> Grand is thy mission, O America!
> Thou art the Moses of the nations, and
> Thy mighty duty is to head the way
> To the rich regions of the promised land!
> Thou art responsible for the command![104]

The direction in which America was destined to lead remained unspecified in most of these verses. Generalized objectives such as the following were typical:

We fight for the wide world's right,
To enlarge life's scope and plan,
To flood the earth with hope and light,
To build the kingdom of man.[105]

The many hymns to American destiny that crowded the pages
of centennial commemorations were typified, if not in skill, at
least in their effusive vagueness, by Harriet Monroe's contribution to the World's Columbian Exhibition at Chicago:

. . . thou [Columbia] shalt win
Glory and power and length of days.
The sun and moon shall be thy kin,
The stars shall sing thy praise.
All hail! we bring thee vows most sweet
To strew before thy winged feet.
Now onward be thy ways![106]

Among those poets who depicted a special American destiny,
but who stopped short of militarism or imperialism, could be
found some few who mirrored the quality Merle Curti has
labeled "progressive patriotism," the identification of national
loyalty with "devotion to humanity and democracy, peace and
freedom" rather than unthinking idolization of the state.[107] This
quality was also mirrored to some extent by those poets who
wrote for peace and against empire, but it was expressed more
positively in the lines of those who urged on America a stand
for liberty, freedom, and human rights as opposed to "Oppression, Hatred, Ignorance . . . Fear."[108] Patriotism was likewise
identified with equality of opportunity ("Thou knowest no
color, thou askest not man's creed"[109]) and with equal rights
for rich and poor. Included in the list of targets for American
opposition were tyranny, slavery, and materialism:

'Tis yours to bear the World-State in your dream,
To strike down Mammon and his brazen breed,
To build the Brother-Future, beam on beam;
Yours, mighty one, to shape the mighty Deed.[110]

Although these objectives tended to be no more concrete than in other patriotic verses, the "progressive patriots" at least directed their sentiments toward humanitarian rather than chauvinistic ends.

Poets who wrote like this, however, were far outnumbered by colleagues bent on composing unrestrained litanies celebrating America's divinely appointed destiny. Ignoring more mundane causes, these poets attributed America's eminence to the patronage of the Archangel Michael, to the appearance of a second cloud of Mt. Sinai, and to the intervention of God Himself. Inextricably intermingling religious with patriotic themes, these poets sought to demonstrate the divine identity of their own land:

> All the grace of heaven blending,
> Man arising, Christ descending,
> While God's hand in secrecy
> Builds thy bright eternity.[111]

According to the logic of these poets, Christianity was the religion of the common man, freedom and democracy had been God's special gift to America, and the combination of these God-given political and religious institutions fitted us above all others for becoming the New Jerusalem where God's promise to man would be fulfilled. Geography also was made to argue for this American millennium, not only on account of the scenic splendor it provided, but also because it gave us an impartial place between East and West, whence the Word could readily emanate to all mankind, be they heathen or saved. For these poets the mission of America was so undeniably celestial that the phrase "God-and-country," upon emerging from their pens, became blurred into a single concept.

At the extremes of chauvinism were those poets who either removed the "God" from "God and country" or even reversed the word order in this well-worn phrase. In place of the cross and crown they raised the stars and stripes to mark the "dazzling shrine/Of human liberty," or to serve as an "Idol of the Brave."[112] Here stood, unflinchingly and uncompromisingly, the cult of the flag. Decorating their volumes with replicas of Old Glory as large and as colorful as their printers could devise, these versifiers persuaded not so much by logic as by repetition. Whole volumes of hortatory verse were devoted to such sentiments as "It's the flag of the good and the true," "Forever may our standard wave," or simply "Hurrah for the flag to our hearts so dear."[113] Vying with the Fourth of July as a favorite holiday was "Our Flag Centennial: June, 1877," under which title were offered these forthright lines:

> God keep beneath red, white, and blue,
> A nation true;
> Upholding with its powerful might,
> Only the right.[114]

At all of the great fairs of the Gilded Age, these poets noted first and last Old Glory's proud profile against God's great blue sky.

But the extremes of the flag cult were reached by poets who dismissed depressions and droughts with the blithe reminder that we were, after all, privileged to live under the greatest of flags,[115] or by those who deluged the stars and stripes in a flood of martial bathos. The soldier, feeling his wounds, asks for the "dear flag" as a shroud; the sailor prays to end his "long last cruise" with Old Glory as his "windin' sheet"; the "Dying Flag Bearer" (oh what possibilities here!) phrases more precisely his last request: "Lay the stars beneath my head,/And the stripes upon my breast."[116] This sort of superpatriotism, when expanded beyond the flag cult, led one of our most popular poets to entitle a whole volume, *John Smith, U.S.A.* The title verse pictured an American abroad signing the hotel register with both his own name and his country's in the realization that "There is no prouder boast of man/Than this: 'I am an American!' "[117] In the lines of these poets America was worshipped without subtlety and without restraint. The sun could be consoled for having to leave our shores each evening only with the thought of returning on the morrow. The cannons boomed, the bells pealed, and the national ensign preened itself proudly throughout these lines. Not "God and Country," but "Flag and Country": "My country, right or wrong!"

Not all poets, by any means, participated in—nor even approved of—the flagstaff patriotism which dismissed all ills so long as "We've got a brand new flag."[118] There was a complaint against the brag and bluster which offered so little constructive help and which often concealed incompetence and conceit:

> Perchance the follies of another land
> May help our restless folk to understand
> That our Republic, when all's said and done,
> Is the only perfect country 'neath the sun;
> That all they need to do is—lend their nose
> To the infallible leadership of those
> Who, on the "Fourth," talk of the "Declaration,"
> And *prove* by shouting that they love the nation.
> If any dare to doubt these things, he's sold
> His principles for British gold;
> Or he's an infidel, and would o'erthrow
> The grounds of faith in all we *think* we know.[119]

There was objection against indoctrinating the nation's youth in purblind patriotism, against invoking the Deity in all the country's petty crises, and—indeed—against the "strong impression that/Our Flag's upheld by God's own hand."[120] Yet most poets overwhelmingly endorsed the image of an America especially favored and especially destined. The two major points of disagreement among the poets involved militarism and imperialism: Was war a justifiable means toward the end of greater American destiny? And did this destiny involve political empire?

Militarism, scarcely hidden beneath the flag-waving of the superpatriots, came into its own with those who loved the eagle perched atop the flagpole better than the flag itself. Choosing this fierce, fighting bird for a symbol, the cult of the eagle saw America not only as a foe of wrong but as markedly belligerent in this role. "Europe! Stand Back!" they warned in their milder moments as they reinforced the Monroe Doctrine with threats of military might.[121] Boasting a flag "unconquered in wars," these poets pledged our "Strength of . . . arms 'gainst tyrants when called" and guaranteed American readiness to uphold principle with gunpowder.[122] Justifying war as a training ground for masculine bravery and worth, some felt no constraint at pressing children into militaristic molds:

> The soldier is a splendid man
> When marching on parade;
> And when he meets the enemy
> He never is afraid.[123]

More outspoken was this verse composed for a New Bedford grammar school:

> When another war comes on . . .
> We boys will shoulder arms! and we girls
>   will cheer the boys!
> Fighting for unity and freedom.[124]

Even more blood-curdling was this passage from James Whitcomb Riley's *Book of Joyous Children*:

> I want to be a Soldier, with a sabre
>   in my hand
> Or a little carbine rifle . . .
> As gayly dancing off to war
> As dancing a cotillion. . . .
>
> So, when our foes have had their fill,
> Though I'm among the dying,
> To see The Old Flag flying still,
> I'll laugh to leave her flying![125]

Militarism was not for the young alone. Adults, for the benefit of other adults, rehearsed the history of American military achievement, measured belligerently the armed might of potential enemies, and propagandized for more ships and larger forts. Ideal Americans, they wrote, should ask nothing better than to die for country "with the roar of guns."[126] In time of military need the citizen should willingly and readily sacrifice all other needs and interests, no matter how dear or how holy. America's future was to be, as her past had been, dominated by war: "We came to birth in battle; when we pass,/It shall be to the thunder of the drums."[127] Meanwhile? Meanwhile we shall fight for freedom's cause in the far corners of the globe:

> Forever we're bound
> To fight beneath one flag . . .
> And justice uphold the world around.[128]

However, in spite of the memories of Civil War heroics and of compulsory patriotism at the time of the Spanish-American War, a greater number of verses presented the case against the use of violence in the pursuit of the American mission. The most sweeping manifestoes on behalf of peace came from idealistic pens which depicted a perfect state without "castled forts" which would come with the realization that the true desire of the nations was for universal peace.[129] Steps toward this unarmed utopia were urged for a number of reasons. The economic-minded decried Mars as an enemy of prosperity; the class-conscious pointed out that in war it is always the common people who foot the bill; the religiously oriented opposed war as unchristian; and the humanitarians argued against the sanctioning of mass murder in a society which condemned a single slaying. Even nationalistic arguments were brought into play, as by one who blamed our English heritage for our warlike tendencies and urged us to expunge them. Turning his back on Mother England, he concluded:

> American I am; would wars were done!
> Now westward, look my country bids good-night—
> Peace to the world from ports without a gun![130]

Advocating disarmament, these poets reacted to parades and military reviews as "festal shows of war," labeled a new battleship a "million-dollar coffin," and warned that standing armies could be used at home as well as abroad.[131]

Manliness, the pacifists pointed out, bears no relation to participation in national hysteria:

> Who are you at Washington who presume to
>   declare me the enemy of anybody or to
>   declare any nation my enemy?
> However great you may be, I altogether deny
>   your authority to sow enmity and hatred
>   in my soul. . . .
> When I want enemies, I reserve the right to
>   manufacture them for myself. . . .
> Hypnotize fools and cowards if you will, but
>   for my part, I choose to be a man.[132]

These enemies of militarism and war sounded their most consistent and effective note, however, in their violent and appalling pictures of the battlefield:

> . . . I have cursed
> The sunlight and the breezes and the leaves
> To think of men on stretchers and on beds,
> Or on foul floors, like some starved outrageous lizards,
> Made human with paralysis and rags;
> Or of some poor devil on a battle field,
> Left undiscovered and without the strength
> To drag a maggot from his clotted mouth. . . .[133]

Building on such specific horrors, the poet went on to decry war's harvest of widows and orphans and to sympathize with the warrior who prayed not to see his foe lest the recognition of another human being through his gunsights render him unable to pull the trigger. "They're Training Boys to Murder Down on Army Street," one put it plainly, "in the name of God."[134] With a logic he found unanswerable, the pacifist-poet argued that the only possible fruit of battle was victory; and what was victory?

> Not one of all the purple host
> Who took the flag to-day
> Can tell the definition,
> So clear, of victory,
>
> As he, defeated, dying,
> On whose forbidden ear
> The distant strains of triumph
> Break, agonized and clear.[135]

These poets of peace were not necessarily less patriotic than their more bloodthirsty brethren, nor did they seek to deny America's mission. Their strictures were firm and unflagging, however, in the insistence that this mission be achieved without resort to military measures.

The second point of contention among the poets involved America's eventual commitment to empire. Was America's mission simply to lead? Or did it include territorial expansion and the acquisition of remote provinces? Many poets presented thinly veiled dreams of empire, envisioning an America to whom "empires bow" and "Dynasties and kings shall surrender."[136] Some hinted that an American dominion would come about as a result of a union of nations, and some suggested the naturalness and inevitability of the process:

> As a river floweth downward
> From the mountains to the sea,
> O my country, so each nation
> Floweth ever unto thee.[137]

Some, apologetically, called empire by name:

> To make a State
> Imperial—meaning great
> And good and true . . .[138]

With the term itself came echoes of Kipling—the credo of the "white man's burden" and "the pride of the empires of the Blood."[139] Eventually the watchwords of imperial Britain were themselves adopted: "The Sun Never Sets on Old Glory."[140]

Occasionally utilizing arguments from social Darwinism or drawing other analogies from the world of nature, occasionally pleading idealistic motivations, but most frequently assuming that American expansion was both inevitable and self-evident, the poet spoke his piece for empire:

> E'en as men grow, so do nations; all expansion
>   leaves behind
> Narrow mind and narrow limits for the wider
>   lands and seas . . .[141]

> Needs and wrongs of millions await thy rising,
>   vindicate and save, put forth thy hand,
> For the nations gather sternly watchful . . .
> World dominion is a desperate game,
> Let us shackle fast the lowlier brother, yea,
>   Columbia, even in thy name![142]

> The Flag of Washington leads empires on . . .
> The cause of Man is thine, O Flag . . .
> The cause of God is thine, O Flag, sail on![143]

> Columbia, whose arms encirlce now
> The earth, and clasp the hands of those who need,
> Great is thy calling, worthy of thy deed
> The hour; if thou canst to its mandate bow
> In reverence . . .
> The time is thine and who dare disallow![144]

With or without expressed justification, the poet urged toward empire, restating the worth of our heritage, invoking again the hand of God and the power of patriotism, and underlining the imminence of America's fulfillment. The only unsettled question involved this empire's extent, and here the poet indulged in grand hyperbole:

> How many stars, Old Glory, shalt thou wear?
> How many sands are there along thy sea?
> Thou every nation's galaxy shall bear
> And wave to the borders of eternity.[145]

While most poets contented themselves with rhetorical vagueness, others were specific to the degree of endorsing a North American empire which would welcome additional states from the Caribbean and Pacific islands. The most outspoken verse-imperialist of the Gilded Age wrote grandly of "Uncle Sam's Family" including Ireland, the Orient, and cousins in between.[146] Clearly, these poets had taken the bit of empire firmly between their teeth.

As was the case with the militarists, those who wrote explicitly on the side of empire were outnumbered by those who attacked it. Once again, it is not at all necessary to assume that the anti-imperialists were disloyal or that they lacked conviction concerning America's special destiny. What they opposed was any American commitment to a policy of imperialism. The imperialist attitude they cursed with—to their ears—the most damning of all epithets, "jingo." Pairing "Jingo and Yahoo," these poets attached to jingo maneuvers—whether by diplomats, preachers, or politicians—the opprobrium of demagoguery and crass materialism.[147] The platform jingoist was characterized as a "feller" who

> . . . speechified on Freedom . . .
> And soared the Eagle tel, it 'peared to me,
> She was n't bigger 'n a bumble-bee![148]

The jingo's brag and boast, his spear and buckler, led only to hysteria and hardship, complained the poet; and his motto, "My country, right or wrong!" was condemned as sacrilegiously in conflict with that "larger love of the eternal right" which should serve as mankind's guide.[149] These lines, cited in Chapter VII, depict the jingo characteristically:

A jingo in his fighting gear
Swept with his eye the earthly sphere . . .
He saw the sword and burning brand
Turned loose on many a helpless land,
And, fired with zeal, he cried, "What bliss!
Our country must get in on this."[150]

Rudyard Kipling, that most eminent jingo, met with no friendly welcome from these poets. Dubbing him "Laureat Fog-Horn of the Anglo-Saxon Race," they parodied him in a "Possessional" and a mock prayer to the "Lord God of boasts."[151] Castigating him for not minding his own national business, they denounced his "white man's burden" as the dogma "By which shrewd men enchain/The Plain and poorer people" to rob them of their "fruit of labor."[152] Labeling expansionism a euphemism for "The European Law of Loot," they turned critical eyes on Kipling's country and their own.[153] When America and England, the supposed carriers of civilization's best, looked at each other, they saw not humanity's vanguards but "The ogre visage, wet with human blood,/Of gorged, insatiable Tyranny."[154] The manifest destiny of the Anglo-Saxons was compared to the behavior of thieves:

For we, the tramps of all creation—
Scrubs, without a pedigree—
Will raid and steal of ev'ry Nation
Like the pirates of the sea.[155]

In this frame of mind the poet not only attacked contemporary heroes whom he associated with imperialism but also deflated some of history's supposedly unassailable noblemen. "The Proposed Dewey Arch," wrote one poet, would be a monument to "Liberty betrayed, beguiled, misled."[156] As for America's first hero:

You say, Columbus with his argosies
Who rash and greedy took the screaming main

And vanished out before the hurricane
Into the sunset after merchandise,
Then under western palms with simple eyes
Trafficked and robbed and triumphed home again:
You say this is the glory of the brain
And human life no other use than this?[157]

Like his more aggressive fellows, the anti-imperialist poet might cry out, "Awake, ye Patriots!"; but his idea of the dangers ahead was radically different:

Shield us from imperialist shoals
. . . dwarf the growth of militarism . . .
Nor heed the luring voice of avarice . . .
Shall we enslave the human soul?[158]

Even more impassioned than those who raged against jingo attitudes were those who counted up the consequences of empire. America's message to the world, they pointed out, might read well in a peaceful, idealistic setting; but how would it seem when colored by the violent necessities of empire-building:

Anti-annexationists, clamorers for Empire,
Amateurs in ethics, as you prate the work is done.
He who loads the fountain-pen—he's the man
*   that's settled it,*
But this concerns the chap that loads the gun.
'Tis agreed our pap o' Freedom, as it is shipped,
*   is mild and warm,*
Is it curdled when delivered by the chap in uniform?[159]

The wages of empire, prophesied the poet, is death. To prove this he constructed maudlin parallels with doomed Rome and its "horrible revels"; with fated Troy, that "mighty city, red with ruin and sack"; and with countless Babylons, Sidons, and Tyres.[160] Dominated by lust and violence from conception to decline, the life of empire, as pictured by the poet, bred only increasing greed and bequeathed a legacy of "mouldering bones . . . dying groans" and remembered brutality.[161] On the

basis of these lurid predictions, the anti-imperialists urged
Uncle Sam to steer clear of the "big child-nations" with their
malevolent rivalries, to confine himself to the settling of the
continental nation and the defense of the Monroe Doctrine.[162]

Yet in spite of the firmness of his warnings and the grimness
of his visions, the poet who protested against the course of
empire saw himself more often as a Cassandra than as an
honored oracle. With a great sadness he admitted both the
futility of his words and the extent of his nation's commitment.
The crossings from Tampa to Havana and from San Francisco
to Manila, he noted, were immeasurable simply in terms in
miles; for they represented a fundamental and irrevocable
change in the American condition and outlook. Here, tearfully,
he acknowledged the futility of his opposition:

> We have read in the eyes of the morrow
> The warning of the mirth
> That is born of Pride, and the sorrow
> Of nations of the earth
> That they have built . . .
> With a sharp and bloody trowel
> On the sand.[163]

> America, bride of Change!
> Thy cloistral hour is done;
> Thy shy and innocent foot
> Is white on the stranger's stair:
> Unto what end?—Beloved!
> I have heard thee sigh.[164]

The poets of the Gilded Age held in common a firm conviction of America's special blessings and destiny; but in those
who went on from there, the unanimity was anything but
perfect. Although the verses specifically recommending a
peaceful pursuit of the American mission outnumbered the
outspoken avowals of militarism, it would be unfair to depict the
poet as siding with the dove rather than the eagle. Much of the

verse in praise of the flag or representative of the "my-country-right-or-wrong" attitude would hardly indicate a peaceful mood. Thus, although superficial pacifism outweighed overt militarism, it is equally clear that the poet-patriot, collectively speaking, was a rather bellicose gentleman. The poet's stand in regard to empire was parallel in its complexity; for, although the anti-imperialists produced more verse than those who specifically advocated empire, it would be equally mistaken to place the poet on the side of containment. Though he typically stopped short of committing himself to empire by name, his mood once again—as expressed in his strong sense of mission— was all for American leadership among nations, however achieved and perpetuated. These debates over pacifism versus preparedness and trade versus territorial acquisition, however important, were insignificant alongside the volume of verse propounding the inevitability and inviolability of the American mission.

In defense of this destiny, America was upheld as a regenerative force in a tired, corrupt world, and the extension of her territory was hailed as an extension of freedom. Arguments based on geographical pressures and the need for defense also occasionally appeared. It is interesting that social Darwinism, however attractive it may have been to militarists and imperialists, received scarcely any attention from the poets. And the related rationale of the "white man's burden" came in for abuse more often than for approval.

There were, however, two consistent strains which united poetic justifications of America's mission. One was the idea of America's "manifest" destiny, an approach usually associated with arguments inaugurated half a century earlier. To these poets it was obvious that America was heir to cultural traditions reaching back into antiquity, and that her role was to embody what was best in all of them, affixing the stamp of her own originality, and—in the midst of unmatched physical blessings— bringing to fruition the race-long hopes of all mankind. Thus

many poets argued on the basis of historical—if not biological—
evolution, assuming that history revealed continual progress
toward better things. Thus it followed that the newest of nations
must inevitably become the best. The most popular justification
of all, however, was the religious one. Under this heading was
stressed the Hebraic as well as the Christian heritage; the more
recent past had witnessed the designation of a new and finally
chosen race of Americans, led by God's hand to the promised
land in the West, where the New Jerusalem would at last be
realized. America's mission, to most poets, was an ineluctable
part of the divine plan.

The underlying preoccupations of the poets complement one
another in a way that raises interesting questions concerning
the national character. In both applied science, and in the
material achievements which made it possible, the poet found an
important confirmation of America's special destiny. In the
implications of theoretical science, in the application of materialistic standards, and in the assumptions of aggressive nationalism, however, the poet saw a threat to his traditional allegiance
to humanism, idealism, and democracy. In some ways these
collective attitudes were consistent and commendable; in other
ways they represent a split and immature personality which
could reject the consequences of conditions it had tolerated and
even encouraged. Gratefully accepting the boon of scientific
progress and material convenience, the poet turned his back on
attempts to explain the universe in scientific or materialistic
terms. Uninhibitedly boasting of America's special place in the
world of nations, he shrank from many of the physical and
political consequences of this premise. While the dance went on,
he seemed to think, the piper might remain unpaid.

America, of course, had no monopoly on the development of
contradictory traits of national character. But there did seem to
be something especially indigenous in the degree of naïve
intensity which colored the poetic discussion of all issues

P.G.A.—S

affecting America's public behavior. To these poets America had been and must continue to be exceptional and exemplary, not only for her own sake but for the sake of all civilization; for here was the grand experiment, the supposed culmination of man's long strivings. In this light the most ordinary subject became suffused with an intensity understandable only in terms of extreme national self-consciousness. Should Britain sin, Britain sins; should Spain fall, Spain falls. But should iniquity or failure be associated with the United States, the case of all mankind will have been lost in the balance.

Notes

[1] Hovey, *Poems*, 53–59.

[2] Mackintosh, *Course of Sprouts*, n. pag.

[3] *Proceedings at the Twenty-Fifth Anniversary of the Haverhill Monday Evening Club*, 33. Verse by John Crowell.

[4] Holden, *Ode*, 10.

[5] Booth, *Family of Three*, 170.

[6] *"Reminiscence of '84,"* 17; *Echo of the Seneca*, 91; Hill, *History and Origin of the "Dude,"* n. pag.

[7] Baker, *Vacation Thoughts*, 82–83.

[8] E. A., *Yale Jingle Book*, n. pag.

[9] Kent, *Sunshine and Storm*, 161–66; Holden, *Hand-Book of the Lick Observatory*, 77.

[10] Field, *Four-leaved Clover*, 82–83.

[11] Deem, *Rip Van Fossil*, 23; Helmuth, *With the "Pousse Cafe,"* 47.

[12] Edgerton, *Songs of the People*, 192–93.

[13] Robertson, *Dead Calypso*, 23.

[14] Farquhar, *Libyssa*, 44–47; Donaldson, *Poems*, 145.

[15] Howard, *Later Poems*, 60.

[16] Paine, *Autobiography of a Monkey*, n. pag.

[17] Bragdon, *Undergrowth*, 151–54.

[18] Gilman, *In This Our World*, 78–79.

[19] Fleenor, *In Passing Through*, 27.

[20] Goddard, *Buds, Briers, and Berries*, 111.

[21] Cawein, *Red Leaves and Roses*, 85; Clark, *Book of Poems*, 17–22.

[22] Guthrie, *Songs of American Destiny*, 199. This poet, an evolutionary predecessor of e. e. cummings, capitalized only the first word of each stanza.

[23] *God in Creation and Evolution*, 128; Reynolds, *Poems by Farmer Reynolds*, 83.

[24] Humphrey, *Random Shots*, 19–20.

[25] Fleming, *Gleanings of a Tyro Bard*, 102.

[26] Eddy, *Miscellaneous Writings*, ii.

[27] Ingersoll, *"Intolerant Orthodoxy's Blasphemous Creeds,"* 36–44; Schermerhorn, *Atomic Creation*, 1–54; Stowe, *Poetical Drifts of Thought*, 85–89.

[28] Peckham, *Sea Moss*, 47.

[29] Bragdon, *Golden Person in the Heart*, 20; Cowan, *Southwestern Pennsylvania*, 291–94.

[30] Bedlow, *War and Worship*, 164.

[31] Douglas, *Bird's Eye View*, 3.

[32] Tynan, *Three Score Poems*, 12.

[33] Patton, *Mignonette*, 132–33.

[34] Dickinson, *Poems Second Series*, 136.

[35] Dyer, *Rhymes of a Radical*, 134; Cawein, *Idyllic Monologues*, 103–4.

[36] Mifflin, *Collected Sonnets*, 354.

[37] Watson, *To-day and Yesterday*, 27.

[38] *Proceedings of the Annual Meeting*, 75. Verse by Oscar Mellish.

[39] John S. Davis, *Poems*, 6.

[40] Weare, *Songs of the Western Shore*, 91.

[41] Adams, *Breezy Western Verse*, 88; Easton, *Chicago*, 5.

[42] Abbott, *Wild Roses*, 34; Archibald, *Some Scribbles*, 68; Barbour, *Songs and Sonnets*, 45.

[43] Robinson, *Epic Ballads of the Land of Flowers*, 110–11.

[44] Headland, *Midnight Items*, 37; Farquhar, *Libyssa*, 118.

[45] Cook, *First Mortgage*, 26, 228; Kiser, *Ballads of the Busy Days*, 184.

[46] Brown, *One Dollar's Worth*, 5.

[47] Bien, *Oriental Legends*, 150–51.

[48] Dyer, *Rhymes of a Radical*, 68.

[49] Bowen, *Losing Ground*, 13.

[50] Fleenor, *In Passing Through*, 63.

[51] Carman and Hovey, *Last Songs from Vagabondia*, 73. Verse by Richard Hovey.

[52] Welburn, *American Epic*, 269.

[53] Cheyney, *Poems*, 70.

[54] Brooks, *Margins*, 78.

[55] Sanburn, *Thoughts in Verse*, 60; Elshemus, *Mammon*, 99.

[56] Robinson, *Children of the Night*, 35.

[57] Santayana, *Hermit of Carmel*, 204.

[58] Glanville, *"An Eye for an Eye,"* 55.

[59] Bowen, *Losing Ground*, 3.

[60] Rupp, *Sonnets*, 7.

[61] Kelley, *Age of Gold*, 8.

[62] Major, *Peril of the Republic*, 3.

[63] McIntyre, *Sun-sealed*, 75.

[64] Kirschbaum, *Idyls Crude*, 24.

[65] Smiley, *Meditations of Samwell Wilkins*, 90.

[66] Edgerton, *Songs of the People*, 57.

[67] Maline, *Nineteenth Century*, 9.

[68] Freeman, *Reminiscences of Farm Life*, 35; Field, *Second Book of Verse*, v.

[69] Martin, *Vistae Vitae*, 3.

[70] Doyle, *Moody Moments*, 33.

[71] Crane, *Black Riders*, 61.

[72] Lozier, *Your Mother's Apron Strings*, 19; Kelso, *Poems*, 71.

[73] Lee, *Sphinx of Gold*, n. pag.

[74] Austin, *Devil's Football*, 20.

[75] Carman and Hovey, *Songs from Vagabondia*, 2. Verse by Richard Hovey.

[76] Koopman, *At the Gates of the Century*, 60.

[77] Carter, *Out Here in Ol' Missoury*, 62–63.

[78] Conant, *Poems*, 92.

[79] Kernestaffe, *Pebbles and Pearls*, 89.

[80] Crane, *War Is Kind*, 45.

[81] Donner, *English Lyrics*, 71.

[82] McCann, *Songs from an Attic*, 120.

[83] Fenollosa, *East and West*, 42.

[84] Savage, *At the Back of the Moon*, 34.

[85] Hollister, *Sunflower*, 119, 120.

[86] Crist, *Patchwork*, 221; Hendrix, *Fragments*, 80; Musser, *Poems*, 113.

[87] Grant, *Forget-me-nots*, 80.

88 Cornwall, *Roses and Myrtles*, 93.
89 Savage, *First Poems and Fragments*, 73.
90 Thomas, *Cassia*, 39.
91 Lodge, *Song of the Wave*, 116; Banks, *Quiet Music*, 48.
92 d'Arville, *Omega et Alpha*, 78.
93 Peck, *Greystone and Porphyry*, 46–62.
94 Robinson, *Torrent and the Night Before*, 12.
95 Wilson, *Versatile Verses*, 38; Pearson, *Golden Grains*, 230; Thornton, *Zenobia*, 61; Dennis, *Asphodels and Pansies*, 40.
96 Wadsworth, *Winter Pastoral*, 19.
97 Schultz, *Course of Progress*, 100.
98 Turner, *Pre-eminence of Our American Independence*, 7.
99 Barton, *For Friendship's Sake*, 12.
100 Riehl, *Runes of the Red Race*, 119.
101 Reid, *Heather Bell*, 48–49.
102 Bowen, *In Divers Tones*, 78.
103 Hamilton, *America*, 17; Voldo, *Song of America*, 70.
104 Denton, *Early Poetical Works*, 51.
105 Savage, *Hymns*, 51.
106 Monroe, *Valeria*, 234.
107 Merle E. Curti, *Roots of American Loyalty* (N. Y.: Columbia University Press, 1946), 217.
108 Stevens, *Idyl of the Sun*, 92.
109 Woodward, *Lyrics of the Umpqua*, 1.
110 Markham, *Lincoln*, 53.
111 Woodberry, *My Country*, 12.
112 Hodge, *Stray Shots*, 31; Emmons, *Mingled Memories*, 99.
113 Hancock, *Book of Poems*, 60; Gallagher and Simmons, *Cruise of the "Trenton,"* 66; Dodge, *Echoes from Cape Ann*, 66.
114 Alden, *Lines, Rhymes, or Poetry*, 83.
115 Kiser, "*Budd Wilkins at the Show*," 36–37.
116 Brooks, *Old Ace*, 106; Bate, *Berth-deck Ballads*, 10; Booth, *Family of Three*, 249.
117 Field, *John Smith, U.S.A.*, 9–15.
118 Smith, *Some Simple Rhymes of Leisure Times*, 90.
119 Savage, *At the Back of the Moon*, 17–18.
120 Walker, *Between the Tides*, 215.
121 Barbour, *Songs and Sonnets*, 37.
122 Lambie, *Century*, 31; Delano, *Stone of Whizgig Race*, 15.
123 Baum, *Father Goose*, n. pag.
124 *Stars and Stripes*, 9; verse by Stephen W. Goodhue.
125 Riley, *Book of Joyous Children*, 35–36.
126 Riley, *Afterwhiles*, 116.
127 Hovey, *Along the Trail*, 17.
128 Kenney, *Thusettes*, 113.
129 Cawein, *Moods and Memories*, 271.
130 Woodberry, *Poems*, 4.
131 Moore, *Death of Falstaff*, 68; Johnson, *Now-a-day Poems*, 65.
132 Crosby, *War Echoes*, 4.
133 Robinson, *Captain Craig*, 21.

[134] Lemon, *Ione*, 197.

[135] Dickinson, *Poems* (copyright 1890), 13.

[136] Schultz, *Course of Progress*, 16; Trow, *Prose and Verse*, 21.

[137] Lemon, *Ione*, 335.

[138] Lampton, *Yawps*, 21.

[139] Carman and Hovey, *Last Songs from Vagabondia*, 55. Verse by Richard Hovey.

[140] Edgerton, *Songs of the People*, 46.

[141] Savary, *Poems of Expansion*, 10.

[142] Devine, *"Like a Sun to Illumine the World,"* n. pag.

[143] Cleveland, *Scarlet-veined*, 85–86.

[144] Adams, *Songs and Sonnets*, 102.

[145] Claflin, *Thoughts in Verse*, 28.

[146] Robinson, *Epic Ballads of the Land of Flowers*, 108.

[147] Whiting, *Four Hundred to One*, 125.

[148] Riley, *Poems Here at Home*, 7.

[149] Whitaker, *My Country*, 11.

[150] Burgoyne, *Songs of Every Day*, 125.

[151] Swift, *Advent of Empire*, 33–34.

[152] Bullard, *Cupid's Chalice*, 63.

[153] Wise, *Optimist*, n. pag.

[154] Koopman, *At the Gates of the Century*, 57.

[155] Dickson, *Farmer's Thoughts*, 20.

[156] Crosby, *Swords and Plowshares*, 27.

[157] Stickney, *Dramatic Verses*, 71.

[158] Dibble, *Prairie Poems*, 33.

[159] Day, *Kin O'Ktaadn*, 227.

[160] Cawein, *Idyllic Monologues*, 104; Cawein, *Garden of Dreams*, 20.

[161] James H. Scott, *Poems*, 68.

[162] Le Gallienne, *Cry of the Little Peoples*, n. pag.

[163] Griffith, *Excursions*, 10.

[164] Guiney, *Martyrs' Idyl*, 76.

IX

The Poet and the Age of Guilt

THE POTENTIAL POLARITIES OF PUBLIC RESPONSE TO
the issues and conditions of the Gilded Age, as set forth in
Chapter I, have—in the intervening chapters—resolved themselves into majority and minority points of view. With this
evidence in hand, we have reached a position from which to make
a more general evaluation. In what way does this poetic
response contribute to a broad understanding of the age? What
does it reveal about the nature and extent of the poet's collective
citizenship?

i

In responding to the first of these questions, it will be helpful
to note the extent to which the verse of the Gilded Age confirms, and the extent to which it contradicts, the accepted
interpretations of that era. Although contradictions will be
found to outweigh confirmations, there are many important

ways in which the verse substantiates informed expectations.

Superficially, at least, the themes described in Chapter VIII add evidence to prior judgments passed upon this generation. Lewis Mumford, for example, has prepared us for the fascination with science which pervaded much of the poetry:

. . . new inventions . . . were still almost toys, and before their potentialities had been transferred into slick routines, they had a power to stir the mind, out of all proportion to any of their later effects. The telephone, the electric light, the phonograph, the improved camera, the gas engine, the typewriter, all belonged in their inception, if not in their full development, to the Brown Decades: they had something of the profound fascination that the Leyden jar had in an earlier century: they were wonders of nature before they became utilities.[1]

In many respects, the poetic reaction to the world of science did seem exactly like that of a child with a new toy. In its more mature aspects, as it pertained to scientific theories and their epistemological applications, the poetic preoccupation with science only mirrored another prime characteristic of this scientifically oriented age. The debate over the theory of evolution, which formed a center of poetic interest, constituted an especially representative direction of interest.

There is abundant reason to anticipate, too, the poet's concern with materialism. Mark Sullivan baldly epitomized this condition in his summary of late-nineteenth-century attitudes:

If one should venture so daring an effort as a condensed summary of the forces of American life, one would probably say that at this particular time many of them had to do with money, some away from it; nearly all whirled around it. One large class was making money and finding various uses for it, some enjoyable and some not, some wholesome and some not. Whereas another large group was failing to make money, failing to achieve economic or social parity with the other class, according to what were the standards of the day. With both classes, money was the chief concern. It was undoubtedly an age where money-making was the most prized career.[2]

Mr. Dooley, even more talented at epitomization, pronounced the "crownin' wurruk iv our civilization" to be "th' cash raygister." The heroes of the age, from the actual captains of industry to the fictional tycoons of Horatio Alger,[3] were all symptomatic of a materialistic culture in which the dollar sign approximated the halo as an outward manifestation of grace. The Gospel of Wealth, as a dominant social philosophy, gave its blessing to the worship of the tangible. To the extent that they shared this preoccupation, the poets reflected one of the best-established attributes of their era. Many of them recognized the prevalence of such values, and a few of them went so far as to agree with George Santayana, who in one of his moods found something virtuous in America's peculiar brand of materialism.[4]

The strong strain of patriotism and expansionism which characterized this verse sounded no discordant note to the ear attuned to Gilded Age airs. In the early years of this period any lack of patriotic fervor might have been taken as a deprecation of the effort expended in saving the Union; not to revere that Union could well savor of basest treason, of ingratitude to the gallant dead. As Civil War associations began to fade, a new war arrived to bolster the general sense of almost compulsory national loyalty. Party politics, political philosophies, labor and immigration questions—all were colored by the closed question of national allegiance. Nativistic arguments came into play against Socialists, free-traders, and advocates of unrestricted immigration. On many issues, in fact, patriotic arguments were unabashedly employed on both sides of the same question. Patroitism, in fine, carried the day; in contributing to this nationally dominant theme the poets developed their own tributes to America's historically and religiously sanctioned mission of leading the world into a glorious future.

In more particular ways, too, the verse offers evidence in support of prevalent notions concerning late-nineteenth-century circumstances and attitudes. Obviously, the poetry supports Arnold Toynbee's description of America's "chief myth—that of leaving the city of destruction to move through the wilderness to the promised land."[5] For this generation the promised land lay in the trans-Mississippi West; and the poet waxed enthusiastic about the prospects for a continental nation brought to fulfillment in the midst of the natural grandeur with which he characterized this region. In a way that could have been expected, he translated the nation's successful taming of the continent into a theistically oriented call for manifest destiny.[6] For him this "promised land" denoted no static utopia, but rather a dynamic national achievement with strong international implications.

The "city of destruction," conversely, aroused an adverse response which might likewise have been expected. Impressed though he was by the heterogeneity and vitality of the metropolis, and fascinated though he was by its applications of technological progress, the poet's prevailing response to the city was one of hostility. Whether or not he was a conscious partisan of rural mores, he consistently pictured the city as a dark, noisy, crowded, dangerous, and immoral region, the haunt of drunkards, neurotics, criminals, and scoffers. He saw the pace, the competitiveness, and the impersonality of city life combining to produce a nearly helpless race, almost totally dependent on mechanical contrivances, and thus antithetical to the tradition-honored, independently situated farmer-frontiersman. The poet's revulsion at this newborn urban monster was natural enough; it would have been difficult, however, to foresee the fierce intensity and detailed astuteness of his reaction.

Many poets responded complacently to the economic status quo, accepting the existing distribution of wealth, and holding both rich and poor responsible for their conditions. But while the Gospel of Wealth, and its complementary gospel of poverty, found numerous poetic adherents, the majority report on economic questions must be listed under the heading of the unexpected. In reacting to political conditions the poet evinced even more superficial conformity to expected patterns. In so far

as the political character of the age was determined by a sentimental extension of Civil War associations and by undue
emphasis upon the personalities of candidates for election, the
overwhelming amount of verse devoted to the career and
character of politico-military heroes offers no surprises. Yet
when this primarily occasional verse is seen in its true perspective, the political attitudes of the poet are less subject to easy
generalization. The poet conformed most nearly to expected
patterns when he rejected third parties and "foreign radicalism."
In his loyalty to the two-party system, and in his insistence on
home-grown answers to native problems, the poet revealed
himself as an accurate stereotype for an age which distinguished
itself through its passive and provincial acceptance of some truly
intolerable political abuse. As on the economic front, however,
the principal poetic reaction to political conditions must be
regarded as a departure from the usual preconceptions concerning this period.

It is only the area of humanitarian reform that reveals the
poet behaving in a manner wholly consistent with our impression of this age. The reform program of that era, riddled with
"many glaring gaps and strange oversights,"[7] was accurately
reflected in verse. Here an apathy toward social causes formed a
placid entr'acte between the frothy curtain-raiser of hyper-
activity before the Civil War and the climactic years of
achievement after the turn of the century. There were some
minor surprises in the subjects which received occasional
attention from the verse-reformers, but their principal emphasis
on woman's rights and the temperance-prohibition crusade was
eminently to be expected. Some of the arguments employed in
support of these causes might evoke more than routine interest;
but the emphasis on moral suasion, sentiment, and exhortation
was entirely in keeping the reform temper of the Gilded Age.

In his reaction to international questions the poet conspicuously fails to conform to expected patterns. The prevailing
attitude toward immigration is indicated by the founding in

1887 of the American Protective Association, with the aim of combating Roman Catholicism; the organization in 1897 of the Immigration Restriction League, which opposed the influx from Southeast Europe; and the passage of legislation in the 1880's which excluded Chinese labor. These episodes signalled the growing tendency of the United States to close its doors to the multitudes it had theretofore received almost without discrimination. Recalling the poet's xenophobic reaction to the importation of foreign political and economic ideas, one might have expected him to react in the same way to the immigration question.

But only in two cases was he unsympathetic toward foreign minorities, either as present or as potential neighbors. Of all the Europeans with whom he dealt, only the Italian attracted his antipathy. Not only did the poet's Italophobia coincide with that of labor unions and of other local groups, but it also served to adumbrate that shift in national sentiment which, by the 1920's, had resulted in nearly closing America's doors. In expressing some reservations about Chinese immigration the poet likewise reflected a public attitude which manifested itself not only in regional and occupational hostility but also in legislative enactments. Here, too, future difficulties with Asian minorities on American shores were foreshadowed; but in this case the poets were less than representative or prophetic. Their unfriendliness toward the Chinese consisted only of a strong minority sentiment; most verses on the Chinese question held that these Orientals should be treated equally with all others interested in American citizenship.

When it came to international questions outside our own borders, the poet seldom responded in a manner reflected by governmental policies and actions. In only two instances, one major and one minor, did the collective sentiment of the verse match the official American attitude. The Boxer Rebellion was treated by relatively few poets; but those who did revealed a strong, though not unanimous, sentiment in favor of intervention for the protection of American lives. Along with many other Americans, the poets called long and loud for intervention in Cuba; in fact poetic pleas for intercession against Spanish rule could be read long before the federal government seriously considered action. Once war had been declared, of course, the poet joined gladly with his patriotic fellow citizens in promoting the martial spirit[8] and in lionizing the heroes of the fray, especially Admiral Dewey. Poetic pressure for American action on behalf of Boer and Irish national self-government, although it neither reflected majority sentiment throughout the nation nor led to any serious consideration by federal authorities, did represent one of the era's characteristic pastimes: twisting the tail of the British lion. Where recent Irish immigrants and other anti-British groups offered a source of desirable and sometimes crucial votes, the deliberate cultivation of Anglophobia was by no means uncommon. Although the poet's intention was not always so obvious, he was a frequent participant in the same sport.

In many ways, the verse which related to social, political, and economic questions conformed to expected patterns: in its preoccupation with science, materialism, and national destiny; in its consistent loyalty to the legendary search for the promised land in the wilderness as a refuge from the doomed city; in its occasional acceptance of the economic status quo; in its prevailing dedication to the two-party system; in its continuing, if limited, concern with humanitarian causes; in its representative expression of Italophobia at home and Anglophobia abroad; and in the persistent predication of much of its thought on stereotyped assumptions concerning class and regional differences. Yet, as each successive chapter has shown, the verse of social awareness was often acutely and unexpectedly at variance with the attitudes commonly regarded as typical of the Gilded Age. Some of these exceptions are trifling; some have been anticipated by isolated studies here and there; but their cumulative impact represents the most important contribution of this verse to the appreciation of the age it represents. The nature of this contribution is essentially revisionary.

In assessing the Western experience, for example, the poet reacted in such a way as to contradict our expectations at a number of turns. He did not follow the lead of his prose-writing colleagues in romanticizing the Indian, but consistently commented on the Redman in terms of that trusty frontier proverb, *nisi mortui non boni*. Nor did he romanticize those other heroes of fiction, the cowhand and the lawman. Rather, the poet's hero was the pioneer. This apotheosis of the first white Westerners takes on added interest when contrasted with the poet's portrait of his contemporary Westerners; for, far from reflecting a progressive evolution of character, this contrast showed the bravery, diligence, and asceticism of the pioneer degenerating into cruelty, greed, and self-indulgence.[9] Even more upsetting to standard preconceptions was the manner in which the poet rejected the constructive importance of the agrarian experience in the West, contrasting the plight of the drought- and debt-ridden farmer with the commercial and industrial potential of Western towns and cities.

When removed from a Western context, however, the city took on a set of derogatory associations which could have been more nearly expected. It is in the details of this urban characterization, rather than its general tone, that the poet startles modern readers with the shrewdness of his observations. Here the poetic portrait does not so much contradict as anticipate the interpretations of the Gilded Age applied by historians and sociologists from the vantage point of another generation of experience. Not only did the versifier describe the urban syndrome with sometimes astonishing perceptivity, but he also moved in advance of public attitudes by using the city to exemplify the maladies which he found nationally prevalent. It was from this urban context that there emerged the most dramatic contrasts of wealth and poverty, the most virulent portraits of heartless rich, the most heart-rending accounts of

poverty's consequences. In common with the journalistic muck-
raker who, slightly later, also reveled in the detailed reproduction of urban ills, the poet found little to propose in the way of
constructive remedy. But he does clearly show how irresistibly
the violent economic contrasts of urban life led to social
protest.

It is in the realm of protest that the poetry of the Gilded Age
makes its major revisionary contribution toward an understanding of public attitudes in late-nineteenth-century America.
Although he ignored such meaningful episodes as the Homestead strike, and the march of Coxey's and similar armies, he did
discuss other crucial events, such as the Haymarket affair and
the Pullman strike, with notably more sympathy for the workingman than is typically attributed to the general public or than,
for that matter, could be found either in the contemporary
attitudes of labor organizations or in the accounts of "objective"
historians. Although he was—perhaps justifiably—confused by
foreign and "radical" approaches to economic justice, he did
repeatedly insist that American institutions answer to the call
for true economic equity. Although he paid little attention to
specific labor unions, he did avow many things in common with
them, including the organization of the laboring force as a
means toward better economic ends. Although few poets wrote
so forcefully as Markham, many joined him in spirit by supporting the organization of America's rural citizens for education,
social betterment, and political action. Beneath these particularized expressions of sympathy and programs for action lay a
foundation of extensive discontent which ranged from attacks
on the life of the wealthy to exposures of the environment of the
poor.

Although superficially less evident, the dominant character of
the political verse was remarkably similar to that on economic
subjects. Aside from those many poems inspired by the death—
especially death by assassination—of a politico-military hero,
very few verses revealed a susceptibility to the distractions by

which the professional politician reputedly kept his constituents harmlessly entertained and effectively removed from the truly pertinent issues. The poet refused, that is to say, to condone the extension of the Civil War *as a political issue* after 1876, and he refused to be put off from what he considered more pressing matters by details, however titillating, of candidates' personal lives. His central observation on political America was that representative government had given way to rule by corruption, spoils, and special privilege; and that instead of defending the interests of his constituency, the official typically feathered his own nest with the proceeds forthcoming from his representation of entrepreneurs. The politician and his party, the legislatures and the courts, all were held responsible for this victimization of the common political man.

This picture of corruption and the abuse of political institutions will not seem extreme to anyone who has read the standard political histories of this era. What does come as a surprise is the poetic evidence of resistance to these conditions, for the attitude of the public toward this state of moral laxness has been typically interpreted as careless indeed:

There was the same open public corruption, in a community that shared so many of the vices of its false officials that even the pretense of honesty was absent: those who were caught red-handed showed shame and indignation, not over their peculations, but over the fact that they were caught.[10]

But such complacent lack of resentment against breaches of political morality, so frequently attributed to the general public in the late nineteenth century, was clearly not characteristic of its verse-writing component. Not only did the poet compile a vivid list of the horrors of corruption and improper influence, but he went on to identify and discuss three pertinent issues consistently sidestepped by the major parties and their candidates: the money question, the tariff question, and the problem of domestic taxation.

That the verse writer had the discrimination to select three such pertinent issues out of the welter of shams and distractions which plagued that era is both unexpected and impressive. In so doing he acutely recognized the essentially economic nature of political problems; he urged, in fact, not only that the government regulate industrial and financial enterprise but also that it enter into the economic life of the ordinary citizen. The stand he took on these issues pointed clearly toward the platforms of splinter parties and protest groups of the late nineteenth century as well as toward major party platforms and congressional enactments after the turn of the century. On the currency question, although he opposed the demands of the Greenbackers and silverites (by a narrow margin), he did clearly state the need for a currency so controlled by the government as to respond to the needs of the nation at large rather than to the commands of a small group of bondholders, speculators, and gold-hoarders. On the tariff question he sided with free trade (although not so overwhelmingly as some historians portray the public as having done[11]), identifying protective tariff with special privilege. His arguments on the tax question pointed toward the use of federal control not only to regulate large-scale enterprise but also to aid in an equitable redistribution of the national income.

In his reaction to both economic and political events the poet stood alongside the minority protest groups; however, with a seemingly calculated perversity, he rejected by name these movements with which he seemed philosophically to side. His general point of view, for example, seems to fit nowhere so well as with that of the Populists, if we accept the summary of their chief chronicler:

The Populist philosophy thus boiled down finally to two fundamental propositions: one, that the government must restrain the selfish tendencies of those who profited at the expense of the poor and needy; the other, that the people, not the plutocrats, must control the government.[12]

P.G.A.–T

And yet he nearly laughed the "Popocrats" off his pages. In other ways the poet's attitude suggests other affinities. Certainly his resentment of politics-without-principle coincided with a Mugwump war cry; surely his recognition of the need for increased governmental participation in the economy represented a view more closely associated with the Socialists than with any other contemporary political group. And yet, the Liberal Republican movements were collectively rejected and the Socialist causes received no constructive discussion.

The problem of finding an appropriate label, however, is not hopeless. The solution may be most simply arrived at by realizing that not one but two labels are needed. Since the principal poetic comment on things political and economic was one of protest, and could be most consistently characterized by what it opposed rather than by what it favored, to this extent must we recognize here the prime characteristic of muckraking literature, that school of reform by exposure which is usually associated with the early twentieth century but which obviously typifies much of the verse of the eighties and nineties as well. On the other hand, inasmuch as the poet defined and isolated particular politico-economic issues and causes, we can see emerging from his verse an attitude described by no term more fitting than "Progressive." The body of literature from which these issues came forth with increasing insistence as the century neared its close, would indicate no very great difference between Populists and Progressives, so far as their respective social philosophies are concerned. However, the attitudes most often expressed in verse may be most closely identified with three of Progressivism's main tenets: recognition of the workingman and his associations, purification of the institutions of government and party through better men and more effective laws, and expansion of the role of the government so as to achieve economic justice.[13]

Whereas the poet evinced a true spirit of domestic reform in his reaction to urban, economic, and political problems, he approached the area of humanitarian reform with an attitude which may seem surprising only in its lack of collective enthusiasm and scope. While the verse-reformers limited themselves to a predominantly moral and sentimental defense of those two bellwethers of reform, temperance and woman's rights, their pamphleteering counterparts tended to cover a wider range of subjects with a comparatively hard-headed emphasis on legal, economic, and political arguments.[14] This verse does at least bear witness, however, to the expanding political role of the female citizen, to her growing insistence on the franchise, and to her increasing social pervasiveness. And a small body of enlightened comment on both female status and the use of alcohol at least foreshadows more becoming treatment of these subjects in the present century.

From the very apathy and resistance toward reform which the humanitarian verse so often reveals, we may learn to appreciate the volatile, original, and momentous spirit of protest which pervaded the verse on political and economic subjects. If the humanitarian reform verse illustrates what the historian means when he speaks of the complacency of the Gilded Age, then the dramatically contrasting awareness of the politico-economic verse indicates a direction in which we may need to revise our preconceptions. If the humanitarian reform verse indicates the forbidding height of barriers within the public attitude which had to be surmounted in order to inflame the national conscience, then the politico-economic verse shows an impressive willingness and even some success in the face of such discouraging hurdles.

The general tone of the poet's remarks on immigration and foreign minorities must also be considered surprising in a society which was beginning a program of increasingly restrictive immigration policies. With the quantitatively minor exceptions already noted, the poet reacted favorably to all national groups, and wrote eloquently in favor of ethnic tolerance and the continuance of unrestricted immigration. On international questions beyond American shores, the poet consistently called for a clear commitment to the pattern begun in 1776 with the Colonial struggle for national recognition and reaffirmed, as he saw it, in the efforts to free the slave. He held that America should stand for the achievement of independent nationalism around the globe: in Ireland, in South Africa, in Cuba, and in the Philippines. Since this attitude concurred with the actions of our government on only one occasion, it must certainly be regarded as both interesting and unusual.

In the issues of the Spanish-American War, the question of motivation becomes pertinent. If we went to war with Spain simply to avenge the sinking of the *Maine*, as some historians conclude, then we can hardly claim credit for fostering incipient Cuban nationalism. Both before and after this event, the poet insisted upon America's obligation to end her neighbor's suffering, rather than upon simple retribution.[15] Even more unlooked-for was the poet's sharply divided debate over the rights of the Philippine nationalists.

By now the historians seem fairly well agreed that the voting public, at least, favored American annexation of the Philippine Islands and subjection of the Tagal insurrection.[16] Owing principally to the eminence of William Vaughan Moody's "Ode in Time of Hesitation," there has been, however, a readily accepted generalization to the effect that the creative writer sided overwhelmingly with the foes of annexation.[17] A recent examination of the verse of the 1890's has resulted in the seemingly contradictory assertion that the poets of this decade firmly endorsed America's war in the Philippines.[18] The evidence in the present study argues for modifications in both these assertions: the poets were not overwhelmingly on either side of this question. What their testimony most usefully illustrates is the tenseness of this debate, and the narrow margin by which a choice was made. The mixed ideals and objectives which have formed our concept of national role and function, which today may be strikingly seen in the strangely diverse character of America's national allies, has never been so starkly dramatized as in our debate over the Philippines. The poetry reveals an argument which was both intense and evenly divided; strong reasons were presented vehemently on both sides. This metrical battle was important for the slight numerical backing it gave to the foes of annexation; but it was equally important for the manner in which it dramatized the nearly even split in our international personality at this—probably the last—time when America had the opportunity to avoid the international schizophrenia which has plagued her ever since.

Consistent with his suspicions of business influence in domestic matters was the surprisingly persistent outcry raised against the possibility of improper economic pressures on the development of international policy. The one versifier who argued against our part in suppressing the Boxer rebellion, for example, typified the poet's general suspicion that business greed might taint our actions. In the more complex Cuban and Philippine questions, moreover, the poet responded with acute sensitivity and from a consistently anti-business point of view. America's business leaders were fairly evenly divided on the advisability of our entry into the Cuban conflict;[19] hence the poets berated business leaders both for keeping us out of the war—subverting ideals to material worries—and for encouraging our entry for the sake of profiteering. By the time of the Philippine crisis, when business had made its choice for international expansion, the poet spoke vociferously and voluminously in contempt of wallet-stuffing as a national motive. As long as the business point of view had been divided, the poet's consistent anti-business stand drew him into self-contradictions concerning international policy and motivation; but once our embryo barons of international trade had made clear their own objectives, the poet was able to regain his consistency in enthusiastic opposition to the course proposed by the man of commerce.

Not only in the events and conditions which occupied the poet, but also in the prevailing themes which characterized his more fundamental public personality, we find evidence disturbing to some of our preconceptions. While the poet's interest in science, materialism, and national destiny was to be expected, the manner in which he treated these themes was far from routine. His interest in evolutionary ideas could have been foreseen, for example, but it would have been hard to envisage the summary manner with which he dismissed the application of Darwinian precepts to such fields as economic competition and international relations. The idea of free competition among economic individuals as sanctioned by natural law was used to buttress laissez-faire economics and the Gospel of Wealth throughout the nineteenth century; but the poets brought up this rationale only to exclaim on the cruelty of its implications. Toward the end of the century this same idea of natural selection was brought into support of racism and imperialism in international policy. Here, once again, the poet demurred, preferring instead to hitch his wagon of nationalism to the star of divinely appointed destiny. The kind of evolution he favored smacked of the Enlightenment, or of Comtean positivism, in the sense that this evolution was to be orderly, humane, and consistently evident. Where it differed from these earlier ideas was not in its reliance on scientific parallels but in its inclusion of the nineteenth-century idea of progress and in its consistent emphasis on the presence of God's guiding hand.

The poet's resistance to what he saw as the rising tide of scientism represents a natural poetic attitude, but one unlooked-for in an era obsessed by science. He unhesitatingly accepted the material benefits of science and offered a grudging and noticeably fearful respect to the power of scientific ideas. But instead of accepting what he took to be the broader implications of science as a way of thought, he resisted what he feared were encroachments on beloved traditional grounds. As he tempered his acceptance of evolution by altering it with humanism and religious faith, so he qualified his total reaction to the scientific state of mind with warnings against the attempt of science to control, define, and delimit those elements of life, love, and nature which he held illimitable, indefinable, and of immeasurable value.

Compared to the poet's awed resistance to the inroads of science, his protest against the curse of materialism was overwhelming. Rather than complacently accepting the code of Moloch, like a faithful representative of the Gilded Age, he raised a cry of horror at the manner in which his contemporaries had enslaved themselves to the dollar and allowed the standards of the tangible to corrupt society in all its compartments. Wherever he looked, he saw the curse of Mammon—in Congress and in the church, from Wall Street to Lovers' Lane. While such vehement protest offers evidence that the Gilded Age indeed deserved the name, it also indicates the presence of an active conscience. If the plague was raging, at least the verse-diagnosticians had sounded a full alarm.

Although the poet waved the flag and "soared the eagle" with his fellow citizens of these highly patriotic days, he did show a surprising restraint when it came to debating the ways and means of promoting America's extravagant destiny. If he often seemed belligerently nationalistic, he did decide that militarism constituted an improper avenue of expansion. Although many of his lines suggested a conscious craving for a place in the Kiplingesque caravan of empire, he did decline to identify his nation's future with the imperial parade. Though he cultivated an indisputably patriotic temper in spite of his many domestic discontents, he stopped short of explicitly endorsing a philosophy of military or political aggression.

The most effective way to highlight the poet's collective contribution to a deeper understanding of the Gilded Age—and at the same time to identify his most dominant mood—is to identify an attitude which pervaded this verse even more persistently than those themes discussed in Chapter VIII:

protest. Throughout the verse one sees its various manifestations: protest against the failure of the Westerner to live up to the pioneer heritage; against the hardships of life on the farm and in the city; against the consequences, throughout our economic life, of poorly distributed wealth; against the abuse of political institutions on every level; against the sale of liquor and the subjugation of the female; against international immorality and dedication to the dollar. If there is one single preoccupation which gives to this verse a common tone, it is the sense of persistent objection to things as they appeared to the poet.

The pervasiveness of this protestant mood suggests the importance of understanding the verse in terms of acceptance and rejection. On the one hand was the minority which gave happy approval to the advance of American territory and technology; to the prevalent leadership of inventor, entrepreneur, and war-veteran–president; and to the attractive or picturesque aspect of whatever social outcropping captured the poetic attention. On the other hand was the majority which saw with disappointment nearly every scene and player on which the curtain opened. For them the post-bellum return to America's experiment represented a near fiasco. In their view, the institutions molded in our earlier years had been hopelessly outmoded by the changing social, political, and economic patterns at the end of the century.

Throughout the verse there existed an attitude parallel to that described in summarizing the poet's politico-economic viewpoint. The dominant mood was one of opposition. Relatively few poets, even when they endorsed specific programs, supposed that they had arrived at finally formulated answers to the ills of the day. Typically, even those who marched under the same banner were there because they opposed rather than favored similar things. Mugwumps, anti-annexationists, feminists, neo-Jeffersonians—all were chracterized by their willingness to speak out against prevalent conditions rather than by their unified recommendations for alleviating them. The term "muckraking" could very appropriately apply not only to the politico-economic aspects of this verse, but also to the attitude of criticism and exposure which pervaded almost every discussion. The mixed connotation of this term appropriately suggests both negative and constructive functions: the accumulation of elaborate catalogues of resentment and disappointment, and the particularization of discontent by means of which an effective campaign of concrete reform could be waged.

This constructive aspect must be recognized if the verse is to be fairly appraised; and there are many examples of the poet's astuteness in pinpointing particular targets for his protest. In isolating the "urban syndrome," in elaborating the effects of factory labor, and in identifying government control of the economy and labor organization as important politico-economic issues, the poet proved himself a discerning diagnostician of the times. He was by no means so blindly intent on wielding the muckrake as were the journalists or their unhappy prototype in Bunyan. And his insight into the sources of particular social ills remains impressive in spite of his failure to suggest very much in the way of remedy.

The only noticeable trait of the poetic mind in the late nineteenth century which might seem incongruous is its rather strident patriotism. If, according to the poet, so much was wrong with social, economic, and political America, how could he then indulge himself in such unrestrained paeans of patriotism and uninhibited prophecies of unlimited national destiny? In this apparent contradiction lies a valuable clue to the distinctiveness of the age. To call the age a critical one does not impart the full flavor of shame and desperation of which so many of these verses savor. There is a special, an almost hyperbolic disappointment present in the lines of those who found their America wanting. What better explains this special sense of shame than the disappointment of those high and determined hopes which Americans almost universally held for this paradigm of nations? The interaction of this solemn regard for America's noble experiment with this consistently bitter protest combined to produce a sense of extraordinary shame. To call the eighties and nineties an "age of guilt"[20] is to acknowledge both the atmosphere of intense and persistent criticism of its social institutions and behavior, as well as the accompanying sense of shame that these unfortunate conditions should exist in beloved America for which so much had been hoped and promised.

If the poets defined these decades in terms of guilt rather than gilt, then what becomes of the Gilded Age stereotype? This problem in periodization demands close attention to the diversity of late-nineteenth-century trends. We know that at some time during these years Americans traded the problems of the Reconstruction for the task of bringing a highly productive economy into a position of social responsibility. We know that Americans began to realize that their country's future was to be shaped not by the farmer and his philosophy, nor by the vanishing frontier, but by the city, with its new complex of industrial, commercial, financial, and social problems. With the realization that the settling of the continent had in some measure been completed, came the sense that America must take a place in the international picture equivalent to its enlarged stature. Also with these years there appeared cracks in the foundation of Protestant fundamentalism which had lain solidly beneath the century's prominent rationales; testing its solidity were the power of science and the new religion of humanity. These were the developments which signalled the end of what we call the Gilded Age—a time of lingering naïveté, backward-looking complacence, and social irresponsibility. When did these changes take place?

Answers offered by the verse, fractional as they are, must be accompanied by oft-repeated words of caution; yet these answers do appear with some consistency. The primary answer is the inevitable one: basic and sweeping social changes such as these do not come about suddenly, but enter public awareness only by imperceptible degrees. This truism notwithstanding, the verse does reveal a noticeable shift in its point of view at a rather surprising moment in the early 1880's. This change in the social temper announced itself primarily by contrast. The late seventies offered many opportunities for the recognition of new interests and attitudes, but the poet overlooked them almost entirely. In its backward-looking acceptance of social conditions and its failure to recognize the need for a new social awareness, the verse of the 1870's qualifies admirably for the epithets typically applied to the Gilded Age.

With the coming of the eighties, however, the poetic air was suddenly filled with shocked recognition and shouted protest. What gilt had theretofore covered the surface of widespread social, political, and economic problems was replaced by a guilt resulting from the exposure of these problems to view. In many ways the new era had arrived; not overnight, of course, but with astounding abruptness. The seriousness of politico-economic problems was recognized, the importance of urban conditions was stressed, the scope of international attention was broadened, the wide-ranging implications of science were discussed, and the idea of social responsibility came into prominence.

Much evidence outside the verse substantiates the idea of a marked rise in the social temperature during the 1880's. Indices as varied as the numbers of utopian novels and of industrial strikes point to the early eighties as beginning a period of radically increased protest. But since we are mainly concerned with attitudes rather than with events, we might take more seriously the correlation provided by students who have probed into various corners of this era's composite mind: by Morton White, for example, who calls the eighties and nineties a "period of ignition" in American thought; by Lewis Mumford, who quarrels with his own periodization in order to show how the muckrake cast its shadow across the generation coming of age after 1880; by Henry Steele Commager, who sees a "watershed in American history and thought" in the mid-eighties; and by Eric Goldman, who cites the 1880's as the decade in which liberal reform triumphs became "commonplace" and "lower-income discontent" began to cry out for attention.[21] Yet even these interpreters were not always consistent in locating a major American change of temper near 1880; it remains quite difficult to find historical analyses which might explain the poet's consistency throughout the eighties and nineties as distinguished from what went before. Many of the implications of this verse would not be truly revisionary had they sprung exclusively from the nineties and after. What is unexpected is the idea of a continuing point of view which not only characterized the waning years of the century, but pertained equally to its last two decades.

As for setting a terminal date to the era, the chronological limitations of this study make it necessary to be even more humble. Furthermore, nothing at all decisive or dramatic seems to occur in the social view of the versifier as one reads through the 1890's and into the present century. The common notion that the Spanish-American War distracted the public from the pursuit of domestic problems, thereby providing a hiatus between the Populist and Progressive movements, draws no support from the verse. Nor did the turn of the century itself produce any magic change of heart; certainly no break occurred at the end of this period comparable to that shift in social temper observable at 1880. Changes came about through a process of gradual shifts and emergences, as reform targets were steadily particularized and constructive platforms replaced the negative catalogues of complaint. The poetry provides no clear line of demarcation between Populism and Progressivism, between the protests which characterized the late nineteenth century and those which shaped the early years of the new century. What it shows is a Gilded Age which expired with the 1870's, followed by an age of guilt which began with a recognition of changed conditions and a general protest against the inadequate means for dealing with them. With the approach of the twentieth century, this protest became increasingly constructive and specific.

REFORM BY BICYCLE.

ii

Our final question concerns the social character of the poet. To raise it is to challenge the literary historian, critic, and anthologist who have consigned him to a position of disaffiliation. As is doubtless true of any age, the greater portion of this poetry did not deal with topics of primarily social relevance. Yet, as the Appendix quantitatively affirms, there is unmistakable and extensive evidence of the poet's active concern with the events and conditions of his day. Whether his participation amounted to a lot or a little cannot be easily determined in the absence of any basis of comparison; but that is another matter.

What kind of citizen-commentator was the poet? Although sometimes unpredictable in his omissions and emphases, he did focus quite consistently on what can be regarded, both from his standpoint and from ours, as the important social, political, and economic issues. The historian would endorse the value of his coverage both as to subject matter and as to analysis. It can be cited to his credit that he quite frequently went beyond his contemporaries in his shrewd perception of crucial issues and effects, and reacted to them in a way which often puts the scholar and the chronicler in the shade. It is to be expected, perhaps, that the sensitive side of the poet's nature would be repelled by slum conditions and blatant evidences of money-worship, that the humanistic side of the poetic character might hesitate to accord complete hegemony to science, that the prophetic cast of the poetic disposition would lead to a certain shrillness in his pronouncements on the blighting influence of the city and on the consequences of our foreign policy. But as social analysis, this verse shows a clear recognition of important issues and developments, and mirrors a generally perceptive response.

Is there any clear explanation for the existence of this extensive and interesting body of poetic social comment in the face of the literary historian's presumptions to the contrary? In the first place, it is doubtless true that much of the verse here chronicled would not merit the attention of the critic or literary historian who was interested primarily in aesthetic achievement. In the second place, there inevitably will appear from any survey as comprehensive as the present one a group of "undiscovered" poets who are doubtless below the first rank in aesthetic achievement but who deserve attention for what they have said, provided their mode of expression has not been so completely wretched as to disqualify them. A rather lengthy list might be supplied in this category, made up of such names as Ellen P. Allerton, Herbert W. Bowen, John H. Carter, Ernest H. Crosby, W. E. Davenport, Miles M. Dawson, Louis M. Elshemus, Sam W. Foss, Peter Grant, J. E. Higgins, John H. Hirt, John D. Hylton, J. E. Kelley, Hugh Kelso, Eudorus C. Kenney, William J. Lampton, Emanuel Price, Minot J. Savage, George M. Sloan, Ephraim Terry, J. L. Treuthart, and Drummond Welburn. In view of the inaccessibility of the works in question, there is little reason to extend the list; but there are many more. In general these volumes are chiefly interesting as social documents; nevertheless many of them exhibit a prosodic technique sufficiently accomplished to argue for their notice in anthologies and chronicles of our literary past. To at least some degree it would appear that the literary historian's misconception of the period arises from potentially rewarding avenues left unexplored.

Nor are the men and women of little or no literary reputation the only ones to suffer this neglect. Several of the better-known figures of the day are seldom presented to us as poets. In some cases the loss is trifling; but there are palpable rewards in store for the literary historian who takes the trouble to consider the poems of Hamlin Garland, Stephen Crane, and George Santayana. Somewhat less distinguished, but no less completely ignored, are those of John W. DeForest, Ellen Glasgow, and Thomas W. Higginson. But it is not simply that the historian of letters has allowed us to forget that certain literary figures wrote noteworthy verse; a more important critical shortcoming stems from the assumption of a general absence of social relevance in the verse of this period, and the consequent blindness to it even when it is most evident in the leading lights of the day. Who better, for example, than Emily Dickinson and E. A. Robinson represent the sense of oppressed humanism and

the revolt against the materialism of this age? Who better than
Paul Dunbar and Madison Cawein speak for the passing of a
certain fundamental way of life? Who better than Eugene Field
and Richard Hovey debate the domestic and international
politics of the late nineteenth century? Who better than Stephen
Crane illustrates the disillusion with contemporary standards of
success and valor? Who better than George Santayana probes
the essential character of the age? It is not simply that the
historian has forgotten and overlooked a great many verse-
writers of interest—some aesthetically impeccable, some un-
questionably marginal in their prosodic achievements; it is also
that he has apparently approached this subject with predilections
so firm as to obscure from view the obvious social relevance of
this verse. Edmund Clarence Stedman instructed his colleagues
well as to the importance of poetry's contribution to the understanding of its age. His successors followed his practice in
overlooking this quality rather than his preaching in favor of
stressing it.[22]

The case of the novelist in America's Gilded Age has something in common with that of the poet. The complacent acceptance or avoidance of late-century social problems was typically
felt to be symptomatic not only of the populace and the poet,
but also of the creator of prose fiction. By the early nineteen-
forties, however, sufficient evidence had been presented in
defense of the social awareness of the novelist and short-story
writer that more recent literary historians have approached the
fiction of the Gilded Age with increased respect for its value as
social comment. As early as 1927 Allyn Forbes saw in the
welter of utopian novels in the 1880's and 1890's indications of
a certain kind of social awareness.[23] A doctoral dissertation in
1936 indicated a tradition of economic criticism in American
fiction virtually throughout the nineteenth century; more
extensive bibliographical studies followed.[24] When a contributor
to *American Literature* suggested in 1941 that the fiction of the
Gilded Age needed re-appraisal on account of its unrecognized

contribution to social protest, he was soundly upbraided for reiterating the obvious.[25] In the following year the two most important works on this subject appeared, one centering on the political and the other on the economic importance of the fiction of the 1880's and 1890's. Alfred Kazin, in the first of these works, identified the emerging realistic fiction with Populism and other expressions of protest.[26] The second of these two works also offered a conclusion on the social awareness of the Gilded Age writer:

The idea that American authorship, faced with the grave industrial evils of that time, remained complacent; the idea that the literary fraternity were joined solidly in league with the financial fraternity is simply not supported by the facts; it is, indeed, perilously close to the quality of myth.[27]

These special treatments of fiction do not merely suggest a background for Progressivism in the novels of the 1890's—a condition which had been much better recognized than had the social relevance of verse—but go beyond this to point out the importance of the 1880's as a meaningful decade of literary protest in prose. These revisionary analyses of late-nineteenth-century American fiction provide a parallel for the present study both in their recognition of a long-standing misconception and in their plea for re-appraisal.

It would be tempting, at this point, to launch an attack on any of a number of available straw men in order to illustrate the interpretive extremes to which students of the late nineteenth century have been forced by their ignorance of social relevance in our literature in general and in our verse in particular. It would be fairer, however, to point out a general failure in the histories and interpretations of this period—be they literary, social, or intellectual—to utlilize the wealth of valuable testimony now demonstrably present in both our prose and our poetry for the documentation of alert social attitudes. The comments and reactions of the writer may merely furnish additional

P.G.A.–U

substantiation for well-established views; in other cases they will suggest new traits in the public personality which bear further examination. In any case the full and mature appreciation of this era will continue to elude us until we have taken into account the many sources of understanding available.

Already, however, the over-enthusiasm of the convert to this sort of revisionism has begun to interpose its own distortion of our understanding. In two principal ways a creditable zealousness has resulted in an undesirable exaggeration of the claims to be made for literature-as-document. In the first place it must be remembered that no reliable correlation exists between writer and reader, regardless of sales figures and critical acclaim. Each writer speaks for only one person; attitudes expressed by poets and novelists must appear elsewhere in the society in order to establish themselves as convincingly prevalent. Not only must we remember how fractional, albeit special, is literary evidence, but also how firmly it is tied to point of view rather than to point of fact. Illogical though it obviously is, there are those who would have us re-write the factual record simply because literary attitudes may cast a new and different light. That comments and reactions of the writer have their own peculiar force and effect, is well enough recognized; there is no need to undermine this value by claiming too much.

What this second look at the poetry and the period has provided, then, is evidence that the literary historian should take care in his generalizations concerning social meaning in the verse of these decades. In overlooking certain poets who should have interested even the recorder of aesthetic achievement, and in failing to percieve certain clear strains of social analysis in the poets of reputation whom he did treat, he led his readers to the mistaken conclusion that the verse had little to contribute to an understanding of the age itself. This poetry reveals a discriminating and perceptive reaction to most of the issues and conditions which the historian finds important in the political, economic, and social life of the times. By its very nature as poetry, it is colored by special strengths and special weaknesses, but this collective testimony displays an intimate and profound relation between the artist and his culture where indeed there was thought to be little or none.

Notes

[1] Lewis Mumford, *Brown Decades* (N.Y.: Harcourt, Brace, 1931), p. 35.

[2] Mark Sullivan, *Our Times* (N.Y.: Scribner, 1926), I, 286.

[3] For an interesting synthesis of the Horatio Alger code, which in many respects may be applied to the ethos of the Gilded Age, see Kenneth S. Lynn, *Dream of Success* (Boston: Little, Brown, 1955), pp. 7–8.

[4] George Santayana's particular views on this subject may best be observed in *Character and Opinion in the United States* (N.Y.: Norton, 1934), p. 175. Santayana, to be sure, had much else to say on this subject.

[5] This is from a symposium in *Shenandoah*, X (Autumn 1958), p. 7.

[6] In many ways the verse demonstrates the aptness of Ralph H. Gabriel's delineation of the *Course of American Democratic Thought* (N.Y.: Ronald Press, 1956 [2nd ed.]). Page 180 contains a statement of the nature of America's mission during the "Middle Period" which coincides especially closely with attitudes expressed in verse.

[7] Allan Nevins, *Emergence of Modern America, 1865–1878* (N.Y.: Macmillan, 1928), p. 346.

[8] Merle Curti, in an article called "Literary Patriots of the Gilded Age," *Historical Outlook* (now *Social Studies*) XIX (April 1928), 153–56, states that a "majority of American men of letters . . . condemned the Spanish-American War . . ." The verse confirms this generalization only in relation to the question of Philippine annexation. It is true that many of these poets would hardly qualify as "men of letters," but their overwhelming support of American intervention in Cuba at least partially contradicts Professor Curti's statement.

[9] In assessing the impact of the frontier on the character of their ancestral pioneers the poets agreed fairly well with Professor Turner's famous analysis. In appraising their contemporaries, however, they were more in accord with such interpretations as Lewis Mumford's and Matthew Josephson's: *Golden Day* (N.Y.: Boni and Liveright, 1926), p. 275; *Robber Barons* (N.Y.: Harcourt, Brace, 1934), pp. 21–22.

[10] Mumford, *Brown Decades*, p. 15. On the other hand, see Henry J. Ford, *Cleveland Era* (New Haven: Yale, 1919), pp. 8, 12ff., or Matthew Josephson, *Politicos, 1865–1896* (N.Y.: Harcourt, Brace, 1938), pp. 343ff. Ford and Josephson are exceptional in their recognition of the era after 1876 as a time of public resentment against the abuses of professional politics.

[11] Ford, *Cleveland Era*, p. 158. He declares that public opinion against the protective tariff was sufficiently overwhelming to force the Republicans to yield in matters of principle.

[12] John D. Hicks, *Populist Revolt* (Minneapolis: Univ. of Minnesota Press, 1931), p. 406.

[13] Richard M. Hofstadter's remarks are particularly well adapted to separating "differences" from "distinctions" on the question of Populism versus Progressivism as it appeared in the verse: the verse, in fact, suggests even less of a distinction between these two movements than Hofstadter identifies. See *Age of Reform* (N.Y.: Knopf, 1955), pp. 133–34.

[14] For examples of typical arguments see William D. P. Bliss, ed., *Encyclopedia*

of Social Reform (N.Y.: Funk and Wagnalls, 1897), especially pp. 1404–6; *Cyclopedia of Temperance and Prohibition* (N.Y.: Funk and Wagnalls, 1891), pp. 495, 537ff.

¹⁵ Judging from the verse, America's attitude toward entry into the Spanish-American War is better represented in an account such as Foster R. Dulles, *Imperial Years* (N.Y.: Crowell, 1956), pp. 116–29, than in Ellis P. Oberholtzer, *History of the United States Since the Civil War* (N.Y.: Macmillan, 1937), V, 501–2, or in Mark Sullivan, *Our Times* (N.Y.: Scribner, 1926), I, 303.

¹⁶ See Dulles, *Imperial Years*, pp. 111, 166; Oberholtzer,*History*, V, 589–605; Julius W. Pratt, *Expansionists of 1898* (N.Y.: Peter Smith, 1951), p. 314; James F. Rhodes, *McKinley and Roosevelt Administrations, 1897–1909* (N.Y.: Macmillan, 1922), p. 105; Sullivan, *Our Times*, I, 537.

¹⁷ The scholarly basis for this opinion rests not only on Mr. Curti's article (cited in footnote 8, above) but also on two studies by Fred H. Harrington: "The Anti-Imperialist Movement in the United States, 1898–1900," *Mississippi Valley Historical Review*, XXII (September 1935), 211–320; "Literary Aspects of American Anti-Imperialism, 1898–1902," *New England Quarterly*, X (December 1937), 650–667.

¹⁸ Carlin T. Kindilien, *American Poetry in the Eighteen Nineties* (Providence: Brown Univ. Press, 1956), p. 126.

¹⁹ Pratt, *Expansionists*, pp. 232–33, attempts to resolve the earlier conflict between Harold U. Faulkner and James F. Rhodes on this subject. Dulles (*Imperial Years*, pp. 120, 152) confirms Pratt's point of view: that the business community, while unfavorable to our entry into the war, later seized wartime opportunities for expanding economic horizons and therefore, by the time of the Philippine issue, supported annexation. See also Sullivan, *Our Times*, I, 302.

²⁰ The closest application of this phrase to the present use occurs in Harry Hartwick, *Foreground of American Fiction* (N.Y.: American Book Co., 1934), p. 203. He finds an "age of guilt" in the 1890's following a Gilded Age which had "defaulted on its promises to pay."

²¹ Morton G. White, *Social Thought in America* (N.Y.: Viking, 1949), p. 6; Mumford, *Golden Day*, p. 239; Henry S. Commager, *American Mind* (New Haven: Yale Univ. Press, 1950), p. viii; Eric F. Goldman, *Rendezvous with Destiny* (N.Y.: Knopf, 1952), p. 39.

²² In connection with the relation of belletristic achievement to social value I would like to pass on an observation which struck me as I read through these volumes but which would be impossible to substantiate. If one assumes, only for the sake of this aside, four levels of achievement among poets as they are generally appraised, then one might suggest the following pattern: (1) The first-rate poet, often distinguished by his originality, makes his contribution by forging a new expression of certain ideas and responses. Almost invariably this contribution includes a perceptive and subtle commentary on the important social forces of his day. (2) The second-rate poet typically achieves his level by a kind of imitative excellence within the traditions of his literary form. His subjects tend to be unoriginal, and he seldom reveals much of interest concerning his environment. (3) The third-rate poet will usually offer a prosodic product containing a number of obvious flaws. What value he has will rest most consistently on his specific and concrete reactions to the personalities and issues of his day. (4) The fourth-rate poet will be both aesthetically inept and socially illiterate; he will have little interest for anyone.

This is simply an impressionistic observation. Whether it would bear up under close scrutiny, whether it would apply in other creative genres, in other chronological periods, or in other national settings I could not begin to say. But it did appear from this sample that the poet's contribution to the understanding of his age arose from those aesthetically first-rate writers who made the most profound and subtle observations and from those third-rate writers who drew more specifically and obviously on current events and conditions for their poetic materials.

[23] Allyn Forbes, "The Literary Quest for Utopia, 1880–1900," *Social Forces*, VI (December 1927), 179–89.

[24] Claude R. Flory, *Economic Criticism in American Fiction, 1792–1900* (Phila.: Univ. of Pennsylvania, 1936); Lisle A. Rose, "A Bibliographical Survey of Economic and Political Writing, 1865–1900," *American Literature*, XV (January 1944), 381–410. Mr. Rose had earlier surveyed economic fiction from 1902–9.

[25] Edward E. Cassady, "Muckraking in the Gilded Age," *American Literature*, XIII (May 1941), 134–141; Lisle A. Rose, "Shortcoming of 'Muckraking in the Gilded Age.'" *American Literature*, XIV (May 1942), 161–64.

[26] Alfred Kazin, *On Native Grounds* (N.Y.: Harcourt, Brace, 1942), Chapter I.

[27] Walter F. Taylor, *Economic Novel in America* (Chapel Hill: Univ. of North Carolina Press, 1942), p. 323.

APPENDIX

An Experiment in Quantitative Appraisal

THE FOREGOING CHAPTERS INTERPRET AMERICA'S GILDED Age through the testimony of her poet-citizens. This interpretation has aimed not only to fill out our picture of that era but also to deal with the general problem of bringing literary materials to bear on social questions. Hence this note on method should serve not only to establish a basis for the generalizations presented in the foregoing chapters but also to describe an attack on that difficult and pressing problem involving the historical use of literary and sub-literary materials.

When one considers the entirely new dimension which the widespread use of printing—to name but one factor—has forced upon the student of civilization in the Western world, it is surprising that more efforts have not been bent toward systematizing and controlling the enormous and complex record which man now leaves of himself at the close of each succeeding generation. How can one confidently measure our modern culture when each year the individual scholar encompasses only a startlingly diminished fraction of its record and testimony? In attempting to answer such a question, one comes inevitably to think of apportioning the task, of accepting a certain systematization of attack, and of attempting to provide for a clear channel of communication between the various specialists who must undertake the fractional portions of the chore. In answer to the specific challenge of attempting to make literary materials useful to the historian or social scientist, this study begins by offering an extensive analysis of a closely limited and hitherto unexplored area within the human record; it ends by presenting the results of this analysis in a form most readily accessible to other students of the same civilization regardless of their own special interests.

The study itself is based on the Harris collection of American verse in the John Hay Library at Brown University. This, the most comprehensive collection of American poetry, contains some 70 percent of the materials within its scope. It does not include verse drama (although dramatic verse, intended to be read rather than performed, is included), nor does it include anthologies, broadsides, or uncollected verse appearing in magazines and newspapers. It does include children's verse, American verse published abroad, and mixed volumes of prose and verse, however slight the proportion of the latter. My own study has been further limited by the exclusion of verse in languages other than English, and of that by Canadian authors (Bliss Carman was included only as collaborator with Richard Hovey).

The comprehensiveness of the Harris collection frees it from regional, aesthetic, or political bias and makes it an ideally broad and impartial basis for generalizations. Such a basis, moreover, makes possible direct quantitative analysis without the compromises and qualifications necessary when a smaller or more special sample has been used.

The arrangement of the Harris collection involves a certain problem in chronology. In order to keep intact the work of individual poets, the output of each has been shelved according to the date of his *first* published volume. The materials so arranged have been separated into periods covering roughly a quarter of a century. Thus, the works I examined were those of poets whose first volumes appeared between 1876 and 1901. In order to keep within the limits of the period, I arbitrarily excluded verse published after 1905. Thus the study covered the years from 1876 through 1905, but concentrated most heavily on the years from 1880 through 1901. This chronological definition provided a reasonable concentration on the heart of the Gilded Age— the late eighties and the nineties—with diminishing attention to the still-important fringe years in the 1870's and the beginning of the present century.

Also crucial to the quantitative meaning of this study was the establishment of clear categories in which to record the poetic comment. The first step consisted in determining which subjects had been treated most often in the verse of the period. Once the prevalence of a particular subject had been established, the category was broadened so as to include its larger context. For example, once it became apparent that the verse offered sufficient and significant reaction to the status of labor, the focus here was widened to include the whole economic scene. Although the contemporary importance of an event or issue furnished one criterion for its inclusion, emphasis was also placed on the interest of each topic to succeeding generations. Thus the poet's participation in public events was frequently ignored when the significance of the event—a commemorative occasion, a minor election—was largely local or temporary. On the other hand, such subjects as the impact of urbanism, or America's increasing involvement in international affairs, qualified more readily for inclusion because of their continuing subsequent importance. Some hoped-for categories—involving education and religion, for example—did not appear with sufficient strength to merit consideration. Some themes which did appear—such as Civil War reminiscences and Reconstruction issues—were ruled out because of their backward-looking quality and because the chronological limitations precluded any coverage approaching completeness. Within the limitations already noted, the poetry was allowed to speak for itself, not only in establishing its own categories but also in providing its own unique portrait of its age.

The establishment of these categories formed, admittedly, the most controversial step in this process. Any historian with an interpretive interest, any social scientist with a commitment toward a pre-arranged set of compartments, might wish to subject these materials to differing alignments and stresses. That no two of them might profit equally from any single method of organization suggests some support for the idea of approaching the materials with an uncommitted interest and with a determination to discover what the verse itself could best divulge. Admittedly, the poet could be made to answer questions of social relevance which do not appear under the present organization. On the other hand, the questions and issues around which the comment has been arranged do provide, at least, a measure of the poet's own evaluation of relative importance, the poet's own emphasis on the themes and topics which were to him most pressing and pervasive.

The technique employed in bringing the materials of the Harris collection into these categories began with a shelf-reading. Any volume or pamphlet which qualified for consideration under the terms described above was examined for such social comment as it might contain. In this manner 5,883 separate works were perused, of which 1,804 were found to contain material of relevance to one or more of the categories finally dealt with. Thus, based on the number of volumes, one can estimate that the poet's participation in the discussion of social issues amounted to 30.7 percent.

Record was made of comment within each volume on any of the themes or issues under consideration; the comments on these themes contained in the 1,804 volumes amounted to 4,200 distinct topical references. Based on the total social commentary represented by this latter figure, the statistics which follow summarize not simply the extent, but also the nature and proportions, of the poet's social participation. Each chapter has been identified with a percentage representing its fraction of the total; within each chapter further subdivisions have been made in order to demonstrate the quantitative response to more minute headings as well as to indicate the preponderance of poetic opinion on one side or the other of controversial issues or evaluations. For each subdivision, the percentage refers to the total comment on that particular issue only, as should be apparent from the manner in which these summaries have been arranged.

In any project which contains so much of a subjective or interpretive nature, one cannot with any seriousness offer up a column of statistics with pretensions of decimal-point accuracy. It is also obvious that, in the absence of studies with which the following statistics may be compared, these figures often lack something in the way of full meaning. Yet one must start somewhere; the present tabulation may readily afford grounds for future comparisons. Furthermore, these figures do at least have a firm meaning in relation to other figures within this survey; they do impart a definite sense of proportion in determining the poet's interest and in measuring his commitment. Also, an exact statistical answer, even allowing for a reasonable margin of fallibility and interpretive latitude, does provide a much more usable index than do those necessarily vague and generalized impressions based on more limited evidence and less exact methods of categorization. This tabulation, then, is accompanied by some necessary apologies; but it is provided in the hope that it may offer something toward defining attitudes and testing techniques.

*   *   *   *   *   *   *   *

Chapter II, "Westward to Destiny," represented 8.8 percent of the total social comment. It described the poet's reaction in terms of negative and affirmative response as follows:

Negative reactions:
To the Indian	1.1%
To the plight of the farmer and rancher	5.6
Mixed reactions to contemporary character traits ..	13.3

Positive reactions:
To the virtues of the explorer and pioneer ..	32.3
To the prospertity of city and town, commerce and industry	13.3
To the general impact of the West, its scenic geography, its virtues, its potential stimulus to the realization of an exalted American destiny	34.4
	100.0%

*   *   *   *   *   *   *   *

Chapter III, "Gotham and Gomorrah," accounted for 7.6 percent of the total social comment. All but the first of the following categories represented preponderantly negative reactions to urban conditions and characteristics:

Tributes to urban achievement..	19.0%
Contrasts of rural virtues with urban vices	13.6
Reactions to the unpleasant physical characteristics of the city and their attendant evils	22.8
Attempts to characterize the city sociologically and psychologically	33.8
Prophecies of urban doom	10.8
	100.0%

*   *   *   *   *   *   *   *

Chapter IV, "Progress and Protest," accounted for 20.5 percent of the poet's social comment. It presented a reaction to economic conditions by dividing the commentary into two broad groups.

The first consisted of reactions which suggested support for the economic status quo 37.5%
These reactions were distributed as follows:

Tributes to American economic achievement and its begetters 64.6

Acceptance of contemporary conditions of labor and poverty 20.0

Condemnation of philosophies and organizations unfriendly to unrestrained free enterprise 4.6

Praise for industrial leaders and for the concept of "stewardship of wealth"   10.8

_____

100.0%

A second group represented protests against various characteristics and consequences of the economic system 62.5
These protests can be described as follows:

Acknowledgment of agrarian discontent   12.5%

Protest against:

Poverty 15.8

Poor living conditions 6.3

Poor working conditions 8.5

Condemnation of the upper economic class for its:

"Stewardship of wealth" philosophy   3.5

"Conspicuous consumption"   ..   3.3

"Leisure class" behavior 5.4

Attacks on large-scale business 9.7

Censure of financial practices 15.8

Recommendations for governmental control over the economy 2.8

Advocacy of organized labor 16.4

_____   _____

100.0%   100.0%

*   *   *   *   *   *   *   *

Chapter V, "Statesmen and Spoilsmen," made up 12.3 percent of the total social comment and was discussed under four principal headings:

Estimates of individuals on the political scene .. 55.5%
  Sentiment was divided as follows:

			Favorable	Unfavorable
Garfield ..	..	..	23.5%	1.3%
Grant ..	..	..	20.5	2.4
McKinley	..	..	7.4	3.2
Others ..	..	..	23.5	18.2
Subtotals	..	..	74.9%	25.1%
				74.9
				100.0%

Sweeping and overlapping protests against the politician, his institutions, and the atmosphere in which he operated 22.7

Reactions to minor parties and their platforms .. 6.1
  Sentiment was divided as follows:

			Favorable	Unfavorable
Socialists..	..	..	16.1%	14.2%
Populists..	..	..	14.4	18.9
Liberal Republicans	..		5.9	10.3
Others ..	..	·..	5.8	14.4
Subtotals	..	..	42.2%	57.8%
				42.2
				100.0%

Discussions of political issues, philosophies, and remedies 15.7
  Particular issues were:

The money question	..	..	42.4%	
Import tariff	..	..	29.7%	
Domestic taxation	..	..	15.3	
Others ..	..	..	12.6	
			100.0%	100.0%

*   *   *   *   *   *   *   *

Chapter VI, "Wine and Women, a Song of Reform," made up
11.3 percent of the social comment and arranged itself as follows:

Generalized and miscellaneous approaches to
    reform 4.7%

    Praise for the idea of reform and
       the reformer 33.6%

    Attacks on the idea of reform and
       the reformer 31.4

    Reform of the legal system   ..   15.7

    Miscellaneous specific reform
       interests 19.3

                                   100.0%

Woman's rights 29.3

    Arguments for the franchise   ..   16.4%

    Arguments against the "double
       standard," social and sexual   ..   9.3

    Generalized and miscellaneous
       arguments on behalf of woman's
       rights 36.4

    Arguments against the advance of
       woman's rights   ..   37.9

                                   100.0%

Temperance and prohibition 66.0

    Moral and religious appeals 34.6%

    Social appeals 26.0

    Political appeals 12.7

    Physical health appeals 8.6

    Emphases on the drunkard's
       reform..   ..   ..   ..   4.7

    Resistance to temperance and
       prohibition 9.6%

    Miscellaneous appeals, including
       arguments on the use of tobacco   3.8%

                         100.0%   100.0%

*   *   *   *   *   *   *   *

Chapter VII, "Immigration and Internationalism," accounted for 11.1 percent of the poet's total comment and was considered under three major headings:

Attitudes toward immigration and foreign
minorities 33.1%
Attitudes toward groups of foreign origin:

	Favorable	*Unfavorable*
Scottish	2.4%	0.6%
French	2.4	0.6
German	7.1	2.3
Irish	8.5	2.9
Jewish	10.4	4.2
Italian	1.7	3.0
Chinese	8.5	7.9
Others	1.1	0.5
Remarks on tolerance and assimilation	20.7	1.2
Opinions on continuing un-limited immigration ..	7.9	6.1
Subtotals	70.7%	29.3%
		70.7
		100.0%

Comments on various international causes and
crises 20.9
Attitudes toward causes of local national
sovereignty:

	Favorable	*Unfavorable*
The cause of Irish inde-pendence	62.9%	3.1%
The cause of the Boers ..	22.8	1.2
The cause of the Boxers ..	1.0%	4.0%
Subtotals	86.7%	8.3%
		86.7
Other causes and issues		5.0
		100.0%

Discussions pertinent to the Spanish-American
   War and the Philippine insurrection 46.0%
Sympathy for the Cubans in
   earlier revolts 2.5%
Encouragement for the Cubans and
   condemnation of the Spaniards in
   Cuba after 1895 ..   ..   ..   14.2
Urgings of American intervention
   in Cuba as revenge for the *Maine*
   disaster 10.8
Protests against American interven-
   tion 5.5
Support for the war after American
   entry, and appraisal of its results   12.0
Celebrations of war heroes   ..   42.2
Support for the conduct of the war
   against the Philippine insurgents   6.0
Criticisms of the war against the
   Philippine insurgents 6.8

                              100.0%   100.0%

*   *   *   *   *   *   *   *

Chapter VIII, "For Darwin, for Mammon, and for Country," contained three distinct headings and may best be summarized under these separate headings. The chapter as a whole represented 27.2 per cent of the poet's total social comment.

Reactions to the world of science 15.6%
Evidence of the intrusion of the
   world of science into the world of
   the poet: 26.5%
Relative interest in various
   branches of science:
      Psychology 1.4

Physics	1.5
Chemistry	1.8
Astronomy	5.7
Pseudo-science, the occult ..	5.8
Geology	6.2
Medicine and biology ..	8.1
The evolution controversy: Those who supported evolution and its applications, including those who reconciled newer with older beliefs	20.6
Those who argued against evolutionary ideas and their applications	11.9
Discussion of the general epistemological value of science verses older ideas of learning and knowledge; limitations placed on science's domain	10.5
	100.0%

Concern with materialism		35.6
Evidence of the poet's acceptance of materialistic standards ..	4.8%	
Condemnation of the age in sweeping terms	28.1	
Singling out particular forms of materialistic abuse in:		
Economic life..	19.9	
Religious life	13.1	
Politics and government ..	10.9	
Prestige values	8.6	
The arts	8.4	
Relations between the sexes	6.2	
	100.0%	

Debating America's destiny	..	.. ..	48.8
Establishing America as the favored land	.. .. ..	..	11.5%
Underlining her special mission	..		26.7
Augmenting this sense of destiny with special arguments:			
America as the new holy land	..		8.8
Superpatriotism, the cult of the flag, "my country, right or wrong"	.. .. ..		8.6
The arguments over the legitimacy of violence:			
Militarism	.. ..	..	11.5
Pacifism ..	.. ..	..	14.3
The arguments over empire:			
Imperialism	.. ..	..	6.8
Anti-expansionism	..	..	11.8

                                            100.0%   100.0%

*   *   *   *   *   *   *   *

As a final recapitulation, the following tabulation of the total social comment of the poet, divided by chapters, offers a review of the general proportions of the poet's interest in his environment.

Chapter II, Interpretations of the Western frontier	8.8%
Chapter III, Reactions to the rise of the city ..	7.6
Chapter IV, Reflections of economic issues and conditions	20.5
Chapter V, Depictions of political personalities, institutions, and programs	12.3
Chapter VI, Records of humanitarian reforms ..	11.3
Chapter VII, Comments on international questions	11.1
Chapter VIII, Contributions to underlying themes	27.2
Miscellaneous	1.2

                                                        100.0%

BIBLIOGRAPHY

THE FOLLOWING LIST CONSISTS OF ONLY THOSE VOLUMES of verse which comprise the immediate basis for this study. Many of these volumes have been cited in support of particular points. Together with those not heretofore mentioned they make up the total evidence of the poet's social awareness and thus substantiate the generalizations and conclusions which have been offered. These volumes are a part of the Harris collection of American verse (John Hay Library, Brown University). They are listed alphabetically by author or (author lacking) by title. Actual names have been supplied where available to replace pseudonyms or to identify anonyms. Authors' names, otherwise, have been preserved as they appeared on the title page to the extent of first name and middle initial.

A number of general histories, essays, monographs, compilations, periodical articles, and special studies have helped in the interpretation and appraisal of this poetic evidence. Since these works are of particular rather than general interest, they have not been listed here, but have been cited in full at the textual point of most direct relevance.

ABBOTT, CLIFF and MARY. *Wild Roses*. Grandview, Ind.: Keller Printing Co., n.d.

A. C. J. [pseud.]. *Heart Echoes*. Boston: Rand, Avery, 1880.

ADAMS, CHARLES F. *Leedle Yawcob Strauss, and Other Poems*. Boston: Lee and Shepard; New York: Charles Dillingham, 1878.

ADAMS, GEORGE. *Siouska and Other Poems*. Watertown, N.Y.: Publ. by the author, 1886.

ADAMS, JOHN B. *Breezy Western Verse*. Denver: Denver Evening Post, 1899.

ADAMS, MARY M. *Choir Visible*. Chicago: Way and Williams, 1897.

—. *Songs and Sonnets*. New York and London: Knickerbocker Press, 1901.

ADAMS, ROBERT C. *History of the United States in Rhyme*. Boston: Lothrop, 1884.

—. *Illustrated Story of the Union in Rhyme*. Revised by Herbert Heywood. Boston: Thayer, 1891.

ADAMS, SILAS. *Prohibition: or a "Calm View."* Gardner [N.Y.?]: A. G. Bushnell, 1881.

ADLINGTON, FRANCIS M. *New England Sleighing Frolic and Other Poems*. Ed. Amey M. Hillyer. Boston: Frank Wood, 1884.

AIKEN, JAMES. *Collection of the Poetical Writings of James Aiken*, Lewisburg, Pa.: Cornelius, 1878.

ALCIONE [pseud.]. *California Souvenir and Other Poemettes*. San Francisco: N. publ., 1898–99.

ALDEN, AMASA. *Poems*. Wilton, Me.: Record Job Printing, 1887.

ALDEN, WILLIAM C. *Lines, Rhymes, or Poetry*. Cambridge, Mass.: Riverside Press, 1878.

All About the Fair. N. p.: N. publ., n.d.

ALLEN, GRANT. *Lower Slopes*. London: Mathews and Lane; Chicago: Stone and Kimball, 1894.

ALLEN, JOHN. *Confessions of John Allen*. Chicago: Mandel and Phillips, 1905.

ALLEN, LUMEN. *Sage of Mentor*. Chicago: Harper, 1885.

ALLEN, WILLIAM. *Southland Columbiad and Other Poems*. Nashville, Tenn.: Methodist Episcopal Church, 1897.

ALLERDICE, ELIZABETH W. *Our President*. New York: Dutton, 1881.

—. *Over the Hill to the White House*. New York: Denison, 1881.

ALLERTON, ELLEN P. *Annabel and Other Poems*. New York: Alden, 1885.

—. *Walls of Corn and Other Poems*. Hiawatha, Kans.: Eva Ryan, 1894.

ALLIS, ALMON T. *Uncle Alvin at Home and Abroad*. N. p.: Publ. by the author, 1895.

ALLSWORTH, B. W. *Tales and Legends of Two Republics*. Topeka: Hall and O'Donald, 1889.

AMIDON, JOHN J. *Poems*. Providence: Casey, 1894.

ANAGNOS, JULIA R. *Stray Chords*. Boston: Cupples, Upham, 1883.

ANGNEY, LYDIA F. *California and Other Poems*. Gilroy, Cal.: Eaton, 1900.

ARCHIBALD, HUGH. *Some Scribbles*. New York: Irving, 1897.

ARMSTRONG, CLARA J. *La Porte in June*. Chicago: Donnelley, 1890.

ARMSTRONG, ELMON. *Verses.* N. p.: N. publ., n.d.

ARNOLD, AGNES M. *Rosemary . . . "Remembrance."* Washington, D. C.: Saxton, 1898.

At Campfire. N. p.: N. publ., n.d.

ATWOOD, FREDERICK. *Kansas Rhymes and Other Lyrics.* Topeka: Crane, 1902.

ATWOOD, HENRY D. *Last Arrow and Other Poems.* Taunton, Mass.: Publ. by the author, 1899.

AUSTIN, HENRY. *Hobson's Choice: A Poem.* New York: Fenno, 1898.

—. *In the People's Name and Other Poems.* Boston: Arena, 1893.

—. *Off to the Transvaal!* New York: Bell, 1899.

—. *Devil's Football. A Satire on the World in General with Boston as its Axis.* N. p.: N. publ., n.d.

AYARS, J. E. *In Memoriam of Our Fallen Chief, James A. Garfield.* Philadelphia: Goldy, 1882.

BABCOCK, HARMON S. *Friendship of Learning and Other Poems.* Danielsonville, Conn.: New England Fancier, 1893.

—. *Trifles.* Providence: Providence Press, 1879.

BABCOCK, WILLIAM H. *Lord Stirling's Stand and Other Poems.* Philadelphia: Lippincott, 1880.

BAKER, ISADORA. *Sonnets and Other Verse.* Iowa City, Ia.: N. publ., 1896.

BAKER, MYRON E. *Vacation Thoughts.* Madison, Wisc.: Democrat, 1887.

BAKER, SHELDON S. *Marmondale and Other Poems.* New York: Hurst, 1886.

BAKKE, THORVALD. *Crystal and Crown.* Minneapolis: Press of the "U.V." [?], 1900.

BALDWIN, EMILY F. *Flora and Other Poems.* Hartford, Conn.: Brown and Gross, 1879.

BALDWIN, S. L. *Instruction for Chinese Women and Girls* [reputedly translated from the Chinese of Lady Tsao]. New York: Eaton and Mains, n.d.

BALDY, LIZZIE F. *California Pioneer and Other Poems.* San Francisco: Bacon, 1879.

BALL, ALICE M. *Buttercups and Clover.* Buffalo: Office of Triumphs of Faith, 1885.

BALL, BENJAMIN W. *Merrimack River, Hellenics, and Other Poems.* New York and London: Putnam, 1892.

BALLOU, ADDIE L. *Driftwood.* San Francisco: Hicks-Judd, 1899.

BANCROFT, TIMOTHY W. *Gleanings in Verse.* Providence: Preston and Rounds, 1899.

BANCROFT, WILLIAM H. *Shining Pathways and Other Poems.* Philadelphia: Jacobs, 1899.

BANGS, JOHN K. *Cobwebs from a Library Corner.* New York and London: Harper, 1899.

BANKS, CHARLES E. *Quiet Music.* Chicago: Schulte, 1892.

—. *Sword and Cross, and Other Poems.* Chicago and New York: Rand, McNally, 1899.

BARBE, WAITMAN. *Ashes and Incense.* Philadelphia: Lippincott, 1891.

BARBOUR, GEORGE H. *Songs and Sonnets.* Pittsburgh: Davis and Warde, 1897.

BARBOUR, L. G. *End of Time. A Poem of the Future.* New York and London: Putnam, 1892.

BAKER, ALICE J. *Poems.* Cleveland: N. publ., 1888.

BARNES, ALMONT. *American War Songs and Odes.* Washington, D.C.: Barnes, 1892.

—. *Elysian Fields and Other Stuff.* Washington, D.C.: Adams, 1905.

BARNES, HAROLD. *Book of Verse.* Princeton, Ind.: N. publ., n.d.

BARNES, J. T. *Jephtha and His Daughter, and Other Poems.* New York and Chicago: Barnes, 1887.

BARNES, THOMAS Q. *Southern and Miscellaneous Poems.* Mobile: Daily Register, 1886.

BARRETT, JOHN E. *Fugitives and Other Poems.* Buffalo: Peter Paul, 1897.

BARROWS, ELLEN A. *Friendship and Wayside Gleanings.* Boston: Earle, 1887.

BARTON, ANNA. *For Friendship's Sake.* Kalamazoo, Mich.: Everard, 1882.

BASS, CORA C. *Poems.* Lowell, Mass.: Lawler, 1899.

—. *Songs for All Seasons and Other Poems.* Lowell, Mass.: Lawler, 1901.

BATE, WILLIAM S. *Berth-deck Ballads.* New York: Lockwood, 1898.

BATEHAM, MINNIE D. *Invalid Singer. Life and Writings.* Boston: Earle, 1895.

BATES, ALICE P. *Memory Bells.* Buffalo: Moulton, 1894.

BATES, CHARLOTTE F. *Risk and Other Poems.* Boston: Williams, 1879.

BATES, HERBERT. *Songs of Exile.* Boston: Copeland and Day, 1896.

BATES, KATHARINE L. *College Beautiful and Other Poems.* Cambridge, Mass.: Riverside Press, 1887.

BATTERSBY, J. H. *Poems Patriotic.* New York: Huth, 1894.

Battle. Paterson, N. J.: Bertkau, n.d.

BAUDER, LEVI F. *Passing Fancies: Poems.* Cleveland: Private edition, 1880.

BAUM, L. FRANK. *Army Alphabet.* Chicago and New York: Hill, 1900.

—. *By the Candelabra's Glare.* Chicago: Private edition, 1898.

—. *Father Goose.* Chicago: Hill, 1899 [5th edition].

—. *Navy Alphabet.* Chicago: Hill, 1900.

BEACH, ABEL. *Western Airs.* Buffalo: Peter Paul, 1895.

BEADLE, S. A. *Sketches from Life in Dixie.* Chicago: Scroll, 1899.

BEARD, ALEXANDER B. *Choice Poems.* Manchester, N. H.: Riddle, 1892.

BEARD, EDWIN. *Life Lines.* Watseka, Ill.: Iroquois County Times, 1898.

BEATTIE, CHARLES J. *Our Own General Grant, an Obituary Poem.* N.p.: N. publ., n.d.

BEATTIE, M. C. *Poems.* New Haven: Ryder, 1895.

Beauties of America. N.p.: N. publ., n.d.

BECKENBAUGH, GEORGE A. *Cotton Tails.* New York: Russel, 1900.

BEDLOW, HENRY. *War and Worship; A Poem.* New York: Truth Seeker, 1902.

BEEBE, JOHN W. *Prairie Flowers.* Topeka: Crane, 1891.

BEEGLE, MARY P. *Alethea.* Ocean Grove, N.J.: Publ. by the author, 1886.

BELKNAP, P. H. *Canalero. The Trooper.* Boston: Bouve, 1900.

BELL, MACKENZIE. *Pictures of Travel and Other Poems.* Boston: Little, Brown, 1898.

BELL, MILLIE A. *Melodies of the W.C.T.U. Mother Goose.* Cleveland: W.C.T.U., 1885.

BELL, ORELIA K. *Poems.* Philadelphia: Rodgers, 1895.

BELL, RALCY H. *Aala Deene and Other Poems.* Buffalo: Moulton, 1899.

BELLVILLE, JOHN O. *Dramatis Mortalis.* Pearsall, Tex.: Leader, 1900.

—. *Thorns and Roses.* Evansville [Ind. ?]: Keller, 1895.

BELLROSE, LOUIS. *Poet's Appeal for Protection of Home Industry.* Philadelphia: Syckelmoore, 1884.

—. *Thorns and Flowers.* Philadelphia: Publ. by the author, 1879.

BENEDICT, LAMIRA M. *Thistle Down.* Coventryville, N.Y.: Amateur Press, 1901.

BENEDICT, ROSWELL A. *America*. New York: Mearns, Endler, 1876.

BENJAMIN, R. C. *Poetic Gems*. Charlottesville, Va.: Peck and Allan, 1883.

BENNETT, SANFORD F. *Pioneers. An Idyl of the Middle-west*. Chicago: Donnelley, 1898.

BERNSTEIN, HERMAN. *Flight of Time and Other Poems*. New York and London: Neely, 1899.

BEST, SUSIE M. *Fallen Pillar Saint and Other Poems*. New York: Dillingham, 1889.

BICKNELL, THOMAS W. *Hail and Farewell!* N.p.: N. publ., 1901.

BIELBY, ISAAC P. *Poems*. Utica, New York: Living Issue Steam Print, 1886.

BIEN, H. M. *Oriental Legends and Other Poems*. New York: Brown and Derby, 1883.

BIGNEY, M. F. *Poetical History of Louisiana*. New Orleans: Brandao, 1885.

BILLMAN, IRA. *Bluebird Notes. Poems*. New York: Funk and Wagnalls, 1889.

BIXBY, A. L. *Driftwood: A Modest Collection of Random Rhymes*. Lincoln, Nebr.: State Journal, 1895.

—. *Memories and Other Poems*. Lincoln, Nebr.: State Journal, 1900.

BLACK, EFFIE S. *Heart-Whispers*. Cleveland, N.Y.: Barton, 1900.

BLACKWELL, JAMES D. *Poetical Works*. 3 vols. Philadelphia: Lippincott, 1884.

BLAGDEN, SILLIMAN. *Some Sweet Poems*. Boston: N. publ., 1893.

BLANCHARD, RUFUS. *Abraham Lincoln, the Type of American Genius. An Historical Romance*. Wheaton, Ill.: Blanchard, 1882.

BLISS, R. A. *Labor's Daughter*. New York and London: Neely, 1898.

BLOCK, LOUIS J. *Friendship of the Faiths*. Chicago: Kerr, 1893[?].

—. *New World and Other Verse*. New York: Putnam, 1895.

—. [*El*] *Nuevo Mundo: A Poem*. Chicago: Kerr, 1893.

BLOUNT, EDWARD A. *Poems*. Cincinnati: Elm Street, 1897.

BOAZE, H. *Wonders of Nations. America and Americans*. Grand Rapids, Mich.: Dean, 1894.

BONNEY, FLORENCE P. *Meditations*. Chicago: Open Court, 1900.

BOOTH, EMMA S. *Family of Three, Iesuina, and Other Poems*. Buffalo: Moulton, 1893.

BOOTON, JOHN H. and QUARLES, EDWIN L. *Songs and Fantasies*. Salem, Va.: Roanoke College Annual Staff, 1900.

BORTON, FRANCIS S. [*El*] *Camino Real*. Puebla, Mexico: N. publ., n.d.

BOSFIELD, SAMUEL J. *Colored American in the Presidential Campaigns. Some Reasons Why He Should Support the Democratic Platform and Vote for William Jennings Bryan*. Cambridge, Mass.: Caustic and Claflin, 1900.

BOSWORTH, ELIZABETH A. *Poems*. Chicago: Publ. by the author, 1893.

BOWCHER, M. A. *Jingles from the Far West*. San Francisco: Whittaker and Ray, 1904.

BOWEN, HERBERT W. *In Divers Tones*. Boston: Cupples, 1890.

—. *Losing Ground: A Series of Sonnets*. Boston: Cupples, 1892.

BOWEN, JOHN E. *Songs of Toil by Carmen Sylva, Queen of Rumania*. New York: Stokes, 1888.

BOWMAN, EBENEZER. *Fifteen Direct Shots at the Upas Tree of Intemperance*. Boston: Total Abstinence Rooms, 1882.

BOYD, ASA S. *Poetical Works*. Baltimore: Publ. by the author, 1886.

BOYDEN, EMILY M. *Intermittent Thoughts*. Chicago: Union, 1897.

BOYESEN, HJALMAR H. *Idyls of Norway and Other Poems*. New York: Scribner, 1882.

BOYLAN, GRACE D. *If Tam O'Shanter'd Had a Wheel, and Other Poems and Sketches*. New York: Herrick, 1898.

—. *Kids of Many Colors*. New York: Hurst, 1901.

BOYLAN, WILL M. *Poems*. Eldora, Ia.: Ledger, 1889.

BOYNTON, WARREN. *Poetry and Song, No. 5*. Rockford, Ill.: Publ. by the author, 1878.

BRADFORD, BENJAMIN. *Around the Hub in Rhyme*. Boston: Publ. by the author, 1900.

BRADLEY, L. D. *Wonderful Willie! What He and Tommy Did to Spain*. N.p.: Dutton, 1899.

BRADT, EDITH V. *Songs by the Way*. New York and Washington, D.C.: Neale, 1904.

BRAGDON, CLAUDE F. *Golden Person in the Heart*. Gouverneur, N.Y.: Brothers of the Book, 1898.

BRAGDON, GEORGE C. *Undergrowth*. Oswego, N.Y.: Oliphant, 1895.

BRANCH, HOMER P. *Poems*. Mitchell [state?]: Temperance Power, 1895.

BRAYMAN, MASON. *Selections from the Poetical Writings*. Chicago: Griggs, 1888.

BREEN, P. C. *Hugh O'Nell's War with Queen Elizabeth, Irish National*

Effusions, and Miscellaneous Poems. Chicago: Clark and Edwards, 1882.

BRENDER, MARY W. *Our First Columbian.* Otsego, Mich.: Publ. by the author, 1893.

BRENNAN, DOMINIC. *Heart-tones and Other Poems.* Buffalo: Peter Paul, 1897.

BREYFOGLE, WILLIAM L. *Sense and Satire.* Chicago and New York: Rand, McNally, 1899.

BRIDGES, ROBERT. *Bramble Brae.* New York: Scribner, 1902.

BRIDGES, W. M. *Lights and Shadows of Life.* Atlanta: Franklin, 1897.

BRIDGMAN, L. J. *Jest-nuts.* New York: Caldwell, 1903.

BRODERICK, JOHN T. *Vagrant of Lover's Leap.* Boston: New Nation, 1892.

BROMLEY, ISAAC H. *"Our Chauncey." After Dinner Rhymes.* New York: New York Printing, 1891.

BRONSON, C. H. *Sparkling Light and Other Poems.* Manchester, Ia.: Publ. by the author, 1877.

BROOKS, FRANCIS. *Margins.* Chicago: Searle and Gorton, 1896.

—. *Poems of Francis Brooks.* Chicago: Donnelley, 1898.

BROOKS, FRED E. *Battle Ballads.* San Francisco: Publ. by the author, 1886.

—. *Old Ace and Other Poems.* New York: Cassell, 1894.

—. *Pickett's Charge and Other Poems.* Boston and Chicago: Forbes, 1902.

BROOKS, SAMUEL. *Poems, Ballads, and Songs.* Greenfield, Ind.: Republican, 1881.

BROOKS, WILLIAM G. *Stories in Song and Other Poems.* Lewiston, Me.: Haswell, 1900.

BRORUP, R. P. *Truth and Poetry.* Chicago: International Book, 1897.

BROTHERSON, FRANCES B. *Poems.* Peoria, Ill.: Publ. by her daughter, 1880.

BROWN, A. B. *Bullion in the Campaign of 1880; or Shylock in Verse.* Worcester, Mass.: Brown, 1880.

—. *Soul of Things and Other Poems.* Worcester, Mass.: N. publ., 1882.

BROWN, FREDERICK H. *One Dollar's Worth.* Chicago: Publ. by the author, 1893.

BROWN, GEORGE A. *Ernest and Madeline, and Other Poems.* Hudson, Mich.: Scarritt and Steuerwall, 1880.

BROWN, LELAH H. *Golden Rod.* St. Louis [?]: N. publ., 1892.

BROWN, MATTIE N. *Poems.* Louisville: Kunnecke, 1896 [?].

BROWN, S. A. *Chronological Rhymes in Modern History.* N.p.: N. publ., 1893.

BROWN, THERON. *Life Songs.* Boston: Lee and Shepard, 1894.

BROWN, VALENTINE. *Chieftain and Satires.* Portland, Ore.: N. publ., 1903.

—. *Poems.* Portland, Ore.: N. publ., 1900.

BROWNE, LUCY L. *Prophetic Visions of National Events, and Spirit Communications.* Oakland, Cal.: Publ. by the author, 1882.

BROWNE, WILLIAM T. *Joy Bells.* New York: Dillingham, 1901.

BRUCE, M. E. *Anemones.* N.p.: N. publ., n.d.

BRUCE, WALLACE. *From Grant's Tomb to Mt. McGregor. Patriotic Poems and Addresses along the Hudson.* New York: Bryant Literary Union, 1897.

—. *In Clover and Heather.* Edinburgh and London: Blackwood, 1891 [2nd edition].

—. *Wayside Poems.* New York: Harper, 1895.

—. *Yosemite.* Boston: Lee and Shepard; New York: Dillingham, 1880.

BRUNNER, D. B. *Political History of Berks Country.* N.p.: N. publ., 1902.

BRUNNER, H. D. *Poems.* New York: Scribner, 1896.

BRUNQUEST, WILLIAM. *Poems.* N.p.: N. publ., 1892.

BRYCE, J. W. *Random Rhymes.* Battle Creek, Mich.: Ellis, 1899.

BUCHANAN, JOHN A. *Indian Legends and Other Poems.* San Francisco: Whitaker and Ray, 1905.

BUCK, JEDEDIAH. *Silas Balsam's Letters on Law, Repudiation, and Honor.* New York: Present Problems, 1896.

BUCKHAM, JAMES. *Heart of Life.* Boston: Copeland and Day, 1897.

BUCKINGHAM, EMMA M. *Pearl.* New York: Wells, 1877.

BUELL, GUY A. *Kodaks.* Stockton, Cal.: Record, 1900.

BUELL, MARY E. *Collection of Short Poems.* Milwaukee: Tate, n.d.

BULLARD, FRANK D. *Cupid's Chalice and Other Poems.* New York: Abbey, 1901.

BUNDSCHU, CHARLES E. *Happy New Year to All!* San Francisco: N. publ., 1903–4.

Burdett's Book of Comic Parodies. New York: Hust, 1883.

BURDETTE, ROBERT J. *Smiles Yoked with Sighs.* Indianapolis: Bowen-Merill, 1900.

BURGESS, GELETT. *Chant Royal of California.* San Francisco: Channing Auxiliary, 1899.

BURGOYNE, ARTHUR G. *All Sorts of Pittsburgers.* Pittsburgh: Leader All Sorts, 1892.

—. *Shakespeare up to Date, and Other Latter-day Lyrics.* Pittsburgh: Nevin, 1896.

—. *Songs of Every Day.* Pittsburgh: Pittsburgh Printing, 1900.

Burlingtoniad. N.p.: N. publ., n.d.

BURNETT, JAMES G. *Love and Laughter:* *Being a Legacy of Rhyme.* New York: Putnam, 1895.

BURTON, RICHARD. *Dumb in June.* Boston: Copeland and Day, 1895.

—. *Lyrics of Brotherhood.* Boston: Small, Maynard, 1899.

—. *Message and Melody:* *A Book of Verse.* Boston: Lothrop, 1903.

BUSH, OLIVIA WARD. *Original Poems.* Providence: Basinet, 1899.

BUTLER, GEORGE F. *Isle of Content and Other Waifs of Thought.* Concord, Mass.: Erudite, 1902.

BUTTERFIELD, S. A. *Poems.* Indianapolis: Butterfield, 1880.

—. *Poems.* Indianapolis: Butterfield, 1887.

BUTTERS, MARY E. *Harp of Hesper.* Buffalo: Moulton, 1891.

BUTTS, A. P. *Rhythmical Panorama of Early Pioneer Life.* Rochester, N.Y.: Union, 1890.

BYARS, WILLIAM V. *New Songs to Old Tunes.* South Orange, N.J.: Valley Press, 1897.

—. *Pools at Millburn.* South Orange, N.J.: Valley Press, 1896.

—. *Tennessee.* St. Louis: Tennessee Society, 1899.

BYERS, SAMUEL H. *Happy Isles and Other Poems.* Boston: Cupples, Upham, 1884.

CAKE, LU B. *Devil's Tea Table and Other Poems.* New York: Cake, 1898.

CALDWELL, J. A. *Comprehensive Account and Guide Book of the Pittsburgh, Cincinnati, & St. Louis Railway.* Wheeling: Daily Intelligencer, 1879.

CALVERT, ELIZABETH H. *Boat-Man God and Other Poems.* Seattle: Calvert, 1898.

CAMERON, GEORGE F. *Lyrics on Freedom, Love and Death.* Boston: Moore; Kingston: Shannon, 1887.

Campaign Primer. New York: Harrison, 1880.

CAMPBELL, ALFRED G. *Poems.* Newark: Advertiser, 1883.

CAMPBELL, DUGALD. *Blue Ribbon Lays.* N.p.: N. publ., n.d.

—. *Scot in America: A poem.* Troy, N.Y.: N. publ., 1877.

CAMPBELL, ELIZABETH F. *Children's Bouquet.* N.p.: Publ. by the author, 1901.

—. *Pleasant Thoughts.* Phenix, R.I.: Campbell, 1896.

CAMPBELL, J. A. *Sunbeams.* Chehalis, Wash.: Russell, 1886.

CAMPBELL, JANE. *Club Epic.* N.p.: N. publ., 1887–88.

CAMPBELL, JOHN B. *Nature's Mighty Forces.* Fairmount, Ohio: American Health College, 1896.

CAMPBELL, JOHN P. *Land of Sun and Song.* Topeka: Crane, 1888.

—. *Queen Sylvia and Other Poems.* Cincinnati: Clarke, 1886.

—. *Republica: A National Poem.* Philadelphia: Lippincott, 1891.

CAMPBELL, WALTER L. *Civitas, The Romance of Our National Life.* New York and London: Putnam, 1886.

CAPPLEMAN, JOSIE F. *Heart Songs.* Richmond, Va.: Johnson, 1899.

CAREY, M. F. *Barnstormer's Companion.* Albany: Knickerbocker, 1899.

CAREY, PATRICK. *Poetical Works.* Cohoes, N.Y.: Wallace, 1888.

CARLAND, CONSTANCE P. *King of the Land of Nod and Other Poems.* N.p.: N. publ., n.d.

CARMAN, BLISS and HOVEY, RICHARD. *Last Songs from Vagabondia.* Boston: Small and Maynard, n.d. [copyright 1900].

—. *More Songs from Vagabondia.* Boston: Small and Maynard, 1899.

—. *Songs from Vagabondia.* Boston: Copeland and Day, 1897.

CARNES, MASON. *Lyrics and Verses.* New York: Ireland, 1888.

CARNEY, JIMMY. *Violet Book of Neshobe.* Rutland, Vt.: Publ. by the author, 1883.

CARROLL, WESLEY P. *Moss Agates.* Cheyenne, Wyo.: Daily Sun, 1890.

CARTER, A. A. *Blind Man's Thoughts: Poems.* Worcester, Mass.: N. publ., 1878.

CARTER, JOHN H. *Duck Creek Ballads.* New York: Nixon, 1894.

—. *Log Cabin Poems.* St. Louis: Rollingpin, 1897.

—. *Out Here in Ol' Missoury.* St. Louis: Carter, 1900.

CARTER, SIMEON. *Poems and Aphorisms.* Baldwinville, Mass.: Publ. by the author, 1893.

CASE, JOHN M. *Poems.* Columbus, Ohio: Hann and Adair, 1895.

CASE, VENELIA R. *Grange Poems.* Bloomfield, Conn.: N. publ., 1892.

CASSON, HERBERT N. *Bill Brooks and the Parson.* Lynn, Mass.: Lynn Labor, n.d.

CASTELLE, JOHN W. *Pedagogics Number One.* Chicago: N. publ., 1900.

—. *Schoolmaster and Other Poems.* Blue Island, Ill. [?]: N. publ., 1898.

CASTLE, C. A. *Voices of Song.* Burlington, Ia.: Free Press, 1898.

Catterel Ratterel (Doggerel). New York and London: Putnam, 1890.

CAVANAGH, E. W. *War.* N.p.: N. publ., 1900.

CAVANESS, A. A. and CAVANESS, J. M. *Poems by Two Brothers.* Chetopa, Kans.: Cavaness, 1896.

CAWEIN, MADISON J. *Blooms of the Berry.* Louisville: Morton, 1887.

——. *Garden of Dreams.* Louisville: Morton, 1896.

——. *Idyllic Monologues.* Louisville: Morton, 1898.

——. *Intimations of the Beautiful and Poems.* New York: Putnam, 1894.

——. *Lyrics and Idyls.* Louisville: Morton, 1890.

——. *Moods and Memories.* New York: Putnam, 1892.

——. *Poems of Nature and Love.* New York: Putnam, 1893.

——. *Red Leaves and Roses.* New York: Putnam, 1893.

——. *Triumph of Music.* Louisville: Morton, 1888.

——. *Undertones.* Boston: Copeland and Day, 1896.

——. *Weeds by the Wall.* Louisville: Morton, 1901.

C. B. *Idona, A Collection of Ethic and Religious Poems.* Hamilton [N.Y.?]: Republican, 1890.

CEDELTA [pseud.]. *Medley of Smiles and Tears.* N.p.: N. publ., 1887.

Celebration of the Forty-seventh Anniversary of the Admission of California into the Union by the Society of California Pioneers. San Francisco: Sterett, 1897.

Celebration of the Thirty-eighth Anniversary of the Admission of California into the Union, September 9, 1820, by the Society of California Pioneers. San Francisco: Eastman, 1888.

Celebration of the Thirty-ninth Anniversary of the Admission of California into the Union by the Society of California Pioneers. San Francisco: Eastman, 1889.

Celebration of the Twenty-seventh Anniversary of the Admission of California into the Union. San Francisco: Society of California Pioneers, 1877.

Celebration of the Twenty-third Anniversary of the Society of California Pioneers. San Francisco: Neal, 1883.

Centennalia. N.p.: Rhinebeck Gazette, 1876[?].

Centennial Frog and Other Stories. Philadelphia: Claston, Remsen and Haffelfinger, 1877.

Centennial of the Providence National Bank. Providence: N. publ., 1891.

CHAAPEL, H. HOUGHTON. *Poems*. Rockford, Ill.: Publ. by the author, 1900.

CHADWICK, JOHN W. *Book of Poems*. Boston: Roberts, 1876.

—. *Later Poems*. Boston and New York: Houghton, Mifflin, 1905.

CHAMBERLIN, ALDIN. *Life Thoughts*. Charlevoix, Mich.: Publ. by the author, 1893.

CHAMBERLIN, HENRY H. *Age of Ivory*. Boston: Badger, 1904.

CHAMBERS, AUGUSTA. *My Book*. Buffalo: Publ. by the author, 1880.

CHAMBERS, ROBERT W. *With the Band*. New York: Stone and Kimball, 1896.

CHAMPLIN, EDWIN R. *Heart's Own Verses*. Chicago: Kerr, 1886.

CHANNING, GRACE E. *Sea Drift*. Boston: Small, Maynard, 1899.

CHAPIN, LOU V. *Lover's Anniversary and Other Poems*. Los Angeles: N. publ., 1900.

CHAPMAN, JOHN A. *Within the Vail*. Charleston, S.C.: Walker, Evans and Cogswell, 1879.

CHAPMAN, W. *Few International Historical Sketches of Internal Administration*. N.p.: N. publ., 1895.

CHARLTON, J. *Parody on the Bab Ballads*. N.p.: Chicago & Alton Railroad, n.d.

CHASE, F. E. *Ballads in Black*. Boston: Lee and Shepard, 1882.

CHASE, WHITMAN. *Rough Notes in Rhyme*. Boston: Robinson and Hull, 1881.

CHENEY, WARREN. *Yosemite*. San Francisco: Crocker, 1890.

CHESEBROUGH, ROBERT A. *Reverie and Other Poems*. New York: Little, 1889.

CHESTER, HARRY S. *"When the Light Goes Out" and Other Poems*. Elkhart, Ind.: Truth Publishing House, 1900.

CHEYNEY, JOHN V. *Lyrics*. Boston: Birchard, 1901.

—. *Out of the Silence*. Boston: Copeland and Day, 1897.

—. *Poems*. Boston and New York: Houghton, Mifflin, 1905.

CHILDRESS, RUFUS J. *Woods and Waters*. Louisville: Dearing, 1900.

CHILSON, MYRA. *Revelation Unsealed and Fulfilled*. N.p.: N. publ., n.d.

—. *Water of Life*. N.p.: N. publ., n.d.

CHILTON, ROBERT S. *Poems*. Goderich [state ?]: McGillicuddy, 1885.

CHILTON, WILLIAM P. *Columbia. A National Poem. Acrostic on the American Union*. New York: Authors'; Montgomery, Ala.: White, 1880.

CHITTENDEN, E. P. *Pleroma. A Poem of the Christ.* New York and London: Putnam, 1890.

CHITTENDEN, RUSSELL H. *Verse and Prose.* Brooklyn: Gardner, 1879.

CHITTENDEN, WILLIAM L. *Ranch Verses.* New York and London: Putnam, 1898.

CHRISTIAN, C. RUSSELL. *Mountain Bard.* Huntington, W. Va.: Argus, 1885.

CLAFLIN, SUMNER F. *Thoughts in Verse.* Manchester, N.H.: Publ. by the author, 1893.

—. *Variety from a Canvasser's Note Book.* Manchester, N.H.: N. publ., 1905.

CLARK, ADELBERT. *Our Boys of Company K and Other Patriotic Poems.* Laconia, N.H.: Press of the News and Critic, 1898.

CLARK, ANNIE M. *Verses and Versions.* Lancaster, Mass.: Publ. by the author, 1898.

CLARK, AUGUSTUS P. *Book of Poems.* Cambridge, Mass.: Private edition, 1896.

CLARK, BENJAMIN F. *Poems.* Washington, D.C.: N. publ., 1895.

CLARK, JAMES G. *Poems and Songs.* Columbus, Ohio: Champlin, 1898.

CLARKE, JEAN. *Boss Devil of America.* Boston: Whitney, 1878.

CLARKE, MARY B. *Autumn Leaves.* Buffalo: Moulton, 1895.

CLEVELAND, LUCY. *Scarlet-veined and Other Poems.* New York: Randolph, 1897.

CLINE, WILLIAM H. *"In Varying Moods."* Kansas City, Mo.: Hudson-Kimberly, 1898.

CLINGMAN, NIXON P. *Poet and His Songs.* Baltimore: Arundel, 1900.

CLODFELTER, N. J. *Early Vanities.* New York: Hurst, 1886.

—. *Gotham of Yasmar: A Satire.* Buffalo: Peter Paul, 1897.

CLOSE, LISSIE E. *Home Poems.* Chicago and Cleveland: Wellman, 1876.

CLOYD, DICK. *Voice.* Prescott, Ark.: Picayune, n.d.

COAN, LEANDER S. *Better in the Mornin'.* Great Falls, N.Y.: Lord, 1880.

Coaquanock. Philadelphia: Germantown Social, 1878.

COATES, ELMER R. *Laurel Hill: A Poem.* Philadelphia: N. publ., 1878.

COATES, FLORENCE E. *Mine and Thine.* Boston and New York: Houghton, Mifflin, 1904.

COBB, ELLA W. *Memoir of Sylvanus Cobb, Jr.* Boston: Publ. for his family, 1891.

COBURN, J. G. *Euxemes and Other Poems.* Baltimore: Cushings and Bailey, 1889.

COBURN, WALLACE D. *Rhymes from a Round-up Camp.* Great Falls, Mont.: Ridgley Press, 1899.

COCKE, ZITELLA. *Grasshoppers' Hop and Other Verses.* Boston: Estes, 1901.

COE, CARRIE M. *Charity "Boom."* N.p.: Hahnemann Hospital Free Bed Fund, 1880.

COFFIN, FRANK B. *Coffin's Poems with Ajax' Ordeals.* Little Rock, Ark.: Colored Advocate, 1897.

COLBURN, MARIA S. *Golden Gems.* Oakland, Cal.: Pacific Press, 1891.

COLBY, H. W. *Rhymes of the Local Philosopher.* Taunton, Mass.: Davol, 1899.

COLBY, JOHN S. *Agatha: A Romance of Maine with Other Poems.* Boston: Williams, 1880.

COLE, CHARLES E. *Colonel; A Story in Verse.* Wichita [?]: Hobson, n.d.

COLE, JESSIE A. *Poems.* Denver: Wood, 1885.

COLE, SAMUEL V. *In Scipio's Gardens and Other Poems.* New York and London: Putnam, 1901.

COLES, ABRAHAM. *Man, the Microcosm and the Cosmos.* New York: Appleton, 1892 [4th edition].

COLLIER, ADA L. *Lilith: The Legend of the First Woman.* Boston: Lothrop, 1885.

COLLIER, THOMAS S. *Song Spray.* New London, Conn.: Viets, 1889.

COLLINS, CHARLES H. *Echoes from the Highland Hills.* Cincinnati: Thompson, 1884.

—. *From Highland Hills to an Emperor's Tomb.* Cincinnati: Clarke, 1886.

—. *New Year Comes, My Lady.* Buffalo: Moulton, 1895.

COLLINS, CLINTON. *Poems, Sketches.* Cincinnati: Keating, 1890.

COLLINS, E. L. *Poems.* Memphis: Rodgers, 1883.

COLLINS, JOHN. *1970, a Vision of the Coming Age.* Philadelphia: N. publ., 1891.

COMMELIN, ANNA O. *Of Such is the Kingdom, and Other Poems.* New York: Fowler and Wells, 1894.

CONANT, HENRY R. *Poems.* Kaukauna, Wisc.: Sun, 1893.

CONANT, ISABELLA H. *Field of Folk.* Boston: Badger, 1903.

CONE, JOE. *Heart and Home Ballads.* Cambridge, Mass.: Smart, 1899.

CONNERS, MARIA W. *Wreath of Maple Leaves.* Seattle: Hughes, 1888.

CONOVER, O. M. *Via Solitaria. Reconciliation*. Madison, Wisc.: Cantwell, 1882.

CONRARD, G. HARRISON. *Idle Songs and Idle Sonnets*. Cincinnati: Editor, 1897.

—. *Junior's Poems*. Cincinnati: Methven, 1891.

CONWAY, JOHN D. *Complete Poems*. Lawrence, Mass.: Conway, 1875.

CONWAY, JOHN W. *Thrice Words*. Kansas [no city]: Norton Champion, 1894.

COOK, E. U. *First Mortgage*. Chicago: Rhodes and McClure, 1902.

COOK, FANNY B. *Fancy's Etchings*. San Francisco: Winterburn, 1892.

COOKE, J. EDMUND. *Rimes to Be Read*. Chicago: Conkey, 1897.

COOLBRITH, INA. *Songs from the Golden Gate*. Boston and New York: Houghton, Mifflin, 1895.

COOLIDGE, HENRY D. *Effusion*. Boston: Wright and Potter, 1891.

COOLIDGE, KATHERINE. *Selections*. Boston: Private edition, 1901.

COONLEY, LYDIA A. *Under the Pines and Other Verses*. Chicago: Way and Williams, 1895.

COOPER, W. C. *Tethered Truants*. Cincinnati: Sullivan, 1897.

COREY, ARTHUR D. *A Memorial*. Cambridge, Mass.: Wilson, 1892.

CORNABY, HANNAH. *Autobiography and Poems*. Salt Lake City: Graham, 1881.

CORNWALL, SARAH J. *Roses and Myrtles*. New York: Appleton, 1881.

CORNWALLIS, KINAHAN. *Conquest of Mexico and Peru*. New York: Daily Investigator, 1893.

—. *Song of America and Columbus . . . 1495–1895*. New York: Daily Investigator, 1892.

CORNWELL, M. S. *Wheat and Chaff*. Romney, W. Va.: Cornwell Bros., 1899.

CORSON, GEORGE N. *Great Tangle-ation*. Norristown, Pa: Helffenstein, 1894.

COTHRAN, E. E. *Smiles and Tears*. San Francisco: San Francisco News, 1882.

COUGHLIN, WILLIAM J. *Songs of an Idle Hour*. Boston: Williams, 1883.

COULIN, EMILE D. *America Past and Present*. New York: Wien, 1904.

—. *Poetical Leisure Hours*. Stamford, Conn.: Bradley and Cunningham, 1899.

COWAN, FRANK. *Southwestern Pennsylvania in Song and Story*. Greensburg, Pa.: Publ. by the author, 1878.

COWDEN, WILLIAM F. *Poems*. Baltimore: Boyle, 1888.

COX, J. BRADFORD. *Sadalpha*. San Jose, Cal.: Mercury Steam Print, 1880.

COX, PALMER. *Another Brownie Book*. New York: Century, 1890.

—. *Frontier Humor*. New York: Union, 1889.

—. *Hans Von Pelter's Trip to Gotham*. New York: Art Printing, 1877.

—. *Popular Hero*. New York: Pond's Extract, 1887.

—. *What a Cake of Soap Will Do*. N.p.: Procter and Gamble, n.d.

COYLE, HENRY. *Promise of Morning*. Boston: Angel Guardian, 1899.

CRAIG, B. F. *Rough Diamond*. Kansas City, Mo.: Ramsey, Millet, and Hudson, 1880.

CRANDALL, CHARLES H. *Chords of Life*. Springdale, Conn.: Publ. by the author, 1898.

—. *Wayside Music*. New York and London: Putnam, 1893.

CRANE, OLIVER. *Minto and Other Poems*. New York: Ketcham, 1888.

CRANE, STEPHEN. *Black Riders and Other Lines*. Boston: Copeland and Day, 1895.

—. *War Is Kind*. New York: Stokes, 1899.

CRAWFORD, JOHN W. *Poet Scout: Verses and Songs*. San Francisco: Keller, 1879.

—. *Souvenir of Song and Story*. New York: Buss, 1889.

CREAMER, EDWARD S. *Adirondack Readings*. Buffalo: Moulton, 1893.

CREASY, ARTHUR. *Two Women Wronged*. Parsons, Kans.: Foley Railway Printing, 1900.

CRESSEY, GEORGE C. *Early Morning, The Last Charge, and Other Poems*. Leipsic [state?]: Ackermann and Glaser, n.d.

CREWSON, E. A. *Old Times*. Kansas City, Mo.: Tiernan-Havens, 1893.

CRISSEY, FORREST. *In Thompson's Woods*. Chicago: Blue Sky, 1901.

CRIST, MALEY B. *Patchwork*. Atlanta: Martin and Hoyt, 1898.

CROCHERON, AUGUSTA J. *Wild Flowers of Deseret*. Salt Lake City: Juvenile Instructor Office, 1881.

CROFFUT, W. A. *Prophecy and Other Poems*. New York: Lovell, n.d.

CROSBY, ERNEST H. *Broad-cast*. London: Fifield, 1905.

—. *Plain Talk in Psalm and Parable*. Boston: Small, Maynard [1899, 1st edition], 1901 [3rd edition].

—. *Swords and Plowshares*. New York: Funk and Wagnalls, 1902.

—. *War Echoes*. Philadelphia: Innes, 1898.

CROSBY, POWEL R. *Poems*. Verne, Mich.: Publ. by the author, 1895.

CROSS, MAY. *Pygmalion . . . and Other Poems*. Watertown, N.Y.: Hungerford, 1887.

CROWE, WILL L. *Poems*. N.p.: Publ. by the author, 1893.

CROWNINSHIELD, FREDERIC. *Painter's Moods*. New York: Dodd, Mead, 1902.

—. *Pictoris Carmina*. New York: Dodd, Mead, 1900.

—. *Tales in Metre and Other Poems*. New York: Cooke, 1903.

CROZIER, M. P. *Songs in Earnest*. Washington, D.C.: Soule, 1887.

CRUFF, JOHN F. *Poems and Squibs*. Providence: Townsend, 1900.

"Cuba Libre!" New York: Raymond, n.d.

CUDMORE, P. *Battle of Clontarf and Other Poems*. New York: Kennedy, 1895.

—. *Buchanan's Conspiracy, the Nicaragua Canal and Reciprocity*. New York: Kennedy, 1892.

— *Poems and Songs, Satires and Political Rings*. New York: Kennedy, 1885 [4th edition].

—. *Prophecy of the Twentieth Century*. New York: Kennedy, 1899.

CULBERTSON, ANNE V. *Lays of a Wandering Ministrel*. Philadelphia: Lippincott, 1896.

CUMMINGS, EPHRAIM C. *In Measured Language*. Portland, Me.: Private edition, 1899.

CUMMINGS, ST. JAMES. *Flamborough Head and Other Poems*. Charleston, S.C.: Publ. by the author, 1899.

Curious Adventures of the Man with the Sewing Machine. Cleveland: White Sewing Machine, 1883.

CURREY, AUGUSTUS. *Sower*. Detroit: Riverside Publishing, 1884.

CURRIE, GEORGE G. *Sonnets and Love Songs*. West Palm Beach, Fla.: Dean, 1901.

CURRIER, JOHN M. *Song of the Hubbardton Raid*. Castleton, Vt.: Private edition, 1880.

CURRIER, MARY M. *Among the Granite Hills*. Cambridge, Mass.: Publ. by the author, 1894.

CURTIS, HARRIS G. *Poems*. Appleton, Wisc.: Post Publishing, 1894.

CURTIS, HATTIE J. *Angel Whisperings*. Chicago: Religio-Philosophical Publishing, 1889.

CURTIS, M. B. *Legend of Sam'l of Posen*. New York: N. publ., n.d.

CURTIS, T. D. *Nazarene and Other Rhymes*. Syracuse: Farmer and Dairymen, 1885.

CUSTEAD, E. *Rose and Elza.* New York: Jenkins, 1882.

DAGNALL, JOHN M. *Our American Hash: A Satire.* New York: Publ. by the author, 1880.

DALY, JOSEPH. *Wild Flowers.* Boston: Stanley and Usher, 1883.

DAMON, FANNIE A. *Heart Treasures.* Buffalo: Moulton, 1894.

DANDRIDGE, DANSKE. *Joy, and Other Poems.* New York and London: Putnam, 1900 [2nd enlarged edition].

DANIEL, J. W. *Cateechee of Keeowee.* Nashville, Tenn.: Methodist Episcopal Church, 1898.

DANIELL, IRENE S. *Pastime Poems.* Milwaukee: King-Fowle-McGee, 1896.

DARLING, S. I. *Messages from the Watch Tower.* San Francisco: Carrier Dove, 1890.

DARROW, A. R. *Iphigenia and Other Poems.* Buffalo: Sherill, 1888.

D'ARVILLE, GREVILLE. *Omega et Alpha, and Other Poems.* San Francisco: Elder and Shepard, 1899.

DAVENPORT, W. E. *Beggar-man of Brooklyn Heights and Other Chants.* Brooklyn: Publ. by the author, n.d.

—. *Man: A Poem in Three Parts.* New York: Publ. by the author, 1884.

—. *More Outcries from Brooklyn Hollow.* New York: Publ. by the author, n.d.

—. *Perpetual Fire.* New York: Publ. by the author, 1886.

—. *Poetical Sermons.* New York: Publ. by the author, 1896.

—. *Poetical Sermons, Including the Ballad of Plymouth Church.* New York: Putnam, 1897.

—. *Visions of the City.* New York: Publ. by the author, 1884.

DAVIE, OLIVER. *Odds and Ends.* Columbus, Ohio: Publ. by the author, 1902.

DAVIES, JOHN A. *Success, and Other Poems.* Cleveland: Davies, 1881.

DAVIS, BEN W. *Sea-weed and Sand.* N.p.: N. publ., n.d.

DAVIS, CORA M. *Immortelles.* New York: Putnam, 1887.

DAVIS, DANIEL W. *'Weh Down Souf.* Cleveland: Helman-Taylor, 1897.

DAVIS, DUDLEY H. *Davis's Poems. Songs of the Age.* Baltimore: Publ. by the author, 1891.

—. *Kingdom Gained and Other Poems.* Richmond, Va.: Johnson, 1896.

DAVIS, JACK. *Jack Davis' Poems.* Atlanta: Foote and Davies, 1904.

DAVIS, JOHN S. *Poems.* Montgomery, Ala.: N. publ., n.d.

DAVIS, MILES A. *Among the Muses*. N.p.: Publ. by the author, 1894.

DAVIS, PARKER B. *Tangled Rhymes*. Portland, Me.: Ford and Rich, 1889.

DAVIS, REBECCA I. *Gleanings from Merrimac Valley*. Portland, Me.: Hoyt, Fogg and Donham, 1881.

DAVIS, SAM. *Short Stories*. San Francisco: Golden Era, 1886.

DAWSON, DANIEL L. *Seeker in the Marshes and Other Poems*. Philadelphia: Rees, Welsh, 1893.

DAWSON, MILES M. *Poems of the New Time*. New York: Alliance, 1901.

DAY, DUNCAN. *In School Days and Other Poems*. Baraboo, Wisc.: Luckow, 1895.

DAY, HOLMAN F. *Kin O'Ktaadn*. Boston: Small, Maynard, 1904.

—. *Pine Tree Ballads*. Boston: Small, Maynard, 1902.

—. *Up in Maine*. Boston: Small, Maynard, 1900.

DAY, JOHN W. *Galaxy of Progressive Poems*. Boston: Colby and Rich, 1890.

DAY, MAIE. *Blended Flags*. Danville, Va.: N. publ., 1898.

DAY, RICHARD E. *Lines in the Sand*. Syracuse: Roberts, 1878.

—. *Lyrics and Satires*. Syracuse: Roberts, 1883.

DEAN, C. A. *Inspirational Poems*. Portland, Ore.: Publ. by the author, 1898.

DEAN, JAMES B. *Poems*. Vol. II. Cheshire, Mass.: N. publ., 1896.

DEARDEN, WILLIAM. *Mummy's Plaint and Other Poems*. Northampton, Mass.: Wade, Warner, 1888.

DEARING, LULU S. *Lost Chords*. Chillicothe, Mo.: Publ. by the author, 1900.

DE CLEYRE, V. *Worm Turns*. Philadelphia: Innes, 1900.

DECOSTA, BENJAMIN F. *Pilgrim of Old France*. New York: Private edition, 1894.

Dedication of the W.C.T.U. Mercy Home, Manchester, N.H., January 1, 1890. Exeter, N.H.: Gazette Printing, 1890.

DEEM, FRED. *Rip Van Fossil: A Medical Tragedy*. New York: Alliance, 1900.

DEFOREST, JOHN W. *Poems, Medley and Palestina*. New Haven: Tuttle, Morehouse and Taylor, 1902.

DEKAY, CHARLES. *Hesperus and Other Poems*. New York: Scribner, 1880.

DELANO. GEORGE S. *Stone of Whizgig Race and Selections*. N.p.: N. publ., 1900.

DELEVANTE, MICHAEL. *First Blossoms.* New York: Brentano, 1894.

DEMAREST, MARY L. *Writings.* Passaic, N.J.: Publ. by her husband, 1888.

DENISON, T. S. *Old Schoolhouse and Other Poems and Conceits in Verse.* Chicago: Denison, 1902.

DENNEHY, PATRICK F. *Convict's Story and Other Poems Descriptive of Prison Life.* Providence: N. publ., 1894.

DENNIS, AMANDA E. *Asphodels and Pansies.* Philadelphia: Lippincott, 1888.

DENNIS, ELLEN A. *Poems.* Auburn, Me.: Merrill and Webber, 1893.

DENTON, FRANKLIŃ E. *Early Poetical Works.* Cleveland: Williams, 1883.

DEVENS, WILLIAM H. *Selections of Prose and Verse.* N.p.: N. publ., n.d.

Devil's Visit [attributed to Frederick Hollick]. New York: Excelsior Publishing, 1891.

DEVINE, THOMAS F. *"Like a Sun to Illumine the World."* Waterbury, Conn.: N. publ., 1900.

DIBBLE, F. D. *Prairie Poems and Others.* New York: Neely, 1900.

DICKINSON, CHARLES M. *Children, and Other Verses.* New York: Cassell, 1889.

DICKINSON, EMILY. *Poems.* Boston: Roberts, 1894 [13th edition].

—. *Poems Second Series.* Boston: Roberts, 1892.

—. *Poems Third Series.* Boston: Little, Brown, 1917 [originally publ. 1896].

DICKINSON, MAY L. *Edelweiss.* New York: N. publ., 1876.

DICKSON, JOHN J. *Farmer's Thoughts.* N.p.: N. publ., 1896.

DIEKENGA, I. E. *Between Times.* Boston: Earle, 1882.

DILLMAN, WILL. *Across the Wheat.* Revillo, S.D.: Item, 1898.

DODGE, ELLEN A. *Poems and Letters.* N.p.: Printed for the family, 1894.

DODGE, HANNAH P. *Teacher's Message.* Boston: N. publ., 1896.

DODGE, MARIA J. *Echoes from Cape Ann.* Boston: Cupples and Hurd, 1889.

DOEMAN, ALLEN. *Poems. A Collection of Seven Hundred Miscellaneous Poems.* Chicago: American Publishing, 1892.

DOGGETT, JOHN M. *Hugh Allone, Sailor.* Richmond, Va.: Whittet and Shepperson, 1886.

DOLE, NATHAN H. *Peace and Progress. Two Symphonic Poems.* Boston: Private edition, 1904.

DONAHOE, D. J. *In Sheltered Ways.* Buffalo: Moulton, 1895.

DONAHUE, T. L. *Pedro and Miguel.* Newport, R.I.: Davis and Pitman, 1880.

DONALDSON, SAMUEL. *Poems.* Philadelphia: N. publ., 1885.

DONALDSON, THOMAS B. *Apropos Alphabet.* New York: Sterling, 1900.

DONAN, P. *Utah.* Buffalo: Dodge, 1895.

DONEGHY, GEORGE W. *Old Hanging Fork and Other Poems.* Franklin, Ohio: Editor, 1897.

DONNER, HERMAN M. *English Lyrics on a Finnish Harp.* Boston: Badger, 1902.

DOOLING, JAMES J. *Rhymes without Treason.* Lexington, Mass.: Parsons, n.d.

DORR, JOSEPH W. *Babylon.* Tacoma, Wash.: Commercial, 1897.

DORWARD, WILFRID J. *Mother and Others.* Milwaukee: Sentinel, 1898.

DOUGLAS, HARRIET D. *In Memoriam.* Cambridge, Mass.: Wilson, 1887.

DOUGLAS, MALCOLM. *My Odd Little Folk. Rhymes and Verses about Them.* Philadelphia: Altemus, 1893.

DOUGLAS, SARAH. *Bird's Eye View of the Progress of Science, Religions, and Philosophy.* Providence: Rhode Island News, 1883.

DOWNEY, STEPHEN W. *Immortals.* Washington, D.C.: N. publ., 1880.

DOWNING, ANDREW. *Trumpeters and Other Poems.* Washington, D.C.: Hayworth, 1897.

DOYLE, BURTON T. *Pansies for Thought.* Buffalo: Peter Paul, 1895.

DOYLE, E. A. *Poems and Lyrics Relating to the Spanish and Cuban War.* Winchester, Ohio: Herald, 1898.

DOYLE, EDWARD. *American Soldier, a Poem.* New York: Uptown, 1897.

——. *Haunted Temple and Other Poems.* New York: Knickerbocker, 1905.

——. *Moody Moments, Poems.* New York: Ketcham and Doyle, 1888.

DOZIER, ORION T. *Galaxy of Southern Heroes and Other Poems.* Birmingham, Ala.: N. publ., 1905.

DRAPER, JAMES S. *Sentiment and Song.* Boston: Private edition, 1893.

DREAME, CECIL. *Edith May: A Romant of Colorado.* Pittsburgh: Stevenson and Foster, 1882.

DRESSER, HENRY B. *Captured and Bound.* Worcester, Mass.: N. publ., 1894.

DREW, M. AURILLA. *Spiced Thought-Food.* Winona, Minn.: Jones and Kroeger, 1885.

DRUMMOND, WILLIAM H. *Habitant and Other French-Canadian Poems.* New York: Putnam, 1893.

—. *Johnnie Courteau and Other Poems.* New York: Putnam, 1901.

—. *Voyageur and Other Poems.* New York: Putnam, 1905.

DRUMOCH, SEMAJ. *Hades.* Chicago: N. publ., 1895.

DUBBS, JOSEPH H. *Home Ballads.* Philadelphia: Fisher, 1888.

DUGAN, MAY M. [Annie A.]. *Myrtle Leaves.* Sedalia, Mo.: Democrat, 1885.

DUNBAR, PAUL L. *Lyrics of Lowly Life.* New York: Dodd, Mead, 1896.

—. *Lyrics of the Hearthside.* New York: Dodd, Mead, 1899.

—. *Majors and Minors.* Toledo, Ohio: Hadley and Hadley, 1895.

DUNHAM, SAMUEL C. *Goldsmith of Nome and Other Verse.* Washington, D.C.: Neale, 1901.

—. *Just Back from Dawson and Other Doggerel.* N.p.: N. publ., 1899.

DUNN, GEORGE W. *Temple of Justice and Other Poems.* Kansas City, Mo.: Ramsey, Millett and Hudson, 1882.

DUNROY, WILLIAM R. *"Corn Tassells," A Book of Corn Rhymes.* Lincoln, Nebr.: University Publishing, 1899.

DURANT, HORACE B. *Prohibition Home Protection Party Campaign Songs.* Claysville, Pa.: Durant, 1884.

DURFEE, WILLIAM. *Now and Then.* New Bedford, [Mass.?]: Sherman and Habicht, 1890.

DUTCHER, EDWARD W. *Legend of a City and Other Poems and Fancies.* Fulton, Ill.: N. publ., 1878.

DWINELLE, HESTER S. *Poems.* Florence, Italy: Claudian Press, 1900.

DYE, EVA E. *Stories of Oregon.* San Francisco: Whitaker and Ray, 1904.

DYER, W. L. *Rhymes of a Radical.* Indianapolis: Carlon and Hollenbeck, 1890.

E. A. *Yale Jingle Book.* New York: Sterling, 1900.

EASTMAN, ELAINE G. *Journal of a Farmer's Daughter.* New York: Putnam, 1881.

EASTON, JOHN A. *Chicago.* Benton Harbor, Mich.: N. publ., 1890.

Echo of the Seneca. Geneva, New York: Hobart College, 1886.

ECKERSON, THEODORE J. *When My Ship Comes In.* Cambridge, Mass.: Riverside, 1881.

EDDY, MARY B. *Miscellaneous Writings.* N.p.: N. publ., n.d.

EDGERTON, JAMES A. *Songs of the People.* Denver: Reed, 1902.

—. *Voices of the Morning.* Chicago: Kerr, 1898.

EDMUNDS, ALBERT J. *Songs of Asia Sung in America: Together with Other Poems*: *1880–1895*. Philadelphia: Folwell, 1896.

EISENBEIS, LOUIS. *Amen Corner and Other Poems*. West Chester, Pa.: N. publ., 1897.

ELBING, RAY. *Spirit of Mount Vernon*. Columbus, Ohio: Haak, 1900.

ELDRED, O. P. *Poems Without a Muse*. Cincinnati: Editor, 1899.

ELLARD, HARRY. *Ranch Tales of the Rockies*. Canon City, Colo.: Publ. by the author, 1899.

ELLIOTT, LYDIA L. *Skeleton's Message and Other Poems*. Terre Haute, Ind.: Inland, 1896.

ELLIS, JAMES T. *Poems*. Louisville: Fetter, 1898.

ELLIS, WILLIAM. *Old Wisconse*. Wausau, Wisc.: Philosopher, 1899.

ELLWANGER, W. D. *Summer Snowflake*. New York: Doubleday, Page, 1902.

ELMORE, ALFRED. *Maple Valley Poems*. N.p.: N. publ., 1892 [4th edition].

ELMORE, JAMES B. *Love among the Mistletoe*. Alamo, Ind.: Publ. by the author, 1899.

—. *Lover in Cuba and Poems*. Alamo, Ind.: Publ. by the author, 1901.

—. *Supplement. A Lover in Cuba and Poems*. Nashville, Tenn.: McQuiddy, 1902.

—. *Twenty-five Years in Jackville . . . and Selected Poems*. Alamo, Ind.: Publ. by the author, 1904.

ELSHEMUS, LOUIS M. *"Lady" Vere and Other Narratives*. New York: Abbey, 1897.

—. *Mammon. A Spirit-song*. New York: Eastman-Lewis, 1897.

—. *Moods of a Soul*. Buffalo: Moulton, 1895.

—. *Songs of Spring and Blossoms of Unrequited Love*. Buffalo: Peter Paul, 1895.

EMERSON, ALDALINE T. *Love-bound and Other Poems*. Cambridge, Mass.: University, 1895.

EMERSON, EDWIN. *Poems*. Denver: Carson-Harper, 1901.

EMERSON, FREDERICK W. *Patriotic Songs and Poems*. Marblehead, Mass.: Lindsey, 1892.

EMMETT, R. H. *Song and Ballad Poems*. N.p.: Publ. by the author, 1899.

EMMONS, JAMES G. *Mingled Memories*. N.p.: Publ. by the author, 1889.

EMSWILER, GEORGE P. *Poems and Sketches.* Richmond, Ind.: Nicholson, 1897.

ENGLAND, HOWELL S. *Shots at Random.* New York: Ogilvie, 1899.

ENGLE, W. A. *Poems.* N.p.: N. publ., 1883.

ENGLISH, JOSIAH G. *Poems.* Xenia, Ohio: N. publ., 1888.

ESLING, CHARLES H. *Melodies of Mood and Tense.* Philadelphia: Walsh, 1894.

ESTES, J. E. *Glory to "Old Glory."* Fall River, Mass.: Publ. by the author, 1898.

ESTES, T. J. *Early Days and War Times in Northern Arkansas.* Lubbock, Tex.: Dow, n.d.

EVANS, ALEXANDER. *Fashion and Other Poems.* Louisville: N. publ., 1887.

EVANS, THOMAS J. *Sir Francis Drake and Other Fugitive Poems.* Richmond, Va.: Whittet and Shepperson, 1895.

EWING, WILLIAM G. *Poems on United States History.* N.p.: N. publ., 1880.

FABENS, JOSEPH W. *"Last Cigar" and Other Poems.* New York: Holbrook, 1887.

FABER, FELIX. *American History Versified.* New York and Washington, D.C.: Neale, 1905.

FAIRHURST, A. *My Good Poems.* St. Louis: Christian, 1899.

FALES, EDWARD L. *Songs and Song Legends.* St. Paul: Publ. by the author, 1887.

FALL, CHARLES G. *Village Sketch and Other Poems.* Boston: Cupples, Upham, 1886.

FALT, CHARLES M. *Wharf and Fleet. Ballads of the Fishermen of Gloucester.* Boston: Little, Brown, 1902.

FARGO, KATE M. *Songs Not Set to Music.* New York: Abbey, 1901.

FARQUHAR, EDWARD. *Libyssa.* Washington, D.C.: Publ. by the author, 1898.

FARRALONE [pseud.?]. *Poems of Sentiment, Affection, and Devotion.* Detroit: Graham, 1887.

FARROW, BERTHA S. *College Rhymes.* Indianapolis: Bowen-Merrill, 1893.

FEARING, LILLIAN B. *In the City by the Lake.* Chicago: Searle and Gorton, 1892.

FELLOWS, ODELL T. *Rhymes of Reform.* Pasadena, Cal.: Swerdfiger, 1897.

FENNALL, PATRICK. *Lyrics and Poems.* Oswego, N.Y.: Oliphant, 1886.

FENOLLOSA, ERNEST F. *East and West, the Discovery of America, and Other Poems.* New York: Crowell, 1893.

FENOLLOSA, MARY M. *Out of the Nest.* Boston: Little, Brown, 1899.

FERGUSON, AMOS J. [and wife]. *Pioneer and His Daughter. Bible Poem.* Jamestown, N.Y.: Journal Printing, 1883.

FERRE, ELLA. *Land by the Sunset Sea and Other Poems.* San Francisco: Figel, 1884.

FETTERMAN, J. D. *Street Musings: Or Joe's Romantic Adventures in the Great Midland City.* Kansas City, Mo.: Rigby-Ramsey, 1895.

FIELD, CHARLES K. *Four-leaved Clover, Being Stanford Rhymes.* San Francisco: N. publ., 1899 [3rd edition].

FIELD, EUGENE. *Clink of the Ice and Other Poems.* Chicago: Donohue, 1905.

—. *Culture's Garland.* Boston: Ticknor, 1887.

—. *Hoosier Lyrics.* Chicago: Donohue, 1905.

—. *John Smith, U.S.A.* Chicago: Donohue, 1905.

—. *Little Book of Tribune Verse.* New York: Grosset and Dunlap, 1901.

—. *Little Book of Western Verse.* New York: Scribner, 1892.

—. *My Book.* Chicago: Private edition, 1905.

—. *Second Book of Verse.* New York: Scribner, 1893.

—. *Sharps and Flats.* Two volumes. New York: Scribner, 1900.

—. *Songs and Other Verses.* New York: Scribner, 1903.

FIELD, EUGENE and ROSWELL M. *Echoes from the Sabine Farm.* New York: Scribner, 1904.

Field-Gar-a-Jim. Chicago: Western News, 1880.

Fighting Strength of Nations. Baltimore: Emerson Drug, n.d.

FISH, ANGELINA. *Voices and Echoes of the Past.* Brooklyn: N. publ., 1885.

FISHER, CHARLES A. *Minstrel with the Selfsame Song and Other Poems.* Baltimore: Fisher, 1903 [2nd edition].

FISHER, LAURA H. *Figures and Flowers for Serious Souls.* Buffalo: Moulton, 1888.

FISHER, STOKELY S. *Leilia Lee and Other Poems.* Cambridge, Ohio: Amos, 1888 [2nd edition].

FISHER, W. W. *Poetical Works.* Philadelphia: Publ. by the author, 1876.

FISKE, ALBERT W. *New Year Offering.* Bristol, N.H.: Musgrove, 1880.

FISKE, HORACE S. *Ballad of Manila Bay and Other Verses.* Chicago: University of Chicago, 1900.

FITZGERALD, MARCELLA A. *Poems.* New York: Publ. by the author, 1886.

FITZGERALD, O. P. *California Sketches.* Nashville, Tenn.: Southern Methodist, 1882.

FITZPATRICK, ERNEST H. *Passing of William McKinley. A Poem.* Pontiac, Ill.: News, 1901.

FLAGG, EDWARD O. *Poems.* New York: Whittaker, 1890.

FLATTERY, HUGH. *Pope and the New Crusade.* New York: Knox, 1887.

FLEENOR, CREEDMORE. *In Passing Through.* Bowling Green, Ky.: Courier, 1898.

—. *Poetical Works.* Bowling Green, Ky.: Authors, 1905.

FLEMING, A. M. *Gleanings of a Tyro Bard.* N.p.: Berry, 1890.

FLETCHER, JOSIAH M. *Thousand Songs of Life, Love, Hope and Heaven.* Nashua, N.H.: Parker, 1890.

FLIESBURG, OSCAR and JOHNSON, LEWIS P. *Cristoforo Colon. An Epic Poem.* St. Paul: N. publ., 1893.

Flowers and Flag of Our Country. Denver: Western Lithographing, 1897.

FOLSON, FLORENCE. *Love Lyrics.* Boston: Idea, 1899.

FORD, ANNA M. *Garlands of Thought.* Philadelphia: Flint, 1885.

FORD, ANNA P. *Vesper Voices.* Asbury Park, N.J.: Pennypacker, 1899.

FORDHAM, MARY W. *Magnolia Leaves.* Charleston, S.C.: N. publ., 1897.

FORRESTER, ARTHUR M. *Irish Crazy Quilt.* Boston: Mudge, 1891.

FOSS, SAM W. *Back Country Poems.* Boston: Lee and Shepard, 1894.

—. *Dreams in Homespun.* Boston: Lee and Shepard, 1898.

—. *Songs of War and Peace.* Boston: Lee and Shepard, 1899.

—. *Whiffs from Wild Meadows.* Boston: Lee and Shepard, n.d.

FOSTER, ELIZABETH M. *Poems.* New York: Broadway, 1905.

FOSTER, LEONARD G. *Whisperings of Nature.* Cleveland: N. publ., 1893.

FOWLE, MARY L. *Where Is Heaven? and Other Poems.* San Francisco: Bancroft, 1890.

FOWLER, EGBERT W. *Poems.* Boston: Badger, 1905.

FRAME, NATHAN T. *Under the Lindens. Poems.* Cleveland: N. publ., 1885.

FRANK, HENRY. *Skeleton and the Rose.* Chicago: Brentano, 1886.

FRANKLIN, BENJAMIN [pseud.]. *Free Silver*. New York: Republican National Committee, n.d.

FRANKLIN, JAMES T. *Mid-day Gleanings*. Memphis: Tracey, 1893.

FREEMAN, W. R. *Reminiscences of Farm Life in Western New York, Seventy Years Ago*. N.p.: N. publ., 1894.

FREER, CHARLES H. *Missionary and Other Poems*. Chicago: American Publ., 1892.

FRENCH, ERASMUS D. *Power of Destiny Revealed in Our War with Spain and the Philippines*. Los Angeles: N. publ., 1899.

FRENCH, MYRIAM B. *Stray Leaves and Fragments*. New York: N. publ., 1890.

FRISBIE, ALVAH L. *Siege of Calais and Other Poems*. Des Moines: Mills, 1880.

FRISELLE, FRANK M. *Kismet Poems*. Manchester, N.H.: Clarke, 1898.

FRY, MARY A. *Tennessee Centennial Poem. A Synopsis of the History of Tennessee*. Chattanooga: Publ. by the author, 1896.

FRY, SOL. *Poems*. Pittsburgh: N. publ., 1876.

FULLER, ANGELINE A. *Venture*. Detroit: Williams, 1883.

FULLER, WILLIAM H. *From the Cradle to the Grave and Other Poems*. Ionia, Mich.: N. publ., 1888.

FUNK, HENRY B. *Christopher the Crank, and the Day We Celebrate*. Clay Center, Nebr.: Publ. by the author, 1894.

FURMAN, ALFRED A. *In Vales of Helikon*. New York: Wynkoop, Hallenbeck and Crawford, 1899.

GAILEY, MATTHEW. *Wreaths and Gems*. Philadephia: Spangler and Davis, 1882.

GALLAGHER, JAMES and SIMMONS, THOMAS H. *Cruise of the "Trenton" in European Waters*. New York: O'Keefe, 1881.

GARDNER, ANNA. *Golden Rod and Other Poems*. N.p.: Inquirer and Mirror, n.d.

—. *Harvest Gleanings in Prose and Verse*. New York: Fowler and Wells, 1881.

GARITEE, JOHN. *Poems*. N.p.: N. publ., n.d.

GARLAND, HAMLIN. *Prairie Songs*. Cambridge and Chicago: Stone and Kimball, 1893.

—. *Trail of the Goldseekers*. New York: Macmillan, 1899.

GARY, ANSTISS C. *Year's Singing and Other Poems*. Chicago: Brentano, 1895.

GATES, LAWRENCE G. *Musings.* Troy, Ohio: Democrat, 1886.

GAYLORD, MAY L. *Heart Echoes.* New York: N. publ., 1895.

GEORGE, JESSE. *Our Army and Navy in the Orient.* Manila: N. publ., 1899.

GERRY, CHARLES F. *Meadow Melodies.* Boston: Lee and Shepard, 1887.

GERSON, FELIX N. *Some Verses.* Philadelphia: Stern, 1893.

GIBBONS, J. J. *In the San Juan. Colorado.* N.p.: N. publ., 1894.

GIBSON, A. M. *Leisure Hour Lyrics.* N.p.: Hartford Press, 1899.

GIBSON, R. E. *Sonnets and Lyrics.* Louisville: Morton, 1891.

GIBSON, WILLIAM. *Poems of Many Years and Many Places.* Boston: Lee and Shepard, 1881.

GIFFIN, DAN S. *Story of Pioneer Life.* Chicago: Bartsch, 1898.

GIFFEN, FANNIE R. *Oo-mah-ha Ta-wa-tha [Omaha City].* Lincoln, Nebr.: Publ. by the author, 1898.

GILBERT, HOWARD W. *Aldornere, and Two Other Pennsylvania Idylls; Together with Minor Poems.* Philadelphia: N. publ., 1890.

GILCHRIST, ANNIE S. *Souvenir of the Tennessee Centennial.* Nashville, Tenn.: Gospel Adocate, 1897.

GILL, AUGUSTUS. *Musings by Pequit Brookside.* Boston: Private edition, 1888.

GILMAN, CHARLOTTE P. *In This Our World and Other Poems.* San Francisco: Barry and Marble, 1895.

GILMORE, MINNIE. *Pipes from Prairie-land and Other Places.* New York: Cassell, 1886.

GITTINGS, JOHN G. *West Virginia Lyrics.* Morgantown, W. Va.: Acme, 1902.

GLANVILLE, ALBERT. *"An Eye for an Eye."* Chicago: Francoeur, 1897.

GLASGOW, ELLEN. *Freeman and Other Poems.* New York: Doubleday, Page, 1902.

God in Creation and Evolution, and the Church of Every Age in Light and Shade. New York: Beekman, 1883.

GODDARD, SEXTUS P. *Buds, Briers, and Berries.* Worcester, Mass.: Goddard, 1880.

GOLDEN, PETER. *Criticism of Things in General and Other Poems.* St. Louis: Marnell, 1900 [?].

—. *Voice of Ireland.* New York: O'Conner, n.d.

GOODENOUGH, ARTHUR H. *"Blossoms of Yesterday."* Seattle: Schoenfeld, 1896.

GOODRICH, HENRY A. *Evening Lyrics.* Fitchburg: Emerson, 1902.

GOODRICH, HENRY H. *Memorial Birthday Poem to the Poet Thomas Moore.* Philadelphia: Patterson and White, 1889.

GOODRICH, SAMUEL. *Poems.* Union Springs, N.Y.: Hoff, 1885.

GOODWIN, H. *After Many Days.* Marblehead, Mass.: Lindsey, 1893.

GOODWIN, M. M. *Autumn Leaves.* St. Louis: Christian Publishing, 1880.

GORDON, HANFORD L. *Feast of the Virgins and Other Poems.* Chicago: Laird and Lee, 1891.

GORDON, W. B. *Book of Verses.* West Point, N.Y.: Publ. by the author, 1887.

GORDON, W. S. *Recollections of the Old Quarter.* Lynchburg, Va.: Moose, 1902.

GORHAM, WALLACE A. *Bosky Dells and Sylvan Roads.* Sioux Falls, S.D.: N. publ., 1900.

GORTON, M. J. *Drama of the Cycle and Other Poems.* Boston: Cupples, 1891.

GOSS, CALVIN. *Vision of Tasseo.* Oskaloosa, Ia.: Central, 1878.

GOSSE, JOHN. *Royal Pastoral and Other Poems.* New York: Young, 1883.

GOULD, ABBIE W. *Blossoms from a New Field.* Moline, Ill.: Publ. by the author, 1900.

——. *Flowers of Thought.* Moline, Ill.: Publ. by the author, 1896.

GOULD, ALTA I. *Veteran's Bride and Other Poems.* Grand Rapids, Mich.: Farrell, 1897 [4th edition].

GOULD, GEORGE M. *An Autumn Singer.* Philadelphia: Lippincott, 1897.

GOULD, MARK, *Poems for the Times on Prevalent Custom and Essential Reforms Relating Chiefly to Temperance and the Sabbath.* Worcester, Mass.: Florence, 1891.

GOULDING, LAWRENCE G. *Arthur and the Ghost, with a Synopsis of the Great Battle of November, 7 1882.* New York: Goulding, 1883.

GOURAUD, G. F. *Ballads of Coster-land.* New York: Herald Square, 1897.

GOWING, CLARA. *My Chest.* Reading, Mass.: Twombly, 1899.

Grand Celebration of the Opening of the New Bridge, Penna. Ave. S.E., Washington, D.C. Washington, D.C.: Gibson, 1890.

GRANNISS, ANNA J. *Boy with the Hoe.* Hartford, Conn.: Gaines, 1904.

——. *Sandwort.* Keene, N.H.: Darling, 1897.

——. *Skipped Stiches.* Keene, N.H.: Darling, 1896.

GRANT, GENA F. *Forget-me-nots.* Rockland, Me.: Courier-Gazette, 1899.

GRANT, PETER. *By Heath and Prairie.* Chicago: Magnus Flaws, n.d.

GRANT, PETER S. *Ad Matrem and Other Poems.* New York: Ingalls Kimball, 1905.

GRANT, ROBERT. *Lambs.* Boston: Osgood, 1883.

—. *Little Gods-on-wheels: or, Society in Our Modern Athens.* Cambridge, Mass.: Sever, 1879 [2nd edition].

—. *Yankee Doodle. A Poem.* Boston: Cupples, Upham, 1883.

GRAY, ALBERT Z. *Jesus Only.* New York: Randolph, 1882.

GRAY, EDWARD M. *Alamo and Other Verses.* Florence, N.M.: Publ. by the author; London: Denny, 1898.

—. *Nation's Prayer.* Florence, N.M.: Alamo Publishing; London: Denny, 1898.

GREENE, WILLIAM B. *Cloudrifts at Twilight.* New York: Putnam, 1888.

GREGG, LUCY B. *Poems in Three Departments.* Indianapolis: Patton, 1886.

GREGG, WARREN B. *Poems of the Middle West.* Cedar Rapids, Ia.: Metcalf, 1899.

GREGORY, JOHN G. *Beauty of Thebes and Other Verses.* Milwaukee: Publ. by the author, 1892.

GREGORY, KATE. *Dreamland Hours.* Lafayette [Ind. ?]: Home Journal, 1899.

GRIBBLE, GEORGE D. *Arabesques.* N.p.: N. publ., n.d.

GRIFFIN, WALTER T. *Our Treasure Chest for Girls and Boys.* New York: Union Publishing, 1887.

GRIFFITH, WILLIAM. *Excursions.* Kansas City, Mo.: Hudson-Kimberly, 1900.

—. *Trialogues.* Kansas City, Mo.: Hudson-Kimberly, 1897.

GRIGGS, NATHAN K. *Hell's Canyon: A Poem of the Camps.* Chicago: Schulte, 1899.

—. *Lyrics of the Lariat.* New York, Chicago, and Toronto: Revell, 1893.

GRIMES, EDWARD B. *Poems.* Dayton, Ohio: United Brethren, 1883.

GRISSOM, ARTHUR. *Beaux and Belles.* New York: Putnam, 1896.

GUERRIER, GEORGE P. *"Pipes of Corn."* Boston: Clarke, 1878.

GUILD, CURTIS. *From Sunrise to Sunset.* Boston: Lee and Shepard, 1894.

GUINEY, LOUISE I. *Martyrs' Idyl and Shorter Poems.* Boston and New York: Houghton, Mifflin, 1899.

P.G.A.–Z

GUINEY, LOUISE I. *Roadside Harp.* Boston and New York: Houghton, Mifflin, 1893.

—. *Songs at the Start.* Boston: Cupples, Upham, 1884.

GUNNISON, CHARLES A. *In Macao.* San Francisco: Commercial, 1892.

—. *In the San Benito Hills.* San Francisco: Commercial, 1891.

GUNNISON, MARY S. *Verses and Rhymes.* Jackson [state ?]: N. publ., 1898.

GUSTAFSON, ZADEL B. *Meg: A Pastoral. And Other Poems.* Boston: Lee and Shepard; New York: Dillingham, 1879.

GUTHRIE, WILLIAM N. *Songs of American Destiny.* Cincinnati: Clarke, 1900.

Gynberg Ballads. N.p.: N. publ., n.d.

HAGER, LEVI L. *Forty Years with the Muse.* Dayton, Ohio: United Brethren, 1886.

HALE, ROBERT B. *Elsie and Other Poems.* Boston: Hale, 1893.

HALE, WILL T. *Autumn Lane and Other Poems.* Nashville, Tenn. and Dallas, Tex.: Publishing House of Methodist Episcopal Church, 1899.

HALL, MRS. FRANKLIN. *Yesterday and To-day.* Troy, N.Y.: Dewitt, 1898.

HALL, MARY L. *Live Coals.* Buffalo: N. publ., 1878.

HALL, THOMAS W. *When Love Laughs.* New York: Herrick, 1898.

HAMILTON, AGNES S. *Thoughts and Experience in Verse.* Wilmington, Del.: Lippincott, 1899.

HAMILTON, HENRY. *America and Other Poems.* New York: Putnam, 1885.

HAMMOND, LURANAH. *Voices from Nature.* Strong's Prairie, Wisc.: Publ. by the author, 1894.

HANCOCK, NANNIE P. *Book of Poems.* Roanoke, Va.: Stone, 1900.

HANNA, W. WALKER. *My Early Random Hits.* Philadelphia: Dukes, 1898.

HARDING, A. E. *Garland of Memories.* Pontiac, Ill.: Harding, 1899.

—. *Outside the Gates, or a Tale of a Departed Spirit.* Pontiac, Ill.: N. publ., n.d.

HARK, J. MAX. *Extempore on a Wagon; a Metrical Narrative of a Journey from Bethlehem, Pa., to the Indian Town of Goshen, Ohio, in the Autumn of 1803 by George Henry Loskiel* [translated from the German]. Lancaster, Pa.: Zahm, 1887.

HARLOW, WILLIAM B. *Songs of Syracuse and Other Poems.* Syracuse, N.Y.: Publ. by the author, 1890.

HARMAN, HENRY A. *Freedom's Footprints.* Springfield, Mass.: N. publ., 1899.

HARRIS, JOEL C. *Tar-Baby and Other Rhymes of Uncle Remus.* New York: Appleton, 1904.

HARRIS, SIMON B. *On the Death of President William McKinley.* Lowell, Mass.: N. publ., 1901.

—. *Uncle Sam's Latest Yankee Doodle.* Lowell, Mass.: N. publ., 1899.

HARTWELL, FRANK A. *Some Thoughts in Rhyme.* Louisville: N. publ., 1894.

HARTZELL, JONAS H. *Wanderings on Parnassus.* New York: Whittaker, 1884.

HARVEY, MARGARET B. *Lower Merion Lilies and Other Poems.* Philadelphia: Lippincott, 1887.

HASKELL, GEORGE. *Narrative.* Ipswich, Mass.: Chronicle, 1896.

HASKELL, THOMAS N. *Domestic Poems.* N.p.: Publ. by the author, 1889.

HAWKES, CLARENCE. *Songs for Columbia's Heroes. War Poems for 1898.* Springfield, Mass.: New England, 1898.

HAY, HELEN. *Some Verses.* Chicago and New York: Stone, 1898.

HAY, HENRY H. *Created Gold and Other Poems.* Philadelphia: Newton, 1893.

HAYDEN, HENRY C. *Poems.* Boston: Rand Avery, 1888 [2nd edition].

HAYES, IRVING B. *Work of the Mystic Seven.* Florence, Mass.: Private edition, 1897.

HAYNE, WILLIAM H. *Sylvan Lyrics and Other Verses.* New York: Stokes, 1893.

HAYWARD, EDWARD F. *Patrice: Her Love and Work.* Boston: Cupples, Upham, 1883.

—. *Willoughby.* Boston: Clarke, 1879.

HAYWOOD, JOHN C. *Peter Duikel Spiel and Other Moods More Serious.* Philadelphia: Drexel Biddle, n.d.

HEADLAND, I. T. *Midnight Items, and Spare-Moment Scraps.* Cincinnati: Central, 1886.

HEATH, GEORGIANA L. *Assurance and Other Poems.* Boston: Lothrop, 1886.

HEATON, AUGUSTUS G. *Fancies and Thoughts in Verse.* Boston: Poet Lore, 1904.

HEATON, JOHN L. *Quilting Bee and Other Rhymes.* New York: Stokes, 1896.

HELMER, MYRA B. *Child's Thoughts in Rhyme.* Chicago: Chicago Legal News, 1903.

HELMUTH, WILLIAM T. *"Scratches" of a Surgeon.* Chicago: Chatterton, 1879.

—. *With the "Pousse Cafe," Being a Collection of Post Prandial Verses.* Philadelphia: Boericke and Tafel, 1892.

—. *Yellowstone Park and How It Was Named.* Chicago: N. publ., 1892.

HEMPSTEAD, FAY. *Poems.* Little Rock, Ark.: Allsopp and Paul, 1898.

HEMSTEAD, JUNIUS L. *Musings of Morn.* New York: Neely, 1898.

HENDERSON, ANNA R. *Life and Song.* Buffalo: Moulton, 1900.

HENDERSON, DANIEL M. *Bit Bookie of Verse.* Baltimore: University Book Store, 1905.

—. *Poems, Scottish and American.* Baltimore: Cushings and Bailey, 1888.

HENDERSON, J. R. *Thoughts at Random.* Henderson, Wisc.: Publ. by the author, 1896.

HENDRIX, LILY E. *Fragments.* Mexico, Mo.: Baptist Publishing, 1894.

HENSHAW, SARAH E. *Rhymes and Jingles.* Oakland, Cal.: Printed for the family, 1892.

HERFORD, OLIVER. *Child's Primer of Natural History.* New York: Scribner, 1901.

—. *Fairy Godmother-in-law.* New York: Scribner, 1905.

—. *Overheard in a Garden.* New York: Scribner, 1900.

HERRALD, MICHAEL. *Herrald's Book of War Songs.* Redding, Ia.: Publ. by the author, 1899.

HERSHEY, EUSEBIUS. *Living Poem.* Philadelphia: Craig, Finley, 1882.

HEWETSON, GEORGE B. *Strike and Other Poems.* New York: Putnam, 1896.

HEYLMUN, J. WHEELER. *Musings on a Locomotive.* Williamsport, Pa.: Publ. by the author, 1887.

HIBBARD, GRACE. *More California Violets.* N.p.: N. publ., n.d.

—. *Wild Roses of California.* San Francisco: Robertson, 1902.

HIGGINS, J. E. *Looking Backward in Rhyme and Other Poems.* San Francisco: Carrier Dove, 1892.

HIGGINSON, ELLA. *Snow Pearls.* N.p.: Lowman and Hanford, 1897.

—. *Voice of April-land and Other Poems.* New York: Macmillan, 1903.

—. *When the Birds Go North Again.* New York: Macmillan, 1898.

HIGGINSON, THOMAS W. and HIGGINSON, MAY T. *Such as They Are. Poems.* Boston: Roberts, 1893.

HIGGS, AUSTIN H. *Poem: Or, the Prodigal Son.* Columbia, Mo.: Statesman Book and Job, 1891.

HILDRETH, FRED L. *Echoes from My Song Realm.* Worcester, Mass.: Wesby, 1899.

HILL, BENJAMIN D. *Passion Flowers.* New York: Benzinger, 1898.

HILL, ROBERT S. *History and Origin of the "Dude."* New York: Publ. by the author, n.d.

HILLHOUSE, MARGARET P. *White Rose Knight and Other Poems.* New York: Private edition, 1894.

HILLS, EMILY M. *Pictured Rocks of Lake Superior and Other Poems.* Rome, Italy: Fabriani, 1904.

HILLS, LUCIUS P. *Echoes.* Atlanta: Publ. by the author, 1892.

HINCKLE, HAZEL. *Life's Blue and Gray.* Chicago: Nistle, 1900.

HINES, GEORGE A. *Superscription and Other Verse.* N.p.: N. publ., n.d.

Hints from the Works and Days. New York and Washington, D.C.: Brentano, 1883.

HIRT, JOHN H. *Second Booklet of Social Poems.* Great Falls, Mont.: Publ. by the author, 1902.

——. *Social Poems.* Great Falls, Mont.: Publ. by the author, 1900.

Historical Society of Newburgh Bay and the Highlands. Centennial Number. Newburgh, N.Y.: Newburgh Journal, 1900.

History of Coney Island in Rhyme. New York: Morrison, Richardson, 1878.

History of the Joint Anniversary Celebration at Monterey, Cal. San Francisco: Fraternal Publishing, 1886.

HITT, ADRAIN. *Grant Poem, Containing Grant's Public Career and Private Life from the Cradle to the Grave.* New York: Nassau, 1886.

HOBART, GEORGE V. *Li'l Verses for Li'l Fellers.* New York: Russell, 1903.

——. *Many Moods and Many Meters.* Baltimore: Guggenheimer, Weil, 1899.

HOBBS, MARY E. *Poems.* Chicago: American Publishers, 1891.

HOCKENBERGER, MARGARET. *Ma and Pa and Me.* N.p.: N. publ., n.d.

HODGE, F. O. *Stray Shots.* Worcester, Mass.: Stobbs, 1894.

HODGMAN, FRANK. *Wandering Singer and His Songs.* Climax, Mich.: Publ. by the author, 1898.

HOFFMAN, ELWYN I. *Poems.* Stockton, Cal.: Hummel, 1895.

HOFFMAN, MINTA B. *Memorial Songs.* St. Louis: Western, 1877.

HOLBROOK, JENNIE E. *Ruth Haight and Other Poems.* Milwaukee: N. publ., 1878.

HOLCOMB, WILLIAM H. *Old Mission Rhymes.* San Diego: Frye, Garrett and Smith, 1900.

HOLDEN, E. H. *Original Poems.* New York: Bedell, 1886.

HOLDEN, EDWARD S. *Hand-book of the Lick Observatory of the University of California.* San Francisco: Bancroft, 1888.

HOLDEN, WARREN. *Many Moods.* Philadelphia: Lippincott, 1895.

——. *Ode. Human Brotherhood.* Philadelphia: Lippincott, 1895.

——. *Spiritual Evolution.* Philadelphia: Lippincott, 1889.

HOLFORD, CASTELL N. *Cofachiqui.* Bloomington, Wisc.: Holford, 1884.

Holiday Souvenir. Detroit: Detroit Journal, 1890.

HOLLENBECK, JEREMIAH. *Prohibition. A Temperance Poem.* Mercer, Pa.: N. publ., 1888.

HOLLISTER, J. FLETCHER. *Sunflower.* Plano, Ill.: Herald Steam Book, 1881.

HOLLOWAY, ELVIRA H. *Gleanings from the Golden State.* San Francisco: Publ. by the author, 1893.

HOLMES, CHARLES E. *Happy Days.* Aberdeen, S.D.: New Printing, n.d.

HOOKER, JOHN. *Some Reminiscences of a Long Life.* Hartford, Conn.: Belknap and Warfield, 1899.

HOPKINS, RUFUS C. *Roses and Thistles.* San Francisco: Doxey, 1894.

HOPKINSON, C. BENJAMIN. *Wayside Flowers.* Chicago: Western Methodist Book, 1900.

HORTON, GEORGE. *Songs of the Lowly and Other Poems.* Chicago: Schulte, 1892.

——. *War and Mammon.* Wausau, Wisc.: Philosopher, 1900.

HOSSLER, J. S. *Poetic Musings.* Rochester, Mich.: N. publ., 1901.

HOUGHTON, HORACE H. *Poems.* Galena [state?]: Publ. by the author, 1878.

HOVEY, RICHARD. *Along the Trail.* Boston: Small, Maynard, 1898.

——. *Poems.* Washington, D.C.: Smith, 1880.

HOWARD, ALFRED B. *Rhymes and Sketches.* New York: Private edition, 1891.

HOWARD, CLIFFORD. *Thoughts in Verse.* Buffalo: Peter Paul, 1895.

HOWARD, HATTIE. *Later Poems.* Hartford, Conn.: N. publ., 1887.

HOWARD, HATTIE. *Poems.* Hartford, Conn.: N. publ., 1886.

—. *Poems.* Vol. III. Hartford, Conn.: Hartford Press, 1901.

—. *Poems.* Vol. IV. Hartford, Conn.: Hartford Press, 1904.

HOWARD, WILLIAM M. *Poems.* New York: Knickerbocker, 1900.

HOWE, CAROLINE D. *Ashes for Flame and Other Poems.* Portland, Me.: Loring, Short and Harmon, 1885.

HOWE, LUCRETIA T. *Home Songs and Chronicles of the Ellis.* Rumford Falls, Me.: Rumford Falls Publishing, 1899.

HOWELL, CHARLES B. *Next Door and Other Poems.* Detroit: Publ. by the author, 1888.

HOWELL, JOHN E. *Columbus.* New York: Howell, 1893.

HOYT, THOMAS R. *Cheerful Muse, or, Hoyt's Happy Thoughts.* Goffstown N.H.: Publ. by the author, 1891.

—. *Hoyt's Harp.* Goffstown, N.H.: Publ. by the author, 1886.

HUBBELL, MARK S. *Various Verses.* Buffalo: N. publ., n.d.

HUBBELL, WALTER. *Midnight Madness.* Chicago: Bingham, 1892.

HUCKEL, OLIVER. *Larger Life: A Book of the Heart.* Baltimore: Bridges, 1900.

HUFF, JACOB K. [published under the pseudonym, Faraway Moses]. *Songs of the Desert.* Williamsport, Pa.: N. publ., 1895.

HUIGINN, E. J. *Duxbury Beach and Other Poems.* Boston: Damrell and Upham, 1894.

HULL, MATTIE E. *Spirit Echoes.* Buffalo: Hull; New York: Sunflower, 1901.

HULME, JAMES N. *Alliteration.* Chicago: Chicago Legal News, 1882.

HUMPHREY, NELSON G. *Random Shots.* Bloomington, Ill.: Pantagraph, 1884.

HUNT, EMMA E. *"The Writing on the Wall."* San Jose, Cal.: N. publ., 1900.

HUNTER, MAGGIE. *Pearls of a Woman's Heart.* Peoria, Ill., Franks, 1886.

HUNTINGTON, HELEN. *Folk Songs from the Spanish.* New York: Putnam, 1900.

—. *Solitary Path.* New York: Doubleday, Page, 1902.

HUNTINGTON, IRWIN. *Wife of the Sun.* Mobile: Gossip Printing, 1892.

HURD, HELEN M. *Poetical Works.* Boston: Russell, 1887.

HUSSEY, TACITUS. *River Bend and Other Poems.* Des Moines: Carter and Hussey, 1896.

HYLTON, JOHN D. *Above the Grave of John Odenswurge.* New York: Challen, 1884.

—. *Heir of Lyolynn.* Palmyra, N.J.: Publ. by the author, 1883.

—. *Knights of the Plow.* Palmyra, N.J.: Hylton Grange, 1891.

—. *Motion, Space and Time. An Epic of the Universe.* Palmyra, N.J.: Hylton Grange, 1892.

I'ANSON, MILES. *Vision of Misery Hill. A Legend of the Sierra Nevada and Miscellaneous Verse.* New York: Putnam, 1891.

ILIOWIZI, HENRY. *Quest of Columbus. A Memorial Poem in Twelve Books.* Chicago: Smith, 1892.

Imitators. A Poem of Boston Life. Boston: Cupples, Upham, 1886.

Indictment. Philadelphia: Milliken, n.d.

INGERSOLL, SAMUEL. *"Intolerant Orthodoxy's Blasphemous Creeds." And Other Poems.* Chicago: Tidd, 1892.

JACKSON, HALLIDAY. *Poems.* Philadelphia: Friends' Book Association, 1888.

JACKSON, LYDIA M. *Wild Rose Petals.* Topeka: Crane, 1889.

JACOBY, RUSSELL P. *Poet and His Songs.* Baltimore: Bridges, 1900.

JAMES, BUSHROD W. *Alaskana or Alaska in Descriptive and Legendary Poems.* Philadelphia: Porter and Coates, 1893.

—. *Echoes of Battle.* Philadelphia: Coates, 1895.

JAMES, CHARLES. *Poems.* New York: N. publ., 1903.

JAMES, THOMAS D. *My Neighbor: A Story in Verse with Other Poems.* New York: Carter, 1880.

James Abram Garfield. Memorial Observances. Worcester, Mass.: City Council, 1881.

JEFFERSON, SAMUEL. *Columbus, an Epic Poem.* Chicago: Griggs, 1892.

JEFFREY, ROSA V. *Crimson Hand and Other Poems.* Philadelphia: Lippincott, 1881.

JENKINSON-FRAZEE, ISAAC. *Nahda.* Oceanside, Cal.: Blade, 1898.

JEPSON, FRANKLIN P. *Pot-pourri.* Wheeling: Stanton, 1896.

JEWETT, CHARLES. *Harvest of Rum.* Norwich, Conn.: Publ. by the author, 1877.

JOHNES, EDWARD R. *Briefs by a Barrister.* New York: Putnam, 1879.

JOHNSON, CHARLES F. *What Can I Do for Brady? And Other Verse.* New York: Whittaker, 1897.

JOHNSON, DAVID N. *New Age.* Lynn [Mass.?]: Parker, 1896.

JOHNSON, H. F. *Poems of Idaho.* Weiser, Ida.: Signal Job Printing, 1895.

JOHNSON, H. U. *Seventeen-Seventy-Six and Other Poems.* Cleveland: Brooks, Schinkel, 1877.

—. *Western Reserve Centennial Souvenir.* Cleveland: Taylor-Austin, 1896.

JOHNSON, PHILANDER C. *Now-a-day Poems.* Washington, D.C.: Neale, 1900.

—. *Songs of the G.O.P.* Washington, D.C.: Neale, 1900.

JOHNSON, ROBERT U. *Songs of Liberty and Other Poems.* New York: Century, 1897.

—. *Winter Hours and Other Poems.* New York: Century, 1892.

JOHNSON, SAMUEL. *Belshazzar's Doom.* St. Paul: N. publ., 1887.

JOHNSTON, J. P. *Galileo and Other Poems.* Pittsburgh: Mills, 1878.

JOHNSTON, W. H. *Pagan's Poems.* Peoria, Ill.: Franks, 1884.

JOHNSTON, WILLIAM P. *Seekers After God.* Louisville: Morton, 1898.

JOHNSTONE, E. F. *Original Poems.* Ann Arbor, Mich.: Courier, 1893.

JOHNSTONE, JULIAN E. *Songs of Sun and Shadow.* Boston: Clarke, 1900.

JONES, AMANDA T. *Prairie Idyl and Other Poems.* Chicago: Jansen, McClurg, 1882.

JONES, DAVID M. *Lethe and Other Poems.* Philadelphia: Lippincott, 1882.

—. *Songs for the Hour.* Philadelphia: Lippincott, 1893.

JONES, E. G. *Poems of the Day.* N.p.: N. publ., 1896.

JONES, JOHN A. *Retrospect.* Philadelphia: Lippincott, 1884.

JONES, JULIA C. *Story of the Ship and Mechanic Art.* San Francisco: Bancroft, 1890.

JONES, STACY. *Mnemonic Similiad.* Philadelphia: Boericke and Tafel, 1904.

JOSAPHARE, LIONEL. *Humpback, the Cripple and the One-eyed Man.* San Francisco: Robertson, 1903.

Journey to Alaska. N.p.: N. publ., n.d.

JOYCE, JOHN A. *Complete Poems.* Washington, D.C.: Neale, 1900.

—. *Peculiar Poems.* New York: Knox, 1885.

KAHN, RUTH W. *First Quarter.* Cincinnati: Editor, 1898.

KAPLAN, A. O. *Jonathan's Dream.* Cincinnati: Art Novelty, 1895.

KARN, ESTHER N. *"Snowflakes."* Philadelphia: Lasher, 1900.

—. *Violets.* Chicago: Winona, 1904.

KAUTZ, AUGUSTA. *Ink in Bloom.* San Diego, Cal.: Baker, 1902.

—. *Straggling Thoughts among Homely Duties.* San Francisco: Crocker, 1898.

KAUTZ, AUGUSTA. *World My Own*. San Francisco: Crocker, 1896.

KAYE, JOHN B. *Songs of Lake Geneva*. New York: Putnam, 1882.

KEELER, CHARLES A. *Idyls of El Dorado*. San Francisco: Robertson, 1900.

—. *Light through the Storm*. San Francisco: Doxey, 1894.

—. *Promise of the Ages*. N.p.: N. publ., 1896.

—. *Siege of the Golden City*. Altruria, Cal.: Altrurian, 1896.

KELLEY, J. E. *Age of Gold*. New York: Pryse, 1899.

KELLY, M. A. *Volume of Poems*. Boston: Cupples, 1892.

KELSO, HUGH. *Poems*. Kinderhook, N.Y.: Reeve, 1886.

KELSO, JOSIE A. *Day Dreams*. Cincinnati: Clarke, 1878.

KEMP, ELLWOOD L. *Idyl of the War, the German Exiles and Other Poems*. Philadelphia: Potter, 1883.

KENNEDY, JAMES. *Poems*. New York: Robertson, 1883 [2nd edition].

KENNEY, EUDORUS C. *Some More Thusettes*. Cortland, N.Y.: Democrat Printery, 1905.

—. *Thusettes*. Cortland, N.Y.: Cortland Democrat, 1899.

KENT, CONSTANCE. *Chord and Cadence*. N.p.: Chapin, 1899.

KENT, LUCIAN H. *Sunshine and Storm*. Sandusky, Ohio: Mack, 1883.

KENYON, JAMES B. *At the Gate of Dreams*. Buffalo: Moulton, 1892.

—. *An Oaten Pipe*. New York: Tait, 1895.

—. *Poems*. New York: Eaton and Mains, 1901.

KERCHEVAL, ALBERT F. *Dolores and Other Poems*. San Francisco: Bancroft, 1883.

KERNESTAFFE, CLELAND. *Pebbles and Pearls*. New York: Neely, 1901.

KERR, JOE. *Cheery Book*. New York: Dillingham, 1898.

—. *Jests, Jingles and Jottings*. New York: Allen, 1893.

KIMBALL, HANNA P. *Cup of Life and Other Verses*. Boston: Cupples, 1892.

—. *Victory and Other Verses*. Boston: Copeland and Day, 1897.

KING, BEN F. *Ben King's Verse*. Boston and Chicago: Forbes, 1903.

KING, LINCOLN. *Poems*. Marshalltown, Ia.: Miller, 1886.

KING, PATRICK M. *Ode*. San Francisco: N. publ., 1892.

—. *Verses*. San Francisco: N. publ., 1890.

KINLEY, ISAAC. *Labor Rhymes*. Los Angeles: N. publ., 1886.

KINNEAR, MARY. *Crooked Sticks*. Cleveland: Hubbell, 1897.

KINTZ, HENRY J. *Inauguration of Grover Cleveland*. Alexandria, Va.: N. publ., 1885.

KIRK, s. c. *Musings on the Way.* Philadelphia: Sickler, 1900.

KIRSCHBAUM, E. T. *Idyls Crude.* Worcester, Ohio: Wood, 1894.

—. *Prose and Poetry.* New York: Alden, 1889.

—. *Times.* N.p.: N. publ., 1899.

KISER, SAMUEL E. *Ballads of the Busy Days.* Boston and Chicago: Forbes, 1903.

—. *"Budd Wilkins at the Show," and Other Verses.* Cleveland: Helman-Taylor, 1898.

KNAPP, HARRIETTE H. *Poems.* N.p.: N. publ., n.d.

KNOWLES, FREDERIC L. *Love Triumphant.* Boston: Estes, 1904.

—. *On Life's Stairway.* Boston: Page, 1901.

KNOWLES, WILLIAM. *Poems.* Indianapolis: Carlon and Hollenbeck, 1881.

KNOWLTON, J. A. *Span of Sight.* Franklin, Ind.: Martin and Martin, 1898.

KOOPMAN, HARRY L. *At the Gates of the Century.* Boston: Everett, 1905.

—. *Morrow Songs 1880–1898.* Boston: Everett, 1898.

KOST, HENRY G. *Poems.* N.p.: N. publ., 1885.

KYLE, CHARLES W. *Forest Leaves and Other Poems.* San Francisco: Stanley, 1894.

LACY, FRANCIS D. *Nature's Harmony.* New York: Truth Seeker, 1883.

LAIDLAW, ALEXANDER H. *Soldier Songs and Love Songs.* New York: Jenkins, 1898.

LAMARSH, NORMAN. *Lux Christi: A Sacred Drama.* Bangor, Me.: Daily News, 1895.

LAMBERT, MARY. *La Rabida: A California Columbian Souvenir Poem.* San Francisco: Bancroft, 1893.

—. *Rhyming Oak Leaves.* San Francisco: Bancroft, 1892.

LAMBIE, JOHN. *Century and Other Poems.* Oakland, Cal.: N. publ., n.d.

LAMBIE, WILLIAM. *Life on the Farm.* Ypsilanti, Mich.: N. publ., 1883.

LAMPTON, WILLIAM J. *Yawps and Other Things.* Philadelphia: Altemus, 1900.

LANTZ, DANIEL O. *Peculiar Poems.* Chicago: Lantz, 1883.

LAROCHE, J. H. *From the Way-side and Other Poems.* Binghamton, N.Y.: N. publ., 1896.

Last Strike for Liberty. A Semi-political Satire on the Revolutionary Demands of the "Liberal" Foreign Element. Cincinnati: Publ. by the author, 1886.

LATROBE, JOHN H. *Ode on the Celebration of the Sesqui-Centennial*

Anniversary of the Settlement of Baltimore. Baltimore: Mayland Historical Society, 1880.

Laurel House Pot-pourri. Lakewood, N.J.: Printed and sold in behalf of the Children's Fresh Air Fund, 1885.

LAVELY, HENRY A. *Heart's Choice and Other Poems.* Cambridge, Mass.: Riverside, 1886.

LAWRENCE, IDA E. *Day Dreams.* Cincinnati: Clarke, 1900.

LEANDER, J. *Mental Mirror; or, Rumseller's Dream. A Poem.* Syracuse: Truair, Smith and Bruce, 1877.

LEARY, DANIEL F. *Toil.* San Francisco: Whitaker and Ray, 1900.

LEAVITT, L. M. *Echoes.* Lewiston, Me.: Gordon and Payne, 1885.

LEE, FRANKLYN W. *Dreamy Hours.* St. Paul: Sunshine, 1890.

—. *Sphinx of Gold.* Rush City, Minn.: Post, 1897.

LEE, WILLIAM W. *Metrical Homily.* Meriden, Conn.: Republican Book, 1893.

LEECH, S. V. *Three Inebriates. A Poem.* New York: Phillips and Hunt, 1886.

LE GALLIENNE, RICHARD. *Cry of the Little Peoples.* East Aurora, N.Y.: Roycroft, n.d.

—. *English Poems.* London: Mathew; New York: Cassell, 1892 [2nd edition].

—. *Robert Louis Stevenson—An Elegy, and Other Poems.* Boston: Copeland and Day, 1895.

LEGG, ROBERT. *Future of Seattle as a Commercial City.* Issaquah, Wash.: N. publ., 1893.

LEGGETT, BENJAMIN F. *Sheaf of Song.* New York: Alden, 1887.

LEIFSNAM, FRANCIS M. *Gathered Waifs.* New York: N. publ., 1898.

LEIGHTON, HARRIET W. *Prairie Songs.* Lincoln, Nebr.: N. publ., 1898.

LEMON, DON M. *Ione and Other Poems.* New York: Broadway, 1905.

—. *Plays and Poems.* San Francisco: Roesch, 1899.

LENT, EMMA A. *Chime of Bells.* Albany: Weed, Parson, 1883.

LEONARD, ELIZABETH C. *Poems.* Boston: Ellis, 1889.

LEONARD, MARY H. *My Lady of the Search-light.* New York: Grafton, 1905.

LESSER, MAXIMUS A. *Echoes of Halcyon Days.* Hartford, Conn.: Spencer, 1897.

LEWIS, GEORGE E. *Heart Echoes.* Grand Rapids, Mich.: Tradesman, 1899.

LEWIS, JUAN. *Poems.* Washington, D.C.: N. publ., 1892.

LEWIS, R. J. *Four Centuries and Other Poems.* Kansas City, Mo.: Wright, 1898.

LINCOLN, RIXFORD J. *Historical New Orleans.* N.p.: N. publ., n.d.

—. *Poems and Short Stories.* New Orleans: Williams, 1900.

LINDNER, GEORGE J. *Stray Leaves.* Nashville, Tenn.: Herald, 1891.

LINN, EDITH W. *Poems.* Buffalo: Moulton, 1892.

LINTHICUM, RICHARD. *One-Lunged Man of Buckskin Joe.* Pittsburgh: Eichbaum, 1895.

LIPPINCOTT, MARTHA S. *Visions of Life.* New York: Abbey, 1901.

LITCHFIELD, H. ELIZABETH. *Life's Web and Other Poems.* Bath, Me.: N. publ., 1892.

LITTELL, MARY V. *Tramplets.* New York: Ogilvie, 1899.

LITTLE, DAVID F. *Wanderer and Other Poems.* Los Angeles: Mirr, 1880.

LLOYD, JOHN W. *Psalms of the Race Roots and Songs by the Side of the Great River. A Scripture of the Larger Love.* N.p.: N. publ., n.d.

—. *Red Heart in a White World.* Westfield, N.J.: Publ. by the author, 1898 [2nd edition].

—. *Songs of the Desert.* Westfield, N.J.: Lloyd Group, 1905.

LOCHMAN, CHARLES L. *Address for the Fiftieth Anniversary of an Odd Fellows' Lodge, and Other Poems.* Bethlehem, Pa.: Publ. by the author, 1897.

LOCKHALT, ARTHUR J. *Beside the Narraguagus and Other Poems.* Buffalo: Peter Paul, 1895.

LOCKINGTON, W. N. *Day-dreams.* San Francisco: Publ. by the author, 1880.

LOCKWOOD, VAN BUREN. *Sweet-briar Petals.* Stamford, Conn.: N. publ., n.d.

LODGE, GEORGE C. *Great Adventure.* Boston and New York: Houghton, Mifflin, 1905.

—. *Poems (1899–1902).* New York: Cameron, Blake, 1902.

—. *Song of the Wave and Other Poems.* New York: Scribner, 1898.

LOGAN, F. A. *Poems.* Sacramento: Crocker, 1883.

LOGUE, EMILY R. *At the Foot of the Mountain.* Philadelphia: Kilner, 1898.

LOOMIS, CLARA J. *Verse and Prose.* Springfield, Mass.: Private edition, 1887.

LOOMIS, EBEN J. *Sunset Idyl and Other Poems.* Cambridge, Mass.: Riverside, 1903.

LOOMIS, SUBMIT C. *Poetry and Prose.* New York: Burnham, 1893.

LORD, WILLIAM S. *Blue and Gold.* Chicago: Dial, 1895.

LORING, MATTIE B. *Stranger.* New York: Abbey, 1900.

LORRIMER, LAURA. *Voice from the South.* Nashville, Tenn.: Publ. by the author, 1883.

LOVEMAN, ROBERT. *Book of Verse.* Philadelphia: Lippincott, 1900.

—. *Poems.* Tuscaloosa, Ala.: Burton, 1893.

—. *Poems.* Philadelphia: Lippincott, 1897.

—. *Songs from a Georgia Garden and Echoes from the Gates of Silence.* Philadelphia: Lippincott, 1904.

LOY, DANIEL O. *Poems of the Golden State and Midwinter Exposition.* Chicago: Publ. by the author, 1894.

—. *Poems of the White City.* Chicago: Publ. by the author, 1893.

LOZIER, JOHN H. *Your Mother's Apron Strings.* Cincinnati: Jennings and Pye; New York: Eaton and Mains, 1898.

LUCE, S. S. *Echoes of the Past.* Galesville, Wisc.: Luce, 1881.

LUCE, S. S. and H. G. *Poems.* Trempealeau, Wisc.: Leith, 1876.

LUDERS, CATHARINE. *Voices in the Wilderness.* Philadelphia: N. publ., 1884.

LUDLOW, LORIN. *Original Rum Convention.* Boston.: N. publ., 1900.

LUNT, H. L. *Catalina the Bride of the Pacific.* Los Angeles: N. publ., n.d.

LUTHER, JOHN H. *Old Baylor and Other Poems.* Temple, Tex.: N. publ., 1900.

LUTZ, J. HENRY. *Select Poems.* Baltimore: Murphy, 1896.

LYNCH, MICHAEL. *In the Promised Land and Other Poems.* Boston: O'Farrell, 1897.

MCABOY, MARY R. *Roseheath Poems.* Cincinnati: Clarke, 1884.

MCCABE, CHARLES W. *Poems of Home and Fireside.* San Francisco: Commercial, 1896.

MCCANN, JOHN E. *Songs from an Attic.* New York: Brentano, 1890.

MCCANN, JOHN E. and JARROLD, ERNEST. *Odds and Ends.* New York: Alliance, 1891.

MCCARDELL, ROY L. *Olde Love and Lavender, and Other Verses.* New York: Wieners, 1900.

MCCARTHY, DENIS A. *Round of Rimes.* Boston: Review, 1900.

M'CLELLAN, GEORGE M. *Poems.* Nashville, Tenn.: Publ. by the author, 1895.

MCCLURE, WILLIAM J. *Poems Religious and Miscellaneous.* New York: Pratt, 1888.

MCCLURG, VIRGINIA D. *Colorado Wreath.* Colorado Springs: N. publ., 1899.

MCCORD, JAMES P. *Poems.* Waverly, Ia.: Publ. by the author, 1889.

MCCOURT, DAVID W. *Treasures of Weinsberg.* Buffalo: Peter Paul, 1895.

MCOY, KITTIE C. *Buds and Blossoms.* Pontiac, Mich.: Gazette, 1886.

MCCRAY, HENRY H. *Poetic Gems.* Gainesville, Fla.: N. publ., 1902 [?].

MCCREADY, WILLIAM. *Poems.* N.p.: N. publ., n.d.

MCCREERY, JOHN L. *Songs of Toil and Triumph.* New York: Putnam, 1883.

MCCUE, REBECCA L. *Flowers of Spring.* Minneapolis: Irish Standard, 1888.

MACCULLOCH, HUNTER. *From Dawn to Dusk.* Philadelphia: Lippincott, 1887.

MCDONALD, FRANK J. *Green Mountain Chimes.* Boston: Rich, 1899.

MCDOWELL, KATE G. *Unfolding Leaves of Tender Thought.* Louisville: Morton, 1898.

MCELROY, CROCKET. *Poems.* Chicago: Scroll, 1900.

MCFADEN, MILDRED S. *Blossoms by the Wayside.* Kansas City, Mo.: Hudson-Kimberly, 1904.

MCFARLAND, JAMES. *Miscellaneous Poems.* New York: Parker, 1897.

MCGAFFEY, ERNEST. *California Idyl.* San Francisco: Channing, 1899.

—. *Cosmos.* Wausau, Wisc.: Philosopher, 1903.

—. *Poems.* New York: Dodd, Mead, 1895.

MCGIRT, JAMES E. *Some Simple Songs.* Philadelphia: Lasher, 1901.

MCGLUMPHY, W. H. *Village Verse.* Cincinnati: Editor, 1900.

MCINTOSH, JOHN. *Songs of Liberty and Other Poems.* Chicago: Woodward and O'Leary, 1882.

MCINTYRE, GEORGE P. *Light of Persia or the Death of Mammon.* Chicago: Wage Workers, 1890.

—. *Sun-sealed.* Chicago: Astronomic, 1893.

MCKENNA, MAURICE. *Poems, Rhymes, and Verses.* Fond Du Lac, Wisc.: Palmer, 1890.

MCKINNIE, P. L. *From Tide to Timber-line.* Chicago: Smith, 1895 [2nd edition].

MCKINSTRY, L. C. *Garfield. A Poem.* Boston: publ. by the author, 1882.

MCLEOD, E. M. *Love's Offering*. Lainsburg, Mich.: n. publ., 1900.

MCPHERSON, LYDIA S. *Reullura*. Buffalo: Moultin, 1892.

MCVICKAR, HARRY W. *Evolution of a Woman*. New York: Harper, 1896.

MACE, FRANCES L. *Under Pine and Palm*. Boston: Ticknor, 1888.

MACKEY, FRANKLIN H. *Laus Infantium*. Washington, D.C.: Private edition, 1897.

MACKINTOSH, CHARLES A. *Memorial*. Cambridge, Mass.: University, 1890.

MACKINTOSH, N. *Course of Sprouts*. New York: Francis and Newton, 1899.

—. *Just for Greens*. New York: Francis and Newton, 1898.

MACKLEY, JOHN H. *Idle Rhymings*. Jackson, Ohio: N. publ., 1885.

MACON, JOHN A. *Uncle Gabe Tucker*. Philadelphia: Lippincott, 1883.

MAGEE, ANNIE H. *In the Fields*. Port Austin, Mich.: Publ. by the author, 1893.

MAGEE, LOUIS J. *Songs after Work*. New York: Randolph, 1896.

MAGUIRE, DON. *Poems*. New York: Trow, 1879.

MAJOR, GEORGE M. *Lays of Chinatown and Other Verses*. New York: Kimball, 1899.

—. *Peril of the Republic and Other Poems*. New York: Putnam, 1884.

MAK, KLARENC W. *Ekkoes from the Hart*. Denver: Publ. by the author, 1900.

MALINE, WILLIAM A. *Nineteenth Century and Other Poems*. Cleveland: Burrows, 1898.

MALONE, WALTER. *Songs of Dusk and Dawn*. Buffalo: Moulton, 1895.

—. *Songs of North and South*. Louisville: Morton, 1900.

MANSILL, THOMAS. *DeSoto and Other Poems*. St. Louis: Hildreth, 1879.

MARDEN, GEORGE A. *Poem before the Alumni Association of Dartmouth College*. N.p.: Printed by request of the Association, 1886.

—. *Yeas and Nays*. Boston [?]: Rand, Avery, 1879.

MARINE, CHARLES. *Poems, Heart Songs and Ballads*. Indianapolis: N. publ., 1896.

MARINE, WILLIAM M. *Battle of North Point and Other Poems*. Baltimore: N. publ., 1901.

Mark Loan. A Tale of the Western Reserve Pioneers. Cleveland: Williams, 1884.

MARKHAM, EDWIN. *Lincoln and Other Poems*. New York: McClure, Phillips, 1901.

MARKHAM, EDWIN. *Man with the Hoe·and Other Poems.* New York: Doubleday and McClure, 1899.

MARROW, ZELOTES A. *Memoir.* Augusta, Me.: Kennebec, 1886.

MARSH, E. N. *New Country.* Baraboo [Wisc. ?]: Old Settlers' Association of Sauk County, 1889.

MARSHALL, PERRY. *Launching and Landing.* Chicago: Kerr, n.d.

MARTIN, EDWARD S. *Little Brother of the Rich and Other Verses.* New York: Scribner, 1895.

—. *Poems and Verses.* New York: Harper, 1902.

MARTIN, M. T. *Vistae Vitae.* Merrimack, Wisc.: N. publ., 1886.

MARTLING, JAMES A. *London Bridge: Or, Capital and Labor.* Boston: Earle, 1881.

MARVIN, RICHARD. *Life and Heart Records.* St. Paul: N. publ., 1887.

Massachusetts Charitable Fire Society. Boston: N. publ., 1892.

MASTERS, EDGAR L. *Book of Verses.* Chicago: Way and Williams, 1898.

MATHEWS, F. SCHUYLER. *Rays from Liberty's Torch.* New York: Obpacher, n.d.

MATHIS, JULIETTE E. *Songs and Sonnets.* San Francisco: Murdock, 1899.

MATTOCKS, BREWER. *Songs of Help and Inspiration.* Faribault, Minn.: American News, 1889.

MAXIM, ROSE. *Autumn Leaves.* North Cambridge, Mass.: Publ. by the author, 1890.

MAXWELL, HU. *Idyls of the Golden Shore.* New York: Putnam, 1889.

MAY, CELEST. *Sounds of the Prairie.* Topeka: Crane, 1886.

MAY, CURTIS. *Moly.* New York: Putnam, 1887.

MAY, JOHN W. *Inside the Bar and Other Occasional Poems.* Portland, Me.: Hoyt, Fogg and Donham, 1884.

MAYER, NATHAN. *From Age to Age.* Hartford, Conn.: Case, Lockwood and Brainard, 1892.

M. E. B. *Epic of Travel.* Boston: Adams, 1884.

MEESER, SPEAKMAN. *Sweet Memories.* Philadelphia: Braden, 1889.

Memorial Volume of the World's Columbian Exposition. Chicago: Stone, Kastler and Painter, 1893.

MENARD, J. WILLIS. *Lays in Summer Lands.* Washington, D.C.: Enterprise, 1879.

MERCUR, ANNA H. *Cosmos and Other Poems.* Buffalo: Peter Paul, 1893.

MEREDITH, GULA. *Bunch of Laurel.* Pottsville, Pa.: Beck, Rice, 1890.

MEREDITH, HARRIET R. *Sketches, Life Thoughts, and Incidents.* Philadelphia: Lippincott, 1881.

MERRIMAN, CHARLES G. *Past and Present.* New Haven, Conn.: Peck, 1888.

METCHIM, B. *Wild West Poems.* N.p.: N. publ., 1889.

MEYER, WILHELM H. *Voice of the Prairie.* De Smet, S.D.: Meyer-Henney, 1901.

MICHENER, FANNIE L. *Prose and Poetical Works.* Philadelphia: Lippincott, 1884 [3rd edition].

MIFFLIN, LLOYD. *Collected Sonnets.* London: Frowde, 1905.

——. *Slopes of Helicon and Other Poems.* Boston: Estes and Lauriat, 1898.

MIGHELS, PHILIP V. *Carrier's Address 1896.* N.p.: American Press, 1895.

——. *Out of a Silver Flute.* New York: Tait, 1896.

MIGNONETTE [pseud.]. *Little Gentile: A Deseret Romance of Captive and Exile in the "New Jerusalem."* Chicago: Publ. by the author, 1879.

MILLER, ABRAHAM, P. *Consolation and Other Poems.* New York: Brentano, 1886.

MILLER, FREEMAN E. *Oklahoma and Other Poems.* Buffalo: Moulton, 1895.

MILLER, IRVING J. *Fireside Poems.* Marshalltown, Ia.: Miller, 1887.

MILLER, JOSEPH D. *Verses from a Vagrant Muse.* Hartford, Conn.: Spencer, 1895.

MILLER, MARION M. *Parnassus by Rail.* New York: Putnam, 1891.

MILLER, MARY M. *Poems.* Columbus, Ohio: Hubbard, 1885.

MILLER, SCHUYLER W. *Gallery of Farmer Girls.* Lincoln, Nebr.: Kiote, 1900.

MILLS, HARRY E. *Sod House in Heaven and Other Poems.* Topeka: Crane, 1892.

MILLS, JOANNA E. *Old and New and Other Poems.* Boston: Columbian, 1893.

MILNE, FRANCES M. *For To-day.* San Francisco: Barry, 1905.

MILNE, JOHN C. *First Raymond Excursion of 1882.* Fall River, Mass.: Almy and Milne, 1884.

MILNE, JOHN C. *Massachusetts Legislature.* Boston: Wright and Potter, 1884.

MINKLER, LAURA. *Songs in the Night.* Burlington, Ia.: Burdette, 1891.

MITCHELL, LANGDON E. *Poems.* Boston: Houghton, Mifflin, 1894.

MITCHELL, S. WEIR. *Collected Poems.* New York: Century, 1896. *Modern Tragedy.* N.p.: N. publ., n.d.

MOLINA, JULIA W. *Mingled Sweets and Bitters.* New York: Abbey, 1902.

MOLLAN, MALCOLM. *Poems.* Bridgeport, Conn.: Publ. by the author, 1880.

MONROE, HARRIET. *Valeria and Other Poems.* Chicago: McClurg, 1892.

MONTEVERDE, FRANK L. *Looking Beyond.* Buffalo: Moulton, 1893.

MONTGOMERY, CARRIE F. *Lilies from the Vale of Thought.* Buffalo: Otis, 1878.

MOODY, JOEL. *Song of Kansas and Other Poems.* Topeka: Crane, 1890.

MOODY, WILLIAM V. *Poems.* Boston and New York: Houghton, Mifflin, 1902.

MOORE, CHARLES L. *Odes.* Philadelphia: Publ. by the author, 1896.

MOORE, DAVID. *Poems.* Wappingers Falls, N.Y.: Corson, 1886.

MOORE, L. BRUCE. *Death of Falstaff and Other Poems.* Baltimore: Cushing, 1897.

MOORE, THOMAS J. *Elecampane and Other Poems.* Cincinnati: Clarke, 1898.

MOORE, W. H. *Collection of Jewels.* Jackson, Tenn.: Publ. by the author, 1900.

MORE, PAUL E. *Great Refusal, Being Letters of a Dreamer in Gotham.* Boston and New York: Houghton, Mifflin, 1894.

MOREHEAD, L. M. *Autumn Leaves.* New York: Randolph, 1883.

MORGAN, JOHN E. *Morning Echoes.* N.p.: N. publ., 1900.

MORRELL, CHARLES B. *"Five Dozen Fancies."* Cincinnati: Earhart and Richardson, 1893.

MORRIS, FLORENCE A. *Destruction of the Battleship Maine.* Epping, N.H.: N. publ., 1898.

MORRISON, WILLIAM H. *Fool's Paradise: A Story of Fashionable Life in Washington.* Washington, D.C.: Publ. by the author, 1884.

MORSE, HORACE W. *Poems.* Cambridge, Mass.: N. publ., 1898.

MORSE, JAMES H. *Summer Haven Songs.* New York: Putnam, 1886.

MORSE, JOHN M. *Memories of Childhood and Other Poems.* New York: Lafayette, 1895.

MORTON, EDWIN. *Occasional Poems.* Morges, Switzerland: Lavanchy, 1890.

MOSHER, LEROY E. *"The Stranded Bugle" and Other Poems and Prose.* Los Angeles: Times-Mirror, 1905.

MOSS, JONATHAN W. *Poetical Works*. Cameron, W. Va.: Publ. by the author, 1886.

MOULTON, JAMES A. *Kansas Bandit or the Fall of Ingalls*. Fort Scott, Kans.: N. publ., 1891.

Mugwumpiad. Albany, N.H.: Carey, 1895.

MUIR, HENRY D. *Poems*. Chicago: N. publ., 1897.

MULLER, DONIZETTI. *Links from Broken Chains*. Cambridge, Mass.: Riverside, 1892.

MUNKITTRICK, RICHARD K. *Acrobatic Muse*. Chicago: Way and Williams, 1897.

MURRAY, JOHN C. *Berwick*. North Berwick, Me.: N. publ., 1891.

—. *Vital Thoughts and Other Poems*. Boston: Gorham, 1904.

MUSKERRY, MARK. *Bundle of Ballads and Other Poems*. New York: Cherouny, 1885.

MUSSER, CHARLES. *Poems*. N.p.: Publ. by the author, 1900.

MYERS, JOHN C. *Buds and Flowers*. Cincinnati: Elm Street, 1890.

NAYLOR, ISAAC. *Stars and Stripes of America Insulted and the Union Jack of Britain Dragged in the Dust. A Trumpet Call to Action!* Philadelphia: N. publ., 1894.

NEALON, WILLIAM H. *Silver Rifts*. N.p.: N. publ., n.d.

NESMITH, JAMES E. *Life and Work of Frederic Thomas Greenhalge, Governor of Massachusetts*. Boston: Roberts, 1897.

NESMITH, JAMES E. *Monadnoc and Other Sketches in Verse*. Cambridge, Mass.: Riverside, 1888.

—. *Philoctetes and Other Poems and Sonnets*. Cambridge, Mass.: Riverside, 1894.

NEVILL, WALLACE E. *Some Little 'Rimes' Composed at Odd 'Thymes'*. Sacramento: N. publ., n.d.

NEVIN, DAVID J. *Biographical Sketches of General James A. Garfield and General Chester A. Arthur*. Philadelphia: Pres. [*sic*] Printing, 1880.

NEVIN, ROBERT P. *"Beautiful River" and Other Poems*. Pittsburgh: Weldin, 1899.

New Year's Eve: Or the Story of Little Gretchen. Boston: Breed, n.d.

NEWCOMER, M. S. *Golden Gleanings*. Cedar Papids, Ia.: Daily Republican, 1891.

NICHOLS, A. G. *Iron Door and Other Temperance Songs*. Kingston, N.Y.: Daily Freeman, 1878.

NICHOLS, J. H. *Hours of Leisure*. Milwaukee: Twentieth Century, 1900.

NICHOLS, KATHERINE S. *Bells and Other Poems*. Haverhill, Mass.: Nichols, 1889.

—. *In Sunset Land*. Haverhill, Mass.: Nicole, 1889.

NICHOLSON, KATHLEEN M. *Whispers of the Pines*. Chicago: Hyland, 1898.

NICKELPLATE, NICODEMUS. *Story of a. Broken Ring*. Rutland, Vt.: Tuttle, 1884.

NIMS, GEORGE W. *Declining Village: Or, My Old New England Home*. Boston: Marsh, 1905.

NOGUCHI, YONE. *Voice of the Valley*. San Fra cisco: Doxey, 1897.

NONA, FRANCIS. *Fall of the Alamo and Historical Drama in Four Acts Concluded by an Epilogue Entitled the Battle of San Jacinto*. New York: Putnam, 1879.

NORMAN, JAMES. *Ealien and Lenard*. Philadelphia: Sherman, 1898.

NORRIS, P. W. *Calumet of the Coteau, and Other Poetical Legends of the Border*. Philadelphia: Lippincott, 1884.

Norwalk after Two Hundred and Fifty Years. South Norwalk, Conn.: Freeman, 1901.

NORWOOD, ELIAS. *Political Poems, for the Poor Man's Rights*. Portland, Me.: Publ. by the author, 1884.

NORYS, MYRA V. *Flag That Won*. N.p.: Valentine, n.d.

NUNEZ JOSEPH A. *Songs of the Isle of Cuba*. Philadelphia: Lippincott, 1885.

NYE, EDGAR W. [BILL]. *Bill Nye's Chestnuts Old and New*. Chicago: Conkey, 1894.

O'BRIEN, FITZ-JAMES. *Poems and Stories*. Boston: Osgood, 1881.

O'BRIEN, MATTHEW. *Extracts from the Writings of Yoor "Strooly;" Matt O'B*. Chattanooga, Tenn.: Toof, 1895.

O'BRIEN, PATRICK. *Emerald Isle*. Cleveland: Walsh, 1890.

O'BRIEN, PATRICK. *Birth and Adoption: A Book of Prose and Poetry*. New York: Publ. by the author, 1904.

O'BYRNE, M. C. *Song of the Ages*. LaSalle, Ill.: Wickham, 1897.

O'CONNELL, DANIEL. *Lyrics*. San Francisco: Bancroft, 1881.

—. *Songs from Bohemia*. San Francisco: Robertson, 1900.

O'CONNELL, JAMES J. *Stanzas and Sketches*. Brooklyn: Publ. by the author, 1883.

O'CONNER, JOSEPH. *Poems*. New York: Putnam, 1895.

O'CONNOR, JAMES. *Works*. New York: Tibbals, 1879.

O'DONAGHUE, MARIAN L. *Contrasted Songs.* Boston: Badger, 1905.

—. *Woman's Tribute to the American Shipping and Industrial League.* N.p.: N. publ., n.d.

O'DONNELL, JESSIE F. *Heart Lyrics.* New York: Putnam, 1887.

O'HARE, TERESA B. *Songs at Twilight.* Columbus, Ohio: Columbus, 1898.

O'KEEFFE, KATHARINE A. *Moore's Anniversary.* Boston: Noonam, 1887.

O'MALLEY, RICHARD L. *Wyoming and Indian Melodies, and Other Poems.* Philadelphia: Ketterlinus, 1891.

O'MEARA, HENRY. *Ballads of America.* Boston: Damrell and Upham, 1891.

OPPER, F. *Folks in Funnyville.* New York: Russell, 1900.

OSBORNE, LOUIS S. *Quest of a Lost Type.* Chicago: N. publ., 1888.

OSBORNE, RICHARD B. *Poems of Living Truth.* Philadelphia: Reformed Episcopal Publishing, 1899.

O'SHERIDAN, MARY G. *Conata.* Madison, Wisc.: Atwood, 1881.

OTT, LAMBERT. *Daily Doings.* Philadelphia: Lippincott, 1888.

OWEN, "FRANCIS BROWNING." *Columbian and Other Poems.* Ann Arbor, Mich.: Register, 1893 [2nd edition].

PABOR, W. E. *Wedding Bells. A Colorado Idyl.* Denver: Pabor, 1900.

PAGE, AMIE S. *At the Gates of Light and Other Poems.* San Francisco: Doxey, 1893.

PAINE, ALBERT B. *Autiobiography of a Monkey.* New York: Russell, 1897.

PAINTER, FRANKLIN V. *Lyrical Vignettes.* Boston and Chicago: Sibley and Ducker, 1900.

PALMER, T. SHREWBRIDGE. *Ray of Hope. Poems.* Washington, D.C.: N. publ., 1884.

PARKER, MARIA H. *Poems and Stories.* N.p.: Stone, Huse, 1876.

—. *Stray Thoughts or Poems.* Boston: Cupples, Upham, 1885.

PARMELEE, JOSEPH W. *Then and Now.* Newport, N.H.: Private edition, 1895.

PARRISH, RICHARD P. *Western Wanderer.* New York: Allison, 1888.

PARRISH, ROB R. *Echoes from the Valley.* Portland, Ore.: Himes, 1884.

Parson's Experience in a Parish on Poverty Hill. Brooklyn: Orphan's Press, 1878.

PATTEE, FRED L. *Message of the West.* State College, Pa.: N. publ., 1903.

PATTON, ELLEN. *Mignonette.* Atchison, Kans.: N. publ., 1883.

PAXTON, W. M. *Poems.* Kansas City, Mo.: Beaumont, 1887.

PAYSON, HANNAH W. *Poems.* Boston: Whately, 1895.

PEARRE, O. F. *Poems.* Pontiac, Ill.: Pearre, 1897.

PEARSON, FRANCIS C. *Golden Grains.* Philadelphia: Collings, 1887.

PECK, HARRY T. *Greystone and Porphyry.* New York: Dodd, Mead, 1899.

PECK, SAMUEL M. *Cap and Bells.* New York: White, Stokes, and Allen, 1886.

—. *Golf Girl.* New York: Stokes, 1899.

PECKHAM, LIZZIE C. *Poems.* Los Angeles: N. publ., 1905.

PECKHAM, LUCY C. *Sea Moss.* Buffalo: Moultòn, 1891.

PECKHAM, MARY C. *"Windfalls Gathered Only for Friends" and Other Poems.* Buffalo: Moulton, 1894.

PECKHAM, P. ANNETTA. *Welded Links.* New York: N. publ., 1884 [2nd edition].

PECKHAM, SAMUEL W. *Verses.* Providence: Private edition, 1894.

Peep at Buffalo Bill's Wild West. New York: McLoughlin, 1887.

PEET, C. C. *Whispers and Echoes.* Boston: Publ. by the author, 1882.

PELTON, DANIEL. *Greenwood.* Volume I. New York: Allison, n.d.

PELTON, JOHN C. *Life's Sunbeams and Shadows.* San Francisco: Bancroft, 1893.

PENNELL, ALICE I. *Silver Cloud.* Springfield, Mass.: Springfield, 1887.

PENNELL, D. S. *Wavelets.* Philadelphia: Pile, 1894.

PENNEY, WILLIAM E. *Ballads of Yankee Land.* New York: Crowell, 1897.

PERKINS, ANNIE S. *Thoughts of Peace.* Boston: Earle, 1892.

PERKINS, E. F. *Poems and Prose Compositions.* Dallas, Tex.: Pearre, 1886.

PERRY, GEORGE. *Sheaf of Poems.* New York: Putnam, 1894.

—. *By Man Came Death.* Boston: Crook, 1886.

PETER, MARY L. *Century of Presidents of the United States . . . in Verse.* Buffalo: Publ. by the author, 1892.

PETERS, SARAH E. *Poems.* N.p.: N. publ., 1898.

PETTET, ROBERT S. *Columbia's Apostasy.* Philadelphia: Publ. by the author, 1899.

PHELPS, ALANSON H. *Wedding of the Rails.* Ashland, Ore.: N. publ., 1887.

PHIPPS, I. N. *Lay of the Wraith and Other Poems.* Louisville: Morton, 1895.

PHIPPS, WILLIAM H. *Hamlet on the Hill and Other Poems.* Pittsburgh: N. publ., 1897.

PICKUP, JAMES. *Collection of Poems.* Spencer, Mass.: Sun Office, n.d.

PILCH, FREDERICK H. *Homespun Verses.* Newark, N.J.: Plum, 1882.

PINNEY, LAURA Y. *Within the Golden Gate.* San Francisco: San Francisco Printing, 1893.

PLIMPTON, FLORUS B. *Poems.* Cincinnati: Plimpton, 1886.

Poems. Boston: Daniels, 1889–90.

POLLARD, JOSEPHINE. *Decorative Sisters.* New York: Randolph, 1881.

POPE, J. WILLIAM. *Songs and Satires.* Pittsburgh: Anderson, 1876.

PORTER, DUVAL. *Lost Cause and Other Poems.* Danville, Va.: Blair and Boatwright, 1897.

POTTER, E. C. *Midlothian Melodies.* Chicago: Private edition, 1900.

POTTER, JEFFREY W. *Poems of New England.* Boston: Earle, 1899.

POWELL, EMILY B. *Songs Along the Way.* Buffalo: Peter Paul, 1900.

POWERS, HORATIO N. *Ten Years of Song.* Boston: Lothrop, 1887.

PRAIGG, D. T. *Almetta.* Indianapolis: Baker-Randolph, 1894.

PRATT, ALICE E. *Sleeping Princess California.* San Francisco: Doxey, 1892.

PREBLE, E. W. *Wayside Leaves.* Boston: Ellis, 1892.

Prescott's Plain Dialogues. New York: De Vitt, 1879.

PRENTICE, JAMES. *Little Book of Verse.* Menomonie, Wisc.: Dunn County News, 1899.

PRESSEY, JONATHAN. *Poems.* Newton, N.H.: Heath, 1887.

PRICE, E. B. *Beulah and Other Poems.* Chicago: Laird and Lee, 1891.

PRICE, EMANUEL. *Poetical Works of Peter Peppercorn.* Philadelphia: McKay, 1884.

PRICE, JACOB. *Poems.* San Leandro, Cal.: N. publ., 1889.

PRICE, THEODORE F. *Heroes of the Spanish-American War.* New York: N. publ., 1899.

—. *Songs of the Southwest.* Topeka: Crane, 1881.

Problem of Human Life Here and Hereafter. New York: Hall, 1877.

Proceedings at the Celebration of the Sesqui-Centennial of the Town of Waltham. Waltham, Mass.: Barry, 1893.

Proceedings at the Semi-Centennial Anniversary of the Connection of Caleb Arnold Wall with the Worcester County Press. 1837–1887. Worcester, Mass.: Seagrave, 1887.

Proceedings at the Twenty-Fifth Anniversary of the Haverhill Monday Evening Club. Boston: Cupples, Upham, 1886.

Proceedings in the Celebration at Brattleboro, Vermont, October 21, 1892, of the Four Hundredth Anniversary of the Discovery of America by Christopher Columbus. Brattleboro: Phoenix Job Print, 1892.

Proceedings of the Annual Meeting of the Massachusetts Charitable Mechanic Association. Boston: Massachusetts Charitable Mechanic Association, 1891.

PROUDFIT, DAVID L. *Love among the Gamins and Other Poems.* New York: Dick and Fitzgerald, 1877.

PUTNAM, FRANK. *Banquet: Songs of Evolution.* Chicago: Blakely, 1897.

—. *Lafayette Ode and Later Lyrics.* Boston: National Magazine, 1903.

—. *Living in the World.* Chicago and New York: Rand, McNally, 1899.

—. *Memories and Impressions.* Chicago: N. publ., 1896.

Queer Fish and Other Poems. New York: Davis, 1881.

QUILLIN, HORACE S. *Musings by the Wayside.* Philadelphia: Ramon, 1885.

QUINBY, FRANKLYN. *Columbiad.* Chicago: Conkey, 1893.

RADFORD, BENJAMIN J. *Court of Destiny and Other Poems.* St. Louis and Chicago: Christian, 1883.

RALSTON, HARRIET N. *Columbus and Isabella—The Immortals. A Souvenir Centennial Poem.* Washington, D.C.: Publ. by the author, 1893.

RAND, N. W. and J. P. *Random Rimes: Medical and Miscellaneous.* Boston: N. publ., 1897.

RANDOLPH, LEWIS V. *Survivals.* New York: Putnam, 1900.

RANKIN, GEORGE C. *Sheaf: A Bundle of Poems.* Minneapolis: Rankin, 1882.

Rather Restful Rhymes. Boston: Griggs, 1898.

RATTRAN, B. F. *Poems.* Tacoma, Wash.: Monger, 1895.

RAVEN, NIL. *Two Years in Wall Street: Or, Why Was I Born?.* New York: American News, 1877.

RAZE, FLOYD D. *Poems of Peace and of War.* N.p.: N. publ., 1902.

REA, WILLIAM H. *Crescent City.* N.p.: N. publ., n.d.

READ, WILLIAM, *Re-strung Harp.* Boston: Lakeview, 1889.

REALF, RICHARD. *Poems.* New York: Funk and Wagnalls, 1898.

REAVIS, REBECCA M. *Builders.* St. Louis: Becktold, 1884.

—. *Course of Empire and Other Poems.* St. Louis: N. publ., 1886.

REDMAN, JOHN E. *Miscellaneous Poems*. Philadelphia: Winston, 1895.

REED, ANNA M. *Earlier Poems*. San Francisco: Bancroft, 1880.

—. *Later Poems*. San Francisco: Stuart, 1891.

REED, EDWIN T. *Inland Windfalls*. Chicago and New York: Conkey, 1898.

—. *Lyrics*. Wausau, Wisc.: Philosopher, 1900.

REED, JOSEPH S. *Near Nature's Nooks*. Indianapolis: Hollenbeck, 1905.

REEKIE, CHARLES. *Day Dreams*. New York: Robertson, 1895.

REESE, LIZETTE W. *Quiet Road*. Portland, Me.: Mosher, 1896.

REID, GEORGE L. *Heather Bell and Other Poems*. Menasha, Wisc.: N. publ., 1891.

REIDELBACH, JOHN G. *Bubbles from Tippecanoe*. N.p.: N. publ., 1899.

REMICK, MARTHA. *Miscellaneous Poems*. Malden, Mass.: N. publ., n.d.

—. *Miscellaneous Poems Volume II*. Malden, Mass.: Brown, 1900.

"Reminiscence of '84." Cambridge, Mass.: University Press, 1904.

RENNELL, JENNIE. *Chips*. N.p.: N. publ., n.d.

Report of the Sixteenth Industrial Exhibition of the Mechanics Institute. San Francisco: Thomas, 1881.

RE QUA, HARRIET W. *Stones for the Temple*. Rochester, N.Y.: N. publ., 1885.

REXDALE, ROBERT. *Rhymes*. New York: Revell, 1904.

REYNOLDS, J. MASON. *Poems by Farmer Reynolds*. Grand Rapids, Mich.: Publ. by the author, 1882.

RICE, BERNARD L. *View from Pike's Peak and Other Poems*. Denver: Christian Endeavor Printing, 1898.

RICE, CARRIE S. *Where the Rhododendrons Grow*. Tacoma, Wash.: N. publ. 1904.

RICE, MARTIN. *Rural Rhymes and Poems from the Farm*. Kansas City, Mo.: Millett and Hudson, 1877.

RICE, WALLACE. *Flying Sands*. Chicago: Donnelley, 1898.

RICE, WALLACE and EASTMAN, BARRETT. *Under the Stars and Other Songs of the Sea*. Chicago: Way and Williams, 1898.

RICH, HELEN H. *Dream of the Adirondacks and Other Poems*. New York: Putnam, 1884.

—. *Murillo's Slave and Other Poems*. Chicago: Rand McNally, 1897.

RICHARDS, LYDIA P. *American Monodies*. Franklin, Ohio: Editor, 1899.

RICHARDS, T. J. *Shifting Scenes*. San Francisco: Bancroft, 1889.

RICHEY, ISABEL. *Harp of the West*. Buffalo: Moulton, 1895.

RICHMOND, CYRUS R. *Selections from the Poetical Writings.* Cambridge, Mass.: Private edition, 1886.

RICHMOND, JOHN M. *Free America.* Hartford, Conn.: N. publ., 1892.

RIDDICK, ROBERT A. *Musings of a Bachelor.* Raleigh, N.C.: Raleigh Christian Advocate, 1899.

RIEHL, FRANK C. *Runes of the Red Race.* Alton, Ill.: Melling and Gaskins, 1899.

RILEY, JAMES. *Poems.* Boston: Cleaves, Macdonald, 1886.

——. *Songs of Two Peoples.* Boston: Estes and Lauriat, 1898.

RILEY, JAMES W. *Afterwhiles.* Indianapolis: Bobbs-Merrill, 1887.

——. *Armazindy.* Indianapolis: Bowen-Merrill, 1895.

——. *Book of Joyous Children.* New York: Scribner, 1902.

——. *Days Gone by and Other Poems.* Chicago: Weeks, 1895.

——. *Green Fields and Running Brooks.* Indianapolis: Bowen-Merrill, 1895.

——. *His Pa's Romance.* Indianapolis: Bobbs-Merrill, 1903.

——. *Home-folks.* Indianapolis: Bobbs-Merrill, 1900.

——. *Ne[i]ghborly Poems.* Indianapolis: Bowen-Merrill, 1891.

——. *Poems Here at Home.* New York: Century, 1893.

ROBERTS, ELLWOOD. *Lyrics of Quakerism and Other Poems.* Norristown, Pa.: Willis, 1895.

ROBERTS, SUSAN B. *Short Poems.* Elmira, N.Y.: Empire, 1891.

ROBERTSON, LOUIS A. *Dead Calypso and Other Verses.* San Francisco: Robertson, 1901.

ROBERTSON, SAMUEL L. *Dora . . . and Other Poems.* Birmingham [Ala.?]: Roberts, 1894.

ROBINSON, ALFRED. *California: An Historical Poem.* San Francisco: Doxey, 1889.

ROBINSON, CHARLES H. *Lunar Caustic.* New York: Neely, 1897.

ROBINSON, EDWIN A. *Captain Craig.* Boston and New York: Houghton, Mifflin, 1902.

——. *Children of the Night.* Boston: Badger, 1897.

——. *Torrent and the Night Before.* Gardiner, Me.: Publ. by the author, 1896.

ROBINSON, JOHN B. *Epic Ballads of the Land of Flowers.* Deland, Fla.: News, 1905.

——. *New Woman and Other Poems.* Chicago: Barnes, 1896.

ROBINSON, JOSEPH C. *Dream.* Boston: Publ. by the author, 1889.

ROCHE, JAMES J. *Songs and Satires*. Boston: Ticknor, 1887.

—. *Vase and Other Bric-a-Brac*. Boston: Badger, 1900.

ROGERS, LESTER C. *Golden Link and Other Poems*. New York: Chinn, 1895.

ROGERS, ROBERT C. *For the King and Other Poems*. New York: Putnam, 1899.

—. *Poem Delivered at the Dedication of the Pan-American Exposition*. San Francisco: Elder and Shepard, 1901.

ROGERS, WALTER M. *Stray Leaves from a Larker's Log*. Boston: Private edition, 1897.

ROLLINS, ALICE M. *Aphorisms for the Year*. New York: N. publ., 1895.

RORER, DAVID. *Pastime Poems*. Burlington, Ia.: Private edition, 1892.

ROSE, GEORGE. *Heart and Harp*. New York: Madison Square, 1887.

RUBOTTOM, WILLIAM F. *When I Was Living at the Grange and Other Poems*. Buffalo Gap, Tex.: Girand, 1897.

RUDDOCK, C. A. *Temperance Poems*. Winthrop, Minn.: Publ. by the author, 1895.

RUDE, B. C. *Magnolia Leaves*. Buffalo: Moulton, 1891.

RUDY, BELLE L. *Franchise*. Lima, Ohio: Parmenter, 1895.

RUFFIN, H. G. *Colored Country Poet*. Pushmataha, Ala.: N. publ., 1896.

Ruined by Rum. Hartford: Brown and Gross, 1877.

RULE, LUCIEN V. *Shrine of Love*. Chicago and New York: Stone, 1898.

—. *When John Bull Comes A-Courtin' and Other Poems*. Louisville: Caxton, 1903.

RUPP, ALBERT J. *Sonnets*. Boston: Arena, 1896.

RUSH, EDWIN R. *Hours with My Lyre*. Philadelphia: Globe, 1884.

RUSSELL, IRWIN, *Poems*. New York: Century, 1888.

RYDER, THOMAS P. *Verses and Prose Selections*. Wilkes-Barre, Pa.: Wilkes-Barre Press Club, 1899.

ST. PAUL, J. J. *Gathered by the Way*. St. Paul: Jacobson, 1895.

SANBORN, WILL S. *Chita and the Faith of Jose*. N.p.: N. publ., 1897.

SANBURN, M. P. *Thoughts in Verse*. Kansas City, Mo.: Ramsey, Millett and Hudson, 1881.

SANDERS, JOHANNA M. *Poems and Ballads*. San Francisco: Private edition, 1890.

SANGSTER, MARGARET E. *Lyrics of Love*. New York, Chicago and Toronto: Revell, 1901.

SANTAYANA, GEORGE. *Hermit of Carmel and Other Poems*. New York: Scribner, 1901.

SANTORINI, RISORIUS. *Macte Lister Triumphator!* Boston: Cupples and Hurd, 1888.

SAVAGE, MINOT J. *America to England and Other Poems.* New York: Putnam, 1905.

—. *At the Back of the Moon.* Boston: Lee and Shepard: New York: Dillingham, 1879.

—. *Hymns.* Boston: Ellis, 1898.

—. *Poems.* Boston: Ellis, 1882.

SAVAGE, PHILIP H. *First Poems and Fragments.* Boston: Copeland and Day, 1895.

SAVAGE, RICHARD H. *After Many Years.* Chicago and New York: Neely, 1895.

SAVARY, JOHN. *James Abram Garfield.* N.p.: N. publ., 1881.

—. *Poems of Expansion.* New York: Neely, 1898.

SAXBY, HOWARD [JR.]. *Dulcamara.* Cincinnati: Raisbeck, 1903.

SAXBY, HOWARD. *Wifely Worries and Other Poems.* Cincinnati: N. publ., 1894.

SCARFF, CHARLES W. *Grinding of the Mills and Other Poems.* Sunset Home, Vt.: N. publ., 1899.

SCHAFER, EMMA C. *Thoughts on Social Problems and Scripture Readings in Verse.* Pasadena, Cal.: Publ. by the author, 1900.

SCHERMERHORN, CORNELIUS P. *Atomic Creation and Other Poems.* New York: N. publ., 1883.

SCHOFIELD, CHARLES. *Sketch Book.* San Francisco: Publ. by the author, 1886.

SCHOLES, ADAM. *Thoughts in Verse for Kind Hearts.* Detroit: N. publ., 1899.

SCHORB, GEORGE. *Poems.* Burlington, Wisc.: Free Press, 1885.

SCHULTZ, F. W. *Course of Progress.* New York: Argyle, 1892.

SCHUMANN, CHARLES W. *Emigrant of 1845.* New York: N. publ., 1883.

SCOLLARD, CLINTON. *Old and New World Lyrics.* New York: Stokes, 1888.

SCOLLARD, CLINTON and RICE, WALLACE. *Ballads of Valor and Victory, Being Stories in Song from the Annals of America.* New York: Revell, 1903.

SCOTT, EMMA B. *Poems.* Ohio City, Ohio: N. publ., 1900.

SCOTT, JAMES H. *Calendora and Other Poems.* Chicago: Cushing, Thomas, 1881.

SCOTT, JAMES H. *Poems.* St. Louis: Slawson, 1887 [2nd edition].

SCOTT, WINFIELD L. *Songs of an Idle Hour.* Detroit: Speaker Printing, 1895.

SCRIBNER, A. *Ode on Temperance.* Newport, Vt.: N. publ., 1886.

SCULLY, JAMES. *Songs of the People.* Concord, N.H.: Republican Press, 1893.

SEARS, BETSY M. *Medley of Poems.* Rome, Wisc.: N. publ., 1880.

SEARS, GEORGE W. *Forest Runes.* New York: Forest and Stream, 1887.

SEE, ANNA E. *Golden Harp Strains of California.* Chicago: N. publ., 1900.

Semi-Centennial of Anaesthesia; 1846–1896. Boston: Massachusetts General Hospital, 1897.

SEYMOUR, E. J. *Harrison and Reid Campaign Song Book.* N.p.: N. publ., n.d.

SEYMOUR, MINA S. *Pen Pictures.* Lily Dale, N.Y.: N. publ., 1900.

SHADE, WILLIAM H. *Buckeyeland and Bohemia.* Hillsboro, Ohio: Lyle, 1895.

SHADWELL, BERTRAND. *America and Other Poems.* Chicago: Donnelley, 1899.

SHASTID, THOMAS H. *Poems.* Pittsfield, Ill.: Publ. by the author, 1881.

SHAW, WILLIAM J. *Forward Forever!* New York: Fowler and Wells, 1888.

SHEA, JOHN C. *Songs and Romances of Buffalo.* Buffalo: Moulton, 1900.

SHELBY, HELEN. *Poems.* New York: N. publ., 1891.

SHERAN, WILLIAM, *Pro Poeta and Other Poems.* St. Paul: Payne, Vose, 1891.

SHERMAN, IRA E. *Old Time Memories and Other Poems.* New York: N. publ., 1895.

SHERRICK, FANNIE I. *Star-dust.* Chicago, New York and San Francisco: Belford, Clarke, 1888.

SHERWOOD, KATE B. *Dream of the Ages.* Washington, D.C.: National Tribune, 1893.

SHIRLEY, MOSES G. *Everyday Rhymes.* Manchester, N.H.: Clarke, 1892.

SHOEMAKER, WILLIAM L. [*La*] *Santa Yerba.* Boston: Copeland and Day, 1898.

SHOEMAN, CHARLES H. *Dream and Other Poems.* Ann Arbor, Mich.: Wahr, 1899.

SHORTRIDGE, BELLE H. *Lone-star Lights.* New York: Belford, 1890.

SHUEY, LILLIAN H. *Among the Redwoods.* San Francisco: Whitaker and Ray, 1901.

—. *California Sunshine.* Oakland, Cal.: Pacific Press, 1899 [2nd edition].

SIBYL [pseud.]. *Wandering Jew.* New York: Atlantic, 1881.

SIDERS, J. W. *Songs of a Pleb.* Eaton, Ohio: Publ. by the author, 1883.

SIEGVOLK, PAUL. *Few Verses.* New York: DeVinne, 1896.

SIMMONS, ANNA W. *Heart Whispers.* Denver: N. publ., 1895.

SISCO, MARCIA M. *Gems of Inspiration.* Clinton, Ia.: Publ. by the author, 1898.

SKIDMORE, HARRIET M. *Beside the Western Sea.* New York: O'Shea, 1877.

—. *Roadside Flowers.* San Francisco: Robertson, 1903.

SLEEPER, JOHN F. *Battle of Manilla[sic].* New York: Knickerbocker, 1899.

—. *Freedom's Triumph—Spion-Kop.* N.p.: Sherwood, 1900.

—. *March of Olivier.* N.p.: Sherwood, 1900.

—. *Tocsin.* N.p.: Sherwood, 1902 [copyright, 1899].

SLEYSTER, AARON L. *Hours of Pleasure.* Winona, Minn.: Jones and Kroeger, 1895.

SLOAN, DAVID U. *Fogy Days and Now.* Atlanta: N. publ., 1891.

SLOAN, GEORGE M. *Telephone of Labor.* Chicago: N. publ., 1880.

S. M. F. [pseud.]. *Stray Thoughts.* Boston: Publ. by the author, 1888.

SMILEY, J. B. *Basket of Chips.* Kalamazoo, Mich.: Publ. by the author, 1888.

—. *Meditations of Samwell Wilkins.* Kalamazoo, Mich.: Publ. by the author, 1886.

SMITH, CARL. *Where the Sun Goes Down.* Omaha: Gideon, 1894.

SMITH, CHARLES H. *Libertas.* Brooklyn: Ventres, 1880.

SMITH, EMMA P. *Jets of Truth.* San Francisco: Brunt and Fisher, 1886.

SMITH, FRANCIS S. *Reveries and Realities.* New York: Street and Smith, 1891.

SMITH, HARRY B. *Lyrics and Sonnets.* Chicago: Dial, 1894.

SMITH, J. BYINGTON, *Wayside Poems.* Boston: Earle, 1892.

SMITH, J. C. *Some Simple Rhymes of Leisure Times.* Port Townsend, Wash.: N. publ., n.d.

SMITH, JEANIE O. *Day Lilies.* New York: Putnam's, 1889.

SMITH, MARY. *Poems and Essays.* Mobile: N. publ., 1888.

SMITH, MINERVA C. *Gold Stories of '49.* Boston: Copeland and Day, 1896.

SMITH, T. BERRY. *In Many Moods.* Fayette, Mo.: N. publ., 1900.

SMYTH, JAMES W. *History of the Catholic Church . . . and Selected Poems.* Woonsocket, R.I.: Cook, 1903.

SNOW, ALVIN L. *Songs of the White Mountains and Other Poems.* Creston, Ia.: Gazette, 1892.

Songs of the Cranial Nerves. New York: Trow's Printing, 1878.

SOSSO, LORENZO. *In the Realms of Gold.* San Francisco: Elder and Shepard, 1902.

—. *Poems of Humanity.* San Francisco: Griffith and Sons, 1891.

SOURS, B. F. *Tax-Payer's Songster.* Mechanicsburg, Pa.: Tax-Payer's Friend, 1897.

Souvenir of the Celebration of the 120th Anniversary of the Concord Fight. Acton, Mass.: N. publ., 1895.

Souvenir of the Dedicatory Ceremonies of the New York State Building, at Jackson Park, Chicago . . . New York: Board of General Managers of the State of New York at the World's Columbian Exposition, 1892.

Souvenir Program, Golden Gate Park. San Francisco: N. publ., 1888.

SOUVIELLE, E. M. *Ulyssiad.* Jacksonville, Fla.: Dacosta House, 1896.

SPALDING, WILLIAM A. *My Vagabonds.* Los Angeles: Times-Mirror Printing, 1889.

SPEER, WILL A. *"The Dream," "The Vision" and Other Poems.* Unionville, Mo.: Leader Job Print., 1898.

SPENCER, ARMON. *Opening for a Candidate, with Other Poems.* Newark, N.Y.: N. publ., 1881.

SPOLLON, JOHN. *Mary Ann.* Boston: Wade, 1900.

SPRAGUE, WARD. *Billy Dash Poems.* Sandy Creek, N.Y.: Mungor, 1878.

SPROULL, LYMAN H. *Hours at Home.* St. Louis: Continental Printing, 1895.

—. *In the Land of the Columbine.* Chicago: Scroll, 1900.

—. *Snowy Summits.* St. Louis: Fleming, 1898.

SPURR, GEORGE G. *Land of Gold.* Boston: Publ. by the author, 1883.

STACY, ARTHUR M. *Miser's Dream and Other Poems.* Augusta, Me.: Nash, 1883.

STANLEY, L. M. *Poems.* Alliance, Ohio: Scranton Printing, 1900.

STANLEY, M. VICTOR. *Oshkosh.* Oakland, Cal.: Publ. by the author, 1898.

STANTON, FRANK L. *Comes One with a Song*. Indianapolis: Bowen-Merrill, 1899.

STARKEY, ROBERT. *Sparks of Poetic Fire*. Marshfield, Ore.: Coos Bay News Printing, 1880.

STARRETT, LEWIS F. *Poems and Translations*. Boston: Rand Avery, 1887.

Stars and Stripes. New Bedford, Mass.: Fifth Street Grammar School, 1898.

State Steal and Other Verse. Topham [Me.?]: N. publ., 1880.

STEBBINS, SARAH B. *Galgano's Wooing and Other Poems*. New York: Dillingham, 1890.

STEELL, J. D. *Poems*. San Francisco: Golden Era, 1885.

STEVENS, ORRIN C. *Idyl of the Sun and Other Poems*. Holyoke, Mass.: Griffith, Axtell and Cady, 1891.

—. *Song of Companies and Other Poems*. Holyoke, Mass.: Cady Printing, 1894.

STEWART, MARCUS A. *Rosita: A California Tale*. San Jose: Mercury Steam Print., 1882.

STEWART, T. B. *Coming Conflict*. San Francisco: Winterburn, 1887.

STICKNEY, JULIA N. *One Hundred Sonnets*. Groveland, Mass.: Ambrose, 1894.

STICKNEY, TRUMBULL. *Dramatic Verses*. Boston: Goodspeed, 1902.

Stock Exchange Primer. New York: Sears and Cole, 1882.

STODDARD, A. H. *Miscellaneous Poems*. Kalamazoo, Mich.: Publ. by the author, 1880.

STODDARD, ELIZABETH D. *Poems*. Boston and New York: Houghton, Mifflin, 1895.

STONE, F. *McKinley Songster*. Chicago: N. publ., n.d.

Story of the Itata. San Diego: San Diego Print., 1891.

STOUT, ROBERT W. *Poetical Works*. Buffalo: Moulton, 1892.

STOVALL, DENNIS H. *Heart of the Valley*. Corvallis, Ore.: N. publ., 1899.

STOWE, LYMAN E. *Poetical Drifts of Thought*. Detroit: Publ. by the author, 1884.

STOWELL, FRED W. *Ragtime Philosophy*. San Francisco: San Francisco News, 1902.

STREVELL, J. W. *Poems*. Chicago: Hill, 1899.

—. *Thoughts and Memories*. Buffalo: Peter Paul, 1895.

STRONG, AUGUSTUS H. *Address at the Dedication of Rockefeller Hall*. Rochester: Andrews, 1880.

STRYKER, MELANCTHON W. *Lattermath.* Utica: Smith, 1895.

—. *Song of Miriam and Other Hymns and Verses.* Chicago: Biglow and Main, 1888.

SUNDERLAND, BYRON AND CROFFUT, W. A. *Lord's Day—or Man's?* New York: Truth Seeker, 1897.

SUTHERLAND, HOWARD V. *Bigg's Bar and Other Klondyke Ballads.* Philadelphia: Biddle, 1901.

—. *Jacinta, a California Idyl and Other Verses.* New York: Doxey's, 1900.

—. *Songs of a City.* San Francisco: Star Press, 1904.

SUTTILL, MATTHEW. *Works of the Poet Coachman.* New York: Publ. by the author, 1885.

SUTTON, JOHN. *Songs and Poems.* Wilkes-Barre, Pa.: Wilkes-Barre Leader, 1890.

SWARTZ, JOEL. *Poems.* Philadelphia: Coates, 1901.

SWEET, FRANK. *Poems.* Boston: Publ. by the author, 1882.

SWEET, J. P. *Day on Coney Island.* New York: Cornett, 1880.

SWIFT, MORRISON I. *Advent of Empire.* Los Angeles: Ronbroke, 1900.

TACKENBERG, CHARLES W. *Children of Phantasy.* Cincinnati: Literary Shop, 1899.

TADLOCK, CLARA M. *Solomon Grinder's Christmas Eve and Other Poems.* Boston: Lothrop, 1885.

TANEY, MARY F. *Kentucky Pioneer Women.* Cincinnati: Clarke, 1893.

TARBOX, INCREASE N. [pseud.?]. *Songs and Hymns of Common Life.* Boston: Publ. by the author, 1885.

TAYLOR, BELLE G. *Captive Conceits.* New York: Putnam's, 1896.

TAYLOR, EDWARD R. *Professor Joseph Le Conte at Yosemite.* N.p.: N. publ., n.d. [1901?].

TAYLOR, HENRY W. *White Druse and Other Poems.* Anderson, Ind.: Elizabeth Taylor, 1904.

TAYLOR, JOHN D. *Original Poems.* Charleston, S.C.: Walker, Evans, and Cogswell, 1883.

TEETZEL, FRANCES G. *Vagrant Fancies.* Milwaukee: Publ. by the author, 1893.

Telegraph Messenger's Holiday Greeting. N.p.: N. publ., n.d. [written in 1898].

TELKUT, WILLIAM K. *Jen'ral Welfar Posibl.* San Diego: Publ. by the author, 1896.

TEMPLE, J. W. *Sheaf of Grain.* Knoxville, Ill.: Republican Book and Job Print., 1890.

TEMPLER, WILL. *Some Rustic Rhymes.* New York: Burr, 1900.

TERRY, EPHRAIM. *Our Pumpkin Vine, and Other Poems.* New York: Publ. by the author, 1883.

THAW, ALEXANDER B. *Inaugural Ode.* Nelson, N.H.: Monadnock Press, 1905.

—. *Poems.* New York: Lane, 1901.

THAYER, M. LOUISE. *Poems.* Cambridge, Mass.: Publ. by her children, 1882.

THAYER, STEPHEN H. *Songs from Edgewood.* New York: Putnam's, 1902.

THAYER, WILLIAM R. *Poems, Old and New.* Boston and New York: Houghton, Mifflin, 1894.

Thirty-first Anniversary of the Society of California Pioneers. Santa Cruz, Cal.: Publ. by the society, 1881.

THOMAS, AARON B. *Echoes of Spring.* Rossmoyne, Ohio: Publ. by the author, 1901.

THOMAS, EDITH M. *Cassia and Other Verse.* Boston: Badger, 1905.

—. *New Year's Masque and Other Poems.* Boston: Houghton, Mifflin, 1885.

THOMPSON, ANNIE. *Simplicity Unveiled.* Indianapolis: Douglass and Carlon, 1880.

THOMPSON, MAURICE. *Poems.* Boston: Houghton, Mifflin, 1892.

THOMPSON, SAMUEL. *Soulful Thoughts from Kindly Pen after Three Score Years and Ten.* N.p.: N. publ., n.d.

THORNDYKE, W. L. *Simply Stuff.* Loveland, Colo.: Publ. by the author, n.d. [1899?].

THORNTON, G. H. *Zenobia and Other Poems.* San Francisco: Griffith, 1897.

THORPE, ROSE H. *White Lady of La Jolla.* San Diego: N. publ., 1904.

THORWIS, CARLE [pseud. of Peter Sass]. *Cumaean Sibyl's Prophecy for the Twentieth Century.* New Whatcom, Wash.: Edson and Irish, 1900.

THROOP, JOSEPHINE. *Youths' History of the United States in Verse.* Indianapolis: Carlon and Hollenbeck, 1883.

THURSTON, JULIA G. *Threads of Song.* Chicago: Weeks, 1893.

TIFFANY, OLIVE E. *Lenore, the Belle of Monterey.* Kansas City, Mo.: Hudson-Kimberly, n.d. [1900?].

TILLOTSON, MARY E. *Poems.* Philadelphia: N. publ., 1887.

Togus. [City?]. Me.: National Home for Disabled Veteran Soldiers, n.d.

TOLAND, MARY B. *Tisayac of the Yosemite.* Philadelphia: Lippincott, 1891.

TOLKUT, WILLIAM K. *Doktrin and Practis.* Valparaiso, Ind.: Publ. by the author, 1889.

TOMS, MARY F. *Sacred Gems.* Hartford: Cass, Lockwood, and Brainard, 1888.

TORRENCE, F. RIDGELY. *El Dorado.* New York: Lane, 1903.

Tour of Prince Eblis: His Rounds of Society, Church and State. Chicago: Central, 1879.

TOWNSEND, BELTON O. *Plantation Lays and Other Poems.* Columbia, S. C.: Calvo, 1884.

TRAUBEL, HORACE. *Chants Communal.* Boston: Small, Maynard, 1904.

TRAVIS, STUART. *"Bubble" Jingles.* New York and London: Rhode and Haskins, 1901.

TRESCOTT, GEORGE E. *Chirps.* Troy, Mo.: N. publ., 1895.

TREUTHART, J. L. *Milliad. A Poem of Justice and Liberty.* New York: Argyle Press, 1894.

Tribute of Respect to Its Late President James Abram Garfield. Washington, D.C.: Literary Society of Washington, 1882.

TRIPP, HOWARD C. *Around the Fireside and Other Poems.* Kingsley, Ia.: Times, 1893.

—. *Legends of Lemars.* Lemars, Ia.: Publ. by the author, 1883.

TROW, CHARLES E. *Prose and Verse.* Salem, Mass.: Bary, 1900.

TRUEMAN, ANITA. *Philo-sophia.* New York: Alliance, 1900.

TRUESDELL, AMELIA W. *California Pilgrimage.* San Francisco: Carson, 1884.

—. *California's Hymn.* N.p.: N. publ., n.d.

—. *Legend of Santa Barbara's "Big Grape Vine."* San Francisco: Doxey, 1900.

—. *Song of the Flag.* San Francisco: Doxey, n.d.

TURNER, JOSEPH. *Pre-eminence of Our American Independence.* San Francisco: N. publ., 1897.

TURNER, JOSEPH W. *Orange Blossoms.* East Boston, Mass.: Publ. by the author, 1877.

TURNER, THOMAS S. *Heart Melodies.* Buffalo: Peter Paul, 1895.

Twenty-eighth Anniversary of the Corporate Society of California Pioneers. San Francisco: Publ. by the society, 1878.

Twenty-first Anniversary Mare Island Excursion. San Francisco: Military Order of the Loyal Legion of the United States, 1892.

Twenty-sixth Anniversary of the Corporate Society of California Pioneers. San Francisco: Publ. by the society, 1876.

TYNAN, WILLIAM P. *Three Score Poems.* New York: Hust, 1885.

UPSHAW, WILLIE D. *Earnest Willie, or Echoes from a Recluse.* Atlanta: Publ. by the author, 1893.

UPSON, ARTHUR. *Westwind Songs.* Minneapolis: Brooks, 1902.

URMY, CLARENCE T. *Rosary of Rhyme.* San Francisco: Winterburn, 1884.

—. *Vintage of Verse.* San Francisco: Doxey, 1897.

—. *Wreath of California Laurel.* N.p.: N. publ., n.d.

VAN DERVEER, BELLE. *Soul Waifs.* Buffalo: Peter Paul, 1895.

VAN DUZEE, I. D. *By the Atlantic.* Boston: Lee and Shepard, 1892.

VAN DYKE, HENRY, *Music and Other Poems.* New York: Scribner, 1904.

VANDYNE, WILLIAM J. *Revels of Fancy.* Boston: Grant, 1891.

VAN METER, H. H. *Vanishing Fair.* Chicago: Literary Art, 1894.

VAN NORMAN, INA E. *Minnewaska.* Chicago: Donohue and Henneberry, 1897.

VAN NOSTRAND, D. H. *Poems.* Troy, N.Y.: Lisk, 1884.

VAN SLINGERLAND, NELLIE B. *Love and Politics.* N.p.: N. publ., 1899.

—. *Patriotic Poesy.* New York: Guarantee Publishing, 1905.

VAN VORST, MARIE. *Poems.* New York [?]: Dodd, Mead, 1903.

VAN ZILE, EDWARD S. *Dreamers and Other Poems.* New York: Neely, 1897.

VAUGHN, GEORGE. *Progressive Religious and Social Poems.* N.p.: N. publ., 1880.

VICKERS, GEORGE M. *Ballads of the Occident.* Philadelphia: Parkview, 1898.

VICKERS, ROBERT H. *America Liberata.* Chicago: Kerr, 1896.

VICTOR, FRANCES F. *New Penelope and Other Stories and Poems.* San Francisco: Bancroft, 1877.

VIETT, GEORGE F. *Deeper Harmonies and Other Poems.* Norfolk, Va.: Free-Lance, 1905.

—. *"Thou Beside Me Singing" and Other Poems.* Philadelphia: Ziegler, 1900.

VINTON, J. D. *Poems*. Philadelphia: N. publ., 1884.

—. *Shadows from Life*. Philadelphia: Publ. by the author, 1891.

—. *Vinton's Poems*. Philadelphia: Publ. by the author, 1886.

VOLDO, VENIER. *Poems from the Pacific*. San Francisco: Bancroft, 1888.

—. *Songs of America and Minor Lyrics*. New York: Hanscom, 1876.

VON K., CAMILLA K. *Sea-leaves*. Santa Barbara, Cal.: N. publ., 1887.

VOX BUFFALOREM [pseud.]. *Address to the Hunters after the Ninety Days' Scout*. Reynolds City, Tex.: N. publ., 1877.

WADE, A. ANNIE. *Poetical Works*. Allegheny, Pa.: Wade, 1895.

WADSWORTH, E. CLIFFORD. *Winter Pastoral and Other Poems*. Brooklyn: Berg, 1892.

WADY, CLIFTON S. *Poems*. Boston: Blair and Hallett, 1888.

WAGNER, MADGE M. *At San Diego Bay*. San Diego: Golden Era, n.d.

—. *Debris*. Sacramento: Crocker, 1881.

—. *Poems*. San Francisco: Golden Era, 1885.

WAITE, CAMPBELL W. *Helen*. Chicago: Dibble, 1890.

WALKER, EDWARD D. *Poems*. New York: N. publ., 1893.

WALKER, FRED G. *My Leisure Moments*. Salem: Barry and Lufkin, 1893.

WALKER, HORACE E. *Lady of Dardale and Other Poems*. Manchester, N.H.: Browne and Rowe, 1886.

WALKER, W. S. *Between the Tides*. Los Gatos, Cal.: Walker, 1885.

WALL, ANNIE. *Some Scattered Leaves*. Buffalo: Moulton, 1893.

WALLACE, WILLIAM D. *Idle Hours*. New York: Putnam, 1890.

WALSER, G. H. *Poems of Leisure*. Lamar, Mo.: South-West Missouri Printing, 1890.

WALTER, CARRIE S. *Rose-ashes*. San Francisco: Murdock, 1890.

WARD, J. H. *Ballads of Life*. Salt Lake City: Parry, 1886.

WARD, WILLIAM H. *All Sides of Life*. Des Moines: Iowa Printing, 1886.

WARDER, GEORGE W. *Utopian Dreams and Lotus Leaves*. London: Sampson Low, Marston, Searle, and Rivington, 1885.

WARDWELL, HARRISON B. *Poems*. Portland, Me.: Hoyt, Fogg and Donham, 1879.

WARE, EUGENE F. *Rhymes of Ironquill*. Topeka: Kellam, 1885.

—. *Some of the Rhymes of Ironquill*. New York: Putnam; Topeka: Crane, 1902 [11th edition].

WARMAN, CY. *Mountain Melodies*. Denver: Publ. by the author, n.d.

—. *Tales of an Engineer*. New York: Scribner, 1895.

WARREN, H. VALLETTE. *Afloat with Old Glory*. New York: Abbey, 1901.

WARREN, H. VALLETTE. *There Go the Ships and After Many Days*. Buffalo: Moulton, 1898.

WARREN, M. *Creation*. Boston: Williams, 1878.

WASHINGTON, LUCY H. *Echoes of Song*. Springfield, Ill.: Walker, 1878.

—. *Memory's Casket*. Buffalo: Moulton, 1891.

WASON, H. L. *Letters from Colorado*. Boston: Cupples and Hurd, 1887.

—. *Tale of the Santa Rita Mountains*. Denver: Rocky Mountain Herald, 1904.

WASON, S. THERESA. *Poems*. Manchester, N.H.: N. publ., 1880.

WATERHOUSE, ALFRED J. *Some Homely Little Songs*. San Francisco: Whitaker and Ray, 1899.

WATERMAN, NIXON. *Book of Verses*. Boston and Chicago: Forbes, 1900.

WATERS, GAY. *Poetical Works*. Cincinnati: Standard Publishing, 1887.

WATRES, H. G. *Cobwebs*. Boston: Lothrop, 1886.

WATSON, EDWARD W. *Songs of Flying Hours*. Philadelphia: Coates, 1898.

—. *To-day and Yesterday*. Philadelphia: Coates, 1895.

WATSON, GEORGE A. *Poems*. St. Louis [?]: N. publ., 1884.

WATSON, MOODY M. *Poetical Tribute to Our Naval Heroes Who Fought the Battle of Manila*. Haverhill, Mass.: Publ. by the author, 1900.

WATTS, FLORIDA E. *Varied Grace of Nature's Face*. St. Louis: Private edition, 1895.

WAUGH, LORENZO. *Autobiography*. San Francisco: Taylor, 1885 [3rd edition].

WEARE, W. K. *Songs of the Western Shore*. San Francisco: Bacon, 1879.

WEISSE, JANE L. *Writings for the Aged*. New York: Trow, 1887.

WELBURN, DRUMMOND. *American Epic. A Concise Scenic History of the United States*. Nashville, Tenn.: Private edition, 1891.

WELLES, CHARLES S. *Lute and Lays*. New York: Macmillan, 1899.

WELLESLEY-WESLEY, ERNEST G. *Songs of the Heart*. Boston: Morning Star Publishing, 1899.

WELLINGTON, CARRIE L. *Leaflets Along the Pathway of Life*. Boston: Private edition, 1883.

WELLS, CAROLYN. *Folly for the Wise*. Indianapolis: Bobbs-Merrill, 1904.

WERDEN, E. *Sketches in Prose and Verse*. Pittsfield, Mass.: Sun Printing, 1888.

WEST-LYON, ANNA E. *My First Harvest*. Niagara Falls, N.Y.: Publ. by the author, 1893.

WETHERBEE, EMILY G. *Poems and Addresses.* Lawrence, Mass.: Lawrence Publishing, 1898.

WETMORE, HUGH A. *Cowboy Love Song and Other Poems.* Duluth: Wetmore, 1900.

WHARF, JAMES W. *Promiscuous Poems.* Olney, Ill.: Publ. by the author, 1893.

WHARTON, THOMAS. *"Bobbo" and Other Fancies.* New York: Harper, 1897.

W. H. C. *Leaves of Spring Gathered in Autumn.* Philadelphia: Lippincott, 1883.

WHEELER, KATE L. *Home Poems.* Nashua, N.H.: N. publ., 1897.

WHEELWRIGHT, W. B. and PALMER, H. W. *Harvard Alphabet.* Cambridge, Mass.: Harvard Co-Operative Society, 1902.

WHITAKER, ROBERT. *My Country and Other Verse.* San Francisco: Barry, 1905.

WHITE, EUGENE R. *Songs of Good Fighting.* Boston and New York: Lamson, Wolffe, 1898.

WHITE, GEORGE. *Home Ballads.* Chicago: Warren, 1878.

WHITE, RICHARD E. *Cross of Monterey and Other Poems.* San Francisco: California Publishing, 1882.

WHITING, W. I. *Crowning City.* New York: Publ. by the author, 1899.

—. *Four Hundred to One: Or, Pegasus to Purgatory via Wall St. Abattoir.* New York: Publ. by the author, 1896.

—. *Hardscrabble.* New York: Whiting, 1894.

WHITMAN, ALBERY A. *Four Poems.* N.p.: N. publ., n.d.

—. *Not a Man and Yet a Man.* Springfield. Ohio: Republic Printing, 1877.

WHITMARSH, A. N. *Land of Penn and Other Poems.* New York: Church Press, 1883.

WHITWAM, E. A. *Under the Old Flag.* Abingdon, Ill.: Publ. by the author, 1898.

WICKERSHAM, JAMES A. *Poems.* New York: Brentano, 1882.

WIGGIN, SAMUEL A. *Sprigs of Acacia.* Elkton, Md.: Wright, 1885.

WIGGINS, ALLEYNE H. *Earthly Considerations.* Buffalo: Peter Paul, 1897.

WILDMAN, MARIAN W. *Hill Prayer and Other Poems.* Boston: Badger, 1904.

WILEY, H. W. *Song Book of the Association of Official Agricultural Chemists.* Washington, D.C.: Private edition, 1891.

WILKINSON, JAMES. *Hours in Dreamland.* Buffalo: Peter Paul, 1896.

WILKINSON, WILLIAM C. *Poems.* New York: Scribner, 1883.

WILLIAMS, A. [pseudonym of Mrs. M. E. Rice]. *'49 to '94.* San Francisco: Upton, 1894.

WILLIAMS, FRANCIS H. *Flute-Player and Other Poems.* New York: Putnam, 1894.

WILLIAMS, THEODORE. *Rhymes of a Toiler.* Philadelphia: Lippincott, 1890.

WILLIAMSON, GEORGE. *Gleanings of Leisure Hours.* Detroit: International Publishing, 1894.

WILLING, MRS. CHARLES. *Persephone and Other Poems.* Philadelphia: Lippincott, 1881.

WILSON, GEORGE A. *Versatile Verses.* Nyack-on-Hudson, N.Y.: Publ. by the author, 1894.

WILSON, HARMON D. *Troubles of a Worried Man.* Topeka: Publ. by the author, 1903.

WILSON, J. ALBERT. *Paradox and Other Poems.* New York: Putnam, 1877.

WILSON, JOHN G. *Lyrics of Life.* New York: Caxton, 1886.

WILSON, JOHN W. *After Office Hours and Other Poems.* Columbus, Ohio: Champlin Printing, 1898.

WILSTACH, JOHN A. *Battle Forest.* New York: Mail and Express, 1890.

WING, AMELIA K. *Brooklyn Fancies.* Brooklyn: N. publ., 1890.

WING, JOSEPH A. *"Pluck" and Other Poems.* Montpelier, Vt.: Freeman Steam Printing, 1878.

WINGARD, E. A. *Echoes and Other Poems.* Newberry, S.C.: Lutheran Publishing Board, 1899.

WINSLOW, MILTON, *Poems.* Fairmount, Ind.: Morgan, 1891.

WINTHROP, AUGUSTA C. *"The Bugle-Call" and Others.* Boston: Clarke, 1889.

WISE, HILDA J. *Optimist and Other Verses.* N.p.: N. publ., n.d.

WOLCOTT, JULIA A. *Song-Blossoms.* Boston: Brown, 1899 [2nd edition].

WOLF, GEORGE. *Golden Poems.* St. Louis: Barnes, 1884 [2nd edition].

WOOD, BENJAMIN. *Bugle Calls.* New York: Brentano, 1901.

WOOD, J. G. *Poems and Prose.* Katonah, N.Y.: "The Times" Printing, 1898.

WOOD, MARY W. *During a Life-Time.* Chicago: Halpin, 1893.

WOOD, STANLEY. *Gems of the Rockies.* Chicago: Denver & Rio Grande Railroad, 1889.

WOODARD, LUKE. *Poems for the Fireside.* Richmond, Ind.: Nicholson, 1891.

WOODBERRY, GEORGE E. *My Country.* Cambridge, Mass.: Private edition, 1887.

—. *North Shore Watch and Other Poems.* Boston and New York: Houghton, Mifflin, 1890.

—. *Poems.* New York: Macmillan, 1903.

WOODRUFF, BELLE C. *Collection of Wild Flowers.* Buffalo: Moulton, 1894.

WOODWARD, FREDERICK B. *Miscellaneous Poems.* Watertown, Conn.: N. publ., 1891.

WOODWARD, HENRY H. *Lyrics of the Umpqua.* New York: Alden, 1889.

WOODWARD, MARY C. *Darkness and Dawn.* Dayton, Ohio: United Brethren Publishing, 1903.

WOODWARD, NATHAN A. *Pebbles and Boulders.* Buffalo: Moulton, 1895.

WOORSTER, ARTHUR. *Random Rhymes.* Washington, D.C.: N. publ., 1882.

WRIGHT, ALFRED A. *Nation's Sorrow.* Lynn, Mass.: Leech and Lewis, 1881.

WRIGHT, ANNA A. *More Truth than Poetry.* Chicago: N. publ., 1884.

WRIGHT, DANIEL N. *Miscellaneous Poems.* Avon, Ill.: Stevens and Simmons, 1885.

WRIGHT, DAVID H. *Is Peace on Earth?* Philadelphia: Lippincott, 1892.

—. *Under the Red Cross.* Philadelphia: Drexel Biddle, 1901.

WRIGHT, JULIA M. *Mother Goose for Temperance Nurseries.* New York: National Temperance Society and Publication, 1887.

WRIGHT, STEPHEN W. *Grandpa's Rhymes.* Lowell, Mass.: N. publ., 1885.

WYNKOOP, FRANK M. *Mountain Murmurs.* Denver: N. publ., n.d.

Yankee Doodle. New York: McLoughlin, n.d.

YATES, JOHN H. *Ballads and Poems.* Buffalo: Moulton, 1898.

YOUNG, CLAIBORNE A. *Way Songs and Wanderings.* Boston: Estes and Lauriat, 1897.

YOUNG, JULIA D. *Thistle Down Poems.* Buffalo: Peter Paul, 1893.

YOUNG, SOLOMON E. *Legends and Lyrics.* Boston: Writer Publishing, 1890.

ZEDAKER, CASSIUS M. *Book of Poems.* Cleveland: Leader Printing, 1880.

Index